CONTENTS

LOOKING CLOSER 3
CLASSIC WRITINGS
ON GRAPHIC DESIGN

EDITED BY:

Michael Bierut, Jessica Helfand,
Steven Heller, and Rick Poynor

ALLWORTH PRESS
NEW YORK

04   03   02   01   00   99   5   4   3   2   1

Published by Allworth Press
An imprint of Allworth Communications
10 East 23rd Street, New York, NY 10010

Copublished with the American Institute of Graphic Arts

Cover and book design by Michael Bierut, Pentagram, New York

Page composition by Susan Ramundo, SR Desktop Services, Ridge, NY

ISBN: 1-58115-022-9

Library of Congress Catalog Card Number: 98-74536

Printed in Canada

introspective professional voice. (The articles published in these journals, however, viewed contemporary professional concerns narrowly and practically rather than broadly and philosophically, and were so of the time that they were written that the editors of this volume do not feel that republishing them is relevant for this book.)

From the turn of the century through the 1930s, the United States and Europe saw a significant increase in the number of advertising-design periodicals that sought to balance technical and aesthetic concerns. Commercial art—from quotidian advertising to fine book design—had developed into a dominant means of mass communication with distinct schools, movements, and styles. However, trade press writing was often arcane and mired in technical jargon. Commercial art had further evolved into a competitive industry that commanded top dollar for peak effectiveness, and for this reason, rather than any grand aesthetic or philosophical motivation, the industry encouraged more publishing venues for showcase, analysis, and criticism. As divergent beliefs about the nature of professional practice were championed in both official trade and alternative culture periodicals, many writers divided their attention between the technical aspects of production and the formal issues of traditionalism and progressivism, as well as a reconciliation of the two.

Outlets for diverse opinions provided practitioners with soapboxes on which to express ideas that elevated the level of discourse on, and perception of, the field as an intellectually rigorous one. By the 1920s commercial art was championed by progressive artists who viewed it as more than a mere service to business, but as a force for social transformation. Avant-garde design publications in Europe fostered a union of fine and applied art. Critical essays in these magazines were not only screeds or debates over fashionable colors or trendy typefaces, but addressed the rightness of form, the pros and cons of ornament, the ramifications of propaganda, and the concept of plagiarism versus influence.

The literature of graphic design—the original documents through which the profession can trace its nascency—are found in these early trade and progressive periodicals. Archived in the pages of these publications are some lost and a few preserved texts, written by journalists and essayists, which framed the issues that forged twentieth century design practices. The first two volumes of Looking Closer were concerned with documenting the literature of the recent past. For this third edition the editors have anthologized what we believe are some of the wellsprings of contemporary design discourse—those known and lesser-known texts that are directly cited or indirectly referred to in current critical writing and design history. We have also sought out past writing that is relevant to today's practice but has been virtually lost in the stacks of disintegrating books and periodicals.

The editors scoured a wide range of sources from the United States and Europe, from the turn of the century to the early 1980s (stopping where the previous two Looking Closer volumes began), including trade magazines and institutional journals, mainstream magazines and newspapers, annuals and monographs, alternative and avant-garde manifestos, and conference transcripts and papers. In this first retrospective Looking Closer, the editors have included articles and essays that underscore the history of twentieth century graphic design as it has been recorded, as well as those that extend our understanding of graphic communication in the postwar period—issues that are not addressed in the omnibus overviews of the profession, including such topics as feminism and resistance of commercial orthodoxy.

This anthology is chronologically organized to represent the continuum of thought contributing to a field that was, and is, in constant flux. The selected writers grapple with fundamental distinctions between classicism and modernism, craft and art, service and servitude, and timelessness and timeliness. In tracing almost a century of writing, it is clear that whatever the entity is called—printing art, commercial art, graphic design, or visual communication—it inspired and generated fervent critics along all coordinates of the formal and ideological spectra. Through a range of individual writing styles, each author helped elevate the practice beyond the commonplace. So what is here deemed "classic writing" are texts that deserve to be revisited and reread. Individually, they speak volumes about their respective times and places as seen through the lenses of certain key individuals; collectively, they are integral parts of the multiple histories that comprise the legacy of graphic design.

ACKNOWLEDGMENTS

The editors owe a debt of gratitude to Nicole Potter, editor at Allworth Press, for her hard work and dedication to this project. Further thanks to Bob Porter and Nyier Abdou, also at Allworth, and Tad Crawford, publisher, for his continued enthusiastic support.

For permission to reprint texts, the editors are grateful to:

Gabriella Belli
Paul Bernbach
Joan Black
Gui Bonsiepe
Sheila Levrant de Bretteville
Carol Burtin Fripp
Gwen Chanzit
Helene Fried
Ken Garland
Jennifer Havinden
Michael Havinden
Mark Holt
Jane Howard
Larry Keely
Juliette Kepes

Elaine Lustig Cohen
George Melly
Hattula Moholy-Nagy
Hamish Muir
Nicolette Papanek
Satu Papanek
B. Martin Pedersen
Marion Rand
Jon Savage
Leslie Savan
Piet Schreuders
Susan Sontag
Herbert Spencer
Massimo Vignelli
Wolfgang Weingart

Thanks to the following for help in locating material and obtaining permissions:

Dorothy Abbe
Ralph Caplan
William Drenttel
Robin Kinross
Victor Margolin

Philip B. Meggs
Katherine McCoy
Deborah Murphy
Dugald Stermer
Howard Weingrad

Thanks are given for permission to use the following translations:

DESTRUCTION OF SYNTAX—IMAGINATION WITHOUT STRINGS—
WORDS-IN-FREEDOM
Translated by R. W. Flint. Published in *Marinetti's Selected Writings* (New York: Farrar, Straus and Giroux, Inc., 1971).

PROGRAM OF THE FIRST WORKING GROUP OF CONSTRUCTIVISTS
Translated by Christine Lodder, for the Open University. Published in Charles Harris and Paul Wood, eds., *Art in Theory: 1900–1990* (New York: Blackwell Publishers, Inc., 1993).

THE NEW TYPOGRAPHY
Translated by Sibyl Moholy-Nagy. Published in Richard Kostelanetz, ed., *Moholy-Nagy: An Anthology* (New York: Da Capo Press, Inc., 1970).

TOPOGRAPHY OF TYPOGRAPHY
Translated by Robin Kinross. Published in Robin Kinross, *Modern Typography: An Essay in Critical History* (London: Hyphen Press, 1992). Modified from a translation by Helene Aldwinckle, published in Sophie Lissitzky-Küppers, *El Lissitzky: Life, Letters, Text* (New York: Thames and Hudson, Inc., 1980).

TYPOPHOTO
Translated by Janet Seligman. Published in László Moholy-Nagy, *Painting, Photography, Film* (London: Lund Humphries, 1969).

OUR BOOK
Translated by Helene Aldwinckle. Published in Sophie Lissitzky-Küppers, *El Lissitzky: Life, Letters, Text* (New York: Thames and Hudson, Inc., 1980).

WHAT IS NEW TYPOGRAPHY?
Translation published in Eckhard Neumann, *Functional Graphic Design in the 20's* (New York: Reinhold Publishing Corporation, 1967).

OUTLINE OF THE ART OF ADVERTISING MANIFESTO
Translation published in Maurizio Scudiero and David Leiber, *Depero Futurista and New York: Futurism and the Art of Advertising* (Rovereto: Longo Editore, 1986).

LAY IN—LAY OUT
Translated for this collection by Piet Schreuders with Robin Kinross, 1998.

INTRODUCTION
Rick Poynor

The process of extracting material for republication from the mountain of texts that have been generated on a subject is an activity that can never claim to be all-encompassing or definitive. This is especially the case when the territory is only partially mapped. *Looking Closer 3* is, so far as the editors know, the first anthology of its kind. There have been collections of historical texts relating to typography, but perhaps surprisingly, never a survey that gathers earlier writing relating specifically to graphic design, or that addresses typographic writing from graphic design's point of view. While some well-known texts on typography resurface here, they emerge in significantly different terrain.

Dauntingly large as the task seemed at the outset, our method as prospectors was simple enough. We drew up lists, did our solitary research and reading, distributed our findings to the team, and waited to see what they thought. To make its way into the book a text required the support of at least three out of four editors. There was the possibility to reconsider a selected article at a later stage, in the light of more pressing discoveries, and the opportunity to argue the case for the inclusion of a text that had received only lukewarm backing the first time around. The process of refinement and relegation continued up to the book's final stages.

The general criteria we brought to bear on our reading are easily stated. We set out to include historically significant designers and design commentators, significant ideas and themes in the evolution of graphic design in theory and practice, and significant "moments," such as debates, conferences, and manifestos. Although, again, we make no claim to be definitive, we also endeavored to include a broad selection of important design publications (among them *Merz, Commercial Art, Advertising Arts, PM, Typography, Graphis, Typographica,* the *Penrose Annual, Ulm, Dot Zero,* and *Icographic*) as signposts for the reader's further research. We paid close attention to the literary quality of the writing, though selections are inevitably subject to variation in this respect. We have attempted to maintain a balance between better-known texts that call out for inclusion in any representative survey, and less familiar writing that is unjustly overlooked, or hard to locate outside the most specialized libraries, or both. As a way of opening up the often insular and inward-looking discipline of graphic design to broader cultural scrutiny, we have included several significant instances of writing on the subject by nonprofessional observers.

In addition, each of the editors brought preoccupations of his or her own to the proposal and selection of texts, and these will be apparent from the brief commentaries that introduce each of the articles.

We assumed, at the outset, that the book would be divided into thematic sections, but as the pile of texts grew we decided on a straightforward chronological structure. Instead of tying ostensibly related material into neat categorical bundles, it seemed more suggestive, truer to the fluxes of history, and in some ways more revealing, given the book's ninety-year time span, to allow the chronological framework to determine these editorial juxtapositions and let the dates at the top of the articles speak for themselves. Sometimes confluences of viewpoint and opinion can be seen to appear at particular times. On other occasions, these multivocal and even contradictory texts brush against each other in ways that vividly portray the tensions, uncertainties, and disputes of their period. While there are clearly numerous recurrent themes, and our awareness of them sometimes led to the inclusion of additional, thematically-related texts, an unstructured chronology resists the "closure" of a clearly defined thematic framework and allows latitude for other interpretations of this rich seam of source material.

For this first collection of historical writings we have surveyed only texts written in English, or already available in translation (the one exception is Piet Schreuders's "Lay In—Lay Out," translated for us by the author). This book's primary focus is American and European graphic design, and their interrelationship, seen mainly, though not exclusively, from the American point of view. American graphic design is the product, to a large extent, of European influences filtered through American preoccupations and concerns. One of the issues that this selection serves to highlight is the increasingly problematic nature, as graphic design develops as a professional practice, of the paradigm exemplified by the American commercial approach. If this has not been fully apparent until comparatively recently, it is because graphic design has tended to produce its few historians from within its own ranks, and these accounts both serve and legitimize a "professional" analysis of graphic design thinking and practice. Although dissenting views of the discipline began to emerge in the 1960s, particularly in Europe, and are not hard for the researcher to discover, they have not featured strongly in standard narratives of graphic design.

Yet, as this collection shows, the later postwar tensions within graphic design were implicit in some of its earliest statements of aim. The ways in which European modernism was stripped of its ideological purpose in the United States and realigned with corporate interests and goals is well understood, but two of the earliest texts reprinted here, by F. T. Marinetti (1913) and Alexander Rodchenko and Varvara Stepanova (1921), are startling reminders of the narrowness of graphic practice conceived—as W. A. Dwiggins, coiner of the term "graphic design," would conceive it in 1922—as a commercial sales aid. Marinetti's manifesto proposes nothing less than a new revolutionary poetics to be realized in the medium of typographic design; Rodchenko and Stepanova place Constructivist design in the service of revolutionary politics and the transformation of society.

By the end of the 1920s, a considerably more generalized sense of change permeates designers' writings. Revolutionary poetics and politics have been replaced by something much less extreme and—commercially—much more pliant. For the Italian Futurist Fortunato Depero, lionized in New York, enraptured by visions of pneumatics, motors, magnets, and light, "The Art of the future will be undoubtedly ADVERTISING ART." For Alexey Brodovitch, the publicity artist's task, as a pioneer and leader, is to "force a realization" of the beauty of new images on the "consumer-spectator and the mob." In this reformulation, modernism is no longer conceived as an instrument for effecting fundamental reconstruction of the body politic (or poetic), but becomes instead a new form of perception for a time of vertiginous social, urban, commercial, technological, and scientific growth. Confronted by the pulsating energies of American industry, city life, and communications, modernism's mid-century adherents repeatedly noted the barrage of sensory inputs and the "incomparably greater speed and density to visual experience" (György Kepes) that design must help society to channel, filter, and absorb. El Lissitzky, struggling to visualize the drama of these changes, had foreseen the "explosion" of the traditional form of the book into new structures under the dematerializing pressure of a new age of communications. Forty years later, laying the same stress on speed and extended perception, but reversing the image, Marshall McLuhan took it for granted that electricity had by now "imploded" the global communications landscape: The wired world had contracted to become a new kind of experiential village.

In 1936, the American advertising man Earnest Elmo Calkins declared that "business design is today the greatest field for the artist," and variations on this mantra came to be repeated not only by the more farsighted businessmen—from Container Corporation's Walter Paepcke to IBM's Thomas Watson, Jr.—but by designers themselves. Herb Lubalin and Paul Rand present largely untroubled views of design's sales function in the writings featured here, but more qualified accounts of the designer-client relationship emerge from W. A. Dwiggins's flawlessly modulated ironic treatise on dealing with artists, Misha Black's rare glimpses of life inside a design office, and William Golden's blunt reflections on designers' attitudes to the content of the messages they design for business.

A key word found throughout these texts is "responsibility." For Paul and Ann Rand, the social responsibility of the graphic designer lies in helping to sell the products, processes, or services on which jobs and profits depend. There is shame in selling, the Rands suggest, only if these communications do not meet the designer's standards of artistic integrity (which appear to be essentially aesthetic) or misrepresent what is being sold, though no examples are given. In business, William Golden argues, executives see their first responsibility as being to the corporation, not society, but justify this belief with the assumption that what is good for the corporation must necessarily be good for everyone else, in terms of employment, consumer goods, and taxes paid to fund public services. Other designers resist this simplistic view of the designer's function as being primarily to act as a "propagandist for business" (Golden). In the spirit of revolutionary modernism, György Kepes, writing in 1949, sees the design of man himself—as individual and member of society—as design's most pressing task, and while this utopian view of design as a form of social engineering was not widely held, the conviction that the designer had obligations other than the climbing line on the sales graph grew in the 1960s as graphic design gathered pace as a business activity in its own right. In an essay on the responsibilities of the design profession, Herbert Spencer, editor of *Typographica* and the *Penrose Annual*, criticizes the enclosed "professional mystique" of the design process and reminds designers that the "health and happiness" of society, as well as the economy, deserve their attention. The need for a reversal of priorities and a reallocation of designers' talents and energies is perhaps most tellingly expressed in the *First Things First* manifesto, published in Britain in 1964, which explicitly attacks design's dedication to the "high pitched scream of consumer selling."

The mid-1960s disquiet about design's complicity with advertising—also seen in Gui Bonsiepe's reservations about the "triviality of communicative life"—intensified in the 1970s. In formal terms, the orderly principles of modernist New Typography formulated by Jan Tschichold, and refined in the postwar years by Emil Ruder and other Swiss designers, were now subject to postmodern revision by Wolfgang Weingart, whose seminal 1972 American lecture-tour notes are reprinted here. The same year, an even more fundamental feminist critique of modernism and its institutional masters was broached by the American designer Sheila Levrant de Bretteville. Flying in the face of the male-dominated graphic design profession's most cherished axioms, de Bretteville's groundbreaking essay dares to suggest that the simplicity and clarity espoused by the modernists might, in reality, be repressive. "The thrust to control almost inevitably operates through *simplification*," she argues. "Control is undermined by ambiguity, choice, and complexity, because subjective factors in the user become more effective, and the user is invited to participate. *Participation undermines control.*"

The conviction that design had become a control system which existed to manipulate the market and to benefit design itself rather than its users was developed by ecotheorist Victor Papanek in his essay on the design of myths and the myths of design. For Papanek, designers and design educators had actively conspired in withdrawing design—"a basic human ability to help autonomous self-realization"—from ordinary people by cloaking it, as Herbert Spencer had earlier suggested, in professional mystery and myth. In Papanek's view, as in de Bretteville's, it was essential to make design participatory again by reconnecting it with the mainstream of everyday life. Using withering ironic humor, rather than the denunciatory blasts of the manifesto, Piet Schreuders makes essentially the same point when, at the end of his 1977 notes on graphic design, he urges readers simply to take a piece of paper and start laying out. For Schreuders, graphic designers' self-important appeals to objectivity mask an underlying irrationality and confusion. Graphic design as a profession has no business to exist.

If these polemical attacks, however provocative, were never likely to do more than prick a few designers' consciences, other forms of participation in design by its audiences can be seen in writings included in this collection. Although the discourse of graphic design has, to this day, been conducted largely by designers for the benefit of their colleagues, interested observers have sometimes offered their views. An early example, included here, is novelist Aldous Huxley's argument that the convoluted forms of the New Typography fail to take into account the ordinary reader's resistance to revolutionary change. Not until the 1960s, however, did graphic design start to become the subject of occasional journalistic interest, and even cultural criticism, outside the professional trade press. In George Melly's article on British Pop graphics, first published in a Sunday newspaper, the writer's attention falls as much on the way in which the audience—seen by Melly as a "secret society"—consumes and uses the designs, as on the designers who make these images, and they are in any case shown to be participants in the same music and youth subculture. Susan Sontag's essay on Cuban posters has similar points to make about the way in which the display of collected posters in the private space of the home functions as a code by which members of a "subgroup" announce their allegiances and identify each other. Leslie Savan, writing about Helvetica as the pervasive corporate style of 1970s America, and Jon Savage, excoriating "the age of plunder" in British record sleeves, produce essays in critical journalism finely attuned to the social resonance and political meanings of graphic images in contemporary culture. Years after they were written any of these pieces could still serve as templates for a nonpartisan cultural analysis of graphic communication that is rarely attempted in the generalist press.

Each of these articles, essays, and manifestos has been selected because it helps to illuminate the growth of graphic design as it has been preached, practiced, disseminated, and discussed. These documents offer valuable source material for the historian, and those with historical interests, but in many cases they are striking for their continuing relevance to graphic design as it is undertaken today. The ethical dilemmas confronting designers in the second half of the century, during the years of design's increasing professionalization, have become, in some respects, even more acute. In their different ways, writers such as György Kepes, William Golden, Herbert Spencer, and Ken Garland demonstrate a clear-sightedness about the problems and priorities facing design, communication, and society that still has lessons to impart.

The intense critical debate seen in more recent writing about graphic design (subject of the two previous *Looking Closers*) makes this a particularly significant moment to reclaim writing that has been overlooked in existing professional narratives and historical accounts: Sheila Levrant de Bretteville on women in design, Gui Bonsiepe on rhetoric, dom Sylvester Houédard on concrete poetry. In Houédard's kinetic poetics, for instance, we see a missing link in the dissident graphic tradition that connects Marinetti's "words in freedom" to the typographic experiments of the digital era. Graphic design is often spoken of now, by many students and professionals, and sometimes by those outside design, as though it could have no viable use or purpose other than the branding, packaging, and promotion of commodities for sale. The sense is fading that throughout its varied history graphic communication has often been visualized in other ways, and used for other ends. If this anthology helps to enrich and complicate our picture of graphic design's many intertwining branches, it will have fulfilled its editors' hopes and aims.

★

NOTE ON TEXTS

Most texts in this collection are republished in their entirety. Cases where cuts have been made, for reasons of conciseness or space, are marked by the use of [. . .].

1893
THE IDEAL BOOK
William Morris

WILLIAM MORRIS *(1834–1896) viewed the crafts traditions of the Middle Ages as a way of revitalizing the applied arts of his day. Influenced by the writings of the art critic John Ruskin, he helped to spawn a Gothic revival that had both stylistic and philosophical implications. Morris fervently believed in the honesty of functional materials as a means to ensure high design standards. His progressive ideas about a formal rightness that transcends mere style make him, for Nikolaus Pevsner, a pioneer of* modern design. *In 1888, Morris attended a lecture on type by Emery Walker (1851–1933) at the first Arts and Crafts Exhibition in London; he heard the typographer argue that the standards of fifteenth- and sixteenth-century printing should be adopted to counter the qualitative flaws of contemporary books. Three years later, Morris founded the Kelmscott Press with the aim of imbuing printed work with quality and moral value. Having fought against the dubious results of mass production, he also attacked the false medieval revivals to which his own work gave rise. In this lecture, focusing exclusively on the book, he lambasts the sacred cows of printing and type design.—SH*

By the Ideal Book, I suppose we are to understand a book not limited by commercial exigencies of price: we can do what we like with it, according to what its nature, as a book, demands of Art. But we may conclude, I think, that its matter will limit us somewhat; a work on differential calculus, a medical work, a dictionary, a collection of a statesman's speeches, of a treatise on manures, such books, though they might be handsomely and well printed, would scarcely receive ornament with the same exuberance as a volume of lyrical poems, or a standard classic, or such like. A work *on* Art, I think, bears less of ornament than any other kind of book (*non bis in idem* is a good motto); again, a book that *must* have *illustrations*, more or less utilitarian, should, I think, have no actual *ornament* at all, because the ornament and the illustration must almost certainly fight. Still, whatever the subject-matter of the book may be, and however bare it may be of decoration, it can still be a work of art, if the type be good and attention be paid to its general arrangement. All here present, I should suppose, will agree in thinking an opening of Schoeffer's 1462 Bible beautiful, even when it has neither been illuminated nor rubricated; the same may be said of Schüssler, or Jenson, or, in short, of any of the *good* old printers; their works, without any further ornament than they derived from the design and arrangement of the letters, were definite works of art. In fact a book, printed or written, has a tendency to be a beautiful object, and that we of this age should generally produce ugly books, shows, I fear, something like malice prepense—a *determination* to put our eyes in our pockets wherever we can.

Well, I lay it down, first, that a book quite un-ornamented can look actually and positively beautiful, and not merely un-ugly, if it be, so to say, architecturally good, which, by the by, need not add much to its price, since it costs no more to pick up pretty stamps than ugly ones, and the taste and forethought that goes to the proper setting, position, and so on, will soon grow into a habit, if cultivated, and will not take up much of the master-printer's time when taken with his other necessary business.

Now, then, let us see what this architectural arrangement claims of us. *First*, the pages must be clear and easy to read; which they can hardly be unless, *secondly*, the type is well designed; and *thirdly*, whether the margins be small or big, they must be in due proportion to the page of letters.

For clearness of reading the things necessary to be heeded are, first, that the letters should be properly put on their bodies, and, I think, especially that there should be small whites between them: it is curious, but to me certain, that the irregularity of some early type, notably the Roman letter of the early printers of Rome, which is, of all Roman type, the rudest, does *not* tend toward illegibility: what does do so is the lateral compression of the letter, which necessarily involves the over-thinning out of its shape. Of course, I do not mean to say that the above-mentioned irregularity is other than a fault to be corrected. One thing should *never* be done in ideal printing, the spacing out of letters, that is, putting an extra white between them; except in such hurried and unimportant work as newspaper printing, it is inexcusable.

This leads us to the second matter on this head, the lateral spacing of words (the whites between them); to make a beautiful page great attention should be paid to this, which, I fear, is not often done. No more white should be used between the words than just clearly cuts them off from one another; if the whites are bigger than this it both tends to illegibility and makes the page ugly. I remember once buying a handsome fifteenth-century Venetian book, and I could not tell at first why some of its pages were so worrying to read, and so commonplace and vulgar to look at, for there was no fault to find with the type. But presently it was accounted for by the spacing; for the said pages were spaced like a modern book, *i.e.*, the black and white nearly equal. Next, if you want a legible book, the white should be clear and the black black. When that excellent journal, the *Westminster Gazette*, first came out, there was a discussion on the advantages of its green paper, in which a good deal of nonsense was talked. My friend, Mr. Jacobi, being a practical printer, set these wise men right, if they noticed his letter, as I fear they did not, by pointing out that what they had done was to lower the tone (not the moral tone) of the paper, and that, therefore, in order to make it as legible as ordinary black and white, they should make their black blacker—which of course they do not do. You may depend upon it that a gray page is very trying to the eyes.

As above said, legibility depends also much on the design of the letter: and again I take up the cudgels against compressed type, and that especially in Roman let-ter: the full-sized lower-case letters *a*, *b*, *d*, and *c*, should be designed on something like a square to get good results: otherwise one may fairly say that there is no room for the design; furthermore, each letter should have its due characteristic drawing; the thickening out for a *b*, *e*, *g*, should not be of the same kind as that for a *d*; a *u* should not merely be an *n* turned upside down; the dot of the *i* should not be a circle drawn with compasses, but a delicately drawn diamond, and so on. To be short, the letters should be designed by an artist, and not an engineer. As to the forms of letters in England (I mean Great Britain), there has been much progress within the last forty years. The sweltering hideousness of the Bodoni letter, the most illegible type that was ever cut, with its preposterous thicks and thins, has been mostly relegated to works that do not profess anything but the baldest utilitarianism (though why even utilitarianism should use illegible types, I fail to see), and Caslon's letter, and the somewhat wiry, but in its way, elegant old-faced type cut in our own days, has largely taken its place. It is rather unlucky, however, that a somewhat low standard of excellence has been accepted for the design of modern Roman type at its best, the comparatively poor and wiry letter of Plantin, and the Elzeviers, having served for the model, rather than the generous and logical designs of the fifteenth-century Venetian printers, at the head of whom stands Nicholas Jenson; when it is so obvious that this is the best and clearest Roman type yet struck, it seems a pity that we should make our starting point for a possible new departure at any period worse than the best. If any of you doubt the superiority of this type over that of the seventeenth century, the study of a specimen enlarged about five times will convince him, I should think. I must admit, however, that a commercial consideration comes in here, to wit, that the Jenson letters take up more room than the imitations of the seventeenth century; and that touches on another commercial difficulty, to wit, that you cannot have a book either handsome or clear to read which is printed in small characters. For my part, except where books smaller than an ordinary octavo are wanted, I would fight against anything smaller than Pica; but at any rate Small Pica seems to me the smallest type that should be used in the body of any book. I might suggest to printers that if they want to get more in they can reduce the size of the leads, or leave them out altogether. Of course this is more desirable in some types than others; Caslon's letter, *e.g.*, which has long ascenders and descenders, never needs leading, except for special purposes.

I have hitherto had a fine and generous Roman type in my mind, but after all, a certain amount of variety is desirable, and when you have once got your Roman letter as good as the best that has been, I do not think you will find much scope for development of it; I would, therefore, put in a word for some form of Gothic letter for use in our improved printed book. This may startle some of you, but you must remember that except for a very remarkable type used very seldom by Berthelet, English black-letter, since the days of Wynkyn de Worde, has been always the letter which was introduced from Holland about that time (I except again, of course, the modern imitations of Caxton). Now this, though a handsome and stately letter, is not very easy reading, it is too much compressed, too spiky, and, so to say, too prepensely Gothic. But there are many types which are of a transitional character and of all degrees of transition, from those which do little more than take in just a little of the crisp floweriness of the Gothic, like some of the Mentelin or quasi-Mentelin ones (which, indeed, are models of beautiful simplicity), or say like the letter of the Ulm Ptolemy, of which it is difficult to say whether it is Gothic or Roman, to the splendid Mainz type, of which, I suppose, the finest example is the Schoeffer Bible of 1462, and which is almost wholly Gothic. This gives us a wide field for variety, I think, so I make the suggestion to you, and leave this part of the subject with two remarks: first, that a good deal of the difficulty of reading Gothic books is caused by the numerous contractions in them, which were a survival of the practice of the scribes; and in a lesser degree by the over abundance of tied letters, both of which drawbacks I take it for granted would be absent in modern types founded on these semi-Gothic letters. And, secondly, that in my opinion the capitals are the strong side of Roman, and the lower-case of Gothic letter, which is but natural, since the Roman was originally an alphabet of capitals, and the lower-case a gradual deduction from them.

We now come to the position of the page of print on the paper, which is a most important point, and one that till quite lately has been wholly misunderstood by modern, and seldom done wrong by ancient printers, or indeed by producers of books of any kind. On this head I must begin by reminding you that we only occa-sionally see one page of a book at a time; the two pages making an opening are really the unit of the book, and this was thoroughly understood by the old book producers. I think you will very seldom find a book produced before the eighteenth century, and which has not been cut down by that enemy of books (and of the human race) the binder, in which this rule is not adhered to: that the hinder edge (that which is bound in) must be the smallest member of the margins, the head margin must be larger than this, the fore larger still, and the tail largest of all. I assert that, to the eye of any man who knows what proportion is, this looks satisfactory, and that no other does so look. But the modern printer, as a rule, dumps down his page in what he calls the middle of the paper, which is often not even really the middle, as he measures his page from the head line, if he has one, though it is not really part of the page, but a spray of type only faintly staining the head of the paper. Now I go so far as to say that any book in which the page is properly put on the paper is tolerable to look at, however poor the type may be (always so long as there is no "ornament" which may spoil the whole thing), whereas any book in which the page is wrongly set on the paper is *intolera-*ble to look at, however good the type and ornaments may be. I have got on my shelves now a Jenson's Latin Pliny, which, in spite of its beautiful type and handsome painted ornaments, I dare scarcely look at, because the binder (adjectives fail me here) has chopped off two-thirds of the tail margin: such stupidities are like a man with his coat buttoned up behind, or a lady with her bonnet put on hind-side foremost.

Before I finish this section, I should like to say a word concerning large paper copies. I am clean against them, though I have sinned a good deal in that way myself, but that was in the days of ignorance, and I petition for pardon on that ground only. If you want to publish a handsome edition of a book as well as a cheap one, do so; but let them be two books, and if you (or the public) cannot afford this, spend your ingenuity and your money in making the cheap book as sightly as you can. Your mak-ing a large paper copy out of the small one lands you in a dilemma even if you re-impose the pages for the larger paper, which is not often done I think. If the margins are right for the smaller book, they must be wrong for the larger, and you have to offer the public the worse book at the bigger price: if they are right for the large paper they are wrong for the small, and thus *spoil* it, as we have seen above that they must do; and that seems scarcely fair to the general public (from the point of view of artis-tic morality) who might have had a book that was sightly, though not high priced.

As to the paper of our ideal book we are at a great disadvantage compared with past times. Up to the end of the fifteenth or, indeed, the first quarter of the six-teenth centuries, no bad paper was made, and the greater part was very good indeed. At present there is very little good paper made, and most of it is very bad. Our ideal book must, I think, be printed on hand-made paper as good as it can be made; penury here will make a poor book of it. Yet if machine-made paper must be used, it should not profess fineness or luxury, but should show itself for what it is: for my part I decid-edly prefer the cheaper papers that are used for the journals, so far as appearance is concerned, to the thick, smooth, sham-fine papers on which respectable books are printed, and the worst of these are those which imitate the structure of handmade papers.

But, granted your hand-made paper, there is something to be said about its substance. A small book should not be printed on thick paper, however good it may be. You want a book to turn over easily, and to lie quiet while you are reading it, which is impossible, unless you keep heavy paper for big books.

And, by the way, I wish to make a protest against the superstition that only small books are comfortable to read; some small books are tolerably comfortable, but the best of them are not so comfortable as a fairly big folio, the size, say, of an uncut *Polyphilus*, or somewhat bigger. The fact is, a small book seldom does lie quiet, and you have either to cramp your hand by holding it, or else to put it on the table with a paraphernalia of matters to keep it down, a tablespoon on one side, a knife on another, and so on, which things always tumble off at a critical moment, and fidget you out of the repose which is absolutely necessary to reading; whereas, a big folio lies quiet and majestic on the table, waiting kindly till you please to come to it, with its leaves flat and peaceful, giving you no trouble of body, so that your mind is free to enjoy the literature which its beauty enshrines.

So far then, I have been speaking of books whose only ornament is the necessary and essential beauty which arises out of the fitness of a piece of craftsmanship for the use which it is made for. But if we get as far as that, no doubt from such craftsmanship definite ornament will arise, and will be used, sometimes with wise forbearance, sometimes with prodigality equally wise. Meantime, if we really feel impelled to ornament our books, no doubt we ought to try what we can do, but in this attempt we must remember one thing, that if we think the ornament is ornamentally a part of the book merely because it is printed with it, and bound up with it, we shall be much mistaken. The ornament must form as much a part of the page as the type itself, or it will miss its mark, and in order to succeed, and to be ornament, it must submit to certain limitations, and become *architectural*; a mere black and white picture, however interesting it may be as a picture, may be far from an ornament in a book; while on the other hand, a book ornamented with pictures that are suitable for that, and that only, may become a work of art second to none, save a fine building duly decorated, or a fine piece of literature.

These two latter things are, indeed, the one absolutely necessary gift that we should claim of art. The picture-book is not, perhaps, absolutely necessary to man's life, but it gives us such endless pleasure, and is so intimately connected with the other absolutely necessary art of imaginative literature that it must remain one of the very worthiest things towards the production of which reasonable men should strive.

Paper delivered before the Bibliographical Society on 19 June 1893, and published in Transactions of the Bibliographical Society.

1913
DESTRUCTION OF SYNTAX—IMAGINATION WITHOUT STRINGS—WORDS-IN-FREEDOM
F. T. Marinetti

AT A TIME WHEN *graphic design had yet to emerge as a fully defined commercial practice, the writings and experiments of the Italian Futurist Filippo Tommaso Marinetti (1876–1944) embodied a vigorous alternative set of possibilities for graphic communication. As a poet reacting against his Symbolist predecessors, Marinetti's primary concern was with the free expressive potential of language, and his typographic researches were all conducted to this end (though the approach would later be applied to advertising by Fortunato Depero and others). Marinetti was the self-publicizing author of the first Futurist hymn to speed, dynamism, war, and the end of tradition—published in* Le Figaro *newspaper in 1909— and between 1912 and 1914 he articulated his radical aesthetic agenda in a series of manifestos. This extract, with its section on "typographical revolution," is the most explicit in typographic terms. In the poems collected in his book* Les mots en liberté futuristes *(1919), Marinetti collaged letterforms and fragments into a state of violent agitation, with words moving at the velocity of the trains, planes, waves, and atoms that inspired the Futurists. Verbal language is dematerialized, even as its material aspects are elevated, while the sensibility guiding these paper-bound explosions is cybernetic.—RP*

WORDS-IN-FREEDOM

Casting aside every stupid formula and all the confused verbalisms of the professors, I now declare that lyricism is the exquisite faculty of intoxicating oneself with life, of filling life with the inebriation of oneself. The faculty of changing into wine the muddy water of the life that swirls and engulfs us. The ability to color the world with the unique colors of our changeable selves.

Now suppose that a friend of yours gifted with this faculty finds himself in a zone of intense life (revolution, war, shipwreck, earthquake, and so on) and starts right away to tell you his impressions. Do you know what this lyric, excited friend of yours will instinctively do?

He will begin by brutally destroying the syntax of his speech. He wastes no time in building sentences. Punctuation and the right adjectives will mean nothing to him. He will despise subtleties and nuances of language. Breathlessly he will assault your nerves with visual, auditory, olfactory sensations, just as they come to him. The rush of steam-emotion will burst the sentence's steampipe, the valves of punctuation, and the adjectival clamp. Fistfuls of essential words in no conventional order. Sole preoccupation of the narrator, to render every vibration of his being.

If the mind of this gifted lyrical narrator is also populated by general ideas, he will involuntarily bind up his sensations with the entire universe that he intuitively knows. And in order to render the true worth and dimensions of his lived life, he will cast immense nets of analogy across the world. In this way he will reveal the analogical foundation of life, telegraphically, with the same economical speed that the telegraph imposes on reporters and war correspondents in their swift reportings. This urgent laconism answers not only to the laws of speed that govern us but also to the rapport of centuries between poet and audience. Between poet and audience, in fact, the same rapport exists as between two old friends. They can make themselves understood with half a word, a gesture, a glance. So the poet's imagination must weave together distant things *with no connecting strings*, by means of essential *free* words.

DEATH OF FREE VERSE

Free verse once had countless reasons for existing but now is destined to be replaced by *words-in-freedom*.

The evolution of poetry and human sensibility has shown us the two incurable defects of free verse.

1. Free verse fatally pushes the poet towards facile sound effects, banal double meanings, monotonous cadences, a foolish chiming, and an inevitable echo-play, internal and external.
2. Free verse artificially channels the flow of lyric emotion between the high walls of syntax and the weirs of grammar. The free intuitive inspiration that addresses itself directly to the intuition of the ideal reader finds itself imprisoned and distributed like purified water for the nourishment of all fussy, restless intelligences.

When I speak of destroying the canals of syntax, I am neither categorical nor systematic. Traces of conventional syntax and even of true logical sentences will be found here and there in the words-in-freedom of my unchained lyricism. This inequality in conciseness and freedom is natural and inevitable. Since poetry is in truth only a superior, more concentrated and intense life than what we live from day to day, like the latter it is composed of hyper-alive elements and moribund elements.

We ought not, therefore, to be too much preoccupied with these elements. But we should at all costs avoid rhetoric and banalities telegraphically expressed.

THE IMAGINATION WITHOUT STRINGS

By the imagination without strings I mean the absolute freedom of images or analogies, expressed with unhampered words and with no connecting strings of syntax and with no punctuation.

'Up to now writers have been restricted to immediate analogies. For instance, they have compared an animal with a man or with another animal, which is almost the same as a kind of photography. (They have compared, for example, a fox terrier to a very small thoroughbred. Others, more advanced, might compare the same trembling fox terrier to a little Morse Code machine. I, on the other hand, compare it with gurgling water. In this there is an *ever vaster gradation of analogies*, there are ever deeper and more solid affinities, however remote.)

'Analogy is nothing more than the deep love that assembles distant, seemingly diverse and hostile things. An orchestral style, at once polychromatic, polyphonic, and polymorphous, can embrace the life of matter only by means of the most extensive analogies.

'When, in my *Battle of Tripoli*, I compared a trench bristling with bayonets to an orchestra, a machine gun to a *femme fatale*, I intuitively introduced a large part of the universe into a short episode of African battle.

'Images are not flowers to be chosen and picked with parsimony, as Voltaire said. They are the very lifeblood of poetry. Poetry should be an uninterrupted sequence of new images, or it is mere anaemia and greensickness.

'The broader their affinities, the longer will images keep their power to amaze.'

(Technical Manifesto of Futurist Literature)

The imagination without strings, and words-in-freedom, will bring us to the essence of material. As we discover new analogies between distant and apparently contrary things, we will endow them with an ever more intimate value. Instead of *humanizing* animals, vegetables, and minerals (an outmoded system) we will be able to *animalize, vegetize, mineralize, electrify, or liquefy our style*, making it live the life of material. For example, to represent the life of a blade of grass, I say, 'Tomorrow I'll be greener.'

With words-in-freedom we will have: CONDENSED METAPHORS. TELE-GRAPHIC IMAGES. MAXIMUM VIBRATIONS. NODES OF THOUGHT. CLOSED OR OPEN FANS OF MOVEMENT. COMPRESSED ANALOGIES. COLOR BALANCES. DIMENSIONS, WEIGHTS, MEASURES, AND THE SPEED OF SENSATIONS. THE PLUNGE OF THE ESSENTIAL WORD INTO THE WATER OF SENSIBILITY, MINUS THE CONCENTRIC CIRCLES THAT THE WORD PRODUCES. RESTFUL MOMENTS OF INTUITION. MOVEMENTS IN TWO, THREE, FOUR, FIVE DIFFERENT RHYTHMS. THE ANALYTIC, EXPLORATORY POLES THAT SUSTAIN THE BUNDLE OF INTUITIVE STRINGS.

DEATH OF THE LITERARY I

Molecular life and material
My technical manifesto opposed the obsessive *I* that up to now the poets have described, sung, analyzed, and vomited up. To rid ourselves of this obsessive *I*, we must abandon the habit of humanizing nature by attributing human passions and preoccupations to animals, plants, water, stone, and clouds. Instead we should express the infinite smallness that surrounds us, the imperceptible, the invisible, the agitation of atoms, the Brownian movements, all the passionate hypotheses and all the domains explored by the high-powered microscope. To explain: I want to introduce the infinite molecular life into poetry not as a scientific document but as an intuitive element. It should mix, in the work of art, with the infinitely great spectacles and dramas, because this fusion constitutes the integral synthesis of life.

To give some aid to the intuition of my ideal reader I use italics for all words-in-freedom that express the infinitely small and the molecular life.

SEMAPHORIC ADJECTIVE

Lighthouse-adjective or *atmosphere-adjective*
Everywhere we tend to suppress the qualifying adjective because it presupposes an arrest in intuition, too minute a definition of the noun. None of this is categorical. I speak of a tendency. We must make use of the adjective as little as possible and in a manner completely different from its use hitherto. One should treat adjectives like railway signals of style, employ them to mark the tempo, the retards and pauses along

the way. So, too, with analogies. As many as twenty of these semaphoric adjectives might accumulate in this way.

What I call a semaphoric adjective, lighthouse-adjective, or atmosphere-adjective is the adjective apart from nouns, isolated in parentheses. This makes it a kind of absolute noun, broader and more powerful than the noun proper.

The semaphoric adjective or lighthouse-adjective, suspended on high in its glassed-in parenthetical cage, throws its far-reaching, probing light on everything around it.

The profile of this adjective crumbles, spreads abroad, illuminating, impregnating, and enveloping a whole zone of words-in-freedom. If, for instance, in an agglomerate of words-in-freedom describing a sea voyage I place the following semaphoric adjectives between parentheses: (calm, blue, methodical, habitual) not only the sea is *calm, blue, methodical, habitual*, but the ship, its machinery, the passengers. What I do and my very spirit are calm, blue, methodical, habitual.

THE INFINITIVE VERB

Here, too, my pronouncements are not categorical. I maintain, however, that in a violent and dynamic lyricism the infinitive verb might well be indispensable. Round as a wheel, like a wheel adaptable to every car in the train of analogies, it constitutes the very speed of the style.

The infinitive in itself denies the existence of the sentence and prevents the style from slowing and stopping at a definite point. While *the infinitive is round* and as mobile as a wheel, the other moods and tenses of the verb are either triangular, square, or oval.

ONOMATOPOEIA AND MATHEMATICAL SYMBOLS

When I said that we must spit on the Altar of Art, I incited the Futurists to liberate lyricism from the solemn atmosphere of compunction and incense that one normally calls by the name of Art with a capital *A*. Art with a capital *A* constitutes the clericalism of the creative spirit. I used this approach to incite the Futurists to destroy and mock the garlands, the palms, the aureoles, the exquisite frames, the mantles and stoles, the whole historical wardrobe and the romantic bric-a-brac that comprise a large part of all poetry up to now. I proposed instead a swift, brutal, and immediate lyricism, a lyricism that must seem anti-poetic to all our predecessors, a telegraphic lyricism with no taste of the book about it but, rather, as much as possible of the taste of life. Beyond that the bold introduction of onomatopoetic harmonies to render all the sounds and noises of modern life, even the most cacophonic.

Onomatopoeia that vivifies lyricism with crude and brutal elements of reality was used in poetry (from Aristophanes to Pascoli) more or less timidly. We Futurists initiate the constant, audacious use of onomatopoeia. This should not be systematic. For instance, my *Adrianople Siege-Orchestra* and my *Battle Weight + Smell* required many onomatopoetic harmonies. Always with the aim of giving the greatest number of vibrations and a deeper synthesis of life, we abolish all stylistic bonds, all the bright buckles with which the traditional poets link images together in their prosody. Instead we employ the very brief or anonymous mathematical and musical symbols and we put between parentheses indications such as (fast) (faster) (slower) (two-beat time) to control the speed of the style. These parentheses can even cut into a word or an onomatopoetic harmony.

TYPOGRAPHICAL REVOLUTION

I initiate a typographical revolution aimed at the bestial, nauseating idea of the book of passéist and D'Annunzian verse, on seventeenth-century handmade paper bordered with helmets, Minervas, Apollos, elaborate red initials, vegetables, mythological missal ribbons, epigraphs, and roman numerals. The book must be the Futurist expression of our Futurist thought. Not only that. My revolution is aimed at the so-called typographical harmony of the page, which is contrary to the flux and reflux, the leaps and bursts of style that run through the page. On the same page, therefore, we will use *three or four colors of ink,* or even twenty different typefaces if necessary. For example: italics for a series of similar or swift sensations, boldface for the violent ono-matopoeias, and so on. With this typographical revolution and this multicolored variety in the letters I mean to redouble the expressive force of words.

I oppose the decorative, precious aesthetic of Mallarmé and his search for the rare word, the one indispensable, elegant, suggestive, exquisite adjective. I do not want to suggest an idea or a sensation with passéist airs and graces. Instead I want to grasp them brutally and hurl them in the reader's face.

Moreover, I combat Mallarmé's static ideal with this typographical revolution that allows me to impress on the words (already free, dynamic, and torpedo-like) every velocity of the stars, the clouds, aeroplanes, trains, waves, explosives, globules of seafoam, molecules, and atoms.

Thus I realize the fourth principle of my First Futurist Manifesto (20 February 1909): 'We affirm that the world's beauty is enriched by a new beauty: the beauty of speed.'

MULTILINEAR LYRICISM

In addition, I have conceived *multilinear lyricism,* with which I succeed in reaching that lyric simultaneity that obsessed the Futurist painters as well: multilinear lyricism by means of which I am sure to achieve the most complex lyric simultaneities.

On several parallel lines, the poet will throw out several chains of color, sound, smell, noise, weight, thickness, analogy. One of these lines might, for instance, be olfactory, another musical, another pictorial.

Let us suppose that the chain of pictorial sensations and analogies dominates the others. In this case it will be printed in a heavier typeface than the second and third lines (one of them containing, for example, the chain of musical sensations and analogies, the other the chain of olfactory sensations and analogies).

Given a page that contains many bundles of sensations and analogies, each of which is composed of three or four lines, the chain of pictorial sensations and analogies (printed in boldface) will form the first line of the first bundle and will continue (always in the same type) on the first line of all the other bundles.

The chain of musical sensations and analogies, less important than the chain of pictorial sensations and analogies (first line) but more important than that of the olfactory sensations and analogies (third line), will be printed in smaller type than that of the first line and larger than that of the third.

FREE EXPRESSIVE ORTHOGRAPHY

The historical necessity of free expressive orthography is demonstrated by the successive revolutions that have continuously freed the lyric powers of the human race from shackles and rules.

1. In fact, the poets began by channeling their lyric intoxication into a series of equal breaths, with accents, echoes, assonances, or rhymes at pre-established intervals (*traditional metric*). Then the poets varied these different measured breaths of their predecessors' lungs with a certain freedom.

2. Later the poets realized that the different moments of their lyric intoxication had to create breaths suited to the most varied and surprising intervals, with absolute freedom of accentuation. Thus they arrived at *free verse*, but they still preserved the syntactic order of the words, so that the lyric intoxication could flow down to the listeners by the logical canal of syntax.

3. Today we no longer want the lyric intoxication to order the words syntactically before launching them forth with the breaths we have invented, and we have *words-in-freedom*. Moreover our lyric intoxication should freely deform, refresh the words, cutting them short, stretching them out, reinforcing the center or the extremities, augmenting or diminishing the number of vowels and consonants. Thus we will have the *new orthography* that I call *free expressive*. This instinctive deformation of words corresponds to our natural tendency towards onomatopoeia. It matters little if the deformed word becomes ambiguous. It will marry itself to the onomatopoetic harmonies, or the noise-summaries, and will permit us soon to reach the *onomatopoetic psychic* harmony, the sonorous but abstract expression of an emotion or a pure thought. But one may object that my words-in-freedom, my imagination without strings, demand special speakers if they are to be understood. Although I do not care for the comprehension of the multitude, I will reply that the number of Futurist public speakers is increasing and that any admired traditional poem, for that matter, requires a special speaker if it is to be understood.

First published in Lacerba *(Florence: 15 June 1913).*

1921
PROGRAM OF THE FIRST WORKING GROUP OF CONSTRUCTIVISTS
Alexander Rodchenko and Varvara Stepanova

AS A COMMITTED COMMUNIST, *Alexander Rodchenko (1891–1956) was one of the first artists to support the Bolsheviks after the 1917 Russian Revolution. In 1921, he abandoned easel painting and sculpture to concentrate instead on the more socially useful activities of design, typography, and photography. Rodchenko was a founding member of Inkhuk, the Institute of Artistic Culture, which operated in Moscow from 1920 to 1924, and the Working Group of Constructivists was formed in March 1921 during his time as the institute's director. The Constructivist program, coauthored by Rodchenko and his partner Varvara Stepanova (1894–1958)—also a leading member of Inkhuk—was approved at the group's third meeting in April 1921 and published in slightly modified form the following year. It proposes a basis for working, in the service of "scientific communism," which is diametrically opposed to the ideological imperatives of commercial graphic design as it was then emerging in the United States and would later develop. Old forms of art would wither as "constructive life" became the art of the future.—RP*

The Group of Constructivists has set itself the task of finding *the communistic expression of material structures.*

In approaching its task, the group insists on the need to synthesize the ideological aspect with the formal for the real transference of laboratory work on to the rails of practical activity.

Therefore, at the time of its establishment, the group's program in its ideological aspect pointed out that:

1. Our sole ideology is scientific communism based on the theory of historical materialism.
2. The theoretical interpretation and assimilation of the experience of Soviet construction must impel the group to turn away from experimental activity 'removed from life' towards real experimentation.
3. In order to master the creation of practical structures in a really scientific and disciplined way, the Constructivists have established three disciplines: *Tectonics, Faktura,* and *Construction.*
   A. Tectonics or the tectonic style is tempered and formed on the one hand from the properties of communism and on the other from the expedient use of industrial material.
   B. *Faktura* is the organic state of the worked material or the resulting new state of its organism. Therefore, the group considers that *faktura* is material consciously worked and expediently used, without hampering the construction or restricting the tectonics.

C. Construction should be understood as the organizational function of Constructivism.

If tectonics comprises the relationship between the ideological and the formal, which gives unity to the practical design, and *faktura* is the material, the Construction reveals the very process of that structuring.

In this way, the third discipline is the discipline of the realization of the design through the use of the worked material.

The Material. The material as substance and matter. Its investigation and industrial application, properties and significance. Furthermore, time, space, volume, plane, color, line, and light are also material for the Constructivists, without which they cannot construct material structures.

The Immediate Tasks of the Group

1. In the ideological sphere:
   To prove theoretically and practically the incompatibility of aesthetic activity with the functions of intellectual and material production.
   The real participation of intellectual and material production as an equal element in the creation of communist culture.
2. In the practical sphere:
   To publish a statement.
   To publish a weekly paper, *VIP* [*Vestnik Intellektual'nogo Proizvodstva*; the *Herald of Intellectual Production*].
   To print brochures and leaflets on questions relating to the activities of the group.
   To construct designs.
   To organize exhibitions.
   To establish links with all the Production Boards and Centers of that unified Soviet machine, which in fact practically shapes and produces the emergent forms of the communist way of life.
3. In the agitational sphere:
   i. The Group declares uncompromising war on art.
   ii. It asserts that the artistic culture of the past is unacceptable for the communistic forms of Constructivist structures.

First published in Ermitazh, *no. 13 (Moscow: 1922).*

1922
NEW KIND OF PRINTING CALLS FOR NEW DESIGN
W. A. Dwiggins

BEFORE WILLIAM ADDISON DWIGGINS *(1880–1957) introduced the term "graphic design," descriptions like "printing art," "commercial art," "graphic art," and "advertising design" were used interchangeably to connote the visual output of the advertising profession. In this article, written for a special supplement of the* Boston Evening Transcript *devoted to the graphic arts, and published in conjunction with the city's annual graphic arts exposition, Dwiggins attempted to raise the consciousness of fellow graphic artisans and artists, and establish standards for the field. In the 1920s, he was one of the most influential advertising artists and his arguments resonated within the graphic arts community at the time of publication. However, it was at least another decade before "graphic design" became the preferred style of reference. The essay is also significant for what Dwiggins says about the consequences of new printing technologies and about the rise of the advertising industry on all other forms of graphic design. He argues that designers are responsible not only for serving their commercial clients but for satisfying themselves as artists.—SH*

Old Standards of Excellence Suddenly
Superseded Because of the Complex
of New Processes in the Industry—
Still the Opportunity, However,
for Blending Common-
sense with Artistic
Taste

Enthusiasts of a sentimental turn of mind, inspired by a verbal formula— The Printing Art—and misled by a false interpretation of the same, have worked great confusion with the boundary that divides art from printing. The subtle intoxication of the third word of the phrase induces them to materialize vague near-aesthetic halos upon the heads of various people who undertake to print.

How printed matter looks makes no conscious difference to anybody except to the designer and the connoisseur of printing. When placards are put up at the corner garage announcing the current price of gasoline they do not need to be fine art. They do their work just as they are. All the main purposes of printing can be served without calling upon the help of art. The manufacturer with something to sell has ideas about the good looks of his printing, but his ideas are peculiar unto himself, and do not usually claim any relationship with art. He may be under the illusion that his printing is art. We are not. But as a charitable act let us add him to the printing designer noted above to complete the roster of those who care how printed matter looks. Oftentimes printing seems to tell its story just as well without art.

ARTISTS STAMP THE HISTORY OF PRINTING

Make a record of these two facts—printing is not an art, and art is not essential to printing—and against them as a background let us project the following surprising conclusions. The history of printing is largely a history of individual artists. The names that stand foremost in the biography of the craft are the names of men conspicuous for a fine taste for design. Out of all the mass of printing that must have been done since the invention the only noteworthy relics are those few books ar ' documents that were made by men of artistic mind. Printed paper has been collected an. herished for three hundred years, not because it was printing but because it was printeu art.

Artists have tampered with printing and diverted it to their own ends ever since Gutenberg devised movable types. All through the course of the industry they have brought their faculties to bear upon the problem of turning printing into fine art. They have tampered with it in such a thoroughgoing fashion that—so far as the old work is concerned—the practical reasons for doing printing have been lost sight of, and printed paper is noteworthy chiefly because artists did meddle with it.

It will be perceived at once by the most complex that here are two groups of facts that do not fit together at all. There is more to this matter than appears at first blush. It would seem that there are several distinct classes of things to be examined under the title "printing." There are, verily.

Let us get down to cases and pick the industry apart. We want to find out what art has to do with printing—not historic printing but printing here and now. There are plain lines of cleavage in the modern industry. Working on these we are able to pry the business apart into three rough classes—plain printing; printing as a fine art; and a third large intermediate class of printing more or less modified by artistic taste. Town reports and handbills, telephone directories and school catalogs stand in the first class. The second might be represented by books printed for the Grolier Club by Bruce Rogers. The third class of printing is so wide and so varied that you will have trouble choosing examples to represent it.

PLAIN VARIETY AND FINE ART

Printing of the first class—the plain variety—is the backbone of the industry. This class outbulks the others by an overwhelming tonnage. It performs an imposing and valuable work and performs it in a thoroughly workmanlike manner. The technical excellence of the product of the "plain" printing plant is all that anyone could ask. The class of printing proves the truth of the deduction of the third paragraph. It gets no help from art and does not need it. It is outside the domain of art.

Printing as a fine art is not—as one might rashly assume from a review of the industry—a matter of history only. The thing is still happening. The man of taste—whom our sentimentalist would extinguish by calling him a "printer-artist"—is still to be discovered in the craft. Scattered all through the industry are men of fine artistic taste pursuing printing as an art. And it is to be noted that they do it, in many instances, on an entirely practical basis, and find little handicap, indeed, in their adherence to distinguished traditions. They produce printing that is fine art because they want to—because—one is constrained to say—they are artists.

But the consideration of printing as fine art is not quite the purpose of this note. Printing on that plane is, by its very nature, removed into the province of a critic of the fine arts, and cannot be examined on an equal footing with the product of the industry at large. What contact the industry at large has with art is the question on which we are engaged. We have narrowed our examination down to the third group of printing. We may look for that contact there.

This last group has certain noteworthy characteristics. For one thing it is not made to be sold, it is made to be given away—with a very canny purpose behind the gift. Then, it is a new thing—as new as advertising. It is thoroughly democratic—everybody takes a hand in making it. It goes everywhere and is read by everyone. It probably plays a larger part in forming the quasi-social state that we call civilization than all the books and newspapers and periodicals together. Its function is to prepare the ground for selling something, or to sell something directly itself. By hook or by crook, by loud noise or subtle argument, it might fulfill its mission of getting something sold.

It is really a kind of super-printing. Its requirements have forced the industry to expand itself, to include new and strange functions—critical study of clients' markets—preparation of "literature," descriptive, educational, argumentative—sales always in view at the end. One of the functions that the press has been forced to include is performed by a section known as the art department or art service.

The art department produces something. It is what is called "art work." The expression "art work" is advertising agents' slang. "Art work" might be defined as drawings, decorations, etc., made to complicate the advertiser's message. It seems that in some advertising a plain straightforward statement of the facts will not serve. Little indiscretions must be committed. Little naïve slips and false starts need to be contrived, to catch the victim's eye. Or he must have his back rubbed and his foibles exploited before he can be coaxed into just the right position for the deadfall to get him. One infers that it is the function of the art service to provide these inducements, indirections and subterfuges.

The ingenues of the art services work most skillfully at making pictures and ornamental designs. Their products rank sufficiently high as drawings and designs. But the application of their work slips up in some peculiar way. The big carnival on Main Street needs their help to be a complete affair but their art is off up a side alley doing clever tricks.

In view of the excellent work done by some of the art departments of printing plants the foregoing comment may seem to be pitched too strong. But these people hold a key position in the whole question of art and printing and the public taste, and what they do or misdo is of great moment to the artist. You can almost say that the future of printed graphic art rests in their hands. Illustration used to be spoken of as "the people's art" but advertising "art work" has supplanted it in popular esteem. Estimate how many more people know about Coles Phillips than know about Raleigh or George Wright. If all the talk about the importance of art to the industries of a nation is anything but buncombe it is of the highest importance that the advertising draughtsmen be made conscious of their influence and of their opportunity. Art will not occur in the industries until our fellow citizens learn to know the real thing when they see it. Advertising artists are now their only teachers. Advertising design is the only form of graphic design that gets home to everybody.

The implication is that the advertising artists fail to set the proper tone. The conduct of an art as an adjunct to business is always difficult. These artists, however sound as artists they may be in themselves, are under a pressure from outside that is almost bound to make them unfit as exponents of sound standards. It is unlucky that the job of setting styles for printing should be in their hands, because they are bound by the conditions of their service to set styles on a level lower than the best.

ADVERTISING ARTISTS CAN DO BETTER

But they can better their performance. They have the chance to work ably within the limitations of their handicap. They can bring some pressure to bear at least upon making salesprinting a clearer and more precise medium for the merchant's message. They need to relearn the rules of their game. Let them give ear to the words of the prophet and mend their ways. They have a moral code set down for the department of the just typographer made perfect:

> Cultivate simplicity. Have simple styles of letters and simple arrangements.
>
> In the matter of layout forget art at the start and use horse-sense. The printing-designer's whole duty is to make a clear presentation of the message—to give it every advantage of arrangement—to get the important statements forward and the minor parts placed so that they will not be overlooked. This calls for an exercise of common sense and a faculty for analysis rather than for art.
>
> Have pictures consistent with the printing process. Printers' ink and paper are a convention for light and shade and color. Stay inside the convention.
>
> Be niggardly with decorations, borders and such accessories. Do not pile up ornament like flowers at a funeral. Scheme the white spaces—paper is indeed a "part of the picture." Manipulate the spaces of blank paper around and among the printed surfaces to make a pleasing pattern of areas.
>
> Get acquainted with the shapes of the type letters themselves. They are the units out of which the structure is made—unassembled bricks and beams. Pick good ones and stick to them.

It is easy to formulate rules. It is not so easy to apply them. As a matter of fact, the new kind of printing calls for a new kind of design. The revolution in technical practice is complete. Very little is left of the old methods. The standards of good printing as they stood from the beginning of the craft are suddenly superseded. There is thrust into the printer's hand a complex of new processes—halftone engraving, machine composition, quadricolor, offset, fast running photogravure. The original conception of sound printing design as it stood until the age of the machines has very little bearing on these new processes. The impression of ink upon paper is an entirely new and different thing.

In one generation of printers the continuity of tradition has "faulted." Can we design this new printing with our minds trained in the standards that guided Aldus, or Bodoni, or DeVinne? Must all these things that we looked upon as good go overboard? How much of the old standard of quality can carry across the gap, and how can it be related to the new state of things? Typesetting by hand is about to become as obsolete as spinning thread by hand. Machine composition is a settled fact. How is it to be made good in the old sense? Or is the old sense to be discarded?

Of course all these questions will be answered. The right way will be worked out and a new standard evolved. The point to be stressed is that the new standard must not be a mechanical standard merely, it must also be an aesthetic standard. Artists must take a part in thinking it out—not the art services only, but artists—artists in terms of Holbein and Tory.

HINTS FOR ARTISTS IN MODERN PRINTING

There are hints in the new printing that the artist can profit by. Its material suggests a slighter and sketchier style than we at present affect—things that look like here today and gone tomorrow. Such things can still be good design and good art. The butterfly is justly admired for its good looks but is admittedly scheduled for only a brief stay. Our way of using decorative drawings that appear to have consumed months in their preparation is somehow inconsistent with the fact that the things they decorate are meant to last only for an hour. The enduring volumes of the ancients are the wrong source of inspiration for decorative styles that are to serve a purpose so ephemeral.

The French have caught the spirit of this kind of design. The leakage of their styles over into our picture making will serve us a good turn if we are able to perceive what they are about. The drawing of accessories for the new kind of printing and the layout of the printing itself need to be done at a higher rate of vibration than we are accustomed to. Some few have caught the pitch. The art director of *Vogue* and *Vanity Fair* schemes pages that are consistent with the demands of the new craft.

The problem is stimulating through the very condition of its novelty. New lines have to be run and new charts made. For the time being all fences are down and all rules off. So at least it would seem. But in spite of the completeness of the mechanical revolution, the law of art still runs. Sound design is still sound design, even though it be in novel material. The underlying purpose of printing has not changed, neither has the fundamental problem for the artist. An orderly and graceful disposition of parts continues to be desirable and printed pages are still intended to be read. On these terms the designer will attempt to do for the new printing what he undertook to do for the old. His success will still depend upon a suitable blending of common sense with artistic taste.

First published in the Boston Evening Transcript *(29 August 1922).*

1923
WITH TWENTY-FIVE SOLDIERS OF LEAD I HAVE CONQUERED THE WORLD
Francis Meynell

FRANCIS MEYNELL *(1891–1975), proprietor of the Pelican Press and the Nonesuch Press in England, worked at a time when the hegemony of traditional printing and typography was being challenged by the avant-garde moderns throughout Europe. The Pelican Press was established to produce, as Meynell wrote, "the finest possible printing for commerce" and attempted to bridge traditional and contemporary aesthetics. By example, the Pelican Press had a significant influence in the molding of contemporary commercial typography. In 1923, the Pelican Press issued* Typography, *a specimen book designed by Meynell that included "With Twenty-five Soldiers of Lead I Have Conquered the World" as its introduction. In 1971, Meynell wrote that this is "a typical effusion of a young man now grown a stranger to me." Nonetheless it is not only a typofile's tribute to his craft, but a testament that serves to underscore the passion that Meynell and his generation had for the arts of making and printing letters during a critical transitionary period in the history of design.—SH*

A ★ B ★ C ★ D ★ E ★ F ★ G ★ H
I ★ J ★ K ★ L ★ M ★ N ★ O ★ P
Q ★ R ★ S ★ T ★ U
V ★ W ★ X
Y ★ Z

That dramatic statement is obscure in origin, and (as they say) of a certain age—which means, here as always, of an uncertain age. Who said it, and when? Was it a village-bound boaster with a sudden and wonderful revelation of the dramatic spirit? Or was it in very truth a conqueror of men's minds?

Let those who know forbear to tell us. Let the birthplace of his aunt, the recollections of his schoolmaster, the intrigues which gave him his first start in life, let his habits in face of the bottle (to which he was wont to ascribe so much of his success or failure), his taste in cigars, or sword-hilts, or politics, or religion—let all be left unknown and ungathered. For whoever he was, however he prospered, he said and he did (I'll be bound) nothing else that could justify the sublime arrogance of that declaration—"with twenty-five soldiers of lead I have conquered the world." Anything more of his were a derogation from that assertion, or a flat denial, or (worst of all) a jest thrown at it—a very profanation of his moment of divinity.

One thing only shall be allowed. You who like "internal evidence"—a pleasant relic of school days and Skeat—may consider the number 25. Does that date the phrase? In the mid-seventeenth century the *W* was added to the twenty-five; and the twenty-five itself was promoted from twenty-four only a decade or two earlier by the establishment of J. Therefore, if you wish to put a date to Caesar-Shakespeare, I am prepared to agree to 1640. But my side of the bargain is this: that you do now, and with so much, rest content, and leave unopened the dictionary of phrases, where, doubtless, the thing is indexed, dated, annotated, ascribed, analyzed, historified, and stripped naked for the confusion of all our theory.

With twenty-five soldiers of lead. . . . If it is not individually it is at least generally true. All the heights and depths and breadths of tangible and natural things—landscapes, sunsets, the scent of hay, the hum of bees, the beauty which belongs to eyelids (and is falsely ascribed to eyes); all the immeasurable emotions and motions of the human mind, to which there seems no bound; ugly and terrible and mysterious thoughts and things, as well as beautiful—all are compassed, restrained, ordered in a trifling jumble of letters. Twenty-six signs! The complete equipment of my child of six—and of Shakespeare. Two dozen scratches so chosen and so arranged as to make *King Lear* and the Sonnets! They are common to the greatest, and to us. They are the key to eternity. They are the stepping-stones to the stars. And we use them, one to split his infinitives, one to forge a check, one to write betting-slips, one to compose an article which will consist of just so many words as fulfill the order to write such an Introduction as this.

Pause, gentle reader. Come back from the edge of this profound pool of sentiment and truth. Consider this in mitigation of the wonder. As literature is thus contained by a group of symbols, so life is controlled by another and shorter series. I make bold to declare that with eleven soldiers of lead—eleven, no more—I could conquer the universe. You doubt it? But first behold them:

9876543210£

The following simple summary of the history of type-forms, of their uses and of their technology, is addressed to the buyer of printing (be he author, merchant, secretary of a learned society, or publicity agent) who is at the same time a lover of the craft—an amateur of letters no less than of literature. There are plenty of learned, and it is to be feared pedantic, books for the professional bibliophile; and for the less expert and more open-minded a simpler and a more familiar method may be found of use. In the following pages, then, an attempt is made to assist the amateur to a right appreciation of type-forms, and to direct him towards the beautiful and the useful rather than to the "curious." That it is the work of a printer, and that its material is of necessity a display of his own wares, a well-furbished and furnished shop-window, should not detract, even in an age sensitive to (because governed by) advertisement, from whatever merit it possesses; indeed, it should add thereto. For, whatever this book amounts to, it is realistic, it is representative, it shows what can be commanded into his service by any buyer of printing; and it attempts to demonstrate what a commercial press can do to enrich the craft by ransacking the treasure houses of the past and breathing into old bodies the living spirit of our own day.

First published in Typography *(London: The Pelican Press, 1923).*

1923
THE NEW TYPOGRAPHY
László Moholy-Nagy

LÁSZLÓ MOHOLY-NAGY'S TIME *as a teacher at the Bauhaus, from 1923 to 1928, played a crucial role in the development of his ideas and work. Highly effective as a communicator, the self-taught Hungarian polyartist (1895–1946) practiced in many disciplines— painting, design, filmmaking, photography—and experimented with new materials and techniques. Moholy-Nagy's short text for the Bauhaus exhibition catalog* Staatliches Bauhaus in Weimar, 1919–1923 *is a much-cited statement of the fundamental principles of the New Typography, and he went on to design a number of publications embodying these tenets for the Bauhaus press. (In 1925, after the school moved from Weimar to Dessau, a typography and graphic design workshop was introduced, with Herbert Bayer as professor.) For Moholy-Nagy, the essential aim of the New Typography was efficient clarity purged of aesthetic distraction. Typographic form must be determined by the needs of the content, and to achieve this, "elasticity" of typographic expression was not only possible but* de rigueur.*—RP*

Typography is a tool of communication. It must be communication in its most intense form. The emphasis must be on absolute clarity since this distinguishes the character of our own writing from that of ancient pictographic forms. Our intellectual relationship to the world is individual–exact (e.g., this individual–exact relationship is in a state of transition toward a collective–exact orientation). This is in contrast to the ancient individual–amorphous and later collective–amorphous mode of communication. Therefore priority: unequivocal clarity in all typographical compositions. Legibility—communication must never be impaired by an *a priori* aesthetics. Letters may never be forced into a preconceived framework, for instance a square.

The printed image corresponds to the contents through its specific optical and psychological laws, demanding their typical form. The essence and the purpose of printing demand an uninhibited use of all linear directions (therefore not only horizontal articulation). We use all typefaces, type sizes, geometric forms, colors, etc. We want to create a new language of typography whose elasticity, variability and freshness of typographical composition is exclusively dictated by the inner law of expression and the optical effect.

The most important aspect of contemporary typography is the use of zincographic techniques, meaning the mechanical production of photoprints in all sizes. What the Egyptians started in their inexact hieroglyphs, whose interpretation rested on tradition and personal imagination, has become the most precise expression through the inclusion of photography into the typographic method. Already today we have books (mostly scientific ones) with precise photographic reproductions; but these photographs are only secondary explanations of the text. The latest development supercedes this phase, and small or large photos are placed in the text where formerly we used inexact, individually interpreted concepts and expressions. The objectivity of photography liberates the receptive reader from the crutches of the author's personal idiosyncrasies and forces him into the formation of his own opinion.

It is safe to predict that this increasing documentation through photography will lead in the near future to a replacement of literature by film. The indications of this development are apparent already in the increased use of the telephone, which makes letterwriting obsolete. It is no valid objection that the production of films demands too intricate and costly an apparatus. Soon, the making of a film will be as simple and available as now printing books.

An equally decisive change in the typographical image will occur in the making of posters, as soon as photography has replaced poster-painting. The effective poster must act with immediate impact on all psychological receptacles. Through an expert use of the camera, and of all photographic techniques, such as retouching, blocking, superimposition, distortion, enlargement, etc., in combination with the liberated typographical line, the effectiveness of posters can be immensely enlarged.

The new poster relies on photography, which is the new storytelling device of civilization, combined with the shock effect of new typefaces and brilliant color effects, depending on the desired intensity of the message.

The new typography is a simultaneous experience of vision and communication.

First published in Staatliches Bauhaus in Weimar, 1919–1923 *(Munich: 1923).*

1923
TOPOGRAPHY OF TYPOGRAPHY
El Lissitzky

EL LISSITZKY'S STATEMENT, PUBLISHED *in Hanover, in Kurt Schwitters'* Merz *magazine, is a clarion call from the visionary phase of the New Typography. Its condensed declamations promise to sweep every established convention of bookmaking aside and usher in a new era. In his climactic image of the "electro-library," Lissitzky (1890–1941) fore-sees the hypertextual labyrinths eventually delivered by digital technologies. His demand for new writers able to meet the dynamic visual needs of the reinvented book has been repeat-ed many times, though it has still to find widespread understanding or regular fulfillment in the prolific industries of text and image.—RP*

1. The words on the printed surface are taken in by seeing, not by hearing.
2. One communicates meanings through the convention of words; meaning attains form through letters.
3. Economy of expression: optics not phonetics.
4. The design of the book-space, set according to the constraints of printing mechanics, must correspond to the tensions and pressures of content.
5. The design of the book-space using process blocks which issue from the new optics. The supernatural reality of the perfected eye.
6. The continuous sequence of pages: the bioscopic book.
7. The new book demands the new writer. Inkpot and quill-pen are dead.
8. The printed surface transcends space and time. The printed surface, the infinity of books, must be transcended.

THE ELECTRO-LIBRARY

First published in Merz *no. 4 (Hannover: July 1923).*

1925
TYPOPHOTO
László Moholy-Nagy

AT THE BAUHAUS, LÁSZLÓ MOHOLY-NAGY *(1895–1946) edited the* Bauhausbücher *series of fourteen publications, with director Walter Gropius, and his own* Malerei, Photographie, Film (Painting, Photography, Film), *the eighth volume, was published in 1925. Moholy-Nagy's enormously influential concept of "typophoto"—the close integration, by technical means, of typography and the photographic image—is a central precept of modernist graphic design and a cornerstone of the discipline as it subsequently developed. Punctuating his text with large blobs, bold for emphasis, and heavy arrows, Moholy-Nagy foresees the arrival of a "new visual literature" in which photography will be used, as in his own book design, as "typographic" material alongside, and in place of, words. His prediction that the nonlinear techniques of the newsstand magazine might be used in philosophical works suggests he had something more complex in mind than the ordinary illustrated book.—RP*

N either curiosity nor economic considerations alone but a deep human interest in what happens in the world have brought about the enormous expansion of the news-service: typography, the film and the radio.

The creative work of the artist, the scientist's experiments, the calculations of the business-man or the present-day politician, all that moves, all that shapes, is bound up in the collectivity of interacting events. The individual's immediate action of the moment always has the effect of simultaneity in the long term. The technician has his machine at hand: satisfaction of the needs of the moment. But basically much more; he is the pioneer of the new social stratification, he paves the way for the future.

The printer's work, for example, to which we still pay too little attention has just such a long-term effect: international understanding and its consequences.

The printer's work is part of the foundation on which the *new world* will be built. Concentrated work of organization is the spiritual result which brings all elements of human creativity into a synthesis: the play instinct, sympathy, inventions, economic necessities. One man invents printing with movable type, another photography, a third screen-printing and stereotype, the next electrotype, phototype, the celluloid plate hardened by light. Men still kill one another, they have not yet understood how they live, why they live; politicians fail to observe that the earth is an entity, yet television (Telehor) has been invented: the 'Far Seer'—tomorrow we shall be able to look into the heart of our fellow man, be everywhere and yet be alone; illustrated books, newspapers, magazines are printed—in millions. The unambiguousness of the real, the truth in the everyday situation is there for all classes. **The hygiene of the optical, the health of the visible is slowly filtering through.**

●

What is typophoto?
Typography is communication composed in type. Photography is the visual presentation of what can be optically apprehended.
Typophoto is the visually most exact rendering of communication.

●

Every period has its own optical focus. Our age: that of the film; the electric sign, simultaneity of sensorily perceptible events. It has given us a new, progressively developing creative basis for typography too. Gutenberg's typography, which has endured almost to our own day, moves exclusively in the linear dimension. The intervention of the photographic process has extended it to a new dimensionality, recognized today as total. The preliminary work in this field was done by the illustrated papers, posters and by display printing.

Until recently type face and type setting rigidly preserved a technique which admittedly guaranteed the purity of the linear effect but ignored the new dimensions of life. Only quite recently has there been typographic work which uses the contrasts of typographic material (letters, signs, positive and negative values of the plane) in an attempt to establish a correspondence with modern life. These efforts have, however, done little to relax the inflexibility that has hitherto existed in typographic practice. An effective loosening-up can be achieved only by the most sweeping and all-embracing use of the techniques of photography, zincography, the electrotype, etc. The flexibility and elasticity of these techniques bring with them a new reciprocity between economy and beauty. With the development of **photo-telegraphy,** which enables reproductions and accurate illustrations to be made instantaneously, even philosophical works will presumably use the same means—though on a higher plane—as the present day American magazines. The form of these new typographic works will, of course, be quite different typographically, optically, and synoptically from the linear typography of today.

Linear typography communicating ideas is merely a mediating makeshift link between the content of the communication and the person receiving it:

COMMUNICATION   ←   TYPOGRAPHY   →   PERSON

Instead of using typography—as hitherto—merely as an objective means, the attempt is now being made to incorporate it and the potential effects of its subjective existence creatively into the contents.

The typographical materials themselves contain strongly optical tangibilities by means of which they can render the content of the communication in a directly visible—not only in an indirectly intellectual—fashion. Photography is highly effective when used as typographical material. It may appear as illustration beside the words, or in the form of **'phototext'** in place of words, as a precise form of representation so objective as to permit of no individual interpretation. The form, the rendering is constructed out of the optical and associative relationships: into a visual, associative, conceptual, synthetic continuity: into the typophoto as an unambiguous rendering in an *optically* valid form.

The typophoto governs the new tempo of the new visual literature.

●

In the future every printing press will possess its own block-making plant and it can be confidently stated that the future of typographic methods lies with the photo-mechanical processes. The invention of the photographic type-setting machine, the possibility of printing whole editions with X-ray radiography, the new cheap techniques of block making, etc., indicate the trend to which every typographer or typophotographer must adapt himself as soon as possible.

●

This mode of modern synoptic communication may be broadly pursued on another plane by means of the kinetic process, the film.

First published in Malerei, Photographie, Film *(Munich: Albert Langen Verlag, 1925).*

1926
OUR BOOK
El Lissitzky

AS JAN TSCHICHOLD WAS *quick to acknowledge in his seminal book* Die neue Typographie, *published in 1928, El Lissitzky (1890–1941) was one of the preeminent contributors to the new typographic theory. The enormously energetic Russian artist traveled to Berlin in 1921 and, through his work in photomontage, print-making, graphic design, and painting, went on to play a pivotal role in introducing Constructivist and Suprematist ideas into western European art and design. Lissitzky visited the Bauhaus, wrote articles, gave lectures, collaborated on a double issue of Kurt Schwitters's* Merz *(in which his "Topography of Typography" had earlier appeared), and created the trilingual journal* Veshch (Object) *for the Soviet government—with editor Ilya Ehrenburg—before returning to Moscow in 1925 to teach at the Vhkutemas, the Russian Bauhaus. "Our Book," published the following year, elaborates the themes of Lissitzky's* Merz *manifesto. He accurately predicts the liberating effects of photomechanical processes and struggles with the question of what the contemporary book should become. If dematerialization characterizes the age, he suggests, then the traditional form of the book (jacket, spine, sequential numbered pages) must explode into new configurations capable of expressing the "lyric and epic evolution" of the time.—RP*

Every invention in art is a single event in time, has no evolution. With the passage of time different variations of the same theme are composed around the invention, sometimes more sharpened, sometimes more flattened, but seldom is the original power attained. So it goes on till, after being performed over a long period, this work of art becomes so automatic-mechanical in its performance that the mind ceases to respond to the exhausted theme; then the time is ripe for a new invention. The so-called technical aspect is, however, inseparable from the so-called artistic aspect and therefore we do not wish to dismiss close associations lightly, with a few catchwords. In any case, Gutenberg, the inventor of the system of printing from movable type, printed a few books by this method which stand as the highest achievement in book art. Then there follow a few centuries which produced no fundamental inventions in our field (up to the invention of photography). What we find, more or less, in the art of printing are masterly variations accompanied by technical improvement in the production of the instruments. The same thing happened with a second invention in the visual field—with photography. The moment we stop riding complacently on our high horse, we have to admit that the first daguerreotypes are not primitive rough-and-ready things, but the highest achievements in the field of the photographic art. It is shortsighted to think that the machine alone, that is to say the supplanting of manual processes by mechanical ones, is fundamental to the changing of the appearance and form of things. In the first place it is the consumer who determines the change by his requirements; I refer to the stratum of society that furnishes the 'commission.' Today it is not a narrow circle, a thin upper layer, but 'All,' the masses. The idea which moves the masses today is called materialism, but what precisely characterizes the present time is dematerialization. An example: correspondence grows, the number of letters increases, the amount of paper written on and material used up swells, then the telephone-call relieves the strain. Then comes further growth of the communications network and increase in the volume of communications; then radio eases the burden. The amount of material used is decreasing, we are dematerializing, cumbersome masses of material are being supplanted by released energies. That is the sign of our time. What kind of conclusions can we draw from these observations, with reference to our field of activity?

I put forward the following analogies:

INVENTIONS IN THE fiELD OF THOUGHT-COMMUNICATION	INVENTIONS IN THE fiELD OF GENERAL COMMUNICATION
Articulated speech	Upright walk
Writing	Wheel
Gutenberg's letter press	Animal-drawn vehicle
?	Motor-car
?	Aeroplane

I submit these analogies in order to demonstrate that as long as the book is of necessity a hand-held object, that is to say not yet supplanted by sound recordings or talking pictures, we must wait from day to day for new fundamental inventions in the field of book-production, so that here also we may reach the standard of the time.

Present indications are that this basic invention can be expected from the neighboring field of collotype. This process involves a machine which transfers the composed type-matter onto a film, and a printing-machine which copies the negative onto sensitive paper. Thus the enormous weight of type and the bucket of ink disappear, and so here again we also have dematerialization. The most important aspect is that the production style for word and illustration is subject to one and the same process—to the collotype, to photography. Up to the present there has been no kind of representation as completely comprehensible to all people as photography. So we are faced with a book-form in which representation is primary and the alphabet secondary.

We know two kinds of writing: a symbol for each idea = hieroglyph (in China today) and a symbol for each sound = letter. The progress of the letter in relation to the hieroglyph is relative. The hieroglyph is international: that is to say, if a Russian, a German, or an American impresses the symbols (pictures) of the ideas on his memory, he can read Chinese or Egyptian (silently), without acquiring a knowledge of the language, for language and writing are each a pattern in itself. This is an advantage which the letter-book has lost. So I believe that the next book-form will be plastic-representational. We can say that

(1) the hieroglyph-book is international (at least in its potentiality),
(2) the letter-book is national, and
(3) the coming book will be a-national: for in order to understand it, one must at least learn.

Today we have two dimensions for the word. As a sound it is a function of time, and as a representation it is a function of space. The coming book must be both.

In this way the automatism of the present-day book will be overcome; for a view of life which has come about automatically is no longer conceivable to our minds and we are left suffocating in a vacuum. The energetic task which art must accomplish is to transmute the emptiness into space, that is, into something that our minds can grasp as an organized unity.

With changes in the language, in construction and style, the visual aspect of the book changes also. Before the war, European printed matter looked much the same in all countries. In America there was a new optimistic mentality, concerned with the day in hand, focused on immediate impressions, and this began to create a new form of printed matter. It was there that they first started to shift the emphasis and make the word be the illustration of the picture, instead of the other way round, as in Europe. Moreover, the highly-developed technique of the process block made a particular contribution; and so photomontage was invented.

Postwar Europe, skeptical and bewildered, is cultivating a shrieking, bellowing language; one must hold one's own and keep up with everything. Words like 'attraction' and 'trick' are becoming the catchwords of the time. The appearance of the book is characterized by: (1) fragmented type panel, (2) photomontage and typomontage.

All these facts are like an airplane. Before the war and our revolution it was carrying us along the runway to the take-off point. We are now becoming airborne and our faith for the future is in the airplane—that is to say in these facts.

The idea of the 'simultaneous' book also originated in the prewar era and was realized after a fashion. I refer to a poem by Blaise Cendrars, typographically designed by Sonia Delaunay-Terk, which is on a folding strip of paper, 1.50 meters in length; so it was an experiment with a new book-form for poetry. The lines of the poem are printed in colors, according to content, so that they go over from one color to another following the changes in meaning.

In England during the war, the Vortex Group published its work BLAST, large and elementary in presentation, set almost exclusively in block letters; today this has become the feature of all modern international printed matter. In Germany, the prospectus for the small Grosz portfolio *Neue Jugend*, produced in 1917, is an important document of the new typography.

With us in Russia the new movement began in 1908, and from its very first day linked painters and poets closely together; practically no book of poetry appeared which had not had the collaboration of a painter. The poems were written and illustrated with the lithographic crayon, or engraved in wood. The poets themselves typeset whole pages. Among those who worked in this way were the poets Khlebnikov, Kruchenykh, Mayakovsky, Asseyev, together with the painters Rozanova, Goncharova, Malevich, Popova, Burlyuk, etc. These were not numbered, deluxe copies, they were cheap, unbound, paperbacked books, which we must consider today, in spite of their urbanity, as popular art.

During the period of the Revolution a latent energy accumulated in our young generation of artists, which merely awaited the great mandate from the people for it to be released and deployed. It is the great masses, the semiliterate masses, who have become the audience. The Revolution in our country accomplished an enormous educational and propagandistic task. The traditional book was torn into separate pages, enlarged a hundred-fold, colored for greater intensity, and brought into the street as a poster. By contrast with the American poster, created for people who will catch a momentary glimpse whilst speeding past in their automobiles, ours was meant for people who would stand quite close and read it over and make sense out of it. If today a number of posters were to be reproduced in the size of a manageable book, then arranged according to theme and bound, the result could be the most original book. Because of the need for speed and the great lack of possibilities for printing, the best work was mostly done by hand; it was standardized, concise in its text, and most suited to the simplest mechanical method of duplication. State laws were printed in the same way as folding picture-books, army orders in the same way as paper-backed brochures.

At the end of the Civil War (1920) we were given the opportunity, using primitive mechanical means, of personally realizing our aims in the field of new book-design. In Vitebsk we produced a work entitled *Unovis* in five copies, using typewriter, lithography, etching and linocuts. I wrote in it: 'Gutenberg's Bible was printed with letters only; but the Bible of our time cannot be just presented in letters alone. The book finds its channel to the brain through the eye, not through the ear; in this channel the waves rush through with much greater speed and pressure than in the acoustic channel. One can speak out only through the mouth, but the book's facilities for expression take many more forms.'

With the start of the reconstruction period about 1922, book-production also increases rapidly. Our best artists take up the problem of book design. At the beginning of 1922 we publish, with the poet Ilya Ehrenburg, the periodical *Veshch* ('Object'), which is printed in Berlin. Thanks to the high standard of German technology we succeed in realizing some of our book ideas. So the picture-book 'Of Two Squares' which was completed in our creative period of 1920, is also printed, and also the Mayakovsky-book, where the book-form itself is given a functional shape in keeping with its specific purpose. In the same period our artists obtain the technical facilities for printing. The State Publishing House and other printing-establishments publish books, which have since been seen and appreciated at several international exhibitions in Europe. Comrades Popova, Rodchenko, Klutsis, Syenkin, Stepanova and Gan devote themselves to the book. Some of them work in the printing-works itself, along with the compositor and the machine (Gan and several others). The degree of respect for the actual art of printing, which is acquired by doing this, is shown by the fact that all the names of the compositors and feeders of any particular book are listed in it, on a special page. Thus in the printing-works there comes to be a select number of workers who cultivate a very conscious relationship with their art.

Most artists make montages, that is to say, with photographs and the inscriptions belonging to them they piece together whole pages, which are then photographically reproduced for printing. In this way there develops a technique of simple effectiveness, which appears to be very easy to operate and for that reason can easily develop into dull routine, but which in powerful hands turns out to be the most successful method of achieving visual poetry.

At the very beginning we said that the expressive power of every invention in art is an isolated phenomenon and has no evolution. The invention of easel-pictures produced great works of art, but their effectiveness has been lost. The cinema and the illustrated weekly magazine have triumphed. We rejoice at the new media which technology has placed at our disposal. We know that being in close contact with worldwide events and keeping pace with the progress of social development, that with the perpetual sharpening of our optic nerve, with the mastery of plastic material, with construction of the plane and its space, with the force which keeps inventiveness at boiling-point, with all these new assets, we know that finally we shall give a new effectiveness to the book as a work of art.

Yet, in this present day and age we still have no new shape for the book as a body; it continues to be a cover with a jacket, and a spine, and pages 1, 2, 3. . . . We still have the same thing in the theater also. Up to now in our country, even the newest theatrical productions have been performed in the picture-frame style of theater, with the public accommodated in the stalls, in boxes, in the circles, all in front of the curtain. The stage, however, has been cleared of the painted scenery; the painted-in-perspective stage area has become extinct. In the same picture-frame a three-dimensional physical space has been born, for the maximum development of the fourth dimension, living movement. This new-born theater explodes the old theater-building. Perhaps the new work in the inside of the book is not yet at the stage of exploding the traditional book-form, but we should have learned by now to recognize the tendency.

Notwithstanding the crises which book-production is suffering, in common with other areas of production, the book-glacier is growing year by year. The book is becoming the most monumental work of art: no longer is it something caressed only by the delicate hands of a few bibliophiles; on the contrary, it is already being grasped by hundreds of thousands of poor people. This also explains the dominance, in our transition period, of the illustrated weekly magazine. Moreover, in our country a stream of childrens' picture-books has appeared, to swell the inundation of illustrated periodicals. By reading, our children are already acquiring a new plastic language; they are growing up with a different relationship to the world and to space, to shape and to color; they will surely also create another book. We, however, are satisfied if in our book the lyric and epic evolution of our times is given shape.

Abridged from Gutenberg-Jahrbuch *(Mainz, 1926/7).*

1927
WHAT IS NEW TYPOGRAPHY?
Walter Dexel

WALTER DEXEL *(1890–1973) was a Constructivist painter and advertising designer who organized painting exhibitions for Expressionist artists of aesthetic and political movements—Die Brücke, Der Blaue Reiter, and Der Sturm—as well as for the Bauhaus masters Vassily Kandinsky and Paul Klee. He is, however, a marginalized figure within the group of designers practicing the New Typography and was omitted from Jan Tschichold's* Elementare Typographie *(although the oversight was later rectified in* Die neue Typografie*). In 1925, he was invited to Frankfurt, then a center of progressive practice, as an advertising consultant. While there Dexel published this article on the application of modern typography in a Frankfurt daily newspaper. Like the other well-known progressive manifestos, the article was both a practical and philosophical argument for the rightness of the new methods and a proclamation of ascendancy. Its publication encouraged the directors of the Kunstgewerbeschule (School of Arts and Crafts) in Magdeburg to appoint Dexel in 1928 to fill the post of director of the commercial art program, where he remained for a decade until the Nazis branded him a "decadent artist" and he was discharged.—SH*

The goal of the new typography is an objective and impersonal presentation, free of individuality. In my opinion, neither the imitation of handwriting, nor the use of rare, unusual print, nor the alphabet to which several of our most modern artists attach such great importance, nor new and improved script, nor script used only in lower case fulfill this requirement. We have only one duty: to be objective and typical.

Our highest aim is legibility, and our best type is the one which everybody can decipher quickly. If writing in exclusively lower case letters becomes familiar usage, we shall use it, because we realize its economy. However, as long as it requires a special effort on the part of the average reader, it is not the best possible instrument of communication for us.

Our abilities, our taste, or our artistry are of little interest to the public. Science and art are nowadays taken into account much too often. When our message is that coffee is beneficial or that Elizabeth Bergner will appear in the theater tomorrow, or that such-and-such cigarette costs fifty cents, art is not a question.

When information is transmitted over the radio, we do not require that the announcer give us his own pledge, or that he give his voice one tremolo when talking about Elizabeth Bergner and another when he praises Manoli. We would even object to this greatly and beg this gentlemen, "Sir, do talk clearly and make it snappy!"

In my opinion the same holds true for graphic communication. The message has to be clear, objective, and very short. Floods of words and an excessive use of art have taken hold of the field of typography and publicity, and have stifled these basically simple and obvious matters to such a degree that we have to recapture by hard work, step-by-step, our ability to express something precisely. Only those who are deeply involved in these matters know how hard it is to limit oneself to necessities.

Well-conceived typography transmits a pleasing effect of balance and harmony apart from its contents, which may not be the aim of art, but which shows skill and high-quality workmanship. Our means only seem to be limited; our inability to discriminate is the fault of bad training. We have been bombarded by heavy guns too long. In reality each task requires a particular solution. One can hardly make recipes and we should guard against all dogmas, even the factually correct, such as:

"one reads

from the left top

to the right bottom

and must design

accordingly."

It is not at all essential that a printed communication be read from first word to last in consecutive order. In an announcement of an art club the reader should first learn who is to be exhibited. Then if he is not interested in the artist, he need not read the rest of the announcement.

The announcements of the *Jenaer Kunstverein* shown here serve a double purpose: first they are sent to the homes of club members and second they are converted to posters for display in universities, reading rooms, stores, shop windows, etc., by adding a strip of color glued to cardboard of another color. If it were not essential that they be effective seen from a distance, one could object to the heavy san serif lettering, which is not particularly suitable for a postal card.

The block has already become an emblem which the initiated recognize without reading it, and which, therefore, only concerns the stranger. Therefore, apart from the artist's name, only the dates and the information

KUNSTVEREIN JENA

PRINZESSINNENSCHLÖSSCHEN
MITTWOCHS U. SONNABENDS 3–5, SONNTAGS 11–1
AUSSER DER ZEIT FÜHRUNG DURCH DEN HAUSMEISTER

that the works to be shown are watercolors, graphics, paintings, or whatever remain. The arrangement of the single blocks may be necessary but the design need not be monotonous or stereotyped. It is always possible to highlight the most important information by leaving the largest possible empty space around it or by emphasizing particular lines.

In general one understands today by modern media the type (mostly sanserif in all thicknesses and angles. *Mediaeval-Antiqua, Egyptienne,* and a few other clear scripts), the strokes, dots, squares, and arrows available in the printer's letter-case and above all the surrounding empty spaces which we regard as an active factor in achieving constrasts.

KUNSTVEREIN JENA

PRINZESSINNENSCHLÖSSCHEN
GEÖFFNET: SONNABENDS 3–5, SONNTAGS 11–1
AUSSER DER ZEIT FÜHRUNG DURCH DEN HAUSMEISTER
14. DEZEMBER 1924
BIS 11. JANUAR 1925

OSKAR SCHLEMMER

GEMÄLDE ZEICHNUNGEN BÜHNENENTWÜRFE FIGURINEN

Unter modernen Mitteln versteht man heute im allgemeinen neben der Letter (meist GROTESK in ALLEN STÄRKEN und GRADEN, der Mediaeval-Antiqua, der EGYPTIENNE und einigen anderen klaren Schriften) auch alle Arten von Strichen, Punkten, Quadraten und Pfeilen — kurz allen Zeichen, die sich im Kasten des Setzers finden

On the whole I personally am getting away more and more from the use of strokes and squares in the course of the years. Only in a few cases are they justified. As a rule it is sufficient to have proper distribution of space and great variety in type sizes. There is no doubt

that today there is a misuse of lines set at various angles, arrows, squares, and strokes. These serve as crutches and are "modern gestures" which should be rejected as preventing legibility. Used merely decoratively, as happens only too often, these forms are no better than the ornamental borders and the vignettes found at the end of the program of a small town glee club. If there is a square in bottom center instead of a birdie, nothing, but nothing, has been gained.

The "unrestrained use of all directions of lines" falls in the same category.

These are childish things which we should have discarded by now. If necessary, the usual familiar words like "Hotel" or "Bar" might be put one below another, but only such words which we already recognize when we have read only two letters. In all cases where we are not limited by space other solutions should be found. They are always possible; it is just cumbersome at times to search for them.

In order to emphasize the general layout, or to clarify and define the text, strokes or heavy lines may sometimes be unavoidable. Then they are justified and necessary, as for instance in the case of the card for *Der Sturm,* where there are a great number of hard-to-arrange names and, therefore, a planned composition is required. This was obviously determined by the capital letter *S* of the word "Sturm", which appears in the center of the card as large as possible. But this, too, may be regarded as a trifle which one should not repeat too often.

For all designs which have to fulfill other functions besides communication, such as book covers, magazine titles, letterheads, posters, etc., there are, of course, other rules. Communication through letters alone is a limited and specialized field.

In many cases pictorial representations of the objects will be very much to the point. Particularly suitable are all photographic techniques and mechanical reproductions of pictures because they inform us quickly and at the same time in great detail. In the future they will frequently be preferred to words alone.

First published in the Frankfurter Zeitung *(5 February 1927).*

1927
I AM TYPE
Frederic W. Goudy

A 1933 NEW YORKER *magazine profile described Frederic W. Goudy (1865–1947)*
as the "glorifier of the alphabet." He personally designed 124 typefaces and authored
numerous articles, pamphlets, and books, including The Alphabet *(1908),* Elements of
Lettering *(1921), and* Typologia *(1940). In addition, he founded two journals to adver-*
tise his aesthetic ideas: Typographica: A Pamphlet Devoted to Typography and Letter
Design *and* Ars Typographica. *These self-promotional publications were used to persuade*
printers to buy his type, though they eventually also became a resource for scholarship and
criticism. From 1903 to 1939, Goudy was proprietor of the Village Press in Marlborough,
New York, where he hand typeset and printed many of his own books and keepsakes. One
of his broadsides, "I Am Type," also titled "The Type Speaks," uses a preacher's oratory, cut
with irony, to sum up Goudy's oneness with letters, and illustrates the predominance of type
in the printing and design hierarchy of his day. A few years later, as a Christmas offering,
he printed a comic sequel titled "I Am Tight." Goudy's essays sharply prodded his colleagues
yet were often good humored. Although he wanted type designers to follow his standards, his
essays always asked questions rather than imposed rules.—SH

I AM TYPE! Of my earliest ancestry neither history nor relics remain. The wedge-shaped symbols impressed in plastic clay in the dim past by Babylon-ian builders foreshadowed me. From them through the hieroglyphs of the ancient Egyptians, the lapidary inscriptions of the early Romans, down to the beautiful letters by the scribes of the Italian Renaissance, I was in the making. John Gutenberg was the first to cast me in metal. From his chance thought straying through an idle reverie—a dream most golden—the profound art of printing with movable types was born.

Cold, rigid, implacable I may be, yet the first impress of my face brought the Divine Word to countless thousands. I bring into the light of day the precious stores of knowledge and wisdom long hidden in the grave of ignorance. I coin for you the enchanting tale, the philosopher's moralizing and the poet's visions. I enable you to exchange the irksome hours that come, at times, to every one, for sweet and happy hours with books—golden urns filled with all the manna of the past. In books I pre-sent a portion of the eternal mind caught in its progress through the world, stamped in an instant and preserved for eternity. Through me, Socrates and Plato, Chaucer and the bards become your faithful friends who ever surround and minister to you. I am the leaden army that conquers the world: I AM TYPE!

First published by the Village Press, 1931. Reprinted in A Bibliography of the Village Press
by Melbert B. Cary, Jr. (New York: The Press of the Woolly Whale, 1938).

1928
PRINTING OF TODAY
Aldous Huxley

ALDOUS HUXLEY *(1894–1963) is much better known as the author of the novels*
Point Counter Point *(1928) and* Brave New World *(1932) than for this, his only*
known commentary on printing and typography. But as a writer he was definitely concerned
with the presentation of his texts. When commissioned by Oliver Simon, editor of the
Fleuron, *to write the introduction to* Printing of To-day, *a compilation comparing tradi-*
tional and modernistic sensibilities, Huxley took the opportunity to address contemporary
design in aesthetic, sociological, political, and even spiritual terms ("... good printing can
create a valuable spiritual state in the reader, bad printing a certain spiritual discomfort").
He was particularly disappointed with the West's reliance on repetition of the same "six and
twenty letters." He argued that machines should be exploited to create a modern beauty, and
he believed that "violent typographic revolutions cannot be successful" and cautioned against
the preference among certain typographic reformers for illegible type composition that forced
the reader to slow down. Huxley insisted that it was "the author's duty to make reading less
facile," not the typographer's—a debate that continues to rage today.—SH

I n our enthusiasm for the spirit we are
often unjust to the letter. Inward and
outward, substance and form are not
easily separated. In many circumstances
of life and for the vast majority of human beings they constitute an indissoluble unity.
Substance conditions form; but form no less fatally conditions substance. Indeed, the
outward may actually create the inward, as when the practice of religious rites creates
religious faith, or the commemoration of the dead revives, or even calls into existence,
the emotions to which the ceremonial gives symbolical expression.

There are other cases, however, in which spirit seems not to be so closely
dependent on letter, in which the quality of the form does not directly affect the quality of the substance. The sonnets of Shakespeare remain the sonnets of Shakespeare
even in the most abominable edition. Nor can the finest printing improve their quality. The poetical substance exists independently of the visible form in which it is presented to the world. But though, in this case, the letter is powerless to make or mar
the spirit which it symbolizes, it is not for that reason to be despised as mere letter,
mere form, mere negligible outside. Every outside has a corresponding inwardness.
The inwardness of letters does not happen to be literature; but that is not to say that
they have no inwardness at all. Good printing cannot make a bad book good, nor bad
printing ruin a good book. But good printing can create a valuable spiritual state in
the reader, bad printing a certain spiritual discomfort. The inwardness of letters is the
inwardness of any piece of visual art regarded simply as a thing of beauty. A volume
of the Penny Classics may give us the sonnets of Shakespeare in their entirety; and for
that we may be duly grateful. But it cannot at the same time give us a work of visual
art. In a finely printed edition we have Shakespeare's sonnets *plus* the lovely equivalent

of, say, a Persian rug or a piece of Chinese porcelain. The pleasure we should derive from bowl or carpet is added to that which the poetry gives us. At the same time our minds are sensitized by the contemplation of the simple visual beauty of the letters: they are made more susceptible of receiving the other and more complex beauties, all the intellectual and spiritual content, of the verse. For our sensations, our feelings and ideas do not exist independently of one another, but form, as it were, the constituent notes of what is either a discord or a harmony. The state of mind produced by the sight of beautiful letters is in harmony with that created by the reading of good literature. Their beauty can even compensate us, in some degree, for what we suffer from bad literature. They can give us intense pleasure, as I discovered in China, even when we do not understand what they signify. For what astounding elegances and subtleties of form stare out in gold or lampblack from the shop-fronts and the hanging scarlet signs of a Chinese street! What does it matter if the literary spirit expressed by these strange symbols is only 'Fried Fish and Chips', or 'A Five Guinea Suit for Thirty Shillings'? The letters have a value of their own apart from what they signify, a private inwardness of graphic beauty. The Chinese themselves, for whom the Fish-and-Chips significance is no secret, are the most ardent admirers of this graphic beauty. Fine writing is valued by them as highly as fine painting. The writer is an artist as much respected as the sculptor or the potter.

Writing is dead in Europe; and even when it flourished, it was never such a finely subtle art as among the Chinese. Our alphabet has only six and twenty letters, and when we write, the same forms must constantly be repeated. The result is, inevitably, a certain monotonousness in the aspect of the page—a monotonousness enhanced by the fact that the forms themselves are, fundamentally, extremely simple. In Chinese writing, on the other hand, the ideographs are numbered by thousands and have none of the rigid, geometrical simplicity that characterizes European letters. The rich flowing brushwork is built up into elaborate forms, each form the symbol of a word, distinct and different. Chinese writing is almost the artistic image of thought itself, free, various, unmonotonous. Even in the age of handwriting, the European could never hope to create, by means of his few and simple signs, an art of calligraphy comparable to the Chinese. Printing has rendered the Chinese beauty yet more unrealizable. Where the Chinese freely painted we must be content with reproducing geometrical patterns. Pattern making is a poorer less subtle art than painting. But it is still an art. By someone who understands his business the printed page can be composed into patterns almost as satisfyingly beautiful as those of the carpet or the brocade.

The problem that confronts the contemporary printer may be briefly stated as follows: to produce beautiful and modern print-patterns by means of labor-saving machinery. There have been numerous attempts in recent years to improve the quality of printing. But of these attempts too many have been made in the wrong spirit. Instead of trying to exploit modern machinery, many artistic printers have rejected it altogether and reverted to the primitive methods of an earlier age. Instead of trying to create new forms of type and decoration, they have imitated the styles of the past. This prejudice in favor of handwork and ancient decorative forms was the result of an inevitable reaction against the soulless ugliness of nineteenth-century industrialism. Machines were producing beastliness. It was only natural that sensitive men should have wished to abandon the use of machines and to return to the artistic conventions in vogue before the development of machinery. It has become obvious that the machine is here to stay. Whole armies of William Morrises and Tolstoys could not now expel it. Even in primitive India it has proved itself too strong for those who would, with Gandhi, resist its encroachments. The sensible thing to do is not to revolt against the inevitable, but to use and modify it, to make it serve your purposes. Machines exist; let us then exploit them to create beauty—a modern beauty, while we are about it. For we live in the twentieth century; let us frankly admit it and not pretend that we live in the fifteenth. The work of the backward-looking hand-printers may be excellent in its way; but its way is not the contemporary way. Their books are often beautiful, but with a borrowed beauty expressive of nothing in the world in which we happen to live. They are also, as it happens, so expensive, that only the very rich can afford to buy them. The printer who makes a fetish of handwork and medieval craftsmanship, who refuses to tolerate the machine or to make any effort to improve the quality of its output, thereby condemns the ordinary reader to a perpetuity of ugly printing. As an ordinary reader, who cannot afford to buy handmade books, I object to the archaizing printer. It is only from the man with the machine that I can hope for any amelioration of my lot as a reader.

To his credit be it spoken, the man with the machine has done his duty. He has set himself to improve the sordid typographical surroundings in which the impecunious reader was so long condemned to pass his life. He has shown that cheap books need not necessarily be ugly, and that machinery directed by a judicious mind can do as well as, or much better than, the hand of an uninspired craftsman. There are publishers in business today whose seven-and-sixpennies, regarded as typography, are worth a guinea apiece. (What they are worth as literature is another question.) There are a dozen presses producing fine work at moderate prices. The men behind the machines have used their brains.

Some of our excellent machine-printers are still, it is true, too fond of using decorations borrowed from the past, and types that savor of another age than ours. So long as our sense of period remains as strong as it is, so long as we retain our love of the quaint and its more modern equivalent, the 'amusing,' this tendency to substitute pastiche for original creation is bound to persist. There is an incessant demand for the antique: we should not be too hard on the printers who supply it. If they are sinning, they are at least sinning in company. Let the architects and painters, the interior decorators and the theatrical producers throw the first stone. There are pastichers among the printers, just as there are pastichers among the professors of every art. But there are also more original men, who are prepared to encourage modern decorators and to use types that are elegant and striking without being affectedly archaic.

With this last phrase I may seem to be damning the moderns with the faintest of praise. But the truth is that Typography is an art in which violent revolutions can scarcely, in the nature of things, hope to be successful. A type of revolutionary novelty may be extremely beautiful in itself; but, for the creatures of habit that we are, its very novelty tends to make it illegible, at any rate to begin with. I know a rather eccentric German typographical reformer, for whom legibility is the great enemy, the infamous thing that must at all costs be crushed. We read, he argues, too easily. Our eyes slide over the words, and the words, in consequence, mean nothing to us. An illegible type makes us take trouble. It compels us to dwell on each separate word: we have time, while we are deciphering it, to suck out its whole significance. Putting his theory into practice, this reformer had designed a set of letters so strangely unlike those with which the typographical practice of generations has made us familiar, that I had to pore over a simple English sentence as though it were Russian or Arabic. My friend was perhaps justified in thinking that we read too much and too easily. But his remedy, it seems to me, was the wrong one. It is the author's business to make reading less facile, not the printer's. If the author concentrated more matter into the same number of sentences, his readers would have to read more carefully than they do at present. An illegible type cannot permanently achieve the same result, for the simple reason that it does not permanently remain illegible. If we are prepared to make the effort to read until the novel forms have become familiar, the illegible type will come to be perfectly legible. In practice, however, we are reluctant to make this effort. We demand that typographical beauty shall be combined with immediate legibility. Now, in order that it may be immediately legible, a type must be similar to the types with which we are familiar. Hence, the practical printer, who has to live by selling his wares to a large public, is debarred from making revolutionary innovations in the designs of his type. He must content himself with refining on the ordinary, accepted types of commerce. If he has great typographical reforms in view, he must proceed towards them by degrees, modifying the currently accepted designs gradually, so as not to repel the ordinary lazy reader, who is frightened by the idea of making any unnecessary effort. In other arts, where form and substance are directly associated, revolution is possible, may even be necessary. But the outward form of literature is not typography. The association, in a book, of literature with one of the graphic arts is in the nature of an accident. The printer who would at one stroke revolutionize his art frightens away readers, for whom the idea of revolution in literature, or in one of the graphic arts that is independent of literature, has no terrors. The reason for this is obvious. People buy books for the sake of the literature contained in them and not, primarily, as specimens of graphic art. They demand of the typography that it shall be beautiful, yes; but also that it shall give them immediate and unhampered access to the literature with which it is associated. Printers may desire to be revolutionary; but unless they can afford to sell no books, they are compelled by the force of circumstances to adopt a cautious policy of gradual reform. The Communist must either turn Liberal or retire from business.

First published in Printing of To-Day: An Illustrated Survey of Post-war Typography in Europe and the United States *(London: Peter Davies Limited / Harper and Brothers, 1928).*

1929
THE PHILOSOPHY OF MODERNISM
IN TYPOGRAPHY
Douglas C. McMurtrie

IN THE 1920S, THE *philosophy and ideology that molded avant-garde art and design
was the province of Europeans. Not until after the 1925* Exposition Internationale des
Arts Décoratifs et Industriels Modernes *in Paris, which introduced Americans to the
"modern" and "moderne" styles of architecture, clothing, packaging, and graphics, did
American advertising begin to take heed of European progress, particularly in the realm of
type design. One of the leading proponents was Douglas Crawford McMurtrie (1888–
1944), typeface designer (Ultra Modern, McMurtrie Title), and director of typography at the
Ludlow Typograph Company. McMurtrie promoted "modernism's declaration of independence" and in articles for trade journals debated conservative critics who said that foreign
developments were ugly. Through his book,* Modern Typography and Layout, *a contemporary manual of style (published a year after Jan Tschichold's* Die neue Typographie) *he
attempted to convert commercial artists to modernism. This essay, chapter 4 of that book, laid
the philosophical groundwork. Yet where Tschichold's book itself exemplified the New
Typography, the design of McMurtrie's volume was self-consciously composed in a moderne
style.—SH*

Typography has become a medium of communication for the people as a whole and not solely for some select group. Therefore, not until the new spirit of modernism has quite deeply penetrated the popular consciousness, does printing begin to reflect it. Hence the modern movement has been slow in making its impress on the art of typography. But once the new influences were felt in the printing world, the first rumbles rapidly grew into a roar. Typography, like the other applied arts, has been shaken from its old foundations and is being reconstructed along modern lines. Let us consider, then, what the reconstruction is bringing forth, bearing in mind that the underlying principle of the new design is the dictum "Form follows function."

The primary function of typography is to convey a message to the comprehension of the readers to whom it is addressed. Some of these readers may not be particularly interested in the message; hence it is necessary to set it out in type in such manner that it may be read with the greatest possible ease and speed. Clarity is the essential feature of modern typography. Any form which does not first express the function of legibility is not in the true spirit of modern typography, no matter how striking or "modernistic" it may otherwise be.

In former days there was little reading matter, but there was much time available for reading. Today there is a plethora of printed matter clamoring for the attention of people who live at a tempo that leaves them relatively little time to read. To stand any chance of getting read and understood, therefore, the modern message in type must tell its story just as directly and vividly as possible. The outward form of modern typography is of little importance in itself; the expression of the sense of the copy is vital. Easy comprehension of the message, which in typography represents function, is therefore the determinant of form.

According to the principles of the modern typographers, there is permitted no formalism of arrangement. It would represent but slight advance, they argue, to free ourselves from one formalism only to yield in subjection to another, even though represented in newer and sounder rules. We must be guided solely by interpretation of the copy.

The arrangement must therefore be held fluid, so as to permit indication of the comparative importance of portions of the copy by variations in type size or weight, and the accentuation of individual words or sentences by any sound methods of display.

As all art of any vitality is a reflection of life, the typography which is truly representative of its period is expressive of the life of that period. Perhaps the most typical characteristic of present-day living is the quick tempo at which it moves. The tempo of our typography should be in keeping. It should be dynamic rather than static. Its balance should be that of motion rather than that of rest. The balanced compositions suited to the leisurely contemplation of an earlier generation must give place to arrangements in which the sense of movement is inescapable. For we of the present age must, so to speak, read as we run.

The modern typographer contends that symmetrical layout is an outworn form. If all lines are centered on a median axis, this arrangement argues for a special emphasis or significance in the centers of the lines which, of course, they do not have. Or it brings the eye repeatedly to a point of rest, which impedes the movement of the message. If there is any special emphasis or accent point in lines of open display composition, it is at the beginning—in musical parlance, at the point of "attack."

If we grant this contention, we find that the most rational positioning of display lines is to make them flush at the left of the page or of the advertisement, the point to which the eye automatically returns after reading the preceding line. One advantage of this arrangement is that lines of unequal length will fall more easily into a form which does not offend our sense of fitness, than would the same lines if centered.

In left-hand flush arrangements it seems possible to have lines succeed another with little thought of their relative lengths or sequence and still obtain an attractive and readable layout. [. . .]

"Pretty" layouts on the one hand, and exceedingly bizarre arrangements on the other, are to be frowned upon as diverting attention from the message itself to the physical form of its typography, which is always to be considered not as an end in itself, but only as a means to the end that the message be read.

For like reasons, ornamentation in the usual sense is excluded from the modern typography. The only purpose of ornament is to make of the layout an attractive picture, which is not a proper aim, as the sole object should be to get the printed story comprehended by the reader. Anything standing in the way of this objective must be sacrificed.

There is one exception to this general rule. Ornament that is "organic" to the copy—that is, ornament that promotes comprehension of the copy—is permitted if of extremely simple character, so that it does not become an object of interest in itself.

As to types, the tools of the typographer, the idea is to keep them as elementary as possible in form and design, without eccentricities which will attract attention to themselves, and correspondingly detract from the acuity of attention given to the sense of the copy. The more advanced of the modern typographers would even wish to standardize all types in one simple form, so that all attention to printing would be directed, without distraction of any kind, to the story being told in type.

Finally, in modern typography we are to depend on ourselves alone for the working out of any typographic problem, and not depend on the solutions or practices of another age. We are to do our creative work in the spirit of the present and to let it be truly expressive of our own interpretation of the message we are transmitting to readers through the medium of type.

Such, stated in briefest form, is the underlying philosophy of modern typography. I have stated it theoretically because, in essence, its tenets are sound and will commend themselves to the judgment of open-minded typographers. The following chapters of this book [*Modern Typography and Layout*] will be concerned largely with the practical application of these principles in the working out of everyday problems, and most of these applications will be discussed in detail.

But before passing to the consideration of modern typography in practice, it may be well to remind ourselves that the movement is still in its beginning stages and that a great deal of the current work is patently immature. Even the best of the modern typographers have not as yet found themselves in their new milieu. To express it differently, they are not yet fluent in the new idiom of typographic speech. They have taken a great step forward in achieving real emancipation from the rules and regulations of a codified typography. They have worked out a philosophy they consider sound. But the actual examples of their work fall far short, we must admit, of the idealistic expectations we might conceive from a reading of the manifesto of a modernist typographer.

We have, if you will, so far as execution is concerned, the uncertain steps of an infant Gargantua who, even in his babyhood, has shaken the world of type to its very foundations. Added strength, an increased sureness of step, and a greater degree of wisdom, we may expect with the maturity to which he is approaching nearer day by day.

First published in Modern Typography and Layout *(Chicago: Eyncourt, 1929).*

1929
OUTLINE OF THE ART OF ADVERTISING MANIFESTO
Fortunato Depero

FORTUNATO DEPERO *(1892–1960) was a proponent of Italian Futurism, an early European avant-garde movement that challenged bourgeois notions of beauty and extolled the virtues of machines, speed, and war. He wrote manifestos for newspapers, founded and directed the Futurist art magazine* Dinamo, *and organized Futurist exhibitions. Convinced that product advertising was the best means to stimulate a public dialogue on the new aesthetics he accepted commissions both in Italy—including a series for Campari—and New York, where he established a studio. His work was exhibited in 1929 at the prestigious Advertising Club on Park Avenue. Depero composed this brief outline for a manifesto that heroicized advertising, and in 1931, following his return to Rovereto, Italy, it was published as a longer pamphlet entitled "The Art of Advertising." He proclaimed that all good art was a kind of advertising and that paintings of the past celebrating war, religion, and even love were sales instruments. Believing that the artist must train his audience in visual matters, he resolved to work only for clients that gave him this freedom.—SH*

The Art of the future will be undoubtedly
ADVERTISING ART.

I learnt such an heretical teaching from museums, from the great works of the past.

All the Art of the last centuries has been marked with the exaltation of war and religious element.

They are just flattering documentations of facts, ceremonies, characters, exalted in their victories, in their symbols, in their ranges of splendour and command.

Even their products were in simultaneous exaltation: architectures, courts, thrones, draperies, halberts, flags, armours, arms, badges, paintings of any kind.

There is no ancient work without wreaths of advertising triumphs!

Even today
We have:
>   the kings of pneumatics
>   the princes of cars
>   the kings of magnets
>   the dukes of air fans
>   the emperors of motors.

With mechanical eagles we conquered the ecstasy of space!
With electrical magic we enjoyed the astonishment of miracles!
The Art of the past exalted the past-times!
The Art of today has to exalt our glories, our men, our products.
Speed, practicality, electricity.

Light × Light × Light × Light

Advertising Art
Is free from any academic refrain, it is cheerfully bold, exilarating, hygienic and optimistic.

It is an Art of difficult synthesis where the artist deals with the original creation and the modernity at any rate.

it is fatally necessary;
it is fatally bold;
it is fatally new;
it is fatally paid;
it is fatally lived.

First published as a pamphlet in 1931 in Rovereto, Italy.

1930
NEW LIFE IN PRINT
Jan Tschichold

IN THE OCTOBER 1925 *issue of* Typographische Mitteilungen, *a printer's trade journal, guest editor Jan Tschichold (1902–1974) introduced international examples of* elementare typographie *(elementary typography), the experiments in reductive design practice by the European avant-garde (de Stijl, Constructivism, and the Bauhaus). Three years later, in 1928, he published his most influential book,* Die neue Typographie *(trans.* The New Typography, *1995), a manual for German typographers on how to apply progressive, modern typographic concepts and thus reject antiquated ideas of composition. As codifier of the New Typography, Tschichold was in demand as both practitioner and commentator; he wrote a stream of books, pamphlets, and articles in Germany and abroad. His second book,* Eine Stunde Druckgestaltung, *included an introduction titled "Was ist und was will Die neue Typographie?" ("The new typography: What is it and what does it want?"); published as "New life in print" in the British journal* Commercial Art, *it is considered his most concise discussion on the subject. From 1930 to 1931,* Commercial Art *featured a series of articles by Tschichold that championed the adoption of asymmetry and sans-serif type.—SH*

The general term "The New Typography" embraces the activities of a few of the younger typographers working principally in Germany, the Soviet Union, Holland, Czechoslovakia, and in Switzerland and Hungary. The inception of the movement in Germany reaches back into the war period. The existence of the New Typography can be said to be due to the personal achievements of its initiators; but to me it seems more accurate to regard these as the exponents of the tendencies and practical needs of our time, a view which by no means attempts to underestimate their extraordinary achievements and creative power or the inestimable value of their individual pioneer work. The movement would never have been so widespread, as in Central Europe it incontestably is, had it not served practical contemporary needs, and this it does so excellently because its primary aim is the unprejudiced adaptation of typography to the purposes of the task in hand.

Here I think it necessary briefly to describe the state of prewar typographical development. Following upon the stylistic confusion of the eighties, England gave birth to the Arts and Craft movement (Morris 1892), which at least from a typographical standpoint, was mainly influenced by traditional tendencies (limitation of incunabula). In the "Youth style" (Jugendstil, ca. 1900) an attempt was made, without however any permanent success, to break away from traditional models, arriving at a misunderstood off-shoot of the Natural Form (Eckmann), finally to end in a renovated Biedermeier type (Wieynck)—in a word, in a new traditionalism. Then the traditional models were rediscovered and further imitated, albeit on this occasion with better understanding (German Book Production 1911-14-20). The reverence for traditional forms evoked by a more intensive research-work, resulted naturally in a limitation of creative freedom and forced it at length into inanition. Contrary to expectation, the most important gain resulting from these years was the rediscovery of original traditional faces (Walbaum, Unger, Didot, Bodoni, Garamond, etc.), which for some time and with every justification have been preferred above their "precursors," in reality their imitators.

The natural reaction to the inanition of prewar typography was the New Typography aiming above all at suppleness in its methods of design.

Two aims can be discerned in all typographical work: the recognition and fulfillment of practical requirements—and the visual design. (Visual design is a question of aesthetic; it is senseless to attempt to avoid this expression). At this point typography differs not a little from architecture: it is possible (and it has indeed been done by the best architects) that the form of a house may be determined by its practical purpose, but in the case of typography the aesthetic side in the question of design makes itself clearly manifest. This factor relates typography far more nearly to the domain of "free" design on a plane surface (painting, drawing) than to that of architectural art. Both typography and the graphic arts are always concerned with surface (plane) design. Here at this stage the reason why none other than the "new" painters, the "abstract" painters, were destined to be the initiators of the New Typography. It is too wide a subject here to give any account of the development of abstract painting in this connection: visit any exhibition of their work and its relation to the New Typography is immediately discernible. This connection is not, as many believe, a formalist one but is genetic, a fact which abstract painters themselves have failed to understand. Abstract painting is the "unpurposing" relating of pure color and form without any literary admixtures. Typography signifies the visual (or aesthetic) ordering of given elements (practical requirements, type, pictures, color, etc.), on a plane surface. The difference between painting and typography exists only inasmuch as in the former there is a free choice of elements and the resulting design has no practical purpose. Modern typography therefore cannot be better occupied than with an intensive study of surface composition in abstract painting.

Let us examine the principles followed by prewar typography. The majestic traditional model knew of only one scheme of design—the medial axis, the axial symmetry whose plainest example was the title page. The whole of typography followed this scheme, whatever its immediate task might be, whether printing a newspaper or a circular, letterheads or advertisements.

Only in the postwar period did the dim realization dawn that all these were quite different tasks, making entirely different practical demands to be met creatively by the typographer.

A distinction between the New Typography and the old can only be drawn by means of a negation—the New Typography does not traditionalize. And at the door of the old, whose tendency was purely traditional, the blame for this negation must be laid. But at the same time the New Typography, because of its utter rejection of any formalist limitations, is less antitraditional than nontraditional. For instance, to achieve typographical design it is permissible to use every traditional and nontraditional face, every manner of plane relationship and every direction of line. The sole aim is design: the creative harmonious ordering of the practical requirements. Therefore there exist no limitations such as are imposed by the positing of "permissible" and "forbidden" type conjunctions. The old, unique aim of design to present a "restful" page is also reversed—we are at liberty to present a designed "unrest."

The swift tempo of modern business forces us further to a most accurate calculation of economic presentation. Typography had not only to find a simpler and more easily realizable constructive form (than the medial axis) but at the same time had to make this itself more visually attractive and varied in design. Dadaism, through Marinetti in Italy with his "Les mots en liberte futuriste (1919)" and even earlier in Germany, gave the first impulse to the new development in typography. Even today Dadaism is looked upon as sheer idiocy by many who have not taken the trouble to understand its dynamic; only in time to come will the important pioneer work done by those in the schools of Hausmann, Heartfield, Gross, Hulsenbeck, and other Dadaists, be estimated at their proper value. In any case, the handbills and other publications of the Dadaists (which date back into the wartime) were the earliest documents of the New Typography. In 1922 the movement spread; a few abstract painters began typographical experiments. A further impulse was given by the author's supplement ("Elementare Typographie") of the "Typographische Mitteilungen" (1925, out of print), in which the efforts made and results achieved were demonstrated for the first time and which, published in an edition of 28,000, was broadcast to the printing world. The views of the New Typography were the object of savage attack on all sides—today none but a few disgruntled die-hards ever think of raising their voice against them. The New Typography has won through.

Next to its nontraditional attitude the New Typography is characterized by its preference for new technical processes. It prefers:

typefounder's type	to engraved type
machine setting	to hand setting
machine-made paper	to handmade paper
machine presses	to hand presses
photographs	to drawings
photo process blocks	to woodcuts
standardization	to individualization, etc.

Further, the New Typography, by virtue of its methods of design, embraces the whole domain of printing and not merely the narrow field of pure type. Thus in photography we possess an objective means of reproducing objectivity and one which is comprehensible to all. Photography because it is merely another method of visual speech is also regarded as type.

The method of the New Typography is based upon a clear realization of purpose and the best means of achieving it. No modern typography, be it never so "beautiful," is "new" if it sacrifices purpose to form. "Form" is the result of work done and not the realization of an external conception of form. This fact has not been grasped by a whole troupe of pseudo-moderns. The chief demand of the New Typography is the most ideal adaptation to purpose.

This makes the omission of any decorative ingredients self-understood. Purpose further demands, and this cannot be too strongly emphasized, really good legibility. Lines too narrowly or too widely spaced and set are difficult to read and therefore, if for no other reason, to be avoided. The proper use of the various new processes produces in nearly every case specific forms and it is the typographer's proper study to recognize these and adapt his design to them. Thus a good typographer without a most thorough knowledge of technical requirements is unthinkable.

The present mass of printed matter, circulars (a thing which closely affects the individual as he receives no small part of them), renders the use of a standardized format necessary.

Of the available standing types, the New Typography is most partial to the "grotesque" or "block" type, as this is simply formed and easy to read. The use of others, easily legible, or even traditional faces, in the new sense is quite admissible, as they are "evaluated" one against the other, i.e., if the contrast between them be designed. It is not therefore demanded that everything be set in "grotesque," although in most cases this is indicated as most fitting. This face in its many variations (thin, semi-bold, bold-faced, condensed, expanded, hair-spaced, etc.) is open to many effects which in juxtaposition are capable of rich and varied contrasts. Varying contrasts can be obtained by the introduction of antique faces (Egyptienne, Walbaum, Garamond, Italic, etc.), and there is no reason why these effects should not be used in conjunction. Typescript is also a very peculiar and effective face.

Design is the most legible ordering and the correct choice of type dimensions according to their value within the logical bounds of the text (which can be intensified or diminished). The conscious use of movement by means of type or now and again a thick or thin rule, or group of rules, the visual agitated contrast of upper and lower case, thin and bold face, condensed and expanded type, gray and colored patches, slanting and horizontal, compact, and loose groups of type, etc., are further means of design. They represent the "aesthetic" side of typographical composition. Within the definite limits set by practical requirement and logical structure it is possible to tread various paths so that from this point onwards the visual sensibilities of the typographer must be the deciding factor. Thus it comes about that when several typographers are engaged upon the one definite task, they each achieve a varying result, each of which may have the same practical advantages. The various men whose work is illustrated in this article reveal tremendously varying possibilities, in spite of the use of the same means and methods of design. Thus, means which are practically identical meet with an extraordinary variety of usage. And these examples show that modern methods, in spite of frequent surmise, do not lead to monotony of expression, but on the contrary to results of extreme dissimilarity and which above all possess more originality than those of prewar typography.

Color is just such another effective element as type. In a certain sense the unprinted surface must be reckoned in with it and the discovery of its effectiveness must be put to the credit of the New Typographers. The white surface is not regarded as a passive background but as an active element. Among actual colors preference is given to red; as "The" color it forms the most effective contrast to the normal black. The clear tones yellow and blue must also be given place in the foreground of interest as these two are not diffuse. Color is not used as a decorative, "beautifying" ingredient, but the peculiar psychophysical properties of each are used as a means to heighten (or tone down) effects.

Illustration is supplied by photography. By this means we are given the most objective rendering of the object.

Whether photography is in itself an art or not an art need not concern us here; in conjunction with type and a plane surface it can be an art, as then it is purely a matter of values, of fitness in structural contrasts and relationships. Many people incline to mistrust graphic illustrations; the old (often falsifying) graphic illustrations no longer convince us and their individualistic pose and mannerisms affect us unpleasantly. If it be desired to give several pictorial impressions at the same time, to display several contrasting things, montage must be called into service. For this the same general methods of design as in typography hold good; used in conjunction with type, the photograph becomes a part of the whole and must be properly evaluated in this connection so as to achieve harmonious design. A rare but very attractive photographic possibility is the photogram of which an example is shown. A photogram is taken without a camera simply by placing a more or less transparent object on a sensitized medium (paper, film or plates). Typography + Photography is termed "Typophoto."

The extraordinary adaptability of the New Typography to every conceivable purpose renders it an important phenomenon in contemporary life. Its very attitude and position reveal that it is no mere fashion of a moment but is destined to form the basis of all further typographical progress.

Karel Teige of Prague has formulated the main characteristics of the New Typography as follows:

"Constructivist Typography" (a synonym for the New Typography) means and requires:

1. Freedom from tradition and prejudice; overthrow of archaicism and academicism and the rejection of decoration. No respect for academic and traditional rules unsupported by visual reason and which are here lifeless form ("the golden section," unity of type).
2. A choice of type, more perfect, more legible and cut with more geometric simplicity. Understanding of the spirit of the types suitable and their use in accord with the character of the text, contrast of typographical material to emphasize content.
3. Constant appreciation of purpose and fulfillment of requirement. Differentiation in special aims. Advertisements meant to be seen from a distance require different treatment to a scientific work or a volume of verse.
4. Harmonious disposition of surface and text in accordance with objective visual law; surveyable structure and geometric organization.
5. Exploitation of all means, which are or may be offered by present and future technical discoveries; conjunction of illustration and text by typophoto.
6. The closest cooperation between typographers and experts in the composing room is desirable, just as the designing architect cooperates with the constructional engineer, etc., specialization and division of labor are quite as necessary as close contact.

There is nothing to be added to the above beyond that the "golden section" together with other exact proportional formulas are often far more effective than chance relationships and should therefore not suffer fundamental exclusion.

First published in Commercial Art *(London: July 1930).*

1930
WHAT PLEASES THE MODERN MAN
Alexey Brodovitch

THE INDUSTRIALIZATION AND MECHANIZATION *that characterized the Machine Age of the 1930s presented an implicit conflict for designers. It advocated innovation and progress (a boon to freethinkers) yet at the same time, increased standardization (the enemy of free thought). Advertising served this new wave in many ways, and many designers were adamant in their attempts to define what progress really meant to this discipline. Alexey Brodovitch (1898–1971) was a pioneer of modern advertising in Europe. Born in Russia, he emigrated to the United States in 1930 where he founded the Department of Advertising at the Philadelphia Museum School and, in 1941, the Design Laboratory at New York's New School for Social Research. Brodovitch was a committed educator who possessed an almost evangelical need to communicate the goals of modernism to his students. As art director at Harper's Bazaar (1934–1958), his predilection for dramatic sequencing, bold typography, unusual photography, asymmetrical page composition, and dynamic white space influenced a generation of designers, editors, and photographers.—JH*

P resent-day life: industrialization, mechanization, standardization and consequently, competition and speed, requires astuteness and intensity of thought.

The man of today is of an extremely inventive nature and is seeking for the improvement of living. The precepts of comfort, utility and standardization come first in every field.

Standardization and ever-increasing competition, two factors of modern life, disclose a new and interesting chapter in the history of culture, at the same time bringing into it elements of a paradox: standardization—competition, simplification—elaboration. The solving of these problems in Publicity is of primary importance.

Publicity is full of contrast and paradox. Publicity is born of life and life is learned through publicity. Publicity no longer serves merely for the pushing of single products such as soap, sewing machines and spaghetti. Publicity is bigger, deeper and more universal.

If we think of Publicity as art, I would prefer not to call it Applied-Art, as it is generally known, but rather, I should call it Deep-Art as in contrast to the term Fine-Art.

We are living in the age of research and great achievements: electricity, radio, television, aviation, movies, automobiles, and Einstein, Edison, Marconi, Mussolini, Lenin, and Lindberg.

These achievements on the one hand, have changed our psychology, giving us new images and new understanding; on the other hand, because of the ever-accelerating tempo of life they have dulled our sensitivity to thrills and exclamation. No longer do we marvel at fantastic possibilities when each day on picking up the paper we read of record-breaking cars, or that Marconi on his luxurious yacht near

Naples has touched a button which turns on myriads of electric lights in Australia to announce the opening of the electrical exposition, or again an article on the project of drying up the North Sea.

How much of this new understanding of form, mass, plastic, dynamic, color, light, and shadow and perspective is given us by engineering!

The eye of man is trained and sharpened by his daily work, and has become too much the slave of tradition and atavism.

The projector, the lens, even the simple prism, give us a new aspect of the things about us.

The ray of the spotlight piercing the darkness proves the existence of profundity, it shows the third dimension and possibly even the fourth dimension. It reveals and explains the variety of textures, forms, and reliefs.

The lens of a Kodak presents a new understanding of foreshortening and perspective. The movie camera solves the problems of plastic, dynamic, rhythm, and the aesthetic of deformation of objects in motion.

The spectroscope, or the prism, demolishes the existing signification of color, and offers the possibility of explaining form by a different use of color.

The telescope and the microscope reveal to us the infinity of the greatest and the least.

The airplane forces upon us the understanding of cosmic velocity and space.

The television apparatus proves, with lightning speed, a new and definite idea of distance.

In the monotony and drudgery of our work-a-day world there is to be found new beauty and a new aesthetic:

The blinking lights of the city.

The surface of a revolving phonograph record.

The fantastic reflection of the red taillight and the tread of an automobile tire on the wet pavement.

The romanticism of a night landscape revealed by the light of an automobile.

The lyricism of the steel pistons, connection-rods and cogwheels in motion.

The heroism and daring in the silhouette of an airplane.

The harmonious grace of the wireless tower.

The moving static and grandeur of a liner.

The dynamic immensity of a locomotive.

The aesthetic of duco-lacquer, concrete, and chromium steel.

The rhythm of the barographical or statistical diagram.

The primitive precision of the hieroglyphs of stenography.

The science of the underground railway.

The semaphores, traffic lights, and policemen.

The symbol of the circle on the face of a clock.

The deformation of the wheel circle in becoming an ellipse on the photograph of a racing automobile.

Consider the new aesthetic, the new understanding, rhythm, movement, matter . . . Consider the endless possibilities of these new ideas.

Industry today gives the publicity artist not only a new vision but also a variety of new materials and instruments as a means for realizing advertising ideas.

Zinc, hard rubber, glass, sensitive film and paper, celluloid, galalith, lumarith, and ebonoid can easily and adequately take the place of cumbersome lithographic stone, expensive box-wood and steel and copper which are difficult to work. At the same time these materials offer a new medium of expression and may give entirely new effects.

Industrial lacquers, air brush, a thin ray of light, perfected hard, flexible steel needles, surgical knives, and even dental implements may also adequately take the place of watercolors, undurable and clumsy brushes, and charcoal pens and crayons.

Hand-made engraving and printing are things of the past, and while they have not yet become anachronisms, their proper place should be on the dusty shelves of snobbish collectors.

Modern and contemporary technical methods of reproduction and printing such as tepo, helio, and offset, open up colossal potentialities for the publicity artist.

Study the screens and plates, watch the revolutions of cylinders in a printing press, follow the work of the linotypist, examine even the discarded first proofs and we may find many new and purely graphic possibilities which may endlessly enlarge the horizon of artistic conception.

The publicity artist of today must be not only a fine craftsman with the faculty for finding new means of presentation but he must also be a keen psychologist. He must be able to perceive and preconceive the tastes, aspirations and habits of the consumer-spectator and the mob. The modern publicity artist must be a pioneer and a leader, he must fight against routine and the bad taste of the mob.

Man today lives, works, and revolves in a realm created by himself, finding in it utility and comfort. Tradition has compelled him to search for beauty and art in history, museums, expositions, and on the Rue de la Paix; and subconsciously, he loves and cherishes the fruits of his utilitarian efforts, not even suspecting that by so doing he admits their beauty. To force a realization of this on the man of today is the task of the modern publicity artist.

We are living in an age of industry and mechanization. Standardized images and, at the same time, endlessly diversified images, born of human ingenuity, not only simplify our daily tasks but also mark the path for the understanding and the serving of the new aesthetic, rhythm, construction, conception and composition.

We are learning to see and to feel new images, we are using new tools to work new materials: new and unexpected possibilities are opened up and a new aesthetic is born. This is an achievement. To deepen this achievement is the problem of the publicity artist.

To make a summary of the foregoing, the maxims to be developed by the publicity artist of today are:

1. Individuality.
2. Universality.
3. Feeling and understanding for modern life.
4. Feeling and understanding of the psychology of the consumer-spectator and the mob.
5. Facility to juggle with all the graphic possibilities which come with the study and improvement of modern materials and technique and of modern methods of presentation and reproduction.
6. Facility for realizing the advertising idea in materials by the use of elementary methods of enforcement and by presenting publicity in a utilitarian, simple, new, unusual, and logical manner.

First published in Commercial Art *(London: August 1930).*

1930
WHAT MAKES A MAGAZINE "MODERN"?
M. F. Agha

DR. MEHEMED FEHMY AGHA *(1896–1978) was art director for Condé Nast's* German Vogue *in Berlin before he was brought to New York in 1929 to work on American* Vogue, House and Garden, *and* Vanity Fair. *At* Vanity Fair *he introduced an innovative modern format characterized by wide margins, generous white space, sans serif (Futura) headlines, full-page bleeds, and photographs by Edward Steichen, Cecil Beaton, Edward Weston, and Luise Dahl-Wolfe and caricatures by Paolo Garretto, Miguel Covarrubius, and William Cotton. Agha is credited with creating, in 1930, the first single-image "double-page spread." Yet despite his progressive leanings, he was not a strict modernist, but an urbane cosmopolitan with a contemporary vision. Although he was interested in applying the more functional aspects of the European avant-garde's experiments to American publishing, in "What Makes a Magazine 'Modern?'" he takes a jaundiced view of both the orthodox modern and diehard traditional approaches to magazine design. Agha's writing is peppered with food analogies as he questions European, and especially German, bromides about simplicity and function.—SH*

The proverbial French Rabbit-That-You-Must-Get-First-If-You-Intend-To-Make-A-Rabbit-Stew is an animal which seems to be entirely ignored by the majority of modern typographers. If some of the advertising art directors have heard about this interesting animal, they do not seem to be greatly impressed. As far as the magazine make-up men are concerned, they are rather under the influence of the Scotch-Wine-Grower-Who-Told-His-Children-That-Wine-Can-Be-Made-Out-Of-Anything, Even-Out-Of-Grapes.

In other words, there are, all over the world, a great many magazines which use modern make-up (you may call it modernistic). But there are only very few which use modern material. And you must get modern material first if you intend to publish a really modern magazine.

But some of the modern typographical theorists seem rather to favor the wine-grower's point of view, since the purpose of the new typography is, we are told, to build eternal artistic units out of elementary and "timely materials." They feel that materials do not matter much and that it is the way they are used and organized into an entity that constitutes the difference between the old and the new layout. Therefore, the rejuvenated magazines which naïvely use mid-Victorian photographs in flat-edge, black rules and little dots in an Edwardian text may be perfectly justified in feeling that they have achieved modernity by these simple means—provided they pass the test of "fitness to function"—"asymmetric balance" and other branches of modernistic craft.

I do not think, however, that the large quantities of modernistic Rabbit-Stew with very little Rabbit in it, which have been manufactured lately, are entirely the result of the benediction that certain theorists bestow on that kind of fare. We must consider that the writers who have theories about modern magazine making and typography usually have no magazines at their disposal for experimental purposes, while those who are making up magazines are happily ignorant of the very existence of both theories and theorists.

I thought, therefore, that it might be interesting to present a few pages of rare magazines published in Europe by the same persons and organization which are responsible for the theoretic background of the new typography—as well as for other achievements in the modernistic field. To be fair we must admit that it is easy for them to be and look modern: they are published by modernists for the modernists and deal chiefly with modernism.

The results of the modernistic theories when applied in practice by the theorists themselves are very creditable, even when they tackle the problems of the more complicated kind—such as the make-up of fashion and sport pages. The only thing that you might hold against them is that, from time to time, they put too much instead of too little rabbit in the stew.

If we transfer these problems, apparently solved by the semi-dilettante publications of the modernists to the field of actual publishing—with readers, advertisers and often editors who are anything but worshippers of the sacred cows of modernism, the situation becomes singularly uncertain. Then even the fundamentals of modern art and typography lose that definite and self-contained character which in Europe is supposed to be inherent in them. But do they really?

A few years ago the modernistic gospel seemed to have assumed a definite if not very comprehensible shape. The vagabond theories, originated by the Spaniards in France and exported to Germany via Russia, arrived back in France via Holland and Switzerland, only to settle down in Dessau and be taught to Japanese students by Hungarian professors. To the innocent question, "What is modern?" the answers (or rather manifestos), although of various degrees of fogginess of eloquence (according to the nationality of the answerer), remained essentially the same in France and Germany, and, when translated, even the same in America.

Modernists *will* have manifestos. Here is one of them that answers indirectly the other question: "what should comprise the material of a modern magazine!"

The fundamental change of our mental attitude concerning the New World has produced a definite change in our means of expression.

Today we suppress the materials, shapes and tools of Yesterday; instead of the uncertain blow of an axe—we have the chain-saw; instead of a charcoal line—the precise line of a T-square; instead of the wood horn—a saxophone; instead of copying the reflected lights—the creation of lights, in the photos, light-organ, refracted light plays; instead of plastic imitation of movement—the movement itself (light-signs, Eurythmics, Dance); instead of the novel—the short story; instead of sculpture—the building; instead of Opera—the revue; instead of fresco—a poster. . . .

All this sounded convincing until even a year ago. But today, if you have a very sensitive ear, you may discover a little note of uncertainty in this declamation. The "age of industry and standardization," the "cult of the machine," the "typo-photo" and the "graphisms," the "form that follows function," and all the rest of sacred dogmas are still on the flowing banners, but the dreadful word "reaction" is being whispered by "those in the know." The change in women's fashion, in a direction precisely opposite to that which every self-respecting modernist would advise was a terrible blow to the faith which was built on the creed of "simple clothes—simple interiors—simple art—simple typography, etc."

Another symptom. After the very successful Exhibition of German Werkbund in Paris, the French Society of "Artistes Decorateurs Francais" took the liberty of reminding their German colleagues that there are, after all, other things in life and art besides the "cold and organized conception of the technician and manufacturer." In the very heart of the Werkbund, traitors agree with the French point of view; the Werkbund will hold in Stuttgart in October an extraordinary meeting in order to revise its adopted doctrine and decide once and for all what is this thing called "modern."

Does this mean that the modern typographers will have to store away their little dots and black rules and put back frames on their pictures? Or will the modern magazines peacefully follow their own educational campaign, and by trial and error finally achieve harmony between material and its presentation?

This, I am afraid, we will each have to discover by using our own individual and collective judgments.

First published in Advertising Arts *(New York: October 1930).*

1932
THE CRYSTAL GOBLET OR PRINTING
SHOULD BE INVISIBLE
Beatrice Warde

PRIOR TO THE TURN *of the century, practitioners often argued over the virtues of personal style versus neutrality, which was the underlying topic of a lecture given by Beatrice Warde (1900–1969) to the Society of Typographic Designers in London (later published as an essay). Warde, who used the pen name Paul Beaujon, was a respected type historian and critic of the graphic arts industry. In 1927, on the strength Beaujon's writing in the* Fleuron, *she was appointed editor of the* Monotype Recorder, *published in England by the Lanstone Monotype Company. "The Crystal Goblet" is Warde's best-known (and most reprinted) essay on the clarity of type and design. In the introduction to her book of collected writing,* The Crystal Goblet, *she asserts that the essay contains ideas that must be "said over again in other terms to many . . . people who in the nature of their work have to deal with the putting of printed words on paper—and who, for one reason or another, are in danger of becoming as fascinated by the intricacies of its techniques as birds are supposed to be by the eye of a serpent."—SH*

Imagine that you have before you a flagon of wine. You may choose your own favorite vintage for this imaginary demonstration, so that it be a deep shimmering crimson in color. You have two goblets before you. One is of solid gold, wrought in the most exquisite patterns. The other is of crystal-clear glass, thin as a bubble, and as transparent. Pour and drink; and according to your choice of goblet, I shall know whether or not you are a connoisseur of wine. For if you have no feelings about wine one way or the other, you will want the sensation of drinking the stuff out of a vessel that may have cost thousands of pounds; but if you are a member of that vanishing tribe, the amateurs of fine vintages, you will choose the crystal, because everything about it is calculated to *reveal* rather than to hide the beautiful thing which it was meant to *contain*.

Bear with me in this long-winded and fragrant metaphor; for you will find that almost all the virtues of the perfect wineglass have a parallel in typography. There is the long, thin stem that obviates fingerprints on the bowl. Why? Because no cloud must come between your eyes and the fiery heart of the liquid. Are not the margins on book pages similarly meant to obviate the necessity of fingering the type page? Again: the glass is colorless or at the most only faintly tinged in the bowl, because the connoisseur judges wine partly by its color and is impatient of anything that alters it. There are a thousand mannerisms in typography that are as impudent and arbitrary as putting port in tumblers of red or green glass! When a goblet has a base that looks too small for security, it does not matter how cleverly it is weighted; you feel nervous lest it should tip over. There are ways of setting lines of type which may work well enough, and yet keep the reader subconsciously worried by the fear of 'doubling' lines, reading three words as one, and so forth.

Now the man who first chose glass instead of clay or metal to hold his wine was a 'modernist' in the sense in which I am going to use that term. That is, the first thing he asked of this particular object was not 'How should it look?' but 'What must it do?" and to that extent all good typography is modernist.

Wine is so strange and potent a thing that it has been used in the central ritual of religion in one place and time, and attacked by a virago with a hatchet in another. There is only one thing in the world that is capable of stirring and altering men's minds to the same extent, and that is the coherent expression of thought. That is man's chief miracle, unique to man. There is no 'explanation' whatever of the fact that I can make arbitrary sounds that will lead a total stranger to think my own thought. It is sheer magic that I should be able to hold a one-sided conversation by means of black marks on paper with an unknown person halfway across the world. Talking, broadcasting, writing, and printing are all quite literally forms of *thought transference*, and it is this ability and eagerness to transfer and receive the contents of the mind that is almost alone responsible for human civilization.

If you agree with this, you will agree with my one main idea, i.e., that the most important thing about printing is that it conveys thought, ideas, images, from one mind to other minds. This statement is what you might call the front door of the science of typography. Within lie hundreds of rooms; but unless you start by assuming that *printing is meant to convey specific and coherent ideas*, it is very easy to find yourself in the wrong house altogether.

Before asking what this statement leads to, let us see what it does not necessarily lead to. If books are printed in order to be read, we must distinguish readability from what the optician would call legibility. A page set in 14-pt. Bold Sans is, according to the laboratory tests, more 'legible' than one set in 11-pt. Baskerville. A public speaker is more 'audible' in that sense when he bellows. But a good speaking voice is one which is inaudible *as* a voice. It is the transparent goblet again! I need not warn you that if you begin listening to the inflections and speaking rhythms of a voice from a platform, you are falling asleep. When you listen to a song in a language you do not understand, part of your mind actually does fall asleep, leaving your quite separate aesthetic sensibilities to enjoy themselves unimpeded by your reasoning faculties. The fine arts do that; but that is not the purpose of printing. Type well used is invisible *as* type, just as the perfect talking voice is the unnoticed vehicle for the transmission of words, ideas.

We may say, therefore, that printing may be delightful for many reasons, but that it is important, first and foremost, as a means of doing something. That is why it is mischievous to call any printed piece a work of art, especially fine art: because that would imply that its first purpose was to exist as an expression of beauty for its own sake and for the delectation of the senses. Calligraphy can almost be considered a fine art nowadays, because its primary economic and educational purpose has been taken away; but printing in English will not qualify as an art until the present English language no longer conveys ideas to future generations, and until printing itself hands its usefulness to some yet unimagined successor.

There is no end to the maze of practices in typography, and this idea of printing as a conveyor is, at least in the minds of all the great typographers with whom I have had the privilege of talking, the one clue that can guide you through the maze. Without this essential humility of mind, I have seen ardent designers go more hopelessly wrong, make more ludicrous mistakes out of an excessive enthusiasm, than I could have thought possible. And with this clue, this purposiveness in the back of your mind, it is possible to do the most unheard-of things, and find that they justify you triumphantly. It is not a waste of time to go to the simple fundamentals and reason from them. In the flurry of your individual problems, I think you will not mind spending half an hour on one broad and simple set of ideas involving abstract principles.

I once was talking to a man who designed a very pleasing advertising type that undoubtedly all of you have used. I said something about what artists think about a certain problem, and he replied with a beautiful gesture: 'Ah, madam, we artists do not think—we *feel*!' That same day I quoted that remark to another designer of my acquaintance, and he, being less poetically inclined, murmured: 'I'm not *feeling* very well today, I *think*!' He was right, he did think; he was the thinking sort; and that is why he is not so good a painter, and to my mind ten times better as a typographer and type designer than the man who instinctively avoided anything as coherent as a reason.

I always suspect the typographic enthusiast who takes a printed page from a book and frames it to hang on the wall, for I believe that in order to gratify a sensory delight he has mutilated something infinitely more important. I remember that T. M. Cleland, the famous American typographer, once showed me a very beautiful layout for a Cadillac booklet involving decorations in color. He did not have the actual text to work with in drawing up his specimen pages, so he had set the lines in Latin. This was not only for the reason that you will all think of, if you have seen the old typefoundries' famous *Quousque Tandem* copy (i.e., that Latin has few descenders and thus gives a remarkably even line). No, he told me that originally he had set up the dullest 'wording' that he could find (I dare say it was from *Hansard*), and yet he discovered that the man to whom he submitted it would start reading and making comments on the text. I made some remark on the mentality of Boards of Directors, but Mr. Cleland said, 'No: you're wrong; if the reader had not been practically forced to read—if he had not seen those words suddenly imbued with glamour and significance—then the layout would have been a failure. Setting it in Italian or Latin is only an easy way of saying "This is not the text as it will appear."'

Let me start my specific conclusions with book typography, because that contains all the fundamentals, and then go on to a few points about advertising.

The book typographer has the job of erecting a window between the reader inside the room and that landscape which is the author's words. He may put up a stained-glass window of marvelous beauty, but a failure as a window; that is, he may use some rich superb type like text gothic that is something to be looked at, not *through*. Or he may work in what I call transparent or invisible typography. I have a book at home, of which I have no visual recollection whatever as far as its typography goes; when I think of it, all I see is the Three Musketeers and their comrades swaggering up and down the streets of Paris. The third type of window is one in which the glass is broken into relatively small leaded panes; and this corresponds to what is called 'fine printing' today, in that you are at least conscious that there is a window there, and that someone has enjoyed building it. That is not objectionable, because of a very important fact which has to do with the psychology of the subconscious mind. This is that the mental eye focuses *through* type and not *upon* it. The type which, through any arbitrary warping of design or excess of 'color,' gets in the way of the mental picture to be conveyed, is a bad type. Our subconsciousness is always afraid of blunders (which illogical setting, tight spacing and too-wide unleaded lines can trick us into), of boredom, and of officiousness. The running headline that keeps shouting at us, the line that looks like one long word, the capitals jammed together without hair-spaces—these mean subconscious squinting and loss of mental focus.

And if what I have said is true of book printing, even of the most exquisite limited editions, it is fifty times more obvious in advertising, where the one and only justification for the purchase of space is that you are conveying a message—that you are implanting a desire, straight into the mind of the reader. It is tragically easy to throw away half the reader-interest of an advertisement by setting the simple and compelling argument in a face that is uncomfortably alien to the classic reasonableness of the book-face. Get attention as you will by your headline, and make any pretty type pictures you like if you are sure that the copy is useless as a means of selling goods; but if you are happy enough to have really good copy to work with, I beg you to remember that thousands of people pay hard-earned money for the privilege of reading quietly set book-pages, and that only your wildest ingenuity can stop people from reading a really interesting text.

Printing demands a humility of mind, for the lack of which many of the fine arts are even now floundering in self-conscious and maudlin experiments. There is nothing simple or dull in achieving the transparent page. Vulgar ostentation is twice as easy as discipline. When you realize that ugly typography never effaces itself, you will be able to capture beauty as the wise men capture happiness by aiming at something else. The 'stunt typographer' learns the fickleness of rich men who hate to read. Not for them are long breaths held over serif and kern, they will not appreciate your splitting of hair-spaces. Nobody (save the other craftsmen) will appreciate half your skill. But you may spend endless years of happy experiment in devising that crystalline goblet which is worthy to hold the vintage of the human mind.

Address to the Society of Typographic Designers, formerly the British Typographers Guild, London, 1932. Published in Beatrice Warde: The Crystal Goblet—Sixteen Essays on Typography *(Cleveland and New York: World Publishing Co., 1956).*

1935
TOWARDS A UNIVERSAL TYPE
Herbert Bayer

BEGINNING IN THE 1920S, *German type reformers sought ways of replacing the national alphabet—the spiky Blackletter—with simplified gothic letters. A leading advocate was Austrian-born Herbert Bayer (1900–1985), who was educated at the Bauhaus in Weimar and later taught at the Bauhaus in Dessau, where, from 1925 to 1928, he was director of the school's department of typography and advertising. During this time, his interests—and the department's emphasis—shifted from lithography and hand-printing to more mechanical processes and more inventive typographic exploration. A devout modernist who was profoundly influenced by the De Stijl movement (1917–1932), Bayer railed against the redundancy of serifs and capital letters, arguing instead for the efficiency of lower-case and the economy of a sans-serif alphabet. His universal alphabet of 1925–1927 emphatically illuminates this argument. In this article, published seven years after the Bauhaus was closed, Bayer—who was at this time living in Nazi Germany—explains the practical conveniences of a typographic system that mirrors the functional requirements of modern life. Here, a renunciation of thick-to-thin strokes is contrasted by a celebration of the purity of geometric form.—JH*

One glance at the specimen book of types issued by even an up-to-date printing firm, reveals a collection of the most varied sorts of letters, which as a whole constitute a conglomeration of style of the worst kind. arranged in groups and compared with other expressions of the periods from which they have descended, they remind us that:

today we do not build in gothic, but in our contemporary way.

no longer do we travel on horseback, but in cars, train and planes.

we do not dress in crinolines nowadays, but in a more rational manner.

every period has its own formal and cultural features, expressed in its contemporary habits of life, in its architecture and literature. the same applies to language and writing. we recognize clearly enough that literary forms of past ages do not belong to the present times. a man would make himself ridiculous who insisted on talking today in the manner of the middle ages.

later, we shall see that the type designs of tradition do not respond to the essential requirements of type suitable for use today. we look back upon a long line of development in type design, and we have no intention of criticizing the heritage which now oppresses us. but we have reached a stage when we must decide to break with the past. when we are confronted with a collection of traditional styles we ought to see that we can turn away from the antiquated forms of the middle ages with a clear conscience to the possibilities of designing a new kind of type more suitable to the present and what we can foresee of the future.

in the course of the centuries our language has changed. it has become shorter, sound-changes have taken place, new words have been coined, new concepts have been formed. language itself needs complete reorganization—but this is a tremendous subject. we shall not enter upon it, but limit ourselves to consideration of type-design.

out of the conglomerate mass of type faces, some of which are illustrated, there has emerged, as a last phase, the form of classical roman type, with variations until we arrive at the simplified form without serifs, popularly known as "sans-serif" or "sans." in england the most familiar type of this order is commonly known as "gill sans," after the name of its designer, eric gill. sans-serif type is the child of our period. in form it is in complete harmony with other visible forms and phenomena of modern life. we welcome it as our most modern type. we cannot set about inventing an entirely new form of type, as this would have to be parallel with a radical reorganization of the language. we must remain true to our basic letter-forms, and try to develop them further. classic roman type, the original form of all historical variations of type, must still be our starting point. all the variations of shape have been formed freely according to the style and the calligraphy of the type designer, and it is just this freedom which has been responsible for so many mistakes. geometry, however, gives us the most exact forms. albrecht dürer's endeavours to resolve both the roman and the german gothic type into their constructive basic elements, unfortunately were never carried beyond their experimental stage. the *bayer-type* produced by the berthold type foundry represents a practical attempt to give a modern expression to classical roman type by means of geometrical construction of form. a tremendous amount of reading is done today and there should be no difficulties put in the way of the reader. some things have to be read from afar, and letters must be visible from considerable distances. it is not without reason that oculists use clear cut type faces when testing the state of the patient's eyesight.

much has been written about the legibility of type. oculists can offer no definite proofs, because their experiments are influenced by habits to which patients are accustomed. for example, it is found that old people with bad eyesight often read complicated gothic type more easily than clear roman type, because they are used to the former. but from research, however, it has been concluded that the more the individual letters resemble one another in shape, the less visible is the type. this conclusion may be wrong, as it would be easy to find illegible type-faces in which the individual letters differ very widely from one another, if that be the only consideration. and then where shall we look for harmony of form and the fundamental constructional form of our types? other research has established that whole groups of letters—not single letters, but words—are taken in by the eye at one glance. if we carried this conclusion to its logical end we should have optical word pictures (similar to chinese signs) and no type with separate letters. personally, i believe in the following logical conception: the simpler the shape of the letter, the easier the type is to see, read, and learn. in classic times capital letters (the only letters in use) were drawn with a slate pencil and incised with a chisel. no doubt their form was intimately associated with these tools. lower case developed in the early middle ages from the use of the pen, and therefore inherits the characteristics of handwriting. later, both alphabets adapted themselves, and we observe in all types up to the present the characteristic basic element of the thin up-stroke and the thick down-stroke. these characteristics have preserved themselves up to this day. but do we need such a pretense of precedent at a time when 90 percent of all that is read is either written on a typewriter or printed on a printing press, when handwriting plays only a secondary role, and when type could be much simpler and more consistent in form?

hence, i believe the requirements of a new alphabet are as follows:

geometric foundation of each letter, resulting in a synthetic construction out of a few basic elements. avoidance of all suggestion of a hand-written character, uniform thickness of all parts of the letter, and renunciation of all suggestions of up and down strokes. simplification of form for the sake of legibility (the simpler the optical appearance the easier the comprehension).

a basic form which will suffice for diverse applications so that the same character is adaptable for various functions: printing, typewriting, hand and stencil writing, etc.

these considerations will explain the attempt to design a new type. but why do we write and print with two alphabets? a large *and* a small sign are not necessary for one sound. we do not speak a capital a and a small a.

we need a one-letter type alphabet. it gives us exactly the same result as the mixed type of capitals and lower-case letters, and at the same time is less of a burden to school children, students, professional and business men. it can be written considerably more quickly, especially on the typewriter, where a shift key would be unnecessary. typewriting would therefore be more easily learned. typewriters would be cheaper because of simpler construction. typesetting would be cheaper, type cases smaller; printing establishments would save space. writing and addressing done in offices would be much cheaper. these facts apply with special force in the english language, in which the use of capital letters occurs so infrequently. it seems incomprehensible why such a huge amount of apparatus should be necessary for such little use of capitals. if it is considered necessary to emphasize the beginnings of sentences, this could be done by heavy type or wider spacing. proper names could also be shown in another way, and for the "i" a uniform sign would have to be created. pursuing this thought to its logical conclusion we perceive that the sound of the language ought to be given a systematic optical shape. in order to aim at a simplified type, as against that used today, syllables that frequently recur, and combined sounds (diphthongs, etc. should be given new letter signs). THE CAPITAL LETTERS OF ANCIENT TIMES ARE HARDLY LEGIBLE WHEN THEY ARE FORMED INTO SENTENCES. THEY CANNOT, THEREFORE, BE TAKEN INTO CONSIDERATION. there remains only the small letters of our present-day lower case alphabet. this must be the foundation of our one-letter alphabet. and is not a sentence in a one-letter alphabet, which intrinsically possesses a formally compact construction, more harmonious, logically, than a sentence consisting of two alphabets, which completely differ from each other in shape and size?

First published in PM *4, no. 2 (December–January 1939–1940).*

1936
ADVERTISING ART IN THE UNITED STATES
Earnest Elmo Calkins

THE PROfiT MOTIVE, RATHER *than any utopian ethic or aesthetic ideal, paved the way for commercial modernism in the United States. In no small measure modernism was introduced to the conservate American marketplace, in the late 1920s, through advertising created by Earnest Elmo Calkins (1868–1964), an advertising pioneer and founder of Calkins and Holden Advertising Co., in New York. Calkins was not an artist or designer, but he keenly understood the influence that the image of creative packaging and promotion could have on popular attitudes. He admired the Europeans for their skill at synthesizing avant-garde innovations and commercial needs; the results, he said, were not always beautiful "but diabolically clever." Calkins promoted such marketing ideas as "consumption engineering," "forced obsolescence," and "styling the goods." He often wrote critically about the limitations of advertising as a creative force, and vigorously promoted the view that modernity was the best means to increase consumerism, and therefore productivity.—SH*

A selection for whatever purpose of pictures and designs used in advertising is always eclectic. It is never a cross-section, but merely the cream skimmed off the top. A cross-section would show a great body of ugly, stupid, commonplace work with a frosting on top of better art more intelligently used.

In order to present what has been accomplished in applying design to business, and especially to advertising, we make a selection of the best examples of each genre and ignore the rank and file. It is significant that each time such an appraisal is made the number of examples of good work has increased so that choice is increasingly difficult, and that now no exhibition of average proportions is large enough to represent all of the really excellent work that is being done. Thousands of designs are produced monthly by the art departments of advertising agencies and by independent freelance artists working in their own studios, and more and more of these productions are satisfying from the aesthetic point of view, and what is more important, more of them are more definitely and intelligently adapted to their purpose of selling goods.

It was once thought to be an achievement when the business man could be persuaded to allow an artist to make a good picture for him. This picture was then framed in type to compose the advertising page as skillfully as possible under the circumstances, and sometimes very pleasing results were obtained. Having won the advertiser to the point of buying and paying for good art and allowing the artist to express himself according to his own talent, the advertising art director has gone further and made the picture or design, not merely a detached work of art, but an integral part of his page. The art work and the typography have been woven together to produce a unit so that credit for many of the best pages in the American magazines must be divided between the art director, the layout man, and the artist.

This has greatly broadened the use of art in advertising and has been the opportunity for an infinite number of ingenuities. Instead of one picture and one block of text, pictures, frequently in color, have been scattered through the text, greatly brightening the effect and giving it a liveliness and a lightness in harmony with a high-keyed, rapidly moving age. Thus advertising tends to express not only the goods offered but also the tempo, the spirit of the customers who buy them.

The highest pitch of excellence in advertising art is reached in the magazine pages. We do not have in the United States any such poster work as is common in Europe for several reasons. The first is the shape and size of our billboards. Instead of the smaller and better proportioned sheet that is used in Europe, we have a large oblong sheet which doesn't lend itself to good designing. More than that, for some reason, there is not the same freedom of expression, the same daring and originality used in poster designing that is manifest in the advertising pages of magazines. So our best work is not found on the billboards as it is in Europe, but in the color pages which adorn the magazines and successfully compete in interest and attractiveness with the editorial features of the book.

Black-and-white designing for newspaper use is improving. More and more attention is paid to techniques that will print well under the exacting conditions of the newspaper press, but here the advertisements are subject to the standards of make-up which prevail in newspaper work and the limits imposed by rapid press work. The advertisements are seen more in conjunction with other advertisements and with the heavy display used for news, and do not have that completeness and isolation which is theirs when they occupy a page in a magazine.

The use of color in magazines is increasing, spurred by the tremendous improvement in color printing adopted by magazine publishers and by the obvious advantage that color gives to the advertiser, not merely for the realistic presentation of his goods, but more particularly as an eye catcher. The tendency toward high key color, interesting patterns produced by intelligent use of the goods themselves, a movement initiated by Rene Clarke, has begun to characterize a great deal of the color advertising in the magazines. This tendency is often confused with modernism, and is much used for modernistic design, but it is not what is technically known as modernism so much as it is an expression of contemporary life. The work of Rene Clarke is not modernistic. It belongs to no school. It is the individual expression of an artist working in his own way, reflecting the world as he sees it, making interesting patterns of everyday common-place objects and producing new effects, revealing how much beauty there is in ordinary things when they are combined in fresh patterns or viewed from new angles. It was this leadership in pioneering a fresh treatment of advertising design with its infinite possibilities that was responsible for the award to him last year of the Bok Gold Medal.

Modernism, or what is conceived to be modernism, has profoundly influenced American advertising design in both the pictorial treatment and the typography. A good deal that is merely eccentric, the attempt to be different, is wrongly classed as modernism, but principally the movement is an effort to shake off the old realistic treatment which has reached such a dead level of excellence in still life painting as to render it difficult to give an advertisement by the old methods the distinction and individuality it should have.

More and more art directors have striven to express not merely things, but ideas, not so much the picture of a motor car as motion, action, transportation; not so much a vanity product as lure, charm, fascination; not so much a breakfast food as gustatory delight, vigor, health, vitamins, sunlight. The most successful results are had when art director, layout man, and artist work in perfect sympathy and the completed advertisement is a composite thing perfectly united, the skillful use of art, type, white paper, copy, headline, and idea, to produce emotion in the beholder. The lines of the whole advertisement, both type and picture, focus the eye unerringly on the high spot—the name, the product, its use. Speed is suggested in things that are fast, comfort in things that give comfort, smartness in the materials of style—suggested, implied, rather than stated. This cooperative teamwork is recognized in many ways. For instance, in the Bok awards the honor is frequently divided between the two or three men who contributed to the complete result. It should be noted that the greater intelligence that has been introduced into advertising design has profoundly affected not merely the packages in which goods are sold, but the goods themselves. The styling of manufactured goods, which has become such a widespread movement in this country, is a by-product of improved advertising design. The styling of goods is an effort to introduce color, design, and smartness in the goods that for years have been accepted in their stodgy, commonplace dress. The purpose is to make the customer discontented with his old type of fountain pen, kitchen utensil, bathroom, or motor car, because it is old fashioned, out of date. The technical term for this idea is obsoletism. We no longer wait for things to wear out. We displace them with others that are not more efficient but more attractive.

This has offered a new field to our artists and designers which has become a profitable one. The telephone company, one of the largest corporations in the United States, has been much impressed by the substitution by its customers of the so-called French telephone for the standard American type, even though its installation carried a penalty of an additional fifty cents a month rent. The public was influenced partly by the convenience of the one-piece telephone and partly by its more attractive shape. Accepting this mandate from the consumer, the telephone company commissioned a selected few artists of national reputation to design a telephone in the French telephone manner which could rightly take its place among the furnishings of the modern home or office. Something like this is happening in every business, and as the products themselves acquire a certain modicum of good taste, the work of the advertising designer in presenting them attains new heights of daring and inventiveness.

It is undoubtedly true that business design is today the greatest field for the artist. No other department, or all of them together, offers such large rewards in money or such gratifying publicity. Today a man who creates the physical appearance of a motor car receives as much credit as the sculptor of a statue. The man who paints a successful advertising picture is held to be as much of an artist as a man who paints a mural. There is no longer a gap between the business artist and the art artist. They are both the same artist.

In New York City there is an organization known as the Guild of Free Lance artists with some 350 members, comprising the best of the younger men in the city. These men are available for advertising design or magazine and book illustration. Their work extends frequently beyond the mere making of pictures for a book. It includes suggestions for the layout, the format, type page, cover design, the end papers and the book jacket. They are practical men while still artists. They are as legitimate an outgrowth of the age as were the numerous painters of religious subjects which made up the art world of the fifteenth century.

The younger men have grown up in the tradition of business art. They have learned that they can accept it without sacrifice of artistic ideals, but that it is a technical field which requires study and approach for the proper application of artistic ability, exactly as architecture and mural painting. The men who are furnishing the best art to advertising are also painters of pictures for their own satisfaction, which are exhibited in galleries exactly as were those of the old academic school of artists. There is one advertising agency in New York which has among the men on its staff an art club known as The Islanders with eighteen members whose annual exhibitions are duly criticized and commented upon by the art editors of the newspapers and magazines exactly as though they were easel artists pure and simple with no other outlet for their energies or abilities.

The artist who works in advertising design is no longer entirely at the mercy of the business man whose criticisms once paralyzed all his sources of inspiration. Even when the advertiser is not equipped to judge art work, he has a growing appreciation of the powerful part art can play in advertising his business, and more and more these arbiters of destiny are beginning to get a glimmering of art principles. But more than that, there stands today between the artist and the advertiser the art director who is a competent judge of art work from the point of view of the artist, and at the same time has a vivid understanding of the part the art work must play in the advertisement. He is able by his sympathy, knowledge and diplomacy to bring about a welding of the two, the advertiser's aims and desires—the artist's ability and integrity. The result is that as much sincere, able, inspired work is being put into advertising design today as in any other form of art.

As has been said before, this doesn't mean that all advertising art is good. The greater proportion of it is still ordinary and commonplace. Only a few in the vanguard are using it intelligently and to the full capacity of the artist, but each year shows that good designing is more effective than bad in selling goods. More and more advertisers come to this point of view. The Harvard Awards pay especial attention and give special recognition to physical appearance in advertising. The Art Directors' annual exhibition finds increasing difficulty in selecting 350 designs from several thousand that are good enough for display on their walls. New magazines devoted to the aesthetic side of advertising are appearing. Brass founders, motor car manufacturers, cabinet makers, perfumers, camera makers, and others are calling upon the very artists who have been supplying the better advertising designs for advice and help in styling their goods. As an interesting instance of the prevalence of the idea that good taste is a factor in selling goods, note the manufacturer of an electric hearing device for the deaf who has had an artist redesign his instrument.

Almost as much attention is given to places in which goods are sold as to the goods themselves and the advertising thereof. Many old buildings, both for manufacture and retail selling, have been designed in the modern spirit throughout. All these manifestations of a new spirit of design in commerce have grown from the initial impulse of putting the best obtainable art into advertising design. The movement taken in its entirety is slowly transforming industrial America. It is the one hope we have of beauty in the machine age.

First published in the Studio Yearbook *(London: The Studio, 1936).*

1938
VISUAL EXPRESSION
Ashley Havinden

IN THE 1920S AND 1930S, *Ashley Havinden (1903–1973) was the leading exponent of modernist influences on British commercial art. As art director at the W. S. Crawford
advertising agency, he created campaigns for Chrysler cars, Simpson of Piccadilly, and the
Milk Marketing Board informed by the spirit, if not the exact visual procedures, of
Tschichold, Moholy-Nagy, and the Bauhaus. Ashley, as he was known, was a staunch early
advocate of the need for graphic designers to study painting, sculpture, and architecture for
guidance and inspiration in the creation of contemporary visual forms, as his essay for Robert
Harling's journal* Typography *(1936–1939) shows. His article is also unusual for its period
in the stress it lays on the relationship between writer and designer, and for its cautionary observations on the pitfalls of reducing dynamic Continental design styles to visual mannerism
at the expense of linguistic meaning. In his prescient remarks, Havinden anticipates the postwar development, and dilemmas, of design as a professional activity.—RP*

I have called these notes 'Visual Expression' because that seems to me the best
description for the work of the designer in the field of publicity and advertis-
ing. His job is to communicate ideas to the public in terms of pictures and words. His
problem is to create visual forms which are an amalgam of the two, and which are
suitable for multiplication by the printing press.

Most designers derive from artists; and the training of an artist, plus his own
inclinations towards expression, leads him to produce works which are complete in
themselves, without the addition of any words, and which are also ends in themselves
in whatever material they are done.

Therefore, the process of printing and multiplication—as well as the introduction of words, either as display or text—brings a new element into the designer's outlook.

He begins to study the subject of printing and finds that printers have been
at work for some hundreds of years. The early printers brought great integrity to their
job, and naturally a certain tradition of form and craftsmanship grew up as a standard
for future printers.

This standard of craftsmanship has varied somewhat in different ages; sometimes it has been high and sometimes very low. Perhaps its lowest level was reached
as a result of the Industrial Revolution. And we all know how William Morris endeavored to get back to a good standard again by taking the form of the medieval book
as his model.

But his fight was a hard one and, in some ways, a losing one, because he did
not take into account the changing conditions caused by the advent of machinery and
the consequent new demands on the printer. He could not see that, in the same way
that the machine was invading other industries of handcraftsmanship, it would also
invade the printing one—changing it from a craft into an industry.

As his influence was very great, I think that in some ways he is responsible for many of the aesthetic troubles that still face commercial printing.

To Morris, like many of his time, culture seemed inseparable from hand-craftsmanship, and the coming of mechanical invention could only mean the death of culture! So that instead of encouraging the progress of printing inventions with his creative genius, he simply tried to hold the tide back by reaffirming the traditions of the medieval printer.

The cultural outcry led by Ruskin and Morris had the effect of making this growing industry falter in its stride somewhat. Ashamed of its apparently anti-cultural tendencies, it tried to save its face by endeavoring to cast its machine-made forms in the image of the handmade models of the past.

This attitude helped to prevent any genuine aesthetic emerging as a result of the new techniques. I think this aesthetic might have emerged more rapidly if the men working in the new techniques had been less influenced by traditional idealism.

I think we all recognize today that new forms, and indeed new standards, are needed if we are to adapt ourselves to the changed conditions of today.

A good example of this change of conditions was demonstrated in the Pavilon de Publicité at the Paris Exhibition. The demonstration consisted of a comparison between posters designed in the past and posters designed to meet conditions of today. This comparison was made by means of three moving bands, one above the other.

The lower one had the old design on it and moved slowly (about ten miles an hour, which is roughly the speed of an observer of thirty years ago). The design was perfectly comprehensible—but when this same poster was shown on the middle band going by at about forty miles an hour (roughly the speed of a contemporary observer in a motor car) it had become just a blur—nothing emerged!

Above it on another forty-mile-an-hour band was a good contemporary poster, the design of which had been organized to convey its message rapidly, and we found that at this speed it remained perfectly legible and comprehensible.

This demonstration idea was, I believe, one of Jean Carlu's and succeeded admirably in proving the point—namely, that altered conditions mean a new approach on the part of the designer.

Commercial printing exists on the enormous scale of today entirely because of the demands made on it by mechanized industry, and because it is itself mechanized to meet that demand.

New forms, therefore, are more likely to arise spontaneously from new methods if the mind is unhampered by preoccupations with the forms created by the old methods.

The early printer worked on the assumption that if he produced his book, pamphlet, or broadside efficiently enough, it would be studied by the public (who were literate) out of a genuine interest to understand what he had printed.

This is, of course, still true today of the average book, because when people buy a book—provided it is sufficiently legible—they intend to read it. If they give up in the middle, it is because the writer fails to interest them and not because the printer has failed to make the appearance of the pages attractive enough.

Aesthetically, therefore, the fine tradition of good paper (hand-made, if possible, as an ideal), well-proportioned legible type faces, simply and symmetrically arranged, with generous margins, still holds good for contemporary book production. Except, of course, for certain types of instructional books—and books illustrated by photographs. These may require entirely different treatment.

Now, in contrast to this, a wholly new and vast field of printing and designing expression has been opened up by the needs of commercial enterprise and competition.

In the past, before large-scale commerce loomed so big in the affairs of men, the printer himself was the designer-producer of what printing there was to be done! It was the struggle of the printer trying to cope with masses of new design problems with only his book traditions to draw upon, that led to the chaotic and muddled appearance of much of the commercial printing of the early part of this century.

The printer who tried to be true to his traditions resented the introduction of art paper, for example, which he found he had to use if he was to produce a catalog which had halftone blocks of photographs in it. The very presence of the halftone alone seemed to be an anachronism—quite apart from the use of the abominable 'art' paper!

To add further to his troubles, his client wanted to put in more material in the way of headlines, text, and slogans than could be decently accommodated on the few sheets of paper which the cost of the job allowed.

Either his client had to be educated or the printer had to do the job and put up with it. He found, in fact, that his client did not want to be educated. He wanted a booklet that would make sales for his product—not a booklet that would make printing history!

How can a modern refrigerator catalog, for example, be a good piece of printing and sales promotion material if its appearance is based upon the aesthetic of a medieval broadsheet? Or, for that matter, how can a Press advertisement be a convincing statement if it is pretending to be a page out of an eighteenth-century book of *belles-lettres*? Particularly if the product to be sold is supposed to be the latest thing in high-speed motor cars.

The designer working in the commercial field, today, therefore, is faced with a problem of no mean proportions. He sees that the demands of commerce have encouraged the invention of means of reproduction to keep pace with other inventions in modern life.

The desire to reproduce the photograph quickly led to the invention of the halftone block. The old laborious method of making wood engravings from artists' drawings was superseded by the photographically made line block. Then there is photogravure; the tricolor block; off-set litho; the big rotary letterpress machine, printing from rolls of paper; the Monotype machine, the Linotype machine; the Ludlow process; and experiments are now in progress to perfect a means of typesetting by photography; the Jean Berté process; the silkscreen process; methods of printing on glass; on cellophane; on metal; the development of plastics for display and packaging; the electric sky signs of Neon; the Franco sign; the spiral binding; the metallic papers; flock paper; wood veneer papers; and so on. . . .

All this wealth of technical invention is at the service of designers today. Surely something new and remarkable can be done with it all! In fact, the reason why the commercial designer has come to exist is because someone is needed to exploit these remarkable new resources.

But if he is wealthy in the possession of such resources—how much also does he need their utmost aid? For he is faced today with an unprecedented competition for public attention. Publicity is his job—but he soon finds that a great many people are engaged in the same job. The evidence is all around him.

Confronting him in the streets are great electric sky signs surrounded by hoardings crowded with posters!

Shop windows are crowded with showcards and display pieces!

His letterbox is stuffed with catalogs, booklets and pamphlets of all kinds!

His daily newspaper is almost incomprehensible because there are so many advertisements in it.

And even the magazines at his barber's shop or his dentist's waiting room are bulging more with advertisements than with editorial.

It is obvious, therefore, that if any of these methods of publicity are to be effective in holding the public's attention, they must first catch it!

This fact constitutes the designer's first problem—and can very easily be his first pitfall—because at this point he comes up against the *writer* who, being usually a bookish fellow, is fond of words, and thinks the public shares his enthusiasm!

It must be understood that the designer's chief collaborator is the writer, and it is from this collaboration that the designer hopes to achieve the amalgam of words and pictures referred to at the beginning of this paper.

But the writer is a very engaging talker, since the convincing use of words is the very basis of his craft. He tends to hold the whip hand in any conversation with the designer!

The overinfluenced designer can, therefore, very easily imagine that his problem is to try and attract attention by illustrating literally whatever text the writer gives him.

At this early stage in his collaboration with the writer he is not yet aware of the fundamental difference between graphic ideas and literary ones—and as the writer has no knowledge of graphic ideas at all, he is not in a position to inform the designer of their significance.

I will try and give you an example of the sort of thing I mean, which, although exaggerated, is fairly typical. Let us suppose the writer has given the designer a piece of text for a newspaper advertisement on these lines:

'The lasting quality of Smith's Socks is as enduring as the Pyramids!'

This is the designer's big opportunity; remember, he is anxious to attract attention to this statement!

The idea of illustrating the socks seems to be *too* obvious, and also not unusual enough. But the Pyramids—ah! There's something dramatic—it has scale, too, and plenty of artistic possibilities; furthermore, it is obviously the crux of the writer's argument for the public buying Smith's socks!

What could be better then than a superb drawing of the Pyramids? Their triangular shape, too, suggests all sorts of cubist opportunities to give the picture a really modern look!

This modern look the writer is not so sure about—but the designer is quite certain that it is essential.

The design is done and, the text being short, a minimum of room is left below the picture to accommodate it. It is, of course, set in an Egyptian letter to match the picture.

We must assume, for the purpose of my illustration, that the client Mr. Smith is duly pleased with this ingenious idea of associating his socks with the world-famous Pyramids. He feels it is dignified, impressive, and adds luster to the reputation of his business!

We must remember at this point that Mr. Smith is a manufacturer of socks, not an advertising expert, so it is quite natural for him to rely on the advice of his advertising collaborators—in this instance our writer and our designer.

The advertisement, therefore, goes in to the newspapers, so that on the following day the eyes of the bewildered public light on this dramatic announcement. The designer has certainly succeeded in his job. His picture *does* attract attention.

But the point he overlooked was this: that the curious thing about a literary image is that it evokes only an abstract association in the mind, which serves to bring out the significance of the idea.

The writer's image about the Pyramids was quite legitimate—but the designer's elaboration of that image into a tangible reality causes the mind to be led off the subject, because there is no real association between the Pyramids and Mr. Smith's socks.

Since the graphic image is visually more rapidly comprehended than the text matter, the mind is in danger of going off down other avenues of thought . . . such as 'wouldn't it be fun to go to Egypt next holidays!' Consequently the return to the more mundane consideration of Smith's socks is an unwilling one.

The original effort, therefore, to attract the public's attention rapidly to the merits of Smith's socks has been largely dissipated by the designer.

If we assume that the writer's phrase was really sufficient to sell Mr. Smith's socks, surely it would have been better to set it out boldly, using up the whole advertising space, thereby letting it rely on its scale and brevity to attract attention to itself.

Or perhaps better still, if Mr. Smith's socks are as enduring as the Pyramids, why not have a picture of two hands stretching the sock to its fullest capacity, thus symbolizing the strength of the sock; in other words, finding a graphic equivalent for the significance of the phrase, instead of actually illustrating the words themselves.

Now, if the designer would expend the same care on getting the utmost force of expression out of a graphic equivalent of this kind, as he did in the delineation of the Pyramids, and combine it well with the setting out of the text, so that he creates a structural unity—he will not only have an advertisement which attracts attention, but which is a true piece of visual expression in terms of Mr. Smith's socks.

What happens to the designer—as the instance about Smith's socks shows—is that in the course of trying to solve these problems he tends to get too preoccupied with the artistic possibilities of his work at the expense of its clarity.

You remember how he wished to design those Pyramids so that he got what he called a modern effect.

This is because he has probably seen at different times posters by McKnight Kauffer, Cassandre, or Jean Carlu. He may even have come across booklets designed by Jan Tschichold or Moholy-Nagy.

The appearance of this work has struck him as being new and revolutionary and has, moreover, certain points of similarity with cubist and abstract painting.

The modern movement in the arts is obviously influencing commercial designing.

Anxious to progress, he embraces these tendencies with avidity. In his enthusiasm, however, he forgets that the medium of publicity in which he works is only a means to an end.

Unconsciously it becomes for him an end in itself; a vehicle for modern forms, for the sake of modern forms.

He now starts on a geometric pattern-making era—in which all the writer's headlines and text become inextricably woven together with cubist shapes and symbolic drawings, the whole becoming a complete mixture of forms and colors. Very dramatic, very modern—but far from clarifying the subject in which it is desired to interest the public.

Or again, he may be influenced by seeing a Continental design made up of three words in German (a language he doesn't understand) in which the force of the design lay in the arrangement of the words—so that the center word stood out very much more prominently than the rest—obviously a key word in the sense of the phrase.

Suppose now, that by some coincidence his next problem turns out to be a poster on which is to be used a short phrase.

A golden opportunity—so instead of trying to design one of his usual geometric and colorful bombshells, he decides that he will use the phrase itself as the basis of his design.

We'll suppose the phrase to be something like this: 'Walk more in the country.'

The designer is disappointed that the phrase has more than three words in it—but it can't be helped.

Still inspired by his German model he sets to work to arrange these words—the fact that they make a sentence which means something is completely forgotten in his enthusiasm.

The important thing to him is to make the center words stand out.

He paints his background a bright red because it's always an eye-catching color. He then airbrushes a white circular fusz in the middle of it.

Across the whole design he letters the phrase (at an angle because it adds vigor) 'Walk more in the country.' The words 'Walk' and 'Country' are painted in black caps, about an inch high on the red ground and in the white circle are the words 'more in the' in blue caps, about nine inches high.

Blue was used, of course, as a good contrast to the red background.

Now, on the face of it he certainly has an unusual poster.

He has a line of capital letters very dramatically arranged on a colorful background. . . . But . . . although the phrase 'Walk more in the country' is quite legible if one stands only a few feet away—anybody at any distance from it, however, is only able to read the words 'more in the,' which makes about as much sense to the observer as the words in the original German model made to the designer who was influenced by its appearance!

It can be seen from the foregoing that our designer has got a long way away from his aspirations to make the medium of publicity a constructive means of keeping the general public informed about the products and services of modern industry.

From all I have said you will perceive that too great an infatuation with modern forms for the sake of their modernity can be as great a pitfall to the designer as was the Edwardian printer's obsession with medieval book forms as a solution to commercial brochures, etc.

The contemporary designer stands or falls according to the degree to which his use of modern form and color contributes to the rapid comprehension of the ideas that the advertiser wishes to convey.

The advertiser is, of course, a businessman—who, apart from his own gain, exists in the world to the degree to which he anticipates the need of the people, and supplies the right goods accordingly.

To do this successfully he requires the help of the designer. He is not really interested in whether a design is old-fashioned or modern; artistically good or bad. But what he is interested in is whether it serves the purpose for which it is done. That is, does it work—does it come off?

Whatever the issue, therefore, whether it is a call to national fitness, the claims of a political party, or merely the virtues of a good pork sausage, the problem to the designer is the same—namely, the resolving of all those elements, tangible and intangible, literary or graphic, that in some given shape will express the central idea with absolute clarity.

He must evolve a kind of streamlining of the idea, so that its optical reception on the part of the observer is easy and rapid.

In other words, I believe the only ideal a designer should work to is complete clarity of expression. Not only clarity of words, or clarity of picture, but 'idea' clarity.

Whatever is to be expressed must be thoroughly understood before it can be successfully communicated.

A great many designers, if they were to be completely sincere with themselves, with their hands on their hearts, would be hard put to justify their latest job at the bar of true clarity of expression.

If this ruthless analysis of the problem is carried out honestly, the result is far more likely to be unusual and original than by any self-conscious attempt on the designer's part to be original as an end in itself.

Clear thinking is the road to inventive ideas.

A good instance of how clear thinking can produce an original solution to a difficult graphic problem is provided by Jean Carlu, when he was commissioned in 1929 to design a New Year greeting card.

The essence of our attitude towards the New Year is, of course, the passing of time. The difficulty that confronted Carlu, therefore, was to find some symbolic form which would freshly convey that idea.

How archaic were the symbols which he rejected!

The old man with the long robes and tattered beard carrying a sinister scythe over his shoulder, chased by the New Year in the person of a little boy with a pink sash conveniently arranged around his nakedness.

Then there was the egg boiler with the sand running low . . .

Archaic symbols, yes—and so worn out that their significance has sunk as low as that sand.

Now, what did Carlu do?

He took the small trip-meter of the motorcar speedometer as the basis of his idea.

In a sharp and arresting three-color design, worked by airbrush, he showed the 2 and 9 being flicked upwards by the 3 and 0, leaving, of course, the 19 stationary.

He thus symbolized the most striking fact about the New Year—which is the change of date. He did it on the very terms which our swift-moving motor car age most readily understands and appreciates. And—this is a point of importance on which I shall enlarge—the modern symbol lent itself to modern treatment, to a vivid interpretation.

You can't airbrush Father Time's beard or his lugubrious expression. Such an elaborate literary symbol was for armchair contemplation—you can't revamp it for people in a hurry. On all grounds, Carlu was indeed wise to drop it—and take up the clean incisive forms of today.

It is clear, then, that the kind of thinking which produces a constructive result is most likely to emerge when the designer is himself in sympathy with all the manifestations of contemporary life.

He should be familiar with all forms of modern expression in fields other than his own, because it is through the influence of modern architecture and the experiments of the purer arts of painting and sculpture that the new visual forms will be found. In other words the designer should be a man of the world and of his time.

For example, Lubetkin's penguin pond at the Zoo shows clearly the beautiful and compelling shapes that arise out of an exact solution to a problem—free from prejudice and romantic associations. Unlike the pseudo-Elizabethan building I came across in America which had an old sign dangling and creaking over the doorway with the words "Ye olde Radio Shoppe" displayed on it in ancient Gothic letters!

Again, thanks to painters like Picasso and Braque, a designer's knowledge of pure form and color, as well as texture, is greatly increased.

In the poster, for example, the great work of McKnight Kauffer alone is proof of the forcefulness of modern forms when handled by a master designer.

Furthermore, abstract painters like Mondrian, Ben Nichoson and Moholoy-Nagy have opened up new possibilities in spatial expression, the study of which should be of inestimable value, particularly to the layout man and typographer.

Their work tends to be of necessity asymmetric in form because an advertisement or pamphlet cannot be a slow sequence of ideas like a book, but is often five or six ideas all to be seen at once.

The sorting and relating of these ideas, so that they lie down together without conflict becomes a problem of ingenious placing and arrangement if the result is to be a balanced whole.

The abstract shape formed by groups of words in headlines and text can only be seen to their best advantage when arranged by typographers sensitive to the subtlest asymmetric balance of forms in space.

Again, in many of the abstract sculptures of Gabo, new spatial rhythms are discovered through the interpenetration of solid and transparent materials. These works are not only an inspiration to the architect, but also to the display designer, whether for exhibitions, shop windows or electric sky signs.

One can see the beginnings of this new spatial approach in the ESSO light sign on the side of the building facing one, if one walks on the left-hand pavement towards Leicester Square from Piccadily Circus, almost at Leicester Square.

I would like to end this paper by stating that as a designer, I personally welcome these trends and manifestations of our age. I am convinced that, through the inventive skill of scientists and engineers, collaborating with the designer, a new world of visual pleasure is growing up around us.

First published in Typography *no. 7 (London: Winter 1938).*

1940
HARSH WORDS
T. M. Cleland

THOMAS MAITLAND CLELAND *(1880–1964) was a respected editorial and adver-*
tising designer and typographer who adapted a French and Italian Renaissance aesthetic to
contemporary graphic design. He was also affiliated with a group of Americans who, inspired
by the Arts and Crafts movement, sought to return to excellence in printing through fealty
to historical models. In the late 1920s, the New Typography was introduced through trade
magazines and books as a clear challenge to these traditional values. At the American
Institute of Graphic Arts the schism between classicist and modernist members shaped the
agenda—debates for and against were common. Cleland strongly rejected European mod-
ernism and advocated a return to classical methods. His loquacious attack on the new aes-
thetic, a last gasp of sorts, was presented to an audience of traditional book designers who
feared the loss of their professional influence—and jobs. By the late 1930s, however, with
the immigration to the United States of former Bauhaus teachers and students as well as a
growing number of young American designers who embraced modernism, the war against the
new was just about over.—SH

I realize that, nominally at least, my subject must be that of printing and typography as exemplified by the selection of
the fifty best books of the year which we
are here to celebrate; and I suppose, by comparison to deplore the fifty thousand worst
books which may be seen elsewhere. But by what may seem a very odd paradox, I don't
quite know how to stick to this subject without wandering a good way off it. Or, perhaps I should say that I cannot approach it directly except by a very roundabout way.

If I have a thesis for these remarks, I can only develop it in terms of a tree.
This is because I do not believe that invention in the arts can be picked from empty
space like objects in a prestidigitator's act. Fruits really grow on trees and trees have
roots in the earth. The tree I have in mind is cultural civilization: one of its limbs is
art and a branch of this we call the graphic arts, and a twig on this branch is printing
and typography. I promise not to dig into the roots of this tree, but I may be found,
monkey-wise, climbing all over it before I am through.

I am at some disadvantage in that I do not belong to any organizations for
the advancement of typography and the graphic arts—not even to this one—and I am
ill-informed and out of touch with what is going on in these fields except by casual
observation. But as members of this very useful organization, you are not engaged in
printing or other graphic arts, I take it, solely for each other, but for the enjoyment
and delectation of the world at large. So there is a partially compensating advantage
in my being "at large" myself, and thus able to speak of present trends in the graphic
arts as they appear from the outside, looking in. But this advantage may in turn be
offset by the fact that I cannot honestly speak of what I see with much enthusiasm. I
can bring you no message of hope or light of inspiration. Much as I am filled with

admiration and respect for many individual talents and accomplishments that still contrive to exist, they seem to me to stand unhappily isolated in what I can't help viewing as artistic bankruptcy and cultural chaos. Among them are printers making
beautiful books and other things about as well as these things have ever been made.
But as to the general volume of printing, no-one has asked me, to be sure, what I
thought was the lowest point of artistic taste in the five hundred years of its existence
which we are celebrating this year, but if anyone *should* ask me, I would be bound to
say that we have reached that point just about now. Things may get worse, but it's hard
to see how they can. To paraphrase a remark in the concluding chapter of Updike's
classic work on printing types, it has taken printers and publishers five hundred years
to find out how wretchedly books and other things can be made and still sell.

I am not forgetting that there were some very benighted periods of taste in
other centuries that would seem to refute this sweeping assertion. Perhaps it is worth
noting here—and the fact is peculiarly ironical—that the design and style of official
and governmental things—money, postage stamps, bonds and stock certificates—was
created and solidified into a seemingly unalterable convention at that hitherto all-time
low point of the decorative arts in the mid-nineteenth century. So powerful is this
convention that we would be suspicious of a ten dollar bill that was not visually sat-
urated with ugliness. A counterfeiter with aesthetic sensibilities must not only sweat
blood but weep tears over the job of imitating one. But in the sadly perverted taste
of that epoch there was a kind of innocence: standards were still respected, and
proficiency, though overworked and misdirected, was recognized and not condemned.

Today when I look about in the bookstore, and more especially on the news-
stands, or open the pages of most of the magazines with the biggest circulations, I
want to do what the little boy did in the story which was a favorite of my friend, the
late Hal Marchbanks. The little boy had been to his first party, and when he arrived
home, his mother said: "Did mama's little boy have a nice time at the party?" "Yep,"
he replied. "What did mama's little boy do at the party?" "I thow'd up."

Against this steady decline in both taste and workmanship, your fifty books
selection and exhibit each year has been a noble effort, and in this country, almost the
only concerted one of consequence to uphold some standards. You have inspired both
publishers and printers to earnest endeavor to improve their products with frequently admirable results. But these are only fifty books out of how many other books and
other printed things. Without this good work of yours, one wonders if any standards
at all would survive the flood of cheap and easy mechanization, careless workmanship
and bad taste. Not that there is anything wrong with machines. The first hand press,
it should be remembered by its sentimental admirers, was also a machine. We have not
learned to use the machines at their best, but accepted them like fruits in the Garden
of Eden, and thought of nothing but how much we could get out of them in speed
and quantity and profit. Because we can do with them easily what formerly demanded time and pains to do at all, we have too easily assumed that they delivered us from
the need of any time or pains.

Before I go any farther on or off the track with these random remarks, I
should like it to be understood that I am addressing them particularly to any students
and beginners in the graphic arts that may be present, rather than to those who are
arrived. I am a student and still a beginner myself, and so my interest and my heart is
naturally with my own kindred. I speak as an old beginner to younger ones. I am at
a great disadvantage with regard to the number of years I have left in which to get
started, and if I have any advantage at all, it is only in experience with the bewilder-

ments and illusions that clutter our common way in learning and trying to practice one or more of the graphic arts. The confusions and distractions of this day make the path of the student and beginner rough and tortuous. Having traveled it for more years than I like to admit, when I look backward, I am astonished to discover the number of twists and turns and pitfalls I might just as well have spared myself.

Perhaps the most foolish of these was the fear of not being original—what Romain Rolland calls "the fear of the already said." The notion that I must do something new every day, or I would not be creative—forgetting that God made the planets all the same shape as far as we can see, and that the oak tree does not alter the form of its leaves from year to year. There is no supposition so pathetically misleading as that creative originality is within your own volition—the notion that it can be acquired leads to deplorable results. It distracts the mind and energies of the young student from gaining needful technical competence—from learning his trade, and in more mature stages tempts the would-be artist into vulgar mannerisms and formulas which he will call his "style."

The idea that originality is essential to the successful practice of the graphic arts is more prevalent today than it ever was in the days when the graphic arts were practiced at their best. The current belief that everyone must now be an inventor is too often interpreted to mean that no one need any longer be a workman. Hand in hand with this premeditated individualism goes, more often than not, a curious irritation with standards of any kind. The conscious cultivator of his own individuality will go to extravagant lengths to escape the pains imposed by a standard.

But of all the perils that lie in wait for adolescent artists there is none more seductive than the bewildering array of *ologies* and *isms* that leer and beckon to him at every crossroad of his journey. Just as *isms* and *ologies* have taken the place, in social and political life, of right and wrong; so have they become the accepted terms of the arts. In fact, nonsense is now so universally the language of art that it is nearly hopeless to try to make oneself understood in any other.

Brood mare to all of these extravagancies—and I have lived to see many of them come and go—is that one which achieves the super absurdity of calling itself "modernism;" and none has been expounded and exploited in more contradictory and antic ways. To deliberately call oneself "modern" is no less ludicrous than something an old Danish friend told me years ago about a line in one of the books of a very prolific writer of historical romances in his country. In a tale with a medieval setting this writer had one of his knights in armor cry out to another: "We men of the middle ages never take insults, etc."

Embraced with fanatic enthusiasm by many architects and designers is the current quackery called "Functionalism." It, in common with its many predecessors, offers a new gospel for the regeneration of our aesthetic world by restricting all design to the function of its object or its materials. Like the new religions and philosophies that have paraded in and out of our social history for countess generations, it purports to be an original concept. It has brought to us such gladsome gifts as concrete boxes with holes in them for buildings, chairs of bent pipe with no hind legs, glass fireplaces, beds of cement blocks joined by structural steel, the queer agglomeration of unsightly edifices we call the World's Fair and many other specimens of stark and forbidding claptrap. Unless all signs are misleading me, it is another mass vulgarity like the age of golden oak and mission furniture, even now on its way to the junk pile or the attic, perhaps to be someday rediscovered there and dragged out by future generations in search of quaintness.

It seems to me, ladies and gentlemen, that *all* art was *modern* when it was made, and still is if it is suitable to life as we now live it; and I look in vain for any applied art worthy the name that was not also, in some sense functional. From the buttresses of a gothic cathedral to the gayest Chippendale chair one finds, upon analysis, a perfect work of engineering perfectly adapted to its purpose. If this were not so, these things would hardly have endured for so long a time. So that common regard for function which has always been the basic principle of first-rate design, assumes the impressive aspect of a religion, with high priests and ritual, by the simple addition of an *ism*. As students and beginners in search of truth, we are today being pushed and pulled about by no end of such bogus preachments—familiar faces with false whiskers—old and common principles dolled up with new names and often used to account for incompetence and laziness.

And what is the meaning of this term "functionalism"? Must a design be related to no functions except mechanical and material ones? Might not the most fantastic and elaborate works of the geniuses of the baroque and rococo styles have also been functional in that they expressed the spirit and fitted perfectly the life they were intended to serve?

We hear much holy talk of "simplicity" in this day and the idea of simplicity expressed by a total absence of everything not essential to mechanical function has been elevated to a fetish. We have divorced simplicity from its old mate charm as we might break up the happy relationship of ham and eggs or pork and beans. But in this reverent renunciation of all adornment not strictly functional in this limited sense, have we paused to ask whether we are in fact following a basic human instinct, or merely attempting to make a virtue out of poverty of invention? There is no evidence that man is imbued with an instinctive love of simplicity in the objects with which he finds it useful to surround himself. Indeed, our museums are bulging with evidence to the contrary. From the Cro-Magnon cave to gothic cathedrals, from the temples of India to the palace of Versailles, the earth has been made to flower with man's inherent love of ornament. It would seem then that ornamentation is deeply rooted in the human instinct since no tribe, however primitive in other respects, is without it. The restraint of this instinct and the tempering of it with what we call taste is a cultivated faculty like the restraint of our other appetites; but to be a teetotaler in ornament or in anything else, is to confess to either weakness of control or incapacity for enjoyment. "A teetotaler," said Whitman, "is just another kind of toper."

This instinctive yearning for ornamentation is well demonstrated in the case of our own Rockefeller Center; where it has been catered to with peculiar ineptitude. Here all the important structures have been piously stripped of everything nonessential to mechanical function. Pillars, pilasters, cornices and moldings—ornaments that at least have their genesis in structural functions—have all been piously renounced. And then because it was found that the human spirit could not tolerate such barren starkness, and business might suffer from it, ornaments have been pasted around its doorways and approaches like gold paper lace on a pasteboard box—ornaments completely unrelated to any structural function of any kind. Sculptures, fountains, trees, flowers, and awnings have all been pressed into service to compensate for this spurious simplicity. Many of these things are beautiful in their own right like Mr. Manship's golden figure of Prometheus. One of the little office girls that further decorate the scene at the noon hour was overheard the other day explaining to another that this was a statue of "Promiscuous escaping from Responsibility."

So under this wildly flapping banner of "modernism" marches a quaint array of worn and shabby synthesis for art, each day parading a new dress and a new alias. The common urge for self-expression can always find one or another of them at its service. For those who are particularly deficient in the talent, energy, and patience demanded for the mastery of an art, something called "nonobjective" art has been invented. For this the only things required are a box of paints, brushes, and a surface to exercise them on. With these simple and easily procurable tools you express your own inner emotions and need not trouble yourself with anyone else's or with what anyone else sees. If you watch the others you will see that it is mostly being done with triangles, circles or vortexes of paint just as it comes from the tube. If you have no paint, toothpaste will do as well. If, after a few minutes of this, you are tired, stop— you will have added spontaneity to its other attractions. The fact that it deals only with your own emotions will not prevent you putting it on exhibition for other people to enjoy. If anyone balks at enjoying it, you smile wanly and shrug your shoulders and pity them for their dumb enslavement to outworn tradition. It works like a charm— no one will dare attack you—they will all be afraid that you've got something there. People have a terror of making mistakes—as if they had not been made by the best people in all ages. It is the most perfect device yet invented for attracting attention to yourself with the least trouble. A generation ago we heard a great deal about "art for art's sake": now it is art for the artist's sake, like bread for the baker's sake or medicine for the doctor's sake. And I say, for God's sake, tell me what art made through the vision of a human eye with a brain behind it is *not* "non-objective"? No two men will ever draw or paint the same picture of the same object. Only the lens of a camera will render it quite objectively, and even the camera in the hands of an artist is capable of some degree of subjectivity.

[. . .]

While I thus brazenly deny the existence of anything really new, and fail to recognize what is called "progress" and deplore the waste of talent and energy that is dissipated in striving for these things, I am far from blind to the value of revolt. Our creative sense is all too prone to doze off into dreams of past glories. From these, and the sterile copying of them, we may be awakened and rescued by even the crudest of revolutions. We may benefit from them provided we do not let them tear up our roots—provided we still can recognize an illusion when we meet it. The squirrel in his revolving cage must have some illusion of progress, else he would not take any exercise, and without exercise he would fatten and sicken and die.

And, remember, there is always progress to be made within yourselves, no matter if it is the same progress in the same direction that has been made by count-less other souls. And there will, I hope, always be things new to you, as there are every day things new to me, even if the sun has seen them all before. I don't want to live a day longer than I can learn.

There is no reason to suppose that there is not today as much latent talent for the arts in existence, as at any time in their history. But talent for art is not talent for being an artist—one may have much of the one, without much of the other. It seems to me that there are more temptations and distractions working against the talent to be an artist today than ever before. More alluring short cuts and seductive philoso-phies—a disturbing babel of undigested ideas and indigestible objectives. If in this riot you can keep your heads and not lose sight of the important difference between "a grain of truth" and the whole truth, if you can grow in understanding of what it is you want to do, you may, even now, have a good chance of doing it.

But what has all this to do with printing and typography and their related graphic arts? I seem by now to be so far off the track that it will take a derrick and wrecking crew to get me back on again. As a matter of fact I have not forgotten the subject altogether and have, in my lumbering way, been working toward it. But because I can't think of typography as an art in itself, unrelated to all the other arts, I could not approach it except by the way I have.

All of these things that I have been complaining about in the other arts, have their counterparts in present-day typography and printing. The same restless craving for something "new," the same preoccupation with *isms*, the same monotonous sameness. But this poison is aggravated in the case of printing and typography, by the fact that of all the arts, it is, by its very nature and purpose, the most conventional. If it is an art at all, it is an art to serve another art. It is good only in so far as it serves well and not on any account good for any other reason. It is not the business of type and printing to show off, and when, as it now so frequently does, it engages in exhibitionistic antics of its own, it is just a bad servant.

For this reason the embarrassing ineptitude of the current efforts toward a "new typography" are even more distressing than similar contortions in other fields. Typography, I repeat, is a servant—the servant of thought and language to which it gives visible existence. When there are new ways of thinking and a new language, it will be time enough for a new typography. When we have altered all of our manners and social customs, only then will it be time to radically alter the well grounded conventions of this very minor art. Within them there is now ample room, as there always has been, for the exercise of ingenuity, skill and individual taste. I suggest that those who cannot abide the conventions of typography are mostly those who have never tried them.

In what does the newness of this new typography consist? It seems to be new as the neu in neurosis from which it largely derives. It is new as it would be new for a man to enter the dining room on his hands instead of his feet, and instead of eating his soup, to pour it into his hostess's lap. It is as new and agreeable and pleasing to look at as delirium tremens which it closely resembles. The new typography engages in such side-splitting pranks as putting the margins of a book page in just the opposite arrangement to that which practical utility and well founded tradition have always placed them. It might with equal reason and originality, turn the type page upside down. In advertising display it makes use of that highly original and refreshing device of printing what is to be read at a cockeyed angle. The makeup expert indulges that other fresh and original dodge of bleeding pictures off the edge of the page so that a flat two dimensional photograph is viewed without a frame on two of its sides and must compete with a background of all the three dimensional things in the room.

I refuse to bore you or myself by enumerating all the tiresome stock-in-trade eccentricities of the typographic expert in search of something new—the epileptic fits he throws to attract attention to himself at the expense of the words he is printing. You see enough of them every day to know what I mean. Nearly every magazine and newspaper page, not to mention a good many books present the same revolting spectacle—the order of the day it seems, is disorder.

And speaking of magazines, it has fallen to my lot from time to time in the past thirty-five years to design and redesign a number of periodicals of one kind and another. Such jobs require really very little actual work—it's by endless argument and conference that they can wear you to the bone. My simple purpose with these things has always been to bring any measure of order the case will permit out of the disorder in which I generally find it. My mission, if I have any, is to suppress typography, not to encourage it—to put it in its place and make it behave like a decently trained servant. I find magazines rolling in the gutter covered with the accumulated mud of years of dissipation. I pick them up and brush them off, give them a cup of black coffee and a new suit of clothes and start them off on respectable typographic careers. But like other missionaries, more often than not, I find them a year or so later, back in the same gutter, drunk and disorderly and remorselessly happy about it.

If the philosophy of functionalism has hit the new typography as it has the other applied arts, I see no evidence of it. On the contrary, in this field, anything goes, so long as it is eccentric, free from the restraints of reason, and can successfully discourage the reader from reading. All the distortions of the roman alphabet that were discarded a half century ago—in fact any types which are as nearly unreadable as types can be made—have been dragged out again and called "modern." These range from the elaborately ornamental letters of the most depraved periods of design to the stark diagrams of letters that were called by typefounders in my youth: "Printer's lining gothic"—as absurd a misnomer as could be imagined since they have nothing whatsoever to do with gothic letters or any other letter forms known to history. Laymen called them, more accurately, "block letters"; but in the new typography they are elegantly referred to as "sans serifs" because, among other features of the roman alphabet which they lack, is a total absence of serifs. They bear the same relation to roman letters as would an engineer's drawings for a trolley track. At the moment they are very much in vogue and are widely believed to be modern and to be a simplification in harmony with the new architecture, furniture, and other things. They are supposed to represent the spirit of our day like the noise of riveting hammers in a modern musical composition. They simplify the traditional forms of type as you might simplify a man by cutting his hands and feet off. You can no more dispense with the essential features of the written or printed roman alphabet, ladies and gentlemen, than you can dispense with the accents and intonations of human speech. This is simplification for simpletons, and these are block letters for blockheads.

The users of typography and printing, the publishers and advertisers, are also confused by illusions of their own. Foremost among these is the notion that they require every week new types to give freshness and effectiveness to what they print and publish. This wholly unwarranted assumption is undoubtedly a godsend to the typefounders, however disastrous it is to the development of a sane and ordered typography. It has peopled the earth with typographic experts who know "the latest thing" and not much else, and it has relieved the designers of printing from the burden of knowing anything about design. It is so much easier to buy new types than to learn how to use effectively the types we already have. And if, instead of flooding our composing rooms with new types, which are seldom more than variations upon old themes of distortion, our typefounders would give us at least twice as many sizes as they now make, of a few good types, we should have a really flexible medium to work in. We would have to make fewer compromises with good design, and they might profit commercially, as typography surely would profit artistically.

And this constructive suggestion reminds me that I ought perhaps to temper this hurricane of destructive criticism with some further helpful hints. At the moment I can only think of two that might relieve the dreadful situation that I have pictured. One is that we organize a program of all type designers—a little hard on them perhaps, but they would gain martyrdom to a cause—and the other is that we establish a concentration camp in which to intern all those who think up or think they think up new ideas in typography for such time as it will take them to recover from their delusion. There they might while away pleasant hours in the distinguished company of the inventors of paper towels, pasteboard milk bottles, and beer in cans.

With my younger colleagues still in mind, I ought to say something of the practical problems that we encounter in professing and practicing one or other of the graphic arts. We are, or should be, if we are really artists, more concerned with what we give to our art than with what we get out of it. But we have to live—or think we do—and to do that by the practice of art is certainly no easier now than it ever was. If anything, it's a little harder. Beyond that inner satisfaction with what we can give—and there is only a little of that and at rare intervals—the only two things to be got *out* of art are money and fame; and I daresay there are few of us who would not welcome a little of both. But we must compete today with a great many of those who work for nothing else; and who, under the banner of one or another of these *isms* of which I've been prating, can concentrate upon that unique objective unhampered by any serious interest in art itself. They are devotees of success, like their commercial brethren, and by means of the same promotional paraphernalia they succeed so well that one is tempted at times to believe that the only living art is the art of self promotion.

Another curious development of these times is the classification of artists according to political ideology. We hear now of "left wing" artists. As nearly as I can discover, these are to be recognized by their contempt for any sort of craftsmanship and a peculiar inability to keep their drawings clean. They make penury—the unhappy lot of nearly all artists—a pious virtue, and they are not infrequently big with pretension to being the only serious interpreters of life and truth. These are balanced on the other end of the political seesaw by a school of "economic royalists" who have made of art a commercial opportunity. As Industrial Designers with large staffs and control boards and troops of indefatigable press agents, they have welded art and commerce so successfully that it is nearly impossible to tell them apart. Somewhere between the two is the artist; and he is as often as not a forgotten man. Not quite poor enough to be picturesque or heartrending, just well enough off to keep his collar and his drawings clean, he must nevertheless spend an exorbitant part of his life and energies in worrying about bills.

And now to stop the clamor of the butcher, the baker et al., to whom must we sell our graphic arts? For the most part, I suppose, it will be to publishers, industrialists and advertising agents. The publisher is a pretty decent sort, on the whole, but if he is a book publisher, he can generally be recognized as such by the fact of having very little money to spend on art. In my own experience, the most generous and appreciative customer for our wares has been the industrialist. What you do for him can often increase his profit very materially, and he is not slow to recognize that fact.

The advertising agent, speaking very generally and with the particular exception of one very dear friend in mind, deals largely in what might be called scientifically organized fraud. I am aware that to say this now is to risk being called a "communist transmission belt"—whatever that may be. It has even been suggested that by these animadversions upon advertising, I am biting the hand that fed me; but I suggest that I am biting the hand that I have fed until I am fed up on feeding it. It may be that you will find, as I sometimes have, in the ranks of these shock troops of deception, sympathetic and amiable clients for your work who can deal differently with artists than they deal with the public—but not very often. Each of them employs what is called an Art Director whose importance is derived, not so much from art as from the financial size and number of advertising accounts towards which he directs it. It is his duty to furnish you with what he calls "ideas," upon the theory that an artist is not mentally up to having any of his own. Ten to one he will end by altering your drawing to give it the "wallop" thought to be essential to all advertising. A public already groggy and half-blind from the incessant battering of advertisements with a punch, will hardly notice the difference.

"To think at all," says the Spanish philosopher, Ortega y Gasset, "is to exaggerate." A careful measurement of anatomical detail in the drawings and sculptures of Michelangelo will reveal startling exaggerations of fact, but these enlargements upon fact are but his medium for truthful expression. He gives us the figure of a man or woman more essentially true than could be made by any anatomist with micrometer calipers. So, I humbly pray, ladies and gentlemen, that you will apply no instruments of precision to my words—they are the best I could find in this emergency for saying what I believe to be true. If you think me guilty of exaggeration, the foregoing remarks are my only defense. But if you accuse me of being facetious, I will tell you that I have never been more serious in my life.

Address delivered to The American Institute of Graphic Arts, New York, on 5 February 1940. Published in two separate booklets by the AIGA and The Carteret Book Club, both in 1940.

1941
A TECHNIQUE FOR DEALING WITH ARTISTS
W. A. Dwiggins

WILLIAM ADDISON DWIGGINS *(1880–1956) combined a multi-disciplinary type and design practice with a prolific output as a writer, commentator, and satirist. Whether under his own byline, or the* nom de plume *Hermann Püterschein (i.e., pewter shine), he attacked a variety of design issues in pamphlets, magazines, and books, including* The Art of Layout in Advertising *(published in 1928, the same year as Jan Tschichold's* Die neue Typographie*) and* Towards a Reform of the Paper Currency Particularly in Point of Its Design *(1934). One of the earliest designer author/critics, Dwiggins refused to suffer fools or tolerate indignities. Combining a rapier wit and acute irony, he wrote this essay as a handbook on the care and feeding of "artists," not because he had any hope of convincing clients (whom he considered "know-everything-yet-know-nothings") to change their view of designers, but rather to "keep sane those artists who have to deal with businessmen." Like many of his commentaries, it addresses an enduring problem (for designers) with considerable humor and a delicate touch.—SH*

Amerian captains of industry—such ones at least as direct the manufacture and sale of household wares—have been obliged to do that thing that turns the heads of captains gray, namely: to change the tactical scheme in the heat of battle. . . .

In the last ten years a curious change has swept across the fancy of the buying public. The people who buy—that is to say, the women of the country—suddenly think they want *art* mixed in with their purchases. A kitchen range cannot any longer be sold merely as a kitchen range. It has to be offered as a kitchen range *plus*.

The plus part is *art*.

Whether the manufacturers and merchandisers themselves are to blame for this radical change in the consumer-fancy is a question: how far, for example, were certain individuals of the group tempted to travel outside the bounds of sound conservative practice into regions of "esthetics"? How far, by so traveling, did they muddle up the merchandising game?

. . . But the change has occurred, and the result of the change is . . . chaos.

Machines have been used in the facture of domestic wares—utensils, materials, tools, *les meubles*—for one hundred years. Never, in that whole time, has it been necessary at any moment for a proprietor of machines to ask anybody's advice about how the machines should be used. All problems in the operation were solved by the manufacturing proprietor himself or by people in his immediate employ. For all matters that concerned the shapes and finishes of his product he could rely on his own judgment. If he thought an article needed to look handsomer he told his people how to make it handsomer. If he wanted floral encrustations on a cast-iron column so blemishes wouldn't show, he called in the help of the ever-available female relative who had taken lessons in china-painting. If he thought a paint-stripe was needed on a wagon-wheel, he said what color the stripe was to be and where it was to go. His determination of style was final. His taste was as good as any other man's taste. The country was a democracy.

But now—with this demand for *art* as an essential part of the product—the manufacturer finds himself dangling over an abyss that he can neither plumb nor bridge. . . . The new fancy for art-varnish on merchandise puts a strain on the old system that it can't stand up under. The manufacturer, by hook or by crook, has got to provide art. *He* can't supply it—his office-force can't supply it—his telephone girl is flabbergasted—the men in the shop are dazed, insulted, by the simple word—organization helpless, owner to errand-boy—square miles of machines to make things: not a soul on the premises to say how the machines are to make *artistic things*. . . .

There is only one course for the proprietor to pursue: go outside his organization and *call in an artist!*

He does so. He faces the music. He turns his back on tradition—on his own carefully assembled working force. He calls in an artist. And finds . . . what?

He finds that he is not able to deal with this person on any rational terms whatsoever.

He finds that artists talk a foreign tongue—think alien thoughts. That what they aim to do and how they aim to do it are matters absolutely outside his experience, or his comprehension.

He finds that he just can't get along with artists at all.

Now, something will have to be done about this. Some way will have to be found to bridge the chasm between artist and merchant-manufacturer. Obviously the material for the structure will be mutual understanding. If the businessman can get some kind of clue to the artist's mental processes—just a hint—he will be able to whip the artist's contribution into shape to fit the merchandising scheme, and things will move along comfortably. This pamphlet undertakes to provide the clue.

A TECHNIQUE FOR DEALING WITH ARTISTS

WHAT IS AN ARTIST?

The study here undertaken proceeds from the business side of the problem. What we want to do is to arrive at a set of rules for guiding businessmen in their transactions with artists. The logical first step in the undertaking will be to find out what artists are like, why they behave as they do, what they think, how they perform.

PROPOSITION I. An artist is an anomaly in the present civilization because he is moved by a craving outside the universal and rational craving to make money.

The impulse that moves an artist to use up his energy laboring toward an end not measurable in terms of money may be compared with the passion that might possibly move a businessman to perfect an organization or to refine a process—without expecting, for the time being, any economic return from his effort. In the case of the businessman such a passion would be kept within bounds, subordinated to his main effort (i.e., his effort to increase the funds of himself or of his corporation). In the case of the artist the impulsion might not always be so controlled: in the case of the artist his urge to exercise his distinguishing faculty might very likely outrun and displace a craving for money.

II.   The factors of prime importance to a man of business are (1) money, its movement toward him or away from him, and (2) men in terms of money, as removing money from him (employees), or bringing money to him (customers). An artist works, not with men and money, but with materials (i.e., actual substances, wood, metal, glass), with sensory impressions, and with ideas.

III.   Part of the impelling forces that moves an artist along his peculiar line of effort is the pleasure he gets from manipulating materials or from marshalling ideas—the pleasure of seeing things take shape under his hand. A man of business may have this same kind of satisfaction, but in a less degree, because with him that kind of satisfaction will be held strictly subordinate to the satisfaction of accumulating funds.

IV.   An artist aims at a *practical performance* of the fabric he makes. If he makes a chair, his aim is to make a chair that people can sit in comfortably. It is hard for a businessman to think of a fabric as fitted for a use, and sound in itself (except when it is for his own use). The merchant-manufacturer thinks about his product as *merchandise*—something to sell; the artist thinks about his product as something *to be used*. One measures it in units of exchange value; the other measures it in units of performance value.

WHY DOES ART HAVE MARKET VALUE?

Art (the product of artists) may occur in an abstract form, such as music or poetry. Abstract forms of art are not of any use to a businessman. But art may be "applied" to the practical machinery of life (e.g., architecture) sometimes increasing the value of the machinery.

V.   Art in the applied form, therefore, comes within the range of commercial interest because it contributes value to merchandise.
          It is hard for a businessman to understand why art applied to the practical machinery of life should make that machinery more valuable. The value of an internal combustion engine will not be increased by having its parts designed according to one of the esthetic systems. But the value of the vehicle that the engine moves is increased if artistic taste enters into the vehicle's design. Why?

VI.   Artistic quality has commercial value because it panders to an owner's pride. (As in the above instance: the stylish automobile gratifies the owner's pride.) One may stop with that. Other explanations on higher levels of human performance are of less practical value to the businessman.

WHAT DO ARTISTS VALUE?

If the artist is not inclined to appraise his product (art) in terms of dollars and cents, by what standard does he appraise it? What value does he see in it?

An artist's estimate of the value of his product has no relation whatever to the commercial value of art. It is important here only because it throws a light upon the peculiarities of artists.

VII.　　An artist finds a value in the pleasant appearance of things. An object is valuable to him if its shape and proportions please his eye. This sense of grace and satisfactory proportion is not a faculty of artists alone; but in artists it is trained and developed more than in non-artists. The intrinsic value of the material of an object is of less moment to an artist than the object's form, color, etc. Why, and how, the shape of an object pleases an artist and makes the object valuable to him is another story, not pertinent to this discussion.

VIII.　　An artist values "style" in a design or construction or performance. Style in this connection has a special meaning. There is a best way to strike a golf ball, to play tennis, to swim, to walk. In the realm of sport this best way is universally recognized as *form*. Transferred to the region of art this best way of doing things becomes *style*. Style is the simplest, the most graceful, the most forceful way to apply the effort and accomplish the end; style is, therefore, a quality of performance. It is also an end product: objects have style according to the good fortune of their design. Locomotive engines, automobiles, ships, often have great style. A sense of the value of style is not confined to artists alone.

IX.　　An artist finds value in a nice *technical* performance. The way the paint is laid on the canvas; the way the wood is cut by the carving tool—operations of that kind, when done simply by a sure hand, add value to an object in the eyes of an artist; they are contributory to the quality called style.

These are examples of the standards of value that an artist uses in appraising his product.

DO ARTISTS THINK?

It is assumed that an artist's work calls for no use of the reasoning faculties—that he proceeds solely upon a basis of "feeling," achieving his ends by intuition. This assumption is incorrect.

X.　　The artist is a rational creature. His impulse to create a work of art emerges first in the region of intuition; and intuitive choices and decisions operate throughout the process of evolving a work of art. But that process is directed and expanded by reason. The end aimed at is a rational end. (See Proposition IV)

The fabric that an artist builds must perform in a practical way; otherwise he is not suited. The practicality is a result, partly of intuition, but mostly of a rational study of the end to be served. Your proper artist is always half engineer. A sense of weights and stresses, of structural fitness, of the right handling of materials, is as much a part of an artist's equipment as an intuitive sense of rhythmic spaces and graceful lines. If an artist is actually an artist—not a mere esthete—you may rest easy about his rationality.

HOW TO CHOOSE AN ARTIST

Choosing the right artist is, of course, *the* critical operation of the whole technique of dealing with artists. Artists as a class are not trained in the details of business

XXIV.   The best way to revive interest is to keep the artist in touch with the progress of the work in the shop or on the site. Trial proofs, trial specimens, photographs of advancing patterns, experimental data, all tend to keep the artist's interest alive.

XXV.   If there are two or more projects to be undertaken in sequence, carry the artist's interest over from job to job by sending him full data (photographs of finished work, specimens of the completed article, copies of the printed hook, etc., etc.) concerning completed Project No. 1, as he enters upon Project No. 2.

In every case it is wise to show the artist how his design turns out as soon as the work is completed. When it happens repeatedly that an artist makes designs and sends them off into space and never hears of them again, his work seems to him futile and he loses interest. (See Proposition IV: An artist is interested in the *performance* of his design.)

The dispatch of this "revival" material to an artist needs to be done systematically, as a regular part of the program—not left to the chance of somebody's remembering to do it.

HOW TO LOWER THE CONCEIT OF AN ARTIST

XXVI.   To diminish an artist's importance in his own eyes shape your discourse after this fashion. Suppose that you are talking to a celebrated sign-painter. Ask him: "Do you know Jones' work in sign-painting? In my opinion Jones is the greatest sign-painter we have. The only others that approach him at all are _____ and _____. (Not mentioning the artist you are talking to.) Then proceed to describe various of Jones' successes great length. Few professionals can stand up to this ordeal.

If the artist is of a lower order and will not wilt—but, instead, tries to prove that he also is a great sign-painter by showing you photographs of his masterpieces, run through his prints rapidly, without comment, and then take up the tale of Jones' sign-painting again. The second injection will lower the artist's conceit to zero.

HOW TO COMMEND AN ARTIST

XXVII.   If you like the work an artist shows you, do not try to express your approval in the form of apt technical comment. Confine yourself to the simple formula: "I like that"; or grunt in an approving way.

COROLLARY. On the other hand you may use apt technical comments to give expression to a *luke-warm* interest: "I like the way you have managed the perspective in the fly's left foot," etc. The artist will see that you care very little about it and will readily pass on to a discussion of battle-averages, or whatever.

HOW TO FLATTER AN ARTIST

Flattery is effective with artists of minor rank. As an artist's ability rises in degree the effect of direct flattery diminishes. Some great artists are gluttons for flattery; but usually an artist of large dimensions has been fed so much of it that he can no longer taste it. In many cases, no great degree of finesse is required; but speaking in general, the administration of flattery calls for a delicate touch and a sure hand.

XXVIII.   If the first encounter with an artist occurs in his workshop, ask to see his work—using the formula: "I'd like mighty well to see some of the stuff."—not "Oh, *won't* you show me some of your work," etc. If you meet him in the world outside, use the formula: "So-and-so tells me I ought to get in touch with you and see some of the things you are doing," etc.

XXIX.   At the first encounter *do not mention other artists in the same line*—or, if the names of other artists are introduced by the artist himself, deal with them briefly.

XXX.   *Do not disparage the work of other artists in the same line* under the mistaken impression that disparagement of his peers will flatter an artist.
    After you become acquainted with an artist you may discuss other artists freely. But, even in such free discussion, it is wise to let the artist himself take the lead in dismembering other artists—he may secretly be flattered by your dissection of his contemporaries; but use the knife sparingly.

XXXI.   When an artist shows you his work for the first time do not try to shape your comments along technical lines. Use the natural language God gave you, If, by a lucky fluke, you hit upon a point that is the artist's particular pride, do not try to expand or amplify the fortunate stroke. Leave it just as it stands. Artists, flattering each other, use simple phraseology: "That's bully" or "I like that" so-and-so. The less jaw-jaw the better.

XXXII.   An effective form of flattery, in a case where the fee charged is really disproportionately small, is to add slightly to the amount of the artist's charge. Coming in this way, in terms of the businessman's own standard of values, the approval is particularly emphatic.

HOW TO PAY AN ARTIST

XXXIII.   If an artist keeps up his end of the bargain, delivers his work promptly, and gives general satisfaction, you will do well to separate his invoices from the usual sixty days dossier, and treat them as professional bills, i.e., cash on presentation. His receipt of prompt payment for work done promptly will give him a sense of action all along the line and will stimulate him to increased effort to make his end of the job snap.

XXXIV.   Do not try to discipline an artist by holding up payment for his work. He will be irritated by the procedure, to be sure, but not in the way you intend, because he is not so sensitive in the region of the pocket-nerve as you may have anticipated. (See Proposition I)

XXXV.   If the artist is naive, money can be saved by having him make an agreement with you that you will pay for only such part of his work as you may accept and use. This will relieve you from paying for what is really the most time-consuming and laborious part of a designer's job, namely, the preliminary study and preparation of alternative sketches and designs to clarify his plan. You can, of course, reject his finished working-drawings when the study is complete, retaining careful memoranda of various valuable points developed.

XXXVI.   If the artist is young and inexperienced tell him that, while you can't pay much for the design, it will be used widely and seen by millions of people: the wide publicity will greatly benefit him. If the artist is very young this argument may induce him not to charge any fee at all.

XXXVII.   An older artist—particularly the kind that is engrossed by the technical details of his craft—may be induced to take less than his usual fee if you can contrive to make the commission highly interesting on its technical side (if it involves some novel and experimental manipulation, for example). It will be worth your while to surrender some point that you have insisted on—particularly a point that involves merely pride or stubbornness on your part—if the surrender will add some attractive technical feature to the project.

XXXVIII. An artist of long experience whose work is in great demand will have arrived at a fixed scale of prices and cannot be influenced to change them. He will occasionally do work *gratis* if the spirit moves him. The spirit that moves him will be some peculiar feature of the project that engages his interest—but the feature will be too peculiar and unexpected for you to be able to contrive it in advance as bait.

XXXIX.   A simple way to get a lot of art (of a sort) for little or no outlay is to set up a Prize Competition for a given project. Some very excellent artists go in for Prize Competitions, but as a general rule the key men in a field have no time to bother and the designs that come in are second grade. Often a second grade design will be better for your purpose than a strictly first class article; and there will be Honorable Mentions to be saved for later use, and many good ideas that you can use not Mentioned at all.

First published in pamphlet form (New York: Press of the Woolly Whale, 1941).

1946
ART IN INDUSTRY
Walter P. Paepcke

WHILE BUSINESSMEN LIKE *Earnest Elmo Calkins made the case for modern design as a way of improving a company's financial results, others championed the idea of client as patron, commissioning good design as a way of not only selling goods but improving society. Walter Paepcke (1896–1960), president of the Chicago-based Container Corporation of America, was the influential model for a group of corporate leaders in mid-century America who legitimized the formal attributes of modern design as the acceptable expression of forward-looking world capitalism. Paepcke commissioned progressive architecture, graphic design, and advertising, offered property in Colorado as the site of what became the International Design Conference at Aspen, and, through a series of advertising campaigns, introduced modern design and art to the public. The best known, "Great Ideas of Western Man," offered interpretations of quotes from great thinkers of the Western world by a wide range of modern designers. The "United Nations" series, discussed here, commissioned work from artists based in each of the far-flung countries where CCA did business. Although these campaigns could be rightly criticized as superficial, there is no mistaking Paepcke's commitment to progressive design as an end in itself.—MB*

I n earlier days, including the Golden Age in Greece, the artist and the craftsman were very often one and the same individual. Consequently, the architecture and the products of the craft were functional as well as artistic, and the philosophy of the craftsman and the artist necessarily homogeneous.

During the last century in particular, the Machine Age with its mass production procedures has seemingly required specializations which have brought about an unfortunate divergence in work and philosophy of the industrial producer and the artist. Yet artists and businessmen, today as formerly, fundamentally have much in common and can contribute the more to society as they come to complement their talents. Each has within him the undying desire to create, to contribute something to the world, to leave his mark upon society; each has the necessity to earn and provide a living for himself and his family. Too often it can be said that the business man, during the last few generations at least, has concentrated too much on the latter, while the artist in more recent times has found himself working in a vacuum, without the necessary opportunity to think and create and at the same time to provide adequately for himself and his family. Closer cooperation and understanding should help the business man to produce material things which are not only functional and mechanically sound, but also artistically outstanding, and the artist in turn to share to a greater extent in the earning possibilities which are essential for a happy existence.

Equally important in this particular age is the necessity for representatives of all the nations to learn to understand and respect one another. In the adoption of the "United Nations" series, the opportunity presented itself to invite representatives of many widely scattered foreign countries to participate. The artists who contributed to this exhibit are more than skillful technicians; they are cultivated men, widely traveled, scholarly, introspective, observant, and of good will. In some of their paintings there is the zeal of the patriot, and an indication of real scholarship in others. Some are deeply poetic. All seem to spring from a realistic attitude toward life, an attitude of men who are taking part in the world about them.

It should be made easy, remunerative and agreeable for the artist to "function in society not as a decorator but as a vital participant." The artist and the businessman should cultivate every opportunity to teach and supplement one another, to cooperate with one another, just as the nations of the world must do. Only in such a fusion of talents, abilities, and philosophies can there be even a modest hope for the future, a partial alleviation of the chaos and misunderstandings of today, and a first small step toward a Golden Age of Tomorrow.

First published in Modern Art in Advertising: Designs for Container Corporation of America *(Chicago: Paul Theobald, 1946).*

1949
INTEGRATION, THE NEW DISCIPLINE IN DESIGN
Will Burtin

WILL BURTIN'S EXHIBITION *"Integration, the New Discipline in Design" opened at the A-D Gallery, New York, in 1948, before going on to tour the United States. The dynamic lightweight installation, constructed from steel, colored plastics, and aluminum, was based on the four "realities" that Burtin (1908–1972) identified as fundamental to contemporary visual communications. These principles were later summarized in an article published by the international design journal* Graphis *(founded in 1944). For Burtin, the visualization of scientific information and processes, as an educational aid for the public, was one of the essential tasks of the graphic designer, whose pivotal position gave him, or her, the role and responsibility of "communicator, link, interpreter, and inspirer." Burtin's short text, written at a time when designers such as Ladislav Sutnar and Herbert Bayer were also developing innovative techniques for the transmission of complex information, is a personal manifesto. As consultant to the Upjohn pharmaceutical company, he went on to create functional graphics of exceptional beauty, as well as hugely ambitious exhibition models of a human blood cell and a brain.—RP*

isual communications are based on four principal realities:

- the reality of man, as measure and measurer
- the reality of light, color, texture
- the reality of space, motion, time
- the reality of science

THE REALITY OF MAN

Man in design is both—a measure and a measurer.

The dimensions of his hands, his eyes, his entire body should be seen in relationship to the scale, shape, and volume of anything surrounding him, and directed at him.

He is an integral part of everything we can think of and do. He is the most important part in a design. We depend on his physical, emotional and intellectual response, on his understanding.

As we direct communications to him, we must have a proper appreciation of his character, as an individual, as part of a social group, of his desires and dreams.

Man is the total sum of his experiences. His scale and focus change continuously as he studies, grows, and develops. Therefore, in designing we must realize that steadily changing conditions confront us, to which we can adjust ourselves only by:

1. Constantly developing better and more precise ways of expressing ideas,
2. Investigating anew with each new assignment the entire range of approaches,
3. Understanding the mechanics of vision.

THE REALITY OF LIGHT, COLOR, TEXTURE

Color is associative in character. One reason for the emotional impact of color lies in
the firm roots it has in the subconscious and intuitive background of man.

The visual recognition of color values develop very slowly. Rembrandt's
brown, the Victorian purple, Degas' pastel blues and pinks, the beige of the early 20s
are some examples which show how much time passes before specific color perceptions are verbalized, or "become known."

To a physician color means one thing professionally, and something else
esthetically, which also holds for the architect or scientist or carpenter. The first is a
conscious—that is rational—the latter a subconscious definition. The first is knowledge based on actual experience, the second stems from emotional depths. Yet, the
designer must work with both.

Young people employ vigorous, contrasting colors. Advancing years bring a
preference for the sedate. This indicates that the requirements of our nervous system
are balanced through the reaction-focus of our visual nerve, the eye.

Principally, color is light of varying intensity—from white over the prismat-
ic range to black. Its reflecting qualities are intimately linked with its optical structure
and the surface to which applied. Both together appear to our eyes also as texture.
Texture not only influences and dramatizes the color character, but has also structural characteristics of its own, to which our sense of touch reacts. Additionally, through
texture we speculate on what may be behind a surface, what it encloses.

THE REALITY OF SPACE, MOTION, TIME

Understanding of space and time relations is a main requirement in visual organization. In printed design images are superimposed on paper surfaces. The spaces inside
and between letters, between lines of type, their relationship to illustration, are vital
factors, which determine the eye's access to the basic information.

As we read from left to right, a flow develops, which must be utilized to connect the various parts of a message, text and illustration. This movement can be accelerated, by keeping type faces and spacing open, or slowed down, by condensing them.
Thus reading time is as important a measure as the space within which visual communications are organized.

In exhibitions, the adding of a third dimension plus physical motion allows
full employment of the sensations of timing, scale, structure, and volume.

In motion pictures, time can be condensed (one year = one minute) or
stretched (one second = one hour), and the visual image (space) can develop from
realism to illusions of astonishing depth and dexterity.

In stroboscopic images, motion collapses into stages: Time and space melt into
one single unit.

When the effects of multiple motion in space were recognized, the concept of
relativity emerged, which lends time a double meaning—measure of space and evolution—and changes space itself from a linear to a spherical volume. It also abandoned the

idea of absolute positions. Consequently we are able to differentiate between the apparent and true conditions of space, motion, and time and their changing relationships.

THE REALITY OF SCIENCE

The purpose of science is the exploration and prediction of phenomena. In their endeavor to be absolutely clear and economical, scientists have compressed entire processes involving time, space, changes of conditions, density, and speculative thoughts, into abstract symbols of mathematics, thereby creating a visual language of their own.

The extra-sensatory reality of science provides man with new dimensions. It allows him to see the workings of nature, makes transparent the solid and gives substance to the invisible. It has expanded the range of human experience and improved our ability to define and organize data coherently into new visual presentations.

Science is not restricted to engineering, chemistry, medicine, and energy-matter alone. The impact of scientific thinking and procedure is felt increasingly in the fields of social and psychological problems, and in fact in every area of human activity, not excluding that of art.

The designer stands between these concepts, at the center, because of his unique role as communicator, link, interpreter, and inspirer. He deals with their known qualities and quantities, discoveries, processes, ideas, and their effects upon each other.

Through unceasing comparison and interrelation of factors, he gains an understanding and exciting insight into their nature and value, enabling him to depict even that which had been invisible. Thus he creates.

To enlarge and define this vocabulary of visual language, and thereby contribute toward integration of our culture, is his social responsibility as a man, his job as a designer.

[. . .]

First published in Graphis *no. 27 (Zurich: 1949).*

1949
FUNCTION IN MODERN DESIGN
György Kepes

THE BATTLE TO SELL *modernism to the American public began shortly after World War II, led to a considerable degree by the efforts of a number of European immigrants who proclaimed the virtues of practicality, the importance of design principles, and the merits of avant-garde thinking to their students and colleagues at design schools across the United States. Trained as a painter and filmmaker in his native Hungary, György Kepes (b. 1906) emigrated to the United States in 1937, and a year later became Director of the Color and Light Department at the Chicago Bauhaus, under the direction of László Moholy-Nagy. From 1946 to 1974, Kepes taught at the Massachusetts Institute of Technology, and in 1968 founded The MIT Center for Advanced Visual Studies. As author and editor of numerous books on art and perception, he has long been interested in examining how functional design, both in theory and practice, could benefit from a fusion of art and technology. In this essay, Kepes looks critically at the relationship between the utilitarian demands of functionalism and the humanitarian goals of "honest design": it typifies the kind of analysis with which he is most often associated; a combination of creative, pragmatic, and psychological inquiry that lends itself brilliantly to the field of design scholarship.—JH*

Today's obsession for speed and quantity has profoundly influenced the ways in which we think and feel. Mass production and mass communication, with their characteristic standardized thoughts and vision, have overworked ideas, making of them exhausted stereotypes.

We tend to mistake the slogan for truth, the formula for the living form, repetition of habit for cultural continuity. Inertia leads us to carry this dead body of lifeless thoughts around with us. To halt the depletion of the life of the words we use, of the ideas and purposes that guide us, we must constantly overhaul our mental equipment.

Vigilance is needed not only in the spheres where we are vaguely aware of the intentional misuse and manipulation of words and ideas, as in political propaganda or the cheaper aspects of advertising. It is needed also in fields where we assume that we know what we are talking about, in our own profession. Here we must be doubly alert, for we lack the perspective that distance offers.

I have been asked to write about function in design. The words "design" and "function" are prominent in our daily vocabulary. The coupled term, "functional design," is accepted today as the core of professional activities that aim to shape man's physical environment. Has the term "functional design" escaped the fate of other repeated terms? Battles are still fought, and the last skirmishes under the banner "form follows function" are still with us; but there is reason for believing that the underlying thought has lost its living strength.

It seems, therefore, appropriate to begin by asking questions, by examining the fundamental terms that we generally assume have a clear meaning. Taking nothing for granted, let us subject our professional catchwords to strict scrutiny.

What is function in design? To answer this question logically is to answer with relevance to the purpose that initiated the question. To recognize the validity of a logic of design one must first recognize the root purpose.

What is then the purpose of man-made design? Is it sufficient to answer that the purpose of a building is shelter? the purpose of a chair to support the human body? of a book to permit its being read? Can these functions be understood only within the narrow radius of what we consider their function to be, or do we need to inquire still further until we reach a final and common root of all these purposes?

If the roots of those thoughts, which today seem self-evident and which we use frequently in a mechanical repetition, are traced back to the ideas and works of those great pioneers of the recent past who gave us these thoughts, it will become obvious that they meant more than most of us mean today. Louis Sullivan, whose work and writing became the guiding force of contemporary design thinking, was fully aware of the depth and range of the issues involved. He wrote these words about his own goal, "To make an architecture that fitted its function, a realistic architecture based on well-defined utilitarian need—that all practical demands of utility should be paramount as basis of planning and design; that no architectural dictum or tradition or superstition should stand in the way." And he wrote also, putting his own thought in a broader context, "Man perhaps and probably was the only real background that gave distinction to works appearing in the foreground as separated things."[1] For him and for all the great men who paved our way to a healthier thinking, it was always self-evident that design is not for design's sake, that design is for man.

Man was the root of their thought, and human function gave direction and measure to whatever they were doing. They attacked with admirable concentration new structural possibilities, but this technical mastery was only a means to an end and never the end itself. It was not the house function that they built for, but a function of man by means of a building. Not the chair, not the book, which was functioning, but again man, who through his design of the chair and the book could function better, that is, live fuller and freer. And furthermore, it was not merely one aspect of man, not just the feet, the hands, the lungs, or the eyes, but man as a whole. Everything that they conceived was considered in its implications to all the levels of existence of a human being. Although they fully recognized that straightforward thinking in physical and utilitarian terms is a necessary step in putting a design on a healthy basis, they did not forget that the elementary utilitarian functions and the honest use of materials and techniques are conditions only, not ultimate purposes.

Man was in focus; but not man only as he was then. They aimed to satisfy his needs for comfort as a means to help men grow. And we may quote Sullivan again: "The fabricating of a virile, a proud civilization, rich in its faith in man, is surely to constitute the absorbing interest of the coming generation. It will begin to take a functional form out of the resolve of choice, and the liberation of those instincts within us which are akin to the dreams of childhood, and which, continuing on through the children and the children of the children, shall be a guide evermore."

Their work had a living fiber because it was intimately connected with a living human core. For design that integrates life, functioning for man, functions in terms of the materials it uses, the structures it applies, and the form in which it is shaped. Designs which have their root in the heart of man, and not in his pocket, are alive. Designs which grow organically with the calm dignity of honesty, not with the haste of a bad conscience, can only and do only provide the values needed for human growth. They are functional in the truest meaning of the word.

And so let us understand that the issue is not functional design as such, that it is not just the "know how," but the "know why" and the "know what." The crux of the issue is not the mere physical principle, which is as old as nature and history, but the strength and scope of application in the concrete context of genuine human needs. This means that before we proceed to design any object for a given purpose, we should question the purpose itself. The aim of the object should not simply be taken for granted. It should be evaluated in its broadest scope.

Does the so-called functional design which we are so proud of, frequently justly proud, function in this broader sense? We have learned to think honestly in the terms of the materials and tools used and to respect these materials and tools. We are sensitive to new potentialities and zealously follow new materials and new techniques. We design with a simplicity of single-minded purpose, with an economy which is the logic of design, carefully avoiding all waste. The objects we make have visual congruence between the inside and the outside and are transparent in meaning. But did we apply this honesty of thinking, the economy of the making, the alertness to the changing tools and media, to the human material which is the root and purpose, the tool and the user of our designs? Are we devoting as much care to man's need, to his intrinsic nature, as we do to building with reinforced concrete or to bending plywood into furniture?

Has not our concern for the efficiency of the detail led to the neglect of the efficiency of the most important design, the design of man as an individual and as a member of society? It is a brutal paradox of our age that by concentrating all efforts on material products the very heart of all those achievements is neglected; the producing man, the active man, man's happiness, growth, and promise. For how could we hope that all these wonderful, neat, crisp, functional designs that the best designers are creating in their best moments could truly fulfill their function when man becomes used up making the goods which should benefit him? The pleasure in making, that William Morris called "the only birthright of labour," is for most of us only a distant memory of the past. This emphasis on the finished object creates a "ready-made" attitude that rests satisfied with appearances and limited utility. Consequently, the object never seems to take its place in the broader area of total human needs. It is time now for redirection. Let us discipline our thinking by tracing all that we are doing or are intending to do to the original purpose, the human purpose. What we have learned in this recent past we must apply to a broader context. To give functional design a new living meaning we must concentrate on establishing a scale of values. And in the hierarchy of values, the human values should again regain priority. We should recognize levels of functions in which one contains another and keep in mind that the container of all values is man. We must develop a functional thinking, directed toward a design where all levels of human intentions and objects for use are organically interconnected, as only this cohesion will sanction their existence.

What are the possible concrete implications of these thoughts and hopes on designing forms of visual communication, in particular book design? What is the status of contemporary book design in relationship to other designs of today and in relationship to these reorientations that we plead for?

When other man-made objects, not hampered by tradition, went through healthy metamorphoses, when almost every product was revaluated in terms of utilitarian functions, new materials and techniques, the form of the book is barely touched by the recent technological and scientific progress.

It is evident that if the book is to function on those broader terms that we hope for it must first catch up with the temper of the age, with industrial conditions, and must reach a new functional level on a realistic basis. Bookmaking must become efficient in all those means that are now affecting the design of most fabricated objects.

The first task is then to rethink the media in terms of the mechanical inventions and readjust the work to the advanced printing techniques and reproduction methods. If book design will be made with an inventive spirit, fed by the thorough knowledge of advanced production methods, it will inevitably have the stamp of honesty and clarity, the first requisite of functional design. If the designers will conceive their objects with a forward-looking thinking attitude toward their tools, their work will not be sidetracked into the costly fake trimmings of traditional styles, nor will it be necessary to use the patina of the past or the chromium-plated glitter of the present. Book designs which are done with a genuine understanding of mass production give a promise that mass production will serve as a material basis of a democratic society, giving honest service to the largest number of people.

But book design, to catch up with other design, must be efficient not only in its making, but also in its performance. The designer must rethink the book functions in their physical, optical, and psychological aspects. A book has weight, size, thickness, and tactile qualities, qualifies which are handled by the hand, as its optical form is handled by the eye. The physical form of the book will be efficient in its functioning if it fits the need of the hand that uses it. The book can be conceived of in the same sense as a handle of a tool or a utensil, and must be molded so that the hand can "operate" it with perfect control.

As a visual form a book must meet the needs of the eye. The factors influencing visibility and legibility are correlated into functioning visual unity if the size of the page, the type sizes, the distribution of the type, their weight and proportion, the brightness contrast between the color of the paper and the ink, are controlled relationships. But since not an isolated eye alone but an eye with the mind behind it does the reading, the organization of the printed page should be guided by a full understanding of the most advanced knowledge of the findings of psychology. It has been disclosed that one does not perceive patterns and meaning by a piecemeal assembling of the individual parts, but by grasping total relationships. We do not read by piecemeal assembly of the individual letters but by seeing unified wholes, configurations of words or word units. Printing limited by the technical processes of making the letters or casting types and printing them in the mechanical logic of the press cannot meet the requirement of the visual organization processes. The regimentation of reading conditioned by the mechanics of printing, forcing the eye to follow the rigid compulsion of the lines, is not the optimum visual condition of comfortable reading. Eye fatigue is due to the monotony of the visual task. New possibilities of technical inventions and the findings about the laws of visual perception can be synchronized. There is a challenge for coming bookmakers, and there is a hope that printing can undergo a reformulation which will bring book design to a truly contemporary level.

A clear visual structure of the individual pages is not sufficient to make a book integrated. A book commands movement of the reading eye. As a musical composition has a melodic line that binds the tunes into a living continuity, so the book should have a continuity of movement. The dust jacket, the binding, the end papers, the title page, the front matter, the chapter heads, and all the pages should be integrated by an orchestration of the visual sequences. And this directed movement should not be a servitude enforced on reader. A book is not music, which has only one direction. One wants some time to reread a passage or to stay longer at some part. The organization of the visual flow must be flexible enough to escape regimentation.

The linear continuity, however well organized, still cannot fulfill all demands for a unified design. The eye has to take a continuously changing span of attention in following up word, phrase, clause, sentence, paragraph, chapter, and volume. It has various tasks in reading and in looking at pictures. Reading has a changing tempo conditioned by meaning and by the visual keys to read these meanings.

There is an inherent meter and rhythm in the sequence of symbols, words, and images. Books of today very rarely meet a form that corresponds to the living pulsation of the reading eye. Severed from the rhythm of the spoken word, doubly removed from the organic rhythm of a line traced by an organic fluency of the hand, most of our books are dreary tenements of words badly in need of rhythmical accents—accents which exist in the spoken language.

To give a book unity, the graphic form of communication must match in character the ideas of which it is the vehicle. A book can have an integrated personality—its outward face can correspond to its inner content. Today the individuality of the book is only the individual graphic signature of its designer. A genuine face, that is a true unity of spirit, can only be attained by translating verbal content into its appropriate visual terms.

The laws of visual perception are conditioned by the visual habits of the time. Visual communication can be efficient only if it adapts itself to the new landscape and the new psychology of contemporary man. Book design, to be efficient, must make significant adaptations to the contemporary scene.

Machines, motorcars, airplanes, fast-racing trains, flickering light displays, shopwindows, street scenes, motion pictures, television have become common features of the contemporary scene. Together with the new richness of light effects from artificial light sources, the complex dimensions of the landscape with the skyscrapers and their intricate spatial pattern above, and the subways underneath, they give an incomparably greater speed and density to visual experience than any previous environment has ever presented. There is very little time now for perception of unessential details. The duration of the visual impressions is too short. Contemporary man's visual habit underwent a new transformation and developed idioms of simplicity, forcefulness, and structural lucidity. Our vision, to be efficient, learned to see fundamental relationships.

This tendency toward simplicity and precision is further reinforced by certain psychological needs of man living today. We do not see passively; the images we form in our minds are not simple mirrorings of what is outside. We rather see what we are looking for. Our drives, purposes, are guiding our ways of perceiving. Industrial production introduced new objects, machines, and machine-made objects. They were made with utmost precision and control dictated by clearly recognized and respected functional needs, utility, and economy. In a confusing world around and within, these things appeared as the only man-made object of perfection and logic. The mechanical functional clarity of the machine, the perfect harmony of the parts and the unmistakable clear relationships were like an oasis for men searching logic and order in life. Clarity, precision, economy are compelling values in a world suffocating in the fight of cross-purposes. It is not by chance that the most commonly appreciated aesthetic values are in the designs of a motorcar, or airplane, or fountain pen. Visual communication forms, to be efficient in their appeal, have to utilize these qualities of straightforwardness of the visual patterns.

Fitness to function has also another implication. The logic of design is synonymous with economy of design. In the evolution of production, particularly since the industrial age, the division of labor and the functional coordination of unit performances gained increasing significance. Although at present this principle dangerously wounds the integrity of the individual, its essential sense is unquestionable. Today, when a rich range of new vehicles of communications is emerging, it is worthwhile to reconsider the meaning of the distribution of labor. It seems to be essential to understand what form of communication can best fulfill certain aspects of messages. Motion-picture photography and television become major factors in our life. For the time being, they hardly have their proper areas of effective operation. Only recently serious concerns were voiced by leaders of the book industry about the dangerous impact of television on the book industry. Creative thinkers are needed who could guide the proper problems to the proper agents and develop the appropriate distribution of function among the new and old forms of visual communication. There is also chance for a cross-fertilization of ideas, techniques, idioms. It is very possible that book design will benefit greatly from the montage technique of motion pictures as well as from the idioms of television.

Assuming that book design will meet all these and other demands of functional performance and thus will better fill its function, in truly contemporary terms, there are still some distant hopes for meeting also those deeper functions which are anchored in the deepest human needs. What are, then, those aspects of book design which go beyond the mere economy of production and efficiency in utilitarian performance?

Within an ever-increasing wealth of products, man himself became worn out, incapable of benefiting from his labors. Limited to a conveyor belt, he rarely feels the joy of creation. Unable to encompass the metamorphosis of things which take shape under the work of his hands, he forfeits the sense of accomplishment, the unity and thus the harmony in the doing, which might give him true satisfaction. Limited to the mechanical details of one or another singular movement, within the complicated cogwheels of the production machinery, he gradually loses those sensibilities which are the guarantors of his perceiving the richness of life. Drained of the nourishment which is essential to his growing to full human stature, he loses the measure and meaning of his deepest aspirations. Through mass production, which could only be achieved through mechanization, man's sensibility, emotional unity, has been killed or at least dulled and deformed. It is not accidental that in most of our free activities we don't participate with the full vigor of our total self. It is significant that in our arts, or rather in the appreciation of art—movies, the radio, television pictures, and, yes, books—we are passive men, lazy men, armchair onlookers. We perceive only a small fraction of the most vital aspects of life. We do not live any form of creative experience in a total response; we hardly ever participate with our whole sensuous being through eyes, ears, and kinesthetic pleasure. In the age of specialization we also became specialized in our experiences, and have lost the vigor that comes from the coordination of many ranges and levels.

To counteract this shallowness, to achieve a fuller man, we must do everything that helps to rescue and may redevelop man's dulled sensibilities. It is the major function of every man-made design to fit the true purpose of man and help him to

perceive life as an integrated, balanced flow of activity in which his sensuous, emotional, and ideational levels coexist harmoniously. Organic human experiences must
be juxtaposed against the mechanization of man, which pushes and presses him so that
he will fit into the rhythm of the machine.

We must find those feelings in which and through which man's bonds to
nature and to man can again be experienced. Creative experience, man's faculty to
grasp vital organic coherence, is the yeast of the potentially fuller man. Only art, the
joy in creative doing and perceiving, will help to bring back the needed sensibilities
which can safeguard man from being further twisted away from his better nature.
Every man-made object, every element of the man-created environment, will fit to
its deepest function if it is a form of art, if it has unity, proportion, rhythm, and living
symmetry.

What book design ought to aim for is a rhythmical quality conditioned by
appropriate technical and utilitarian limitations. The act of producing our means to
survive, the search for economy of effort, led man to rhythm, and thus to art.
Occupational movements articulated to perfection gave birth to something else
which was broader and richer than its origin. The sweep of the sickle, the meeting of
the hammer with the anvil, the play of the fingers on clay in the process of making a
pot, became dance, song, and ornament. Rhythm, the coordination of individual
motions into an economy of performance, became more than its origin; it became a
symbol of unity between body and mind, material and tools. It became an expression
of interdependence within the individual or within a team of workers. And it can help
book design reach its final functional form.

There is a new challenge in contemporary thinking and vision, a challenge
that springs from the need of a total reorientation of language. A transformation of
vision and thinking is taking place. We are moving toward broader idioms of simultaneity, of transparency, of interpenetration. These are displacing linear perspective in
thinking and seeing. Contemporary painting, architecture, design, writing, and physical science are developing powerful new methods to reach this new operational area.
Transparency in painting, interpenetration of internal and external space in buildings
point toward an even more dynamic visual language of simultaneity. Printed communication has its own contribution to make to this new language, its new place to take
in the new world of vision.

Let there be cooperation among those whose work makes the final form of
a book: the author, the book designer, the printer, the photoengraver. How can a
designer shape the rhythm and personality of a book when he hardly has the chance
to become acquainted with its contents? How can he synchronize his form ideas when
he does not know the problems the other collaborators are facing? A collaborative
team could, in a free give-and-take relationship, develop an integrated spirit, a genuine
craftsmanship on a twentieth-century level. Only such cooperation can stimulate the
writer to consider the book in its true terms. It can help him to think, to write with
consideration of visual rhythms in the development of a new, richer, multi-dimensional
literary art that affects human sensibility on every level of sensuous experience.

Designs for printing are, by sheer quantity, an important factor of our visual
environment. Printed designs inevitably condition man's sensibilities, for better or
worse. It is our task to be alert to what is here involved and to make our designs fit
their total purposes.

If graphic forms are made to function for man's welfare in their fullest range, we may hope that we will one day fulfill our obligation and help make truth truth again and not a slogan. We can create genuine forms, rather than apply formulas. Thus we can bring back the truest meaning of tradition, which is to realize in terms of today a living continuity with the genuine values of the past.

First published in Graphic Forms: The Arts as Related to the Book *(Cambridge, Mass.: Harvard University Press, 1949).*

Notes
1. Louis H. Sullivan, *The Autobiography of an Idea* (New York, 1929).

1954
WHAT IS A DESIGNER?
Alvin Lustig

IN 1954, WHEN ALVIN LUSTIG *(1915–1955) gave this lecture to the Advertising Typographers Association of America, he was virtually blind owing to diabetic complications, and only a year away from death. Yet he was committed to the idea, which governed his professional life and teaching at Black Mountain Summer Institute and Yale University, that design could improve the world by aesthetically enhancing the communication of information. Lustig was described by his friend (and client), the publisher and author Arthur Cohen, as having a strong religious side—"a sense of order in the universe"—and he saw graphic design as one of the tools that could be used to create such order. This essay was one of Lustig's last opportunities to admonish and teach. Addressing advertising art directors who, prior to the advent of the "Creative Revolution" in the 1950s, did not as a rule hold positions of influence, he argues for greater responsibility. They should not succumb to the arbitrary rules and restrictions of the trade, he suggests, but enforce their standing as designers "with a capital D."—SH*

W hat is a designer? The agency art director approaches advertising design with a background of specific market research, the client's particular problems, etcetera, etcetera, etcetera. All these studies that make the advertising wheels go round may prove something, but I doubt it. All they can show is that for some, as yet undiscovered, reason, an ad appears to be successful or not. They don't prove that well-designed ads won't work. They don't prove that ads with less copy won't work. They don't prove that all type ads won't work. As far as the ad design is concerned, I doubt if the tests and studies prove anything at all.

I don't think it's a question of good design or bad design! In order for me to express myself clearly on the subject, I must discuss some things which appear to be entirely unrelated to the problems of advertising. This may seem to be a gobbledygook—but the theory has worked out in practice, as some of my examples may prove.

To begin with, design is related in some way to the world, the society that creates it. Whether you're talking about architecture, furniture, clothing, homes, public buildings, utensils, equipment, each period of design is an expression of the society. People will respond most warmly and directly to those designs which express their feeling and their tastes.

It takes time for people to adjust to design. As recently as ten years ago, "modern furniture" and "modern homes" were thought to be rather cold and weird. Today they are commonplace and are accepted without any feelings of shock and surprise. The great designers anticipated the requirements of their society and expressed them before the society was completely prepared or willing to accept what proved to be something they really wanted. Therefore, the designer does not work completely in the dark. He can't depend on market research. He must blaze his own trails. His greatness is dependent on his being able to recognize ahead of time, almost unconsciously, the trends which will contribute most to the proper expression of the society he lives in.

Now what does this boil down to? If he had depended on market research, twenty years ago, or even ten years ago, he would still be styling traditional furniture, building Victorian houses and nineteenth-century factories. In the graphic arts, he would be limited to cabbage roses, or some such types of visual design. But because he anticipated the future taste of his society, because he correctly predicted what would be fitting and proper, we now have the new forms of design that we accept as characteristic in our time. He both followed and led. He followed his instinct and led the public.

In connection with advertising design it suggests many things. It suggests the unreliability of market research in trying to forecast what the public will buy, what it will like, what will be pleasing to it. All market research can show is *what pleases the public at the moment*. Deductions from that research are probably no more reliable than the intuitive improvisations of the designer. Of course, the agency works in the here and now. It's a rare art director who makes any really significant departures. What appears to be new and significant is, most of the time, very old. It just looks new. And this is probably the way things should be. Whether you're talking about art, layout, copy, type, it is the function of agency personnel to apply their experience and the lessons they have learned to the problems at hand, not to experiment with the client's money. If the client is willing to experiment, then it's time to call somebody whose particular and peculiar talents, abilities and experience have been directed toward the creation of something new and different.

I am not suggesting that the designer is an innovator—period.

This is why you get so many different definitions of the term. There are designers and designers. I would suggest that the designer with a capital D, the kind of designer I've been talking about, is hired because he gives to everything he touches a fresh, new feel. He approaches problems differently. I think an analogy is necessary at this point. It is impossible for a woman to buy at a department store a ready-made dress that is especially styled just for her and her alone . . . that expresses her personality and was made to emphasize her best features. Again, anybody who wants a particular house, something which is akin to a work of art, has to go to a Frank Lloyd Wright or a Gropius. You can't buy one in Levittown.

If we apply this to the graphic arts, and advertising in particular, I must point out that the art director in an agency is a designer, specializing in one particular form. But, for many reasons, all of which are perfectly obvious, he is not a "free" designer. He is exposed to, and must submit to, business factors which control his work. The designer with a capital D is utilized only when a "free" designer is called for—namely, when the peculiar and particular vision of such a designer is in demand. Such a designer might style, or set the pattern, for the pilot ad in a campaign, when a fresh approach or outside thinking is called for. And, speaking for myself, such an approach does not grow out of the considerations that are usually specified as essential to the creation of a successful ad.

I can't and do not want to make any remarks critical of advertising and the inherent problems of the profession. I do think that some of the preconceptions are subject to review. People tend to get in a rut . . . and this applies to designers, art directors, copywriters and businessmen equally. The field of vision narrows and they begin to justify the rut they are in on the basis of scientific or pseudo-scientific laws. Every time I am told that something "must" be done in such-and-such a way, I eventually find out that the "must" doesn't hold quite the weight it's meant to.

The role of the designer and his most important "must" is to remain free, as free as he possibly can, from the prejudices and the ruts which affect so many others in the field of design. He must be constantly on guard, cleansing his mind of the tendency to relax into a routine format, ready to experiment, play, change, and alter forms. If he lacks the inherent ability, the insight, the intuitive selection of what is right for his time, he will not go far and will eventually be forced to enter another field. If he is equipped with these essential characteristics, he will lead the way to new and more effective approaches to design in all its forms.

All I can say about sales, etc., is what has been said before. Good design never hurt sales! I won't take sides on the copy versus art argument, for I feel that the argument itself incorrectly states the problem. Practically, if an all-type ad is well designed, it may work in a proper instance. A fully pictorial ad can be a total failure if poorly executed. What I am concerned with is the important role that the designer (spelled with a capital *D*) can play in introducing fresh thinking into any area of the graphic arts or in any area where design is of importance. The proper use of such a designer is not to make him into another art director, nor another advertising man. If the problem is presented to him, and he is given an opportunity to work it out in his own way, a great many things can be accomplished. You can either tell him exactly what you want, in the way of feeling, objective, etcetera, or you can let him employ his skills and his imagination without precise or specific limitation. Where designers have been employed to the best advantage, a great deal of their success has been as much the result of the contribution of their clients; knowing how to use a designer and work with him is as much a part of the job as what the designer does on his own hook! Using a designer improperly is as fraught with the possibilities of failure as using any skilled consultant improperly. Not only must the designer, who chooses to work in advertising and with advertising agencies, learn some of their techniques and problems, but the agency must learn the meaning of design and its skills as well!

First published in Type Talks *no. 76 (May 1954). Reprinted in* The Collected Writings of Alvin Lustig, *edited and published by Holland R. Melson, 1958.*

1956
THE DESIGNER AND THE CLIENT
Misha Black

THE ROLE OF THE *client is fundamental to the practice of design, but seldom commented on by designers except in the informal telling of self-aggrandizing war stories, where the designer is cast as beknighted hero and the client serves alternately as hapless foil, cunning tormentor, and, occasionally, heavenly muse. One of the few thoughtful commentators on the relationship between client and designer was Sir Misha Black (1910–1977), whom design theorist Reyner Banham once classed with a small handful of practitioners "capable of describing and analyzing their own distinctive businesses with penetration and good sense." In his long career, the Russian-born Black cofounded England's first industrial design firm in 1931, helped organize the Festival of Britain after World War II, and ultimately led one of Europe's dominant consultancies, Design Research Unit, which numbered among its clients London Transport, British Petroleum, and Chase Manhattan Bank. He ended his career as a Professor of Industrial Design at the Royal College of Art, after nearly half a century spent studying, as he does here, the mysterious net "in which the designer and client are inextricably enmeshed."—MB*

It would be instructive for a client to be present, although invisible, when the designer whom he has commissioned sits down alone, or with his colleagues, to start work on a new project. He would be surprised by the transformation. The suave, genial designer who was so accommodating at the conference table and so unsophisticated a companion at dinner would have changed into a serious, engrossed man fanatically concerned with the job in hand.

This assumes, of course, that the designer has a degree of creative ability and is not merely a technician content to imitate or to only efficiently carry out instructions. The purely executant designer has his own merits, but for the moment I wish to consider that smaller band who endeavor to bring to any design problem as much originality as does the chef who slightly varies the cookbook recipe to bring the final dish more to his personal liking.

The client, now as unnoticed as a fly on the wall, would observe three unexpected phenomena: firstly, the self-criticism of the designer as he covers sheet after sheet of paper with preliminary designs, all to be discarded for reasons that would be incomprehensible to his client; secondly, the time taken in developing the finally selected basic design to a stage where drawings and specifications are completed; and lastly, the fact that he, the manufacturer, influences the designer at every stage of the work to a degree that he would hardly credit and of which the designer himself is often unconscious.

In the second-class design office, where expediency controls honesty, the influence of the client is decisive. No more time is spent on the job than the minimum necessary to satisfy the client, and if the client is incapable of judging between a solution that is properly and one only partially resolved, then it is the latter he receives. This is the path of mediocrity, to the rapid deterioration of standards and, for the designer, to an insistent sense of dissatisfaction not compensated by the increasing bank balance that often results from a willingness to produce shoddy work.

When the client is unable to see the difference between a meretricious and a creative solution, the task of the honest designer is insufferably increased. The designer then knows that the acceptance of his work will depend not on rational judgment but on his own powers of persuasion, on his capacity for convincing argument, which often must deliberately falsify the real reason for his decisions. In such circumstances, the designer feels isolated and desperate, knowing that the entire creative energy must come from him alone, with the client as useless as an irresponsible judge. It is therefore not surprising that designers who are doomed to work for blind and dogmatic clients rarely survive the unequal battle and finish up not very different from the second-rate hacks who lack integrity from the start.

Yet even when the client is sufficiently sensitive to judge between a creative and a dreary solution, and when the designer is content to produce only the best work of which he is capable, even then the client exercises so important an influence on the job as to make him almost equal to the designer in determining its final form. The independence of the designer is as illusory as would be the conceit of a motor car that imagines it decides in which direction its wheels shall revolve.

Industrial design is, by definition, creative work, which depends for its materialization on its fabrication by other hands than those of the designer. An idea restricted to visualization in the mind of the designer, or carried no further than a carefully rendered drawing, is as unfulfilled as a play written but never acted or a piano concerto played on a silenced instrument.

This argument could be countered by the deafness of Beethoven when he wrote some of his greatest music or by Cézanne, unhonored in his lifetime; but industrial designers are in a different category. I have yet to meet the designer satisfied or even able to work for any length of time without the stimulus of execution, or capable of development without the experience to be gained only by seeing how the drawing-board design appears after production. But if a chair or refrigerator is to be manufactured, a shop or showroom constructed, or a poster printed, the designer must persuade his client to invest the money necessary for the product to be made or the design otherwise carried out. Then the net is immediately closed, and the designer and client are together inextricably enmeshed.

I am not suggesting that the influence of the client is necessarily harmful. The opposite is often true. When the client and the designer are in sympathy, they can together produce better work than that of which either alone would be capable. The client, particularly if he is an experienced art director, can be the encouragement and the goad, drawing out of the designer, especially if he is young and unpracticed, work of a quality and maturity he would never produce without wise, firm, and experienced guidance. These are positive contributions from the client, but the more useful they are, the more considerable a part does the client play in the production of the final design.

But more often the client lags behind his designer. When his capacity to see what has not before been known is limited, he cannot follow the designer to the frontiers of visual experience where the designer is groping for new shapes, new relationships of planes and colors, new images, which may in fact be what Sir Herbert Read has called the Icon which precedes the Idea. In such circumstances, the client is a shackle dragging the designer back to the standards of the client's world. Then the designer is the anxious leader, able to see the horizon but delayed by the weight of his reluctantly dragging companion, who is fearful to take even a step in the right direction.

This is the moment for the intelligent, farsighted client to shake his head with scarcely contained irritation, to claim that he does in fact give his designers complete freedom and is honored to follow where they lead. But this is an aspiration rather than a fact. Even the most sympathetic client has his likes and dislikes, his quirks and his oddities. Always he is at the designer's elbow, always the designer is worrying, if unconsciously, how his client will react to his proposals, how far he can persuade him to go on the fateful morning when his drawings are taken from the carefully prepared portfolio and exposed to a life-and-death judgment. Then the client, omnipotent, will decide whether the child is to be throttled at birth or allowed to grow to the full manhood of the completed job.

Always under the threat of death in the wastebasket or incarceration in the plan chest, the designer can never be free of his client. As he grows in years and experience, the influence of his client waxes rather than wanes. He becomes more sensitive to the whims of his master, more skilled in satisfying him, more sensitive to the shortness of the steps he can safely take in leadership. The experienced designer is thus able to produce success after success, yet he is always aware, while he accepts the laurel wreath of approbation, of how pitiful has been his tiptoe advance when measured against the great strides he could have taken if his client had been less timid or less restricted by the taste (as he appraised it) of the markets he serves.

It is only at a conference such as this that one is permitted to weep the acid tears of self-pity and flay the earnest features of the successful designer with the lash of self-criticism. But how many designers can truly say they have ever designed and carried to production a job that was finally just as they would have wished to see it?

We, the public designers, are, with the fewest honored exceptions, the great compromisers, the second-layer men, the translators of the real creative work of our time to a more common denominator. There is no harm in that. For every act of creation there must be a thousand adapters. We stretch as a great chain from the artist at the frontier of experience to the base camp where most of our fellow men must live. If the bridge is not weakened by deceit and excessive compromise, ours is a worthy occupation equal at least to that of a competent doctor carefully and painstakingly prescribing the cures that the research scientist has earlier discovered. While engaged in this not unpleasant occupation, let us not deny, however, that the limit of our progress is finitely determined by our clients.

[...]

Address to Sixth International Design Conference, Aspen, 1956. From the archives of the IDCA (International Design Conference, Aspen).

1958
TRADITION: CLICHÉ, PRISON
OR BASIS OF GROWTH?
Herbert Spencer

THE "ART AND SCIENCE *of Typography" conference, organized by the Type Directors Club of New York in Silvermine, Connecticut, and the World Affairs Center, New York, in April 1958, was the first international gathering of its kind. Herbert Spencer (b. 1924), representing Great Britain, was one of seven principal speakers—from Italy, Germany, Japan, the Netherlands, and the United States—invited to analyze the status, function, and responsibility of typographic design as a medium of communication. As founding editor of the journal* Typographica *(1949–1967), Spencer had rapidly established himself as one of postwar Britain's leading advocates of modernist typographic practice by treading a judicious line between the conservative traditions of the country's bookish printers and the dynamic contemporary needs of ephemeral commercial printing, which he believed to be in pressing need of reform. Spencer's paper—the conference's opening address—argues that contentious new typographical tendencies such as asymmetry and the "free spatial disposition of types" have their basis in inviolable principles of composition.—RP*

T o the artist, the architect, the writer, or the composer, I believe tradition is vital to his creative activity.

But excessive respect for tradition becomes traditionalism. And traditionalism kills true tradition.

What, then, is tradition? Tradition is a living, active and vital force in creative activity. It consists not of a code of rigid conventions but of principles based on accumulated experience. These principles we inherit, make use of in our work and modify in the light of our own experience, and then hand on to succeeding generations. Tradition is an inheritance we cannot avoid but which we can easily misinterpret and abuse. It imposes obligations and restrains our formal innovations, yet I do not think we can regard tradition as a prison. It is, I believe, the only sound basis of growth.

But it is vitally important that we should clearly distinguish between *tradition*, which may exercise a healthy restraint upon our innovations, and *traditionalism*, which is indeed a prison, or perhaps more accurately, a cemetery—a graveyard of dead ideas and decaying conventions.

Traditionalism is the negation of tradition. It is the real enemy of healthy tradition. Traditionalism is the product of men devoid of creative ability and incapable of original thought who fail to grasp and to understand the essence of tradition, and who seek therefore to arrest and petrify and preserve the formal expression of tradition at a particular moment. Traditionalism is tradition mummified. It is tradition reduced to a collection of lifeless conventions.

Traditionalism is fostered by men who do not understand tradition but who are awed by it. The creative artist and designer must always and inevitably oppose traditionalism and those who engender it.

The questions raised or implied in the title of this talk are essentially questions of the twentieth century. They are twentieth century questions, not because such issues could not have been discussed in earlier periods than our own, but because the vastly accelerated pace at which established methods and techniques are today being developed gives such questions a relevance and an immediacy peculiar to the present time.

Scientific and technological expansion is today imposing on the printed word and the printed page changes in its presentation more fundamental than any since the change in the fifteenth century from manuscript to type. And we are today witnessing and experiencing not a single change but a whole series of changes, of revaluations and reassessments, and a challenge to established concepts of design and typography.

It is essential that we should fully appreciate the present *tempo* of change, in order to ensure that we do not inadvertently ourselves become supporters of conventions which change has made sterile.

What we have to grasp is that not only are the problems of this century different from those of the last century but that, in actual fact, the requirements of this month are different from those of last month. I am not, of course, here advocating innovation and change for its own sake. What I am trying to stress is that we must be constantly alert to the technical changes now taking place in printing and in methods of reproduction and mass communication generally, and also in the function and requirements of much of the work we design.

Because of today's intensive rate of change it has become inevitable that the designer who relaxes his vigilance, even briefly, will lapse into unrealistic ways of thinking and planning. It is no longer a matter simply of doing a thing well, according to purely formal considerations, but of doing it appropriately. Appropriate, that is, to today's requirements, in harmony with today's methods, and exploiting today's technical opportunities.

You may say that to design well has always implied working in harmony with contemporary conditions and opportunities, and of course this is true. But in periods of less dramatic change it was quite possible for a designer to produce attractive and relevant work simply by embracing an established idiom and without ever consciously questioning the methods and technique he employed.

Today the designer must be conscious of the methods he uses and he must learn constantly to question and reassess his methods and the techniques he employs. This applies, of course, to every field of design activity and in its technical and sociological aspects perhaps most compellingly to architecture.

But in the field of typography and graphic design we must constantly keep in mind the fact that in the Western World we have today the ability and the means to produce and distribute far more words and pictures than we can collectively absorb. And it is a facility we are fully exploiting. Only a fraction of everything printed is read and only a small part of what is read is absorbed and remembered or acted upon.

Today, whether their purpose is to persuade or inform, the printed word and the printed image must be brief, direct, efficient and clear. With the exception only of books read for pleasure or serious study, the printed word is invariably read—or, more accurately, scanned—in a hurry. It has been said that a poster should be designed 'so that he who runs may read.' To the poster I think we can now add popular newspapers and magazines, timetables, instruction manuals, and the whole range of publicity and utilitarian printing.

Nor should we overlook the fact that ephemeral printing of this kind forms the substantially greater part of all printing at present produced in the Western World.

And I think it is now reasonable to speculate on the extent to which such miscellaneous printing influences, and perhaps governs, our reading habits today.

Until relatively recently it could be confidently said that our reading habits were determined by familiarity from an early age with books, either of instruction or entertainment, consisting largely of text. But children are now being taught to a considerable extent by means of the spoken word and visual aids of one kind or another, and recent statistics of the recreational activities of adults in America and Western Europe reveal how contracted has the habit of reading for pleasure become. Even ardent readers today read far more words in magazines and newspapers than in books. It is I think therefore probable that our reading habits are now determined largely by the typography of newspapers and magazines and other forms of ephemeral printing. Although some of the conventions of traditional book typography still survive in the pages of our newspapers and magazines, many others have been discarded or distorted beyond recognition.

A politician has been defined as 'a man who approaches every problem with his mouth open.' The contemporary designer needs to approach every problem with mind and eyes and ears wide open. And in one sense, at least, he must, like the politician, approach every problem with his mouth open too. He must ask why? and how? He must question everything and take nothing for granted. Sound design today demands accurate analysis of the specific problem in hand and proper understanding of the means used to solve it. It cannot be achieved by means of sterile conventions.

In this connection I believe we require a different attitude in the teaching of design subjects in many design schools and colleges. Students must be encouraged to question everything: no design solution, no principle of typography or layout advocated by a teacher should ever be accepted by a student without question. And students must be taught how to question. The art of questioning is to extract the maximum amount of information with the minimum number of questions. After all, in professional practice, the really important thing is not to know *all* the answers but to know how and where to obtain the answers when you need them. In too many schools design subjects continue to be taught by men who are often already out of touch with the current realities of design, and who endeavor to impart a style and a stereotyped technique rather than an understanding and true appreciation of design. It is far less important that a teacher should demonstrate *how* he would solve a given problem than that he should explain *why* he would solve it in his particular way.

It is by asking such questions that we can come to a proper understanding of tradition and can learn to distinguish between living tradition and hollow convention.

There are two principal aspects of typography which tradition may influence. One is the arrangement and disposition of type upon the page and the relation of one page to another. The other aspect is the design of typefaces, the actual letter forms, which are the basic ingredient of typography.

By far the most important development in typographical design in this century has been the consolidation in Europe and America of asymmetrical layout as the basis of most sound and efficient ephemeral printing and of a rapidly increasing amount of bookwork.

This style of typography has evolved slowly and erratically during the last hundred and fifty years. In the process of its evolution it has destroyed many of the conventions imposed by the earlier, rigidly-centered arrangement of types, but it has absorbed many of the sound traditions established in early book typography. And it has now discarded those stylistic conventions, such as heavy rules and geometrical motifs, which it embraced during the twenties and which did much, for a time, to obscure the real merits of asymmetrical layout. The best examples of asymmetrical typography today are virile, rational, and unaffected.

Asymmetrical typography has not merely embraced sound traditional principles of composition and imposition but has, in fact, strengthened many of those principles by brooking no departure from them. Indeed it is true to say that asymmetrical typography has been evolved partly out of respect for tradition. It is incidental that, in the process, it has inevitably destroyed many barren conventions.

Stiffly symmetrical typography enforces upon the page a rigid contour and an artificial pattern. It imposes obstacles upon the arrangement of type which can only be overcome by departing from those principles of composition—such as, for example, close and consistent word-spacing, and the avoidance of unnecessary and misleading word-breaks—which experience has proved to be sound and therefore desirable.

Asymmetrical typography, on the other hand, is flexible. It respects sound traditional principles of composition and regards them as inviolable. And it allows those principles to determine, in harmony with function, the pattern of the page.

In recent years, many of those people who earlier opposed asymmetrical typography have grown to realize that this form of layout provides the most effective vehicle for the setting out of assorted and miscellaneous texts and pictures, and that it is the means by which the greatest use can be made of mechanical composition and other more recent technical innovations. It is now widely understood that asymmetrical typography does not imply *unbalanced* typography and that balance and equilibrium can now be achieved with greater visual interest, and in a more functionally satisfactory way, by means of the free spatial disposition of types.

NEW TECHNIQUES

Today, metal is gradually being eliminated from composition, and by photographic and other means we can now obtain uniformly identical lettering without the use of metal type. In this important new condition the opportunities and advantages of asymmetrical layout are at once apparent. But equally apparent are the potential dangers inherent in the exciting new opportunities now presented. The position today, in this respect, is not unlike that which faced jobbing printers of the mid-nineteenth century when contemporary economic conditions permitted the production of a virtual avalanche of different type designs. Since the invention of the composing machine, the economies of typefounding, as much as improved taste, have forcibly diminished the flow of new type faces. But photography today provides us again with the opportunity of an almost limitless range of cheaply-produced display lettering variations and distortions, and photo-composition of text removes the only slight obstacle—that of combining two different preliminary techniques—to the full exploitation of what we may call photographically-designed lettering.

The typographer's desire for fresh type faces is reasonable and healthy. In advertising, exhibition and display typography, especially photographically-designed lettering, can make a valuable contribution. But the limits are relatively close between which letter forms may be varied if they are to be clear and acceptable to the eye and therefore efficient in function.

Whether the period immediately ahead is one of typographical achievement or, like the mid-nineteenth century, one of typographical chaos may depend to a great extent upon how well we understand and appreciate those principles of letter design which today form our tradition.

But I think that in type design, as in the arrangement and disposition of type, if we can extract from the accumulated experience of the past that is our inheritance those principles which remain valid and vital, then we may be confident that the new techniques of today and of tomorrow will pose not a threat but an opportunity.

First published in the SIA *Journal no. 66 (London: July 1958).*

1959
TYPE IS TO READ
William Golden

WILLIAM GOLDEN *(1911–1959) was art director at the Columbia Broadcasting Company for more than twenty years, where his contributions to the then-emerging field of corporate identity were realized in, among other projects, the art direction of the classic trademark, the CBS Eye, which references both the human eye and a camera lens. Golden was a member of a new breed of art director/designers who, though not strictly modern in the European avant-garde sense, embraced the notions of functionality, clarity, and simplicity. This lecture, given at the Type Directors Club of New York's landmark conference on contemporary typography shortly before Golden's death, testifies to his belief that intelligent design was a corporate duty. These were the early days of crisp, clean design, and Golden (who was also named the club's Art Director of the Year in 1959) was an early proponent of this aesthetic. His observations on typography, style, and content are particularly significant, given the historical moment in which they were delivered. At the dawn of postwar consumer optimism, he argues against designing for designers, and stresses the importance of intelligence, reason, and responsibility in design.—JH*

I f there is such a thing as a "New American Typography" surely it speaks with a foreign accent. And it probably talks too much. Much of what it says is obvious nonsense. A good deal of it is so pompous that it sounds like nonsense, though if you listen very carefully it isn't . . . quite. It is just overcomplicated. When it is translated into prewar English it is merely obvious.

I don't know what it is that impels so many designers to drop their work to write and speak so much about design.

Is it the simple (and perfectly justifiable) instinct for trade promotion? Or have we imported the European propensity for surrounding even the simplest actions with a *gestalt*?

Perhaps the explanation is simpler. The kind of effort that goes into graphic expression is essentially lonely and intensive, and produces, at its best, a simple logical design. It is sometimes frustrating to find that hardly anyone knows that it is a very complicated job to produce something simple. Perhaps we want them to know that we've gone through hell, sweating out a job to reach what seems to be an obvious solution.

And since our professional medium of communication is not verbal, designers don't seem to be lucid writers or speakers on the subject of design.

I have been frequently stimulated by the work of most of the people on this panel, but only rarely by what they have said about it.

While it must be assumed that these endless discussions have values that I am blind to, I am more acutely aware of the dangers they hold for the young. If you have recently interviewed a crop of young designers—the New Renaissance Man in a hurry—applying for their first or second staff job, you will know what I mean.

I was forced to part with one such man on my staff a while ago. He was pretty good, too. But he was another victim of the overseriousness of graphic arts literature. He had all the latest and obscure publications from here and abroad (mostly in languages he couldn't read). He attended all the forums. He would argue endlessly on theory . . . and he was just paralyzed with fright at the sight of a blank layout pad. He could spend as much as a week on a fifty-line newspaper ad. His trouble was, that no matter how he tried, an ad looked very much like an ad, and not any of these almost mystical things he had been reading about.

If there were some way to fix an age limit for attendance at these conferences, in the way that minors are forbidden to attend overstimulating movies, I think they would be relatively harmless, and it might even be pleasant to chew our cud together.

For it has all been said, and said many times, and in a most confusing way, and almost none of it is new. Even the insistence on newness at any cost is in itself familiar.

Perhaps it would be useful for a conference like this to sort it all out. Not merely to summarize this conference, but all of them. If it could be done without padding, I imagine that what is valid about typography would be very brief and relatively simple.

What is right about current typography is so apparent when you see it that it requires no explanation. What is wrong is a little more complex.

It is not as difficult to define what is wrong as it is to find how we got there.

I have my own notion of how we got where we are, and though I have neither the competence nor the ambition to be a typographic historian, this is roughly how it looks from one viewpoint.

Some thirty years ago the rebellious advertising and editorial designer in America was engaged in a conspiracy to bring order, clarity and directness to the printed page. He fought against the picture of the factory, the company logotype, and the small picture of the package that invariably accompanied it. He protested that the copy was too long, and that he was obliged to set it so small that no one would read it. He argued that the normal ad contained too many elements. (He even invented the "busy" page in some effort to accommodate himself to it.) He insisted that this effort to say so many things at once was self-defeating and could only result in communicating nothing to the reader.

He was essentially picture-minded, and only reluctantly realized that he had to learn something about type. It was and still is a damned nuisance, but when he realized how thoroughly its mechanical and thoughtless application could destroy communication of an idea, he had to learn to control it—to design with it.

More and more typography was designed on a layout pad rather than in metal. Perhaps the greatest change in American typography was caused by this simple act—the transfer of the design function of the printer to the graphic designer.

The designer was able to bring a whole new background and a new set of influences to the printed page. He could "draw" a page. There was more flexibility in the use of a pencil than in the manipulation of a metal form. It became a new medium for the designer.

Under the twin impact of the functionalism of the Bauhaus and the practical demands of American business, the designer was beginning to learn to use the combination of word and image to communicate more effectively.

Under the influence of the modern painters, he became aware (perhaps too aware) of the textural qualities and color values of type as an element of design.

And surely a dominating influence on American typography in the prewar years was exerted by the journalists.

Newspapers and magazines were the primary media of mass communication. The skillful development of the use of headline and picture was a far more prevalent influence than the European poster. The newspaper taught us speed in communication. Everyone knew instinctively what the journalists had reduced to a formula: that if you read a headline, a picture, and the first three paragraphs of any story you would know all the essential facts.

The magazine communicated at a more leisurely pace and could be more provocative since it addressed a more selective audience. Because the magazine dealt more in concepts than in news it was far more imaginative. There was more opportunity here, to design within the framework of the two-page spread. But still, the device that bore the main burden of interesting the reader, was the "terrific headline" and the "wonderful picture."

Perhaps it was the growth of radio, a rival medium, that hastened a new effort on the part of the magazine.

Certainly the new technical developments in photography increased the range of its reportage.

But what gave it a new direction and style was not so purely American. I think it was men like Agha and Brodovitch. These importations from Europe set a pace that not only changed the face of the magazine and consequently advertising design, but they changed the status of the designer. They did this by the simple process of demonstrating that the designer could also think.

The "layout man" was becoming an editor. He was no longer that clever, talented fellow in the back room who made a writer's copy more attractive by arranging words and pictures on the printed page in some ingenious way. He could now read and understand the text. He could even have an opinion about it. He might even be able to demonstrate that he could communicate its content better and with more interest than the writer. He could even startle the editor by suggesting content. It wasn't long before he began to design the page before it was written, and writers began to write to a character count to fit the layout.

Whatever successes this revolution achieved were accomplished by demonstration—by individual designers proving to their clients and employers (by solving their problems) the validity of their point of view and the value of their talents. It was accomplished without a single design conference in New York or in Colorado or anywhere else in America.

There were, of course, exhibitions and award luncheons. But the exhibitions were an extension of the process of demonstration, and the arrangers of the award luncheons by some lucky instinct seldom permitted the designer to speak about his work, but rather forced the businessman to discuss it.

But more than any other single factor, I believe the designer won his new status in the business community because he had demonstrated that he could communicate an idea or a fact on the printed page at least as well, and often better, than the writer, the client, or his representative. And he could demonstrate this only if he was at least as faithful to content as he was to style.

During the war and for some time afterward, American typographers made great strides in relation to the Europeans, for the simple reason, I suppose, that there was not only a shortage of paper in Europe but there was a shortage of design. The printers and designers were in foxholes, concentration camps, or dead, and presses and foundries were being bombed.

There was a long period when the bulk of the world's graphic material was being produced in America. Though there was something approaching a paper shortage here, too, there was an excess of profits available to spend on advertising. There were few products to advertise and therefore very little to say about them. But since it was relatively inexpensive to keep a company name in print, it didn't matter too greatly what or how it was said. We produced such a volume of printed material for so long a time, that we were able to assimilate a vast amount of prewar European design, and adapt it to our own language and uses. It had become such a familiar idiom with us that it is now hardly surprising that the announcement of this conference can call contemporary typography purely American.

My first look at postwar typography was fairly bewildering. I had seen and applauded the prewar work by Burtin and Beall. They were developing newer graphic forms, and using words and images on the printed page to communicate. In their hands these images were employed to make a statement clearer, faster.

The new avant-garde was saying nothing and saying it with considerable facility. They could say in their defense that the world was more chaotic than ever, that nobody was saying anything very rational, and that their need to make some kind of order was satisfied to some extent, by creating it on the printed page. It was, largely, an order without content.

There was precedent for this point of view. The determined sales promotion campaign of the abstract expressionist painters was in full swing in America. That it could have been so successful so quickly must surely be due, in part, to its absence of content. In a curious way this revolution was a remarkably safe one—it was so noncommittal.

I have no quarrel with the abstract movement—except with its vociferous intolerance of any other school. But I think the effect on the minds of young designers is a matter of concern. To regard the blank rectangle on a layout pad with the same attitude that the abstract painter confronts his blank canvas is surely a pointless delusion.

The printed page is not primarily a medium for self-expression. Design for print is not Art. At best it is a highly skilled craft. A sensitive, inventive, interpretive craft, if you will, but in no way related to painting.

A graphic designer is employed, for a certain sum of money, by someone who wants to say something in print to somebody. The man with something to say comes to the designer in the belief that the designer with his special skills will say it more effectively for him.

It sometimes develops that as a result of this hopeful transaction, the statement becomes an advertisement for the designer rather than his client. And should there be any doubt about the designer's intention, he will sign it—just as the easel painter does.

Logically enough, this attitude toward design is only tolerated when the client has nothing to say. When his product is no different than anyone else's, and no better. When his company has no "personality"—he borrows the personality of the designer. This is rarely permitted in the mainstream of advertising, but only in the "off-Broadway" arenas.

The immature avant-garde designer seems bitter about the mainstream of American advertising. He hates the "hard sell" and avoids clients who interfere with his freedom. He believes that the role of business should be one of patron of the Arts, and insists that his craft is art.

I do not argue for the return to any form of traditionalism. I do argue for a sense of responsibility on the part of the designer, and a rational understanding of his function.

I think he should avoid designing for designers.

I suggest that the word "design" be considered as a verb in the sense that we design something to be communicated to someone.

Perhaps it would help to clear the air a little if we were conscious that printing and advertising cost a great deal of money. If a designer could pretend that the money to be spent to reproduce his design was his own, I suspect he would subject himself to far more rigid disciplines.

When he examines his work with relation to its function, he wouldn't bury the text and render it illegible on the ground that it is inferior anyway. He will insist, instead, that it be better. If no one will write a better text, he will have to learn to write it himself. For having become, in effect, his own client, he will want to be sure that what he has to say will be clearly understood—that this is his primary function.

He will find that the most satisfying solutions to a graphic problem come from its basic content. He will find it unnecessary and offensive to superimpose a visual effect on an unrelated message.

He might even find that writers, too, have a certain skill, and he might enjoy reading them, and making their work legible.

Perhaps the most important thing that would happen is that all those pointless questions about tradition and modernism, whether our typography is American or European, will become properly irrelevant. All of these influences, and many more, will have become part of the designer's total design vocabulary.

If he applies it successfully, the end product will show no traces of having been designed at all. It will look perfectly obvious and inevitable.

If he is more concerned with how well his job is done than he is about whether or not it is "new," he will even win awards for his performance.

But no matter how many honors are bestowed on him throughout his career, he will never mistake the printed page for an art gallery.

At your conference last year, the most stimulating speaker for me was not a designer at all. He was a semanticist—Dr. Anatol Rapoport of the University of Michigan's Mental Health Research Institute. In trying to analyze our profession, he was pretty close, I think, when he thought of us as intermediaries. He likened us to performers. Actors who speak other people's lines. Musicians who interpret what composers write.

Though he plucked us from the stratosphere and put us in our proper place, he also soothed our ruffled egos by gently suggesting that some performances could be superb.

To the extent that his analysis is correct, it might be useful to quote an old "square" writer on the subject.

I happen at the moment to be working on a reprint of *Hamlet*. Here is what the author demanded of performers:

"Speak the speech, I pray you, as I pronounce it to you . . . For if you mouth it, as many of your players do, I would as lief the town crier spoke my lines.

"Nor do not saw the air too much with your hand, thus; but use all gently. For in the very torrent, tempest, and as I may say, whirlwind of your passion, you must acquire and beget a temperance that may give it smoothness.

"Be not too tame, neither. Suit the action to the word, the word to the action. . . . For anything so overdone is from the purpose of playing, whose end is, to hold, as 'twere, the mirror up to nature.

"And let those who play your clowns speak no more than is set down for them. Go make you ready."

Address to Type Directors Club, New York (18 April 1959); published in the papers of the What is New in American Typography conference, 1960. Reprinted in The Visual Craft of William Golden *(New York: George Braziller, 1962).*

1959
WHAT IS NEW IN AMERICAN TYPOGRAPHY?
Herb Lubalin

THE INTRODUCTION IN THE *United States of photo-type in the late 1950s, and its eventual usurpation of the hot-metal standard, prompted a rash of symposia addressing the new and novel in typography. Among the many design luminaries invited to speak at the 1959 meeting hosted by the Type Directors Club at the Biltmore Hotel in New York, Herb Lubalin (1918–1981) was the most prescient on the subject of television and its effects on America's reading habits. Lubalin, who at that time was an advertising designer/art director at Suddler and Hennesey in New York, was known for his mastery of photo-type and the innovative marriage of headlines and image into unified word-pictures. He was one of the pioneers of the visual "Big Idea" in advertising, the trend toward a single, strong, often witty, image rather than wordy descriptive text. In this talk he demanded that a conservative advertising industry encourage experimentation as a means to increase its impact. He understood that even deliberate ugliness could be used to make eye-catching communications. Lubalin's own experiments in the realm of what he called "distortion and disfiguration" evolved into a distinct American typographic style of the 1960s.—SH*

Typography means different things to different people.

This art of creating impressions on paper through the use of symbols is universally acceptable as a way of communicating, but its acceptability as a creative tool to evoke an emotional response through the physical appearance of words is far from widespread.

I would like to dwell on this subject as it relates to advertising design, since the necessity for earning my livelihood is based on a familiarity with this field.

Here in the United States typography has, in the past few years, assumed an increasingly important role in the creation of advertising. In the past, most advertising consisted of an idea translated in terms of copy (transferred to the printed page by mechanical typographic means) plus an illustration (photography or art) which interpreted the copy message. The typography was used solely as a caption for a picture or the picture was used as graphic means to create a visual image that emphasized the copy message.

Times have changed. With the increasing competition in product marketing in the United States, advertising people are finding it difficult to create ads that do not reflect, either in copy or design, the attitudes of their competitors. Copy claims have become almost indistinguishable. The similarity of each brand of cigarette, liquor, cosmetic or automobile has made it very difficult for creative people to come up with dissimilar claims.

Television has had its effect on the reading habits of the American people. We are becoming more and more accustomed to looking at pictures and less and less interested in reading lengthy copy. The resulting trend in our advertising has been towards large pictorial elements and short sparkling headline copy, with much less emphasis on descriptive product identification.

These influences have created a need for experimentation with new graphic forms in advertising. One of the important results of this experimentation is what I like to refer to as the typographic image. Many designers have found that when the usual means of stimulating the reader into a buying attitude becomes cliché, the use of typography as a word-picture gives them greater creative scope.

In composing a typographic picture, just as in composing a good photograph or illustration, a tight-knit unity of elements is necessary. We have therefore had to take liberties with the many traditional rules and regulations which have come to be accepted as criteria for good typography. These deviations, which include wider measures, elimination of leading between lines, removal of letterspacing, and alteration of type forms have met with violent reaction from traditional typographers and designers to whom these rules are sacred.

In many cases these objections are justified. In the process of experimentation and trial and error, many mistakes are made. In the past few years we have seen more poor typography than at any previous time in advertising history. But we have also seen an abundance of exciting new approaches by a great many designers, where in the past this excitement was provided by an isolated few.

Through typographic means, the designer now presents, in one image, both the message and the pictorial idea. Sometimes, this "playing" with type has resulted in the loss of a certain amount of legibility. Researchers consider this a deplorable state of affairs but, on the other hand, the excitement created by a novel image sometimes more than compensates for the slight difficulty in readability.

The designer, today, has used typography to complement and give meaning to an illustration or photograph, and has used photographs as vital parts of typographic elements. He has resorted to distortion and disfiguration of type forms (harsh words that give fuel to our critics) but the obvious emotional result often lends justification to these disfigurations.

Much of this relatively new concept in typography depends on impact. For this reason many would classify modern American typography as ugly. There is much truth in this observation. But ugliness is not necessarily a deterrent to good advertising. There can be warmth and charm in deliberate ugliness. One has only to look back to early American design and the subsequent Victorian era. The distorted furniture design, the blatant circus and political posters, the ornate gas lamp are becoming more and more appreciated today as an integral part of our modern surroundings. One will undoubtedly get accustomed to the appeal of typography that creates a mood through the spectacular—and even the spectacularly ugly.

One important result of these trends in typography is the reversal of the usual advertising procedure of copy dictating the graphic approach. In many cases the graphic presentation now dictates the copy approach giving an intimate relationship between copy and design. An encouraging result, and one that should prove a boon to future advertising, is that copy people are thinking more in graphic terms while writing and the designer, conversely, thinks in terms of words when designing. This close cooperation is in itself creating a new face for advertising.

I would like to issue a word of warning at this point. The purpose of this essay is to encourage the exploitation of all avenues of creative communications. It is not meant to convey the idea that all knotty design problems can be solved through a specific typographic approach. Typography is not an end product. It is but one of the means to the all important end in advertising—selling goods and services.

Social, political, and economic factors have caused experimentation in many creative areas. In our own small area of typographic design, these influences have resulted in what I believe is the beginning of an American tradition in typography. We have always been strongly influenced by European typographers and designers, and the schools that they represent. I feel that now, for the first time we have emerged with typography that is distinctly American and which is contributing its influence to the rest of the world.

Address to the Type Directors Club, New York (18 April 1959); published in the papers of the What is New in American Typography conference, 1960.

1959
THE NEW TYPOGRAPHY'S EXPANDING FUTURE
Ladislav Sutnar

A PIONEER OF INFORMATION *design, Czech-born Ladislav Sutnar (1897–1976) developed sophisticated design programs during the late 1950s and early 1960s that organized complex data into digestible forms. He insisted on order and logic, and fought to systematize graphic methods. In his book* Visual Design in Action *(1961), he asserts that "the sound basis for modern graphic design and typography . . . was a direct heritage of the avant-garde pioneering of the twenties and thirties in Europe" based on elementary principles of economy and clarity. This was his recurrent theme in numerous essays shorn of verbiage and unnecessary mannerisms. His published texts, personal correspondence, and even the text of this Type Directors Club talk (later the basis of a section in* Visual Design in Action*) were organized into idea-segments that often begin with a subtitle framed by either parentheses or brackets to signal the subject or idea. A letter or number indicates where in the argument's hierarchy the idea belongs. These devices were designed to encourage reading and allowed for efficient skimming.—SH*

N*ew needs demand new means "faster, faster"* (title of book by W. J. Eckert and Rebecca Jones).

1.

1/a. *Mass production the basic cause:* an understanding of the advances in graphic design and typography requires an examination of the causes that produced them. These advances, which have resulted in a new high in dynamic visual information design, have been especially rapid during the last thirty years. They derive from another aspect of our lives which has seen equally striking changes and growth over the same period. This aspect is the rapid developments in industrial techniques which we call mass production.

1/b. *Mass communication the immediate cause:* mass production was not possible without mass distribution, which in turn was not possible without mass selling. Mass selling was impossible without improved forms, and new forms, of communication techniques in newspapers, magazines, radio, and television, and even in the product and its packaging. The changes in these basic elements in our lives have spread to other fields. The architect needs the graphic designer to contribute a system of visual direction and identification to modern schools, stores, and shopping centers. Educators are demanding visual aids. The jet plane pilot cannot read his instrument panel fast enough to survive without efficient typography.

1/c. *Faster visual communication the need:* new means had to come to meet the quickening tempo of industry. Graphic design was forced to develop higher standards of performance to speed up the transmission of information. Like the title of a recent book, appropriately enough on electronic computers, the watchword of today is "faster, faster"—produce faster, distribute faster, communicate faster.

2. *Rejection of the traditional as well as "modernistic"* "most works are most beautiful without ornament" (Walt Whitman).

2/a. *Most approaches not functional:* all of the conventional and other nonfunctional approaches prove inadequate when tested by industry's new need for a dynamic system of information design. They fail to meet the requirements for functional information flow so necessary for fast perception. These requirements are: (a) to provide visual interest to gain attention and start the eye moving, (b) to simplify visual organization for speed in reading and understanding, and (c) to provide visual continuity for clarity in sequence.

2/b. *Traditional approaches inadequate:* traditional approaches are based on arbitrary rules. The Aldus Manutius ideal is "an even, silverish gray of all printing, in title and text, or in ornament." But this is monotonous and uninviting. The formalistic rules of the renaissance period for arranging book title on a middle axis produced static forces of an equilibrium of symmetry. This has to be rejected as too immobile. And the nineteenth century arrangements with fantastic type faces have to be abandoned as irrational, and as false as the meaningless "gingerbread" of American architecture.

2/c. *"Modernistic" approaches not constructive:* modernistic approaches are based on formulas solely concerned with the decorative. From a functional standpoint they represent nothing more than another aspect chinoiserie because they are strictly arrangements for decorative effects. They cannot meet the new needs. The formalistic, the sentimental, the fashionable and the speculative are but short-lived vogues with superficial aims. They do not offer a constructive approach to the design task at hand.

3. *Background of contemporary design* "beauty is the promise of function" (Horatio Greenough)

3/a. *The "new typography:"* a sound basis exists for modern graphic design and typography. It is a direct heritage of the avant-garde pioneering of the twenties and thirties in Europe. It represents a basic change that is revolutionary. This movement was first called "constructivistic," meaning constructed or having a logical structure, as opposed to the improvised or guided-by-personal-feelings. It was also called "functional typography" to emphasize the idea of a design planned to perform a function as contrasted to the use of formalistic rules, or art for art's sake. Later, the clear departure from the apathy of commercial tradition and from obsolete cliché became known as the "new typography." This name still stands for vigor of imaginative experiments, for innovations, and for the invention of new techniques. It reveals new potentials in visual communications.

3/b. *Basis of "new typography:"* as a sort of credo, in 1929 Teige[1] characterized this new typography as follows: (1) freedom from tradition; (2) geometrical simplicity; (3) contrast of typographic material; (4) exclusion of any ornament not functionally necessary; (5) preference for photography, for machine set type and for combinations of primary colors; finally—recognition and acceptance of the machine age and the utilitarian purpose of typography.[2] These points were quoted by Tschichold as a framework of his book "Eine Stunde Druckgestaltung" (A lesson in creative typographical design).

3/c. *The social implications of the "new typography:"* in 1934, in a talk at the opening of an exhibition of Sutnar's graphic work Teige attempted to formulate the new social function of the graphic designer and his relation to his environment. Freely translated, he said: (1) our world is the world of today, on the march to tomorrow; (2) our service is that of a public servant in its best sense, aimed at progressive develop-

ment of higher cultural standards; (3) our work is that of graphic editor, graphic architect, graphic planner, understanding and employing advanced methods of mechanized
printing, collaborating with the expert in the printing plant. He also observed that as
an exception, some visual poems (montage-typography) may resemble the work of
poets. That, where done for utilitarian reasons, the modern typographer's work can be
compared in "the categories of arts in transition" with journalism and with the work
of the architect-planner in the way of thinking and approach.[3]

4. *Principles of contemporary information design* "design is a process of structural
definition" (K. Lönberg-Holm).
    4/a. *Fundamental design principles necessary:* in his book, "vision in motion"
(1947) Moholy-Nagy devotes an entire chapter to discussing the idea that "designing is not a profession but an attitude." In recent years sincere efforts in espousing
the original meaning of the new typography, with its endeavor to create lasting values, have been hampered by blurred imitations. Advertising stunts have ridiculed the
moral forces behind the movement. Even so, progressive evolution of the new typography could not be stopped. An occasional look back to its real origins is necessary
to avoid some present day misconceptions. Bolstered by this knowledge and with
present day experience, principles of sound design for universal application can be
stated.
    4/b. *Fundamental design principles defined:* depending on the requirements of
specific problem needs, the varied aspects of design can be reduced to three interacting, fundamental principles—function, flow, and form. These may be defined as follows: *Function* is the quality which satisfies utilitarian needs by meeting a specific
purpose or goal. *Flow* is the quality which satisfies logical needs by providing a space-
time sequence relationship of elements. *Form* is the quality which satisfies esthetic
needs with respect to the basic elements of size, blank space, color, line and shape.[4]
    4/c. *New design synthesis:* with these three principles as a basis, design is evalu-
ated as a process culminating in an entity which intensifies comprehension. The design
aspects could be analytically polarized further into function versus form, utility versus
beauty, rational versus irrational. The function of design in this regard is established as
one of resolving the conflict of these polarities into a new design synthesis.[5]

5. *The new typography in U.S.A.* "we must obey the time" (Shakespeare).
    5/a. *The "new typography" has taken root:* anyone visiting this country for the
first time cannot avoid being surprised by the multitude of printed matter and by the
diversity of attitudes toward graphic design and typography. Here, now, is an internationally recognized "l'école de New York" in pioneering abstract art. It rivals the older
"l'école de Paris" by the unquestionable merit of its achievements. Here, also, is a
rapidly growing school of "new typography-U.S.A.," inspired by Europe's example
and representing a wealth of new findings in visual communications.
    5/b. *Solutions not found in history:* it is difficult today to visualize any effect that
da Vinci's vision of a flying man can have on modern research in aviation. It is equally difficult to see how the "traditional" or "liberal conservative" should be allowed to
influence further development of the new typography in the U.S. Even in the field of
book design, only emotional prejudice, inertia and conventionalism obstruct design
advances. A book's structural form has not varied for centuries. Even so, the dynamism
of new design standards and the principles of contemporary design are finding their
way into this field. There is just one lesson from the past that should be learned for

the benefit of the present. It is that of the painstaking, refined craftsmanship which appears to be dying out.

5/c. *Opportunity for innovation is unique:* the spectacular complexity and variety of printed communications in this country offers the American designer unparalleled opportunities. Magazines with hundreds of pages, catalogs with thousands of pages, all with their implications of enormous advertising expenditures, are unique to this country. This wealth of work also brings extensive means of reproduction. The larger the opportunity the greater is the danger of opportunism and hesitancy in accepting innovations. But there is no other way to sound design solution than by open minded and educated thinking. This means intensive study and analysis of the needs and extensive research in the design and production means to meet these needs.

6. *Future advances in graphic design* "truth will prevail" (Masaryk).[6]

6/a. *Need is evident and urgent:* with the world becoming ever smaller, a new sense of world interdependence comes sharply into focus. And with it a new need for visual information capable of world-wide comprehension becomes evident. This will require many new types of visual information, simplified information systems, and improved forms and techniques. It will also make urgent the development of mechanical devices for information processing, integration and transmission. These advances will also have their influence on the design of visual information for domestic consumption.

6/b. *Faster progress after agreement on principles:* the way to the advances of tomorrow requires agreement on and ever widening use of basic principles. This is the way accelerated progress came in the natural sciences—Euclid's axioms in geometry, Newton's laws, and Einstein's theories in physics, to name but a few. When these come to graphic design, then the smart gimmicks, the short-lived effects of contradictory modes, the emotional style revivals, the speculative new false styles, the novelties of type face preference, and the assorted variety of "safe" formulas for sure results, all will be quickly forgotten.

6/c. *Progress will be in proportion to our integrity:* we have readily accepted the rapid tempo of advances in science and technology where the inventions of yesterday are today's realities. Similarly, the potential advances of today's new graphic design are building a knowledge of design vocabulary which will be taken for granted tomorrow. And the creative forces at work will find their basic validity in terms of the human values of sincerity, honesty and the belief in the meaningfulness of one's work, in people who disregard material advantages for the sake of new experiments that will make future developments possible.

Address to the Type Directors Club, New York (18 April 1959); published in the papers of the What is New in American Typography conference, 1960.

Notes

1. Karel Teige, writer and editor of magazine and books on modern architecture and art; typographic designer.

2. The English translation quoted is by L. Sandusky, PM Magazine 1938, published by The Composing Room, N.Y.

3. "Sutnar and new typography" *Panorama* magazine. Jan. 1934, Prague.

4. Catalog Design Progress (K. Lönberg-Holm and Ladislav Sutnar, 1950).

5. Ibid.

6. Masaryk. Philosopher, professor of Philosophy Charles University, Prague, founder and first president of the Czechoslovak Republic.

1959
VISUAL ENVIRONMENT OF ADVERTISING
William Golden

MANY DESIGNERS ARE SKEPTICAL *of theory and theorists. This was especially true of CBS's William Golden (1911–1959), who professed to prefer doing design to talking about it. In this speech Golden questions the commitment of any designer—including, in this context, himself—who would forsake the drawing board for the lecture platform. Yet, in terse sentences and the plainest language, he raises the largest possible theoretical issues. What is the relationship of art and design, and of form and content? How can one reconcile the designer's responsibility to society with the demands of the commercial client? By what standards should the profession judge itself? The notoriously taciturn Golden offers few answers. A colleague once described Golden as "a teacher who never taught," but also observed that "the less time he spent at the drawing board the greater contribution he made to advertising." That the questions he raises here are still relevant forty years later reveals the thinking designer behind the consummately practical William Golden.—MB*

I happen to believe that the visual environment of advertising improves each time a designer produces a good design —*and no other way.*

There may, indeed, be some cause for concern about the chaos the designer is bringing to the visual environment of advertising.

I think we tend to do this each time we leave our work for the lecture platform or the typewriter. We tend to overstate our case in the most complicated manner, and to confuse the simple purpose of our perfectly honest, useful, little craft with the language of the sociologist, the psychiatrist, the scientist, the art critic, and sometimes even the mystic.

The obvious function of a designer is to design. His principal talent is to make a simple order out of many elements. The very act of designing exposes elements that are inconsistent and must obviously be rejected. When he is in control of these elements he can usually produce an acceptable design. When someone else controls them the best he can produce is a counterfeit. This is why at some stage of his maturity he feels the need to have a voice in the content itself. If the advertising designer begins to "examine the purposes to which this vast communications machinery is put" (as a prospectus for this conference suggests), he can run headlong into his basic conflict with the business world—a dissatisfaction with the content he is asked to transmit.

For Business the question of content is very simple. Its objective is reflected in its most important single printed document—the Annual Report. This is the yardstick by which all its decisions are measured. If the Report is unfavorable for very long the business will cease to exist. Whatever contributes to its success is right. Whatever endangers the financial statement is wrong.

Thus the morality of Business is clear and reasonably defensible. The morality of the businessman may be something else again, but as Business gets bigger and bigger, his morality is less and less operative. The man himself tends to disappear and in his place the Corporation Executive begins to emerge.

His first responsibility is to the Corporation and not to society. He would say that in our economy what is right for the corporation must inevitably be good for society, because the successful corporation provides more employment, more products and services, and higher tax payments which pay for still more social services. So without having to make a single social decision the corporation executive can tend strictly to business with the comforting assurance that no matter how it is conducted (short of public scandal), his energies will be socially useful—if the business is sufficiently profitable.

The dilemma of the literate advertising designer is that emotionally he is part small businessman and part artist. He isn't strong enough to cut himself off from the world of business to make the personal statement of the artist. He isn't a pure enough businessman to turn his attention completely away from the arts.

He somehow wants the best of both worlds. He becomes a kind of soft-boiled businessman.

When he turns to Business he is told that the content of our time is The Fact. The Fact of Science. The Fact of Business. The Fact is beyond suspicion. It has no views on Art, Religion, or Politics. It is not subject to anyone's opinion. It can be measured and tabulated. It is non-controversial.

In an era of mass marketing, controversy is assumed to be bad for business, for no potential consumer must be offended. Though Business may have no legitimate interest in people, it has an abiding interest in consumers.

The designer for the most part would be willing, I think, to accept The Fact as the content for his work. But he soon discovers that despite the prattle of the public relations expert about "lean, hard facts," the designer is seldom called upon to work with them.

For Business wants him to help create an attitude about the facts, not to communicate them. And only about some of the facts. For facts in certain juxtapositions can offend some portion of the market.

So he finds himself working with half-truths, and feels that he is not using all his talents. He finds that he is part of a gigantic merchandising apparatus in which the media of mass communication have reached a miraculous degree of technical perfection and are being operated at full speed to say as little as necessary in the most impressive way.

And this, too, is what the advertising designer is called upon to do. If he can adjust himself easily to this framework he can work very happily, and may even be handsomely rewarded for his efforts.

If he is reluctant to accept the role of a propagandist for business, but looks further for a deeper meaning for his work, he might find greater solace on the psychiatrist's couch than he will in Aspen.

There is one inviting avenue of escape that seems to give comfort to an increasing number of designers, and certainly to almost all the younger ones. It is that wonderful panacea that came to full flower in a disturbed postwar world: the abstract expressionist school of painting. It is in itself a Fact. It is acceptable because it is Art.

Business can accept it because it is successful, and oddly enough "safe" since it says absolutely nothing. The cynical advertising designer can embrace it because it can help him demonstrate his independence of content. The young designer finds it a wonderful shortcut—a do-it-yourself Art. And anyone can find delight in its total concentration on technique.

But I doubt the necessity to search in so many fruitless directions for a solution to the designer's plight.

Once he stops confusing Art with design for Business and stops making demands on the business world that it has neither the capacity nor the obligation to fulfill, he'll probably be all right. In fact I think he is pretty lucky. In the brave new world of Strontium 90—a world in which craftsmanship is an intolerable deterrent to mass production—it is a good thing to be able to practice a useful craft.

It is a craft that is susceptible to further growth and that can so far do something that neither the Management Executive nor the electronic computer can do.

If he doesn't like the end his craft serves, he can probably find a client whose products or services seem worthwhile. He can "improve the visual environment of advertising" by a flat refusal to do bad work for anyone, and thus maintain the standards of his craft.

He can take pleasure in the fact that the performance of his colleagues in graphic design is improving all the time.

He can even take pleasure, as I do, in the fact that a number of designers are beginning to watch their language.

Maybe they realized that we were beginning to frighten our clients by our strange literature. (After all, it wasn't very long ago that clients were suspicious of any advertising design that merely looked handsome.) Maybe they are finding work more rewarding than talking about it. But whatever the reason, I think (and hope) that there is a detectable change in the climate which once produced the young man who wanted to change the course of the graphic arts.

Even Leo Lionni has become weary of his preposterous invention of the New Renaissance Man, and is ready to embrace anyone who can do one thing well rather than many things badly.

Will Burtin has announced that he just doesn't care whether or not typography is an Art, so long as it does what it is supposed to do.

Saul Bass had admitted that "our typographic designs are . . . ridiculously small expressions of a profound cultural pattern."

Even this present conference concedes that the only way to demonstrate the process of communication "by Image" is by visual exhibit.

It may be useful, however, to reconsider this simplest, most valid, of our group activities. We have annual competitions in which we give each other awards and, by demonstration, set standards for our craft.

This is a sincere but disconcerting activity of perhaps questionable value since the criteria of these exhibitions are usually so poorly defined. Their purpose is to impress and to educate the business community and to honor practitioners in our field.

Yet, who hasn't heard the familiar client refrain: "I don't want an ad that will win a medal. I want one that sells." And who among us hasn't said with some embarrassment, "Sure it's nice to get a medal, but they gave it to me for the wrong job." Obviously we aren't talking to each other very clearly in our exhibitions either.

Let me try to summarize my own experiences as a juror.

In a relatively small regional show, the generous jury found no more than thirty pieces they thought were worth hanging—and only two that seemed to merit recognition. The exhibition committee was aghast. They instructed the jury to hang a predetermined quota of eighty and to award twelve prizes. The jury was thus forced to give its endorsement to pieces that in their opinion had no merit whatever, and an incompetent piece of work could thereafter be cited as having set a standard.

In another regional show, the jury awarded nine of ten prizes to a single man. He was clearly brilliant in every category. The exhibition committee explained that it was not only "unfair" to the others, but that it would so alienate the other local advertising agencies that they would boycott future competitions. The brilliant young man was awarded two prizes.

In a large exhibition with a large jury "democratically representing every school of thought" the jury was broken up into small groups—each to judge different categories. The standards of one group were totally at odds with the next and yet its task was to produce a single cohesive exhibition.

I saw the work of an artist eliminated from one category because he had been represented in the last ten exhibitions and wasn't "new."

In another category he was singled out for special attention by a group that had less interest in novelty than in distinction.

One group was earnestly trying to select a "representative cross-section" of advertising. Another was selecting only those entries that corresponded to their notion of the avant-garde movement.

One refused to hang any part of a large campaign—clearly the best in the show—on the grounds that another single ad in the same series was awarded a prize the year before. Yet another could select the same work in another category because it "continued to maintain the highest standards."

I saw one group reluctantly eliminating work that it admired because their category called for a fixed number of exhibits while another was having trouble finding enough to fill its quota.

On still another occasion the exhibition committee discovered that the jury had failed to find a single example from an industry that was the largest user of advertising in America. This was immediately corrected though nobody before had discovered anything worth hanging.

I have seen jurors sometimes unhappy because memorable work which they had seen in publications never appeared among the exhibition entries. They didn't see how their show could truly reflect the year's accomplishments without the missing work, but they were prevented by exhibition practice, from showing it.

I have even known entrants who prayed that the jury wouldn't select more than one of their entries, because they couldn't afford the hanging fee. They had submitted many entries since they couldn't know whether the jury would be "old guard" or "avant-garde."

Perhaps my most puzzling experience as a juror was to serve with a man I had long admired. He had been demonstrating for years that any page in which the hand of the designer was evident was a bad page—that a good concept flawlessly and simply executed should be the objective of every art director.

The category was "Magazine Advertising: Design of complete unit." I had found an ad which consisted of an outstanding photograph and a single line of copy. It didn't seem to be one of those accidental photographs, but a clearly thought out solution to a problem. My co-juror snorted in derision. "This is nothing but a picture and a caption. Where is the 'design'? Anybody can put a caption under a picture. *He hasn't done anything to it.*"

For me the wheel had turned full circle. Now that we had demonstrated how very difficult it was to produce something simple and were beginning to train our clients to understand it, we had to parade our bag of tricks to demonstrate our agility more obviously.

It would be useful, I'm sure, to discuss ways to define our exhibitions more sharply.

Should they be representative or selective? What standards should they reflect? Is it wiser to have large or small juries? Should there be different jurors and different standards from year to year? Does the practice of awards encourage a community feeling among designers or contribute to their disunity? Shouldn't an exhibition announce its jury and its criteria *before* entries are submitted rather than wade through a mass of material that seems to have been submitted in error?

Must selections be limited by an exhibitor's ability to pay?

I can't help but feel that if these questions can be fully discussed, and solutions are found for them, there would be fewer and more significant exhibitions. And the advertising designer will have taken a great step forward in improving his visual environment.

Address to Ninth International Design Conference, Aspen (21–27 June 1959). Published in The Visual Craft of William Golden *(New York: George Braziller, 1962).*

1959
THE TYPOGRAPHY OF ORDER
Emil Ruder

THE INTERNATIONAL TYPOGRAPHIC STYLE *(also known as Swiss Typography and* Neue Grafik*), which was launched immediately after World War II and was based on Bauhaus teachings, was a progressive movement that employed the grid as the foundation for clarity and efficiency. One of the leading proponents was Emil Ruder (1914–70) who taught at both the Kunstgewerbeschule in Zurich and the Allgemeine Gewerbeschule in Basel. In 1967, Ruder authored* Typographie, *a design manual that demonstrated that the systematic application of type and image based on the grid and sans-serif type was essential to clear communications—its impact was considerable and the book remains in print. Ruder developed an internationally influential method of teaching Swiss modernist design, and more than any other designer in the 1950s, he realized the creative implications of the Univers system of twenty-one related fonts. Both he and his students (including Wolfgang Weingart) showed how to use this visual vocabulary in semantically and syntactically innovative ways. Although* Graphis *had previously featured articles on Max Bill, Armin Hofmann, and Josef Müller-Brockmann, Ruder's illustrated essay provided the first overview of Swiss typography for the magazine's international readership.—SH*

Typography is regarded primarily as a means of ordering the various constituents of a layout. Exacting artistic postulates or creations are no longer involved; the endeavor is simply to find a formally and functionally satisfactory answer to daily requirements. The rule that a text should be easily readable is an unconditional one. The amount of text set on any one page should not be more than the reader can readily cope with; lines that are over sixty letters are considered difficult to read; word and line spacing are closely interrelated and have a most important influence on effortless reading. It is only when these elementary stipulations have been fulfilled that the question of form arises. These rules, however, do not by any means imply any restriction of artistic freedom for the sake of an inflexible system.

Typography, which is characterized by the mechanical manufacture of typefaces and composition to exact dimensions in a rectangular pattern, calls for clear type structures with orderly disposition and terse, compact formulation. The free, untrammeled line of an illustration—a hair or a coil of rope—will then provide the strongest possible contrast to it.

All attempts to infringe these rules are detrimental to good typography. Irregularities in the forms of characters, or alternative letters introduced to give variety to a single typeface, though sometimes excused by citing the 'handicraft' element in typography, are foreign intrusions that have really come in from other reproduction techniques. Typography, perhaps even more than graphic design, is an expression of our own age of technical order and precision.

Interrelation of Function and Form.
When letters are used to build up words,
lines, and type areas, problems of function
and form arise. We shall explain them here
with reference to the German word "buch."

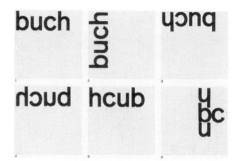

In figure 1, we first read "buch,"
while the graphic pattern is a secondary
matter. Legibility is thus assured as a first
essential. Typography is good when this end
is attained by formally unexceptional means, which is here no doubt the case. In
figure 2, the line is stood on end; legibility is now impaired, while emphasis is placed
on the pattern; form thus comes from function. In figure 3, the inverted line makes
an almost pure pattern of very doubtful legibility. The mirror reflection (figure 4)
though familiar to the compositor, is likewise illegible to the layman and is seen only
as a pattern. By rearranging the letters (figure 5), a pattern of some beauty may be
created, but the word is now quite illegible (a proof that the formal qualities of a type
face are more easily recognized in a strange language). In figure 6, the letters are completely reorganized. Straight lines and curves constitute an interplay of graphic forms
without any communication: typography has lost its purpose.

It is by no means an easy matter to strike the correct balance between function and form, because even a slight weakening of one may result in its being over-
run by the other.

Unprinted Spaces. The white spaces within a character
have an important bearing on its form, and the spacing of
words and lines greatly affects the looks and legibility of a text.
Similarly, an optical impression may very largely depend on the
unprinted spaces.

Our example shows white spaces of various sizes and
with distinct optical values, as they appear when three letters
are set up. The spaces between letters are narrow and therefore intensely bright,
the white inside the *o* is somewhat milder, while the white above the *o* is weakest.
Taken together, the three letters produce a lively and forceful white pattern. The unprinted space accordingly has a value of its own of which deliberate use is made in
typography.

"Overall" Design. All publications that are made up
of a number of pages, such as catalogs, brochures, magazines, and books, require systematic 'overall' designing.
This is not to be limited to any single page but must run
through the whole publication, and it consequently calls
for logical thinking and planning on the part of the
typographer.

The decline of typography about the turn of the
century manifested itself in the failure to create any formal bond unifying all the pages of a printed production.
One of the precepts with which typography has rehabil-
itated itself since the time of William Morris has been
that the lines on the front and back of a leaf should exactly register.

In contemporary typography the very close interconnection of all the parts of a printed production of several pages has come to be taken for granted. If a book is to be furnished with illustrations, these are not to be placed arbitrarily, but in accordance with a quite definite plan. The accompanying six illustrations show a number of single pages taken from a very carefully designed book: (from left to right): bastard title, introduction, principal title page, copyright note, section heading and one standard page of text. The top of the text on the pages with headings has been accepted as a key line throughout the whole book and it is visible also in the principal title page.

A firm's stationery is designed to give the same unified effect. The starting-point here is the sheet of normal letter paper, to which all other stationery, such as invoices and forms, memos, business reply cards and envelopes, are subordinate.

Grid. In printed matter with frequent variations of text, captions and illustrations of differing sizes, the design can be based on the division of a grid. Uncompromising acceptance of the sizes dictated by this grid results in a correct and consistent overall design. The small and more numerous the divisions of the grid, the greater are the possibilities it offers.

The left-hand example shows a grid consisting of thirty-six squares as a basis for a complex pattern of text and illustration. This grid allows of about seventy different illustration sizes and thus gives ample scope for variety in the composition of the page. The right-hand example shows how material consisting of two photographs of different sizes together with accompanying text and subtitle was laid on a page using this grid. [. . .]

Written and Printed Texts. Writing and printing are two fundamentally different techniques which should always be clearly distinguished.

The written character is personal, spontaneous and unique. The printed character, cast in large numbers from the same mould, repeats itself indefinitely in exactly identical form and is

therefore universal and impersonal. Its neutral and reserved nature permits the typographer or designer to use it in many new forms of composition. Any attempt to attain the spontaneity of handwriting with printed characters (more particularly with script types) is doomed to failure, for the two are incompatible.

The two illustrations show a letter from Paul Klee to the art dealer Hermann Rupf written during the war years, expressing his fears and concern for artist friends in France. The agitation of the writer is clearly visible in the hand. The same text composed in type evokes a completely different atmosphere; the communication has become factual and documentary.

Typography in Pictorial Work. In the art of the Far East picture and text form an indivisible whole. Forms are decided in both cases by the brush technique in painting and by the graver in graphic reproduction. Our own position is much less fortunate, and it is often a difficult matter to combine picture and typography. For this reason the achievement of harmony in this respect is one of the preeminent tasks of the contemporary typographer.

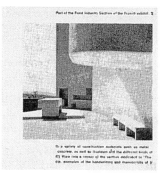

Thus the lettering may make contact with a line drawing by using lines of the same thickness, or the shape of an area of type matter may connect up to some portion of the picture. It is also quite possible to let the picture and the lettering form a contrast with each other, as when the fine gray of type matter is set against the forceful black of the picture.

The example shows how typography makes contact with the pictorial content. The vertical dominant in the left-hand third of the picture is taken up by the two areas of type matter above and below.

First published in Graphis *85 (Zurich: September/October 1959).*

1960
ADVERTISEMENT: AD VIVUM OR AD HOMINEM?
Paul and Ann Rand

PAUL RAND *(1914–1996) was the foremost translator of European modernism into an American vocabulary; the progenitor of the "Big Idea" in advertising; and a pioneer of corporate identity who combined the concept of "less is more" functionality with wit and humor. With Ann Rand (from whom he was divorced at the time), he coauthored this essay for a special issue of the academic arts and culture journal* Daedalus *on "The Visual Arts Today." Harshly critical of poor standards in advertising, their text is an opinionated and typically didactic fusion of Rand's practical, theoretical, and philosophical interpretations of modernism, and a statement of conviction about the rightness of form that guided his teaching at Yale and served as the foundation for his subsequent essays on graphic design. Rand's first book about contemporary advertising,* Thoughts on Design *(1947), was received by fellow designers as a canonical text, but its literary style was terse and betrayed his inexperience as a writer. In this article, he worked with Ann to hone his language, and in the process found a mature voice. He realized that this was an opportunity to reach a broader, perhaps more sophisticated audience addressing design's impact on society.—SH*

> *All that has any significance is the depth and validity of an experience out of which art comes; if it comes out of mere consciously clever ratiocination, it is foredoomed.*
> —Alfred North Whitehead[1]

NEVER in the history of mankind has a visual artist been subjected to such a barrage of sensory experiences as is the commercial artist of today. As he walks through that urban landscape for which his art is designed, he is bombarded with a fusillade of news and noise. He is not merely in contact with people, he is nearly trampled by them. His own art forms (billboard, sign, and advertisement) do not communicate with him, they scream at him from all sides in a crazy cacophony. He is confronted with a massive multiplicity of things—of products and events. Unlike other artists, he cannot detach himself from nor ignore this environment—it is his world. He works in it, with it, and for it.

Can the advertising artist, overwhelmed as he is by so many stimuli, have those deep and valid experiences which are the necessary basis for a genuine art? Such an artist—whose activities range from industrial design to typography—may be loosely described as a sort of professional folk artist; but he differs from the latter, not only in being dependent upon the demands of a mass market and upon using mass means for producing his work, but also in being part of a vastly different cultural climate. The folk artist flourished in relatively stable societies steeped in tradition, in which, although he himself might often remain anonymous, his work was accepted as a normal ingredient of the social matrix. Today, not only do we ask whether the popular artist produces good work, but also whether he should or can be an artist at all. This question is most often discussed in terms of technological change and economic strictures. Yet primarily it is not so much that certain elements within the environment have radically altered, but that our entire way of life and our ways of thinking, feeling, and believing have become utterly different.

The total upheaval in the structure and content of life, announced with such portentous rumblings by the Industrial Revolution, has been with us for a long time, yet we have still not found our bearings. Perhaps "change" is the key word in this new world. Today we are committed to change at so dizzying a speed on all levels, in all directions, and within the lives of all individuals that we are reeling under its impact. We scarcely have time to apprehend changes, let alone evaluate them.

This, however, is precisely what the popular artist has to do if he wants to work effectively. Change is his milieu. As an artist for industry, he designs the myriad products of an industrially productive age. As a painter, he is rarely, and often only incidentally, accepted by men of business. What has aesthetics to do with selling? The probable answer is: very little, directly; indirectly, perhaps a great deal. The commercial artist who wants to be more than a "stylist" must either become clear as to what his cultural contribution may be, or else be overwhelmed by the demands of clients, myths about public taste, consumer research surveys, etc.

To men of former ages, the meaning of life was, so to speak, "given," in part by the relatively unambiguous definition of the individual's vocational role. Clearly, life has meaning for man not only in terms of goals but also in terms of his doing, his functioning as a productive human being. If the artist fails to find goals or cannot manage to function within the cultural climate, not only is his art "foredoomed" but so is he. Precariously perched between economics and aesthetics, his performance judged by the grimly impersonal yet arbitrary "Does it sell?" the commercial artist has great difficult in finding his artistic personality, let alone asserting it. But art has often been practiced under severe constraints, whether those of the community, the church, or the individual patron. Under almost any conditions, short of absolute tyranny, art usually manages to prevail. Even if Lorenzo de' Medici had hated art, it is hard to imagine that Michelangelo would not have found some way to make sculpture and to paint. The artist—easel painter or designer—if he is genuinely committed to his vocation, does not need to be given a reason for existence: he is himself the reason.

Unfortunately he does not always recognize this fact. There are those who believe that the role the designer must play is fixed and determined by the socio-economic climate. He must discover his functional niche and fit himself into it. I would suggest that this ready-made image ignores the part the artist (or for that matter the carpenter or housewife) plays in creating the socio-economic climate. This creative contribution is made by everybody, willy-nilly, but it can become a far more significant one if the individual is aware that he is making it.

Such awareness, furthermore, is a basic source of that human dignity and pride which are prerequisite for the artist's attainment of creative status. The individual who feels himself a hapless, helpless pawn in some obscure life game obviously has trouble believing in either himself or the worth of his endeavor. Unquestionably, as men or artists, we must be able to adapt ourselves to environmental conditions, but we can do this only within certain limits. I would say that an understanding of man's intrinsic needs, and of the necessity to search for a climate in which those needs could be realized is fundamental to the education of the designer. Whether as advertising tycoons, missile builders, public or private citizens, we are all men, and to endure we must be first of all *for* ourselves. It is only when man (and the hordes of individuals that term stands for) is *not* accepted as the center of human concern that it becomes feasible to create a system of production which values profit out of proportion to responsible public service, or to design ads in which the only aesthetic criterion is "How sexy is the girl?"

If the popular artist is confronted too fast by too much, is split, is high-pressured, and is a part of a morally confused and aesthetically apathetic society, it is simple enough to say he can do something about it—but the bigger question is how.

First of all, perhaps, he must try to see the environment and himself in relation to it as objectively as possible. This is not easy. Where the "I" is involved, either specifically or generically, all kinds of resistances are aroused. It is much simpler and often more agreeable to see ourselves and the world through pastel-colored glasses. But if the artist does tumble into the swirling sea of confusion that surrounds his small island of individuality, he can at best only keep his head above water—certainly he will not be able to direct his course. He will no longer have a chance to develop the independence of thought necessary for making valid judgments and decisions.

If he can think independently and logically, the popular artist may come to see continuous and accelerating change, not as confusion compounded, but as the present form of stability. He may also be able to distinguish between the appearance of change and true change.

For the commercial artist such a distinction is vital. As a product designer he is increasingly required to consider what has been called "the newness factor;" as an advertising designer he is told by the copywriter that the resultant product is *New! Amazing! Different! The First Time in History!* All too often this "newness" has nothing to do with the innovation that is genuine change—an invention or an original method of doing or a mode of seeing and thinking. "Newness" frequently consists of contrived and transitory surprise effects such as pink stoves, automobile fins, graphic tricks. The *novelty-for-novelty's-sake* boom, with its concomitants of hypocrisy, superficiality, and waste, corrupts the designer who is taken in by them.

The differentiation of fact from fiction gives the commercial artist a basis for the far-reaching decisions he must often make. It is because of his relationship to industry that these decisions have effects far beyond the immediate aesthetic ones. When the artist designs a product, not only are millions of industry's dollars risked, but so are the jobs of those people involved making the product. Even the graphic artist by "selling" a product helps secure jobs as well as profits. Under these circumstances it becomes a matter of social responsibility for the commercial artist to have a clear and firm understanding of what he is doing and why.

The profession or job of the artist in the commercial field is clear. He must design a product that will sell, or create a visual work that will help sell, a product, a process, or a service. At the same time, if he has both talent and a commitment to aesthetic values, he will automatically try to make the product or graphic design both pleasing and visually stimulating to the user or viewer. By stimulating I mean that his work will add something to the consumer's experience.

While there is absolutely no question that talent is far and away the most important attribute of any artist, it is also true that if this talent is not backed by conviction of purpose, it may never be effectively exercised. The sincere artist needs not only the moral support that his belief in his work as an aesthetic statement gives him, but also the support that an understanding of his general role in society can give him. It is this role that justifies his spending the client's money and his risking other people's jobs, and it entitles him to make mistakes. Both through his work and through the personal statement of his existence he adds something to the world: he gives it new ways of feeling and of thinking, he opens doors to new experience, he provides new alternatives as solutions to old problems.

Like any other art, popular art relates formal and material elements. The material elements may be of a special nature, but, as in all art, the material and the formal are fused by an idea. Such ideas come originally from the artist's conscious and unconscious experience of the world around him. The experience that can give rise to these ideas is of a special kind. As Joyce Carey says, "The artist, painter, writer, or composer starts always with an experience that is a kind of discovery. He comes upon it with the sense of a discovery; in fact, it is truer to say that it comes upon *him* as a discovery."[2] This is reminiscent of Picasso's admonition not to *seek* but to *find*. What both men are saying is that the very act of experiencing is for the artist a creative act; he must bring enough to the experience for it lead him to a discovery about its nature, a discovery he will try to embody and transmit in a work of art. Surfeited by sensory stimuli, the artist today will be helpless to convert experience into ideas if he cannot select, organize, and deeply feel his experiences.

Ideas do not need to be esoteric to be original or exciting. As H. L. Mencken says of Shaw's plays, "The roots of each one of them are in platitude; the roots of *every* effective stage play are in platitude." And when he asks why Shaw is able to "kick up such a pother?" he answers, "For the simplest of reasons. Because he practices with great zest and skill the fine art of exhibiting the obvious in unexpected and terrifying lights."[3] What Cézanne did with apples or Picasso with guitars makes it quite clear that revelation does not depend upon complication. In 1947 I wrote what I still hold to be true, "The problem of the artist is to make the commonplace uncommonplace."[4]

If artistic quality depended on exalted subject matter, the commercial artist, as well as the advertising agency and advertiser, would be in a bad way. For a number of years I have worked with a cigarmanufacturing company whose product, visually, is not in itself unusual. A cigar is almost as commonplace as an apple, but if I fail to make ads for cigars that are lively and original, it will not be the cigar that is at fault.

What is important about visual ideas is that they express the artist's experience and opinions in such a way that he communicates them to others, and that they, in turn, feel a sense of discovery on seeing the work, a sense similar to the artist's own. Only this can enrich the spectator's personal experience. Further, in the case of the graphic artist, these ideas must be so conceived as to help sell the product.

The artist is certainly not alone in facing these problems: they confront the businessman, the scientist, and the technologist. Nor is he alone in his creative drive. The popular artist who sees the world as dominated by mechanistic thinking run amuck, and himself as the machine's victim, feels powerless and alienated. This is unrealistic. The creative, the imaginative, even the aesthetic nature of science is now widely recognized.

If there is reassurance for both artist and scientist in the recognition of this similarity, there is actual danger in the ignoring of it. The mechanistic view of the world saw society as governed by laws similar to what were then believed to be the absolute and immutable "laws" of natural science. It tended to divorce social forces from the actions and decisions of man. The continued popularity of such an attitude is to my mind far more menacing than the physical achievements of science and technology. It is my belief that if we are at the mercy of "social forces," it is because we have put ourselves there. If we have become, or are becoming, "slaves of the machine," it means that we have acceded to slavery.

Even in the astonishing world of the computer and the simulation machine, it must be remembered that, at least initially, it is we who will give them a program. The kind of service they render depends on our decisions, on what we think (given their capacities) they ought to do. The key problem is not with machine or with technology in general, it is with the "ought." For both scientist and artist, as well as the industry that brings them together, it is a matter of over-all aims, specific purposes, and values. It is up to us to decide what we want.

Perception—how we see something—is always conditioned by what we are looking for, and why. In this way we are always faced with questions of value. A turbine must be "scientifically" designed in order to operate, but to design it at all was at one time a matter of decision. Such decisions may or may not be based on needs, but they are surely based on wants. Products do not have to be beautifully designed. Things can be made and marketed without our considering their aesthetic aspects, ads can convince without pleasing or heightening the spectator's visual awareness. But should they? The world of business could, at least for a while, function without benefit of art—but should it? I think not, if only for the simple reason that the world would be a poorer place if it did.

The very *raison d'être* of the commercial artist, namely, to help sell products and services, is often cited by him as the reason he cannot do good work. To my mind, this attitude is just as often the culprit as is the basic nature of the work. The commercial artist may feel inferior and therefore on the defensive with respect to the fine arts. There is undoubtedly a great and real difference between so-called fine art and commercial art, namely, a difference in purpose—a fact that must be recognized and accepted. But there is nothing wrong or shameful in selling. The shame and wrong come in only if the artist designs products or ads that do not meet his standards of artistic integrity.

The lament of the popular artist that he is not permitted to do good work because good work is neither wanted nor understood by his employers is universal. It is very often true. But if the artist honestly evaluates his work and that of the other complainers, he will frequently find that the "good work" the businessman has rejected is not actually so "good." The client can be right: the artist can be self-righteous. In accusing the businessman of being "antimodern" the artist is often justified. But many times "it's too modern" simply means that the client does not know what he is really objecting to. Unbeknown to himself, the client may be reacting to excessive streamlining, an inappropriate symbol, poor typography, or a genuinely inadequate display of the product. The artist must, without bias, sincerely try to interpret these reactions.

If there is nothing wrong with selling, even with "hard" selling, there is one type that is wrong: misrepresentative selling. Morally, it is very difficult for an artist to do a direct and creative job if dishonest claims are being made for the product he is asked to advertise, or if, as an industrial designer, he is supposed to exercise mere stylistic ingenuity to give an old product a new appearance. The artist's sense of worth depends on his feeling of integrity. If this is destroyed, he will no longer be able to function creatively.

On the other hand, it is surely more consoling to the commercial artist to see himself betrayed by the shortsightedness of commerce or to believe he is forced to submit to "what the public wants" than to think he himself may be at fault. The artist

does not wish to see himself as either so indifferent to quality or so cowed by economic factors that he has taken the easy way out—just do what the boss says, and
maybe give it a new twist. Yet actually it may not always be the lack of taste on the
part of client and public that accounts for bad work, but the artist's own lack of
courage.

To do work of integrity the artist must have the courage to fight for what he
believes. This bravery may never earn him a medal, and it must be undertaken in the
face of a danger that has no element of high adventure in it—the cold, hard possibility of losing his job. Yet the courage of his convictions is, along with his talent, his only
source of strength. The businessman will never respect the professional who does not
believe in what he does. The businessman under these circumstances can only "use"
the artist for his own ends—and why not, if the artist himself has no ends? As long as
he remains "useful," the artist will keep his job, but he will lose his self-respect and
eventually give up being an artist, except, perhaps, wistfully on Sundays.

In asking the artist to have courage, we must ask the same of industry. The
impetus to conform, so widespread today, will, if not checked, kill all forms of creativity. In the world of commercial art, conformism is expressed, for example, by the
tenacious timidity with which advertisers cling to the bald presentation of sex, sentimentality, and snobbism, and by such phenomena as the sudden blossoming of fins on
virtually all makes of American cars. The artist knows he must fight conformity, but
it is a battle he cannot win alone.

Business has a strong tendency to wait for a few brave pioneers to produce or
underwrite original work, then rush to climb on the bandwagon—and the artist follows. The bandwagon, of course, may not even be going in the right direction. For
instance, the attention and admiration evoked by the high caliber of Container
Corporation's advertising have induced many an advertiser to say, "Let's do something
like Container," without considering that it might not be at all suited to his needs.
Specific problems require specific visual solutions. This does not mean that an advertisement for a soap manufacturer and one for Container Corporation cannot have
much in common, or that a toaster cannot be designed in terms of the same sound
principles as a carpenter's hammer. Both ads and both products can be made to fulfill
their functions and also to be aesthetically gratifying; both can express respect for and
concern with the broadest interests of the consumer.

It is unfortunately rare that the commercial artist and his employer, be it
industry or advertising agency, work together in an atmosphere of mutual understanding and cooperation. Against the outstanding achievements in design made possible by such companies as Olivetti, Container Corporation, IBM, CBS, El Producto
Cigar Company, CIBA, and a comparatively few others, there stands the great dismal
mountain of average work. The lack of confidence that industry in general evinces for
creative talent and creative work is the most serious obstacle to raising the standards
of popular art. Business pays well for the services of artists who are already recognized
and are consequently "successful." Success is a perfectly legitimate reward for competence and integrity, but if it is a precondition for acceptance, it leaves the beginner
and the hitherto unrecognized innovator in an economic *cul-de-sac*. Moreover, when
business merely asks for something just "a little bit better" or "a little bit different," it
may well inhibit not only artistic creativity, but also all forms of creativity, scientific
and technological included.

From a long-range standpoint, the interests of business and art are not
opposed. The former could perhaps survive without the latter, for a time; but art is a

vital form of that creative activity which makes any kind of growth possible. We are deluged with speeches, articles, books, and slogans warning us that our very survival as free nations depends on growth and progress—economic, scientific, technological. The kind of climate that fosters original work represents an over-all attitude, a general commitment to values that uphold and encourage the artist as well as the scientist and the businessman.

First published in a special issue of Daedalus: The Visual Arts Today, *edited by György Kepes (Winter 1960).*

Notes

1. Dialogues of Alfred North Whitehead, as recorded by Lucien Price (Boston: Little, Brown and Company, 1954), p. 70.

2. Joyce Carey, *Art and Reality* (New York: Harper and Brothers, 1958), p. 1.

3. H. L. Mencken, *Prejudices: A Selection* (New York: Vintage K58, Alfred A. Knopf, 1958), pp. 27 and 28.

4. Paul Rand, *Thoughts on Design* (New York: George Wittenborn, Inc., 1947), p. 53.

1963
CONCRETE POETRY
dom Sylvester Houédard

THE IMPLICATIONS OF THE *international concrete poetry movement, which flourished from the mid-1950s to the mid-1970s, were not lost on the more farsighted designers and typographers of the postwar years. Exponents of visual poetry also viewed the typographic experiments of professional designers such as Brownjohn, Chermayeff, and Geismar with interest. In Britain, Herbert Spencer's internationally distributed journal* Typographica *(1949–1967) regularly published examples of professional and non-professional typography in suggestive juxtaposition. Dom Sylvester Houédard's 1963 essay on concrete poetry's use of graphic space as a "structural agent" was the first to introduce the movement to English-speaking designers. Written in Houédard's poetically compressed style, its idiosyncratic prose brilliantly demonstrates concrete poetry's desire, as Houédard characterized it, to contract and constrict everyday language into new forms of "semantic economy." A Benedictine monk and scholar of world religions, Houédard (1924–1992) was a leading English-language theorist of concrete poetry and created many wordless compositions of his own—called "typestracts"— using an Olivetti manual typewriter.—RP*

'Unfortunately, & especially in germany, concrete poetry has become a fashion in the last years' Eugen Gomringer wrote me in July: in Great Britain the only readers with access to concrete poetry have been subscribers to TYPOGRAPHICA & to *POTH & fishsheet* (edited & designed by Ian Hamilton Finlay & Jessie McGuffie at The Wild Hawthorn Press, Edinburgh): the summer poetry number of *The Aylesford* had Finlay's *valentine.*

Central interest here: relation of new typography & new poetry—place of this in new kinetic/spatial dimensions of art today—significance of fact that Finlay, leading concrete poet in Great Britain, is typographer & toymaker as well as poet.

Contemporary concrete poetry began 1953 with *avenidas mujeres* by Eugen Gomringer, (born in Bolivia 1925, started the eugen gomringer press at Frauenfeld, Switzerland, 1960, where he edits *konkrete poesie/poesia concreta*). The history of concrete poetry can be pushed further back; its roots: the origin of all graphics—cave paintings pictographs ideograms alphabets hieroglyphs—any concrete medium to be looked *at* as well as *through*—any words treated as friends not slaves—as holy not débris. Texts created for concrete use: amulets talismans grigris mani-walls deviltraps kemioth tefillin mezuzahs medals sacred-monograms.

Or mediaeval masons' marks, 18th-century cyphers, 19th-century trademarks—all objects as well as signs. Mysteria & sacramenta—veiling/revealing—forerunners named in 1958 pilot plan: Mallarmé Pound Joyce Cummings Apollinaire: parallel explorers: Webern Boulez Stockhausen & all concrete/electronic musicians (= space intervention in time-art of music); Mondriaan & Max Bill (= time inter-

ventions in spatial, visual arts). 1963 *Manifeste* names Morgenstern Albert-Birot
Schwitters Hugo Ball Seuphor Raoul Hausmann some Surrealists Expressionists
Lettrists. Richard Hamilton in *Typographica 3:* POETS who use layouts to reinforce
poetic ideas (Marinetti Mayakovsky) or make pictures with type (Apollinaire);
ARTISTS who use type to create messages as much pictorial as literary (Schwitters
Picabia van Doesburg Lissitzky Boccioni). This puts concrete in a context that is cur-
rently fascinating critics & historians—the reincarnation of pre-WW/1 creativities in
the post-WW/2 world.

In 100 years since Napoleon III's Salon des Refusés 1863, 2 tendencies in
modern art have been:

(1) the largely WW/1 move to the authentic & non-mimetic, a move powered by its
own built-in nuclear proton-neutron drive:
        (a) the necessary negative anti-past (but still creative) épurations of eg the
dadaists & surrealism, the musique concréte of the Paris club d'essai neo-bruitists &c:
image & sense smashing; iconoclastic & logoclastic: peristaltic, eliminative:
        CONSTRUCTIVE CONTRACTIVE
        (b) the affirmative pro-future creativeness on each side of the emotional/cere-
bral (heart/mind or expressionist/cubist &c/&c) split like f i the fauves constructivists
purists futurists suprematists: the electronic serialism of Radio Cologne musicians.
        CONSTRUCTIVE

(2) The largely post-WW/2 overspill to coexistentialism & mutual interpenetration,
rejection of divides & borders, delight in accepting ambiguity/ambivalence: alive blurring of frontiers between art & art, mind & mind, world & world, mind art & world.
New Dada New Anarchism oecumenical beat-bop P & J, New Directions, New
Departures, New Waves, New Winds, New Typography: humanist planetarization of
this shrinking world.
        SPATIAL COEXISTENTIAL

Pure Concrete
The 3 major statements on pure concrete poetry to date have been: the Gomringer
articles (1954, 56, 58, 60) collected in *the constellations* 1963; the Brazilians' *pilot plan*
1958, and the 2 *manifestes & projet* of Pierre Garnier 1963.
        Concrete poetry is today: it is Afterbeat—history cycle of rhythm-form verse
is closed. Concrete poetry can be semantic (pure) or nonsemantic, mutatis mutan-
dis however, each comes from the 3 tendencies of modern art & is constrictive (con-
tractive), constructive & coexistential. It reduces language (verbiage & syntax) to a
minimum, the LCM of nouns; it makes poem-objects; it overspills in every direction,
primarily to typography 'Ikon & Logos are one' (Hugo Ball 12 june 1916), secondar-
ily to all spatialising art today. New poetry is CONCRETE because it is a poetry of
nouns, words for concrete things: also because it makes poems that are concrete
objects themselves, not windows into souls; it is SPATIAL because it creates its own
space. Pure (semantic) concrete is the poetry of Finlay, of Gomringer, the Brazilians
& Pierre Garnier, of the Japanese Kitasono Katué & Kobayashi.

constricting language: concrete is part of 1963 scene: speaking & writing are getting
shorter, snappier, whole sentences packing in a word, long phrases into initials. Mutual
exchange between speaking & writing, often unnoticed in daily life, needs only to be

pointed out & eg advertisements (pictographs, slogans) become new poetry. This simple direct diction in sign-like new poetry is making literature part of everybody's life (cf Hans Arp on Hugo Ball 1932 trans Eugene Jolas 'thru language too man can grow into life'): it reassets place in society of creative writers.

Absence of inflection & declension in words (infinitives used in french concrete); absence of syntax that gums words together in sentences: syntax replaced by typographic arrangement of words on page. As with ideograms, reader supplies missing links. Poem is kinetic, forces reader to cross border & enter it. This syntax-absence (doubly oriental, like agglutinative Japanese, isolating Chinese) is very like Headlines, Titlepages, Telegrams, Pidgin, Posters. Like contemplation, goal of poetry-purge, was the wordless suprematist *white on white*, *poeme blanc*, concrete fractures linguistics, atomises words into incoherence, constricting language to jewel-like semantic areas where poet & reader meet in maximum communication with minimum words.

Words: hard & lovely as diamonds demand to be seen, freed in space; words are wild, sentences tame them. Every word an abstract painting, read quickly in a phrase words get lost: in concrete, eye sees words as objects that release sound/thought echoes in reader. Opposition PLANE/IRON (AVION/FER) nothing to do with syllable count: difference between comfortable picture of *The tiger on the river bank has come to quench its thirst*, & the power of TIGER. The Logos as one-word poem OM, one-stroke timeless ikon.

constructive: concrete poems just ARE: have no outside reference; they are objects like TOYS & TOOLS (toys can be tools), jewel-like concrete things-in-them-selves, pretiosa; a placed comma, a flower, a blank, something admired in the tokonoma.

Constellations: the simplest possible in use of words—just words groups like star-groups. Concrete poetry is 'I'-less ego-less self-effacing, not mimetic of the poet, not subjective (at least explicitly). Poet: dissolved, issues no *orders* to reader who has to provide his own mind-gum syntax. Readers not bossed—hence new poetry is new anarchy or free symbiosis, like looking at non-demanding nature, viewer sees image of himself. Like mysticism, and zen, breakthru in Oxford semantic problems. Like Ginsberg in *Pa'lante*: 'Give up any poem-practice depending on living inside the structure of language—on words as the medium of conscious being.' Existential source of contradiction (objectivity/subjectivity) disappears.

Concrete poetry communicates its own structure: is an object in & by itself. Its material: word (sound, visual shape, semantical charge); its problem: the function & relation of this material; factors: nearness & similarity—gestalt psychology; rhythm: relational force. Like cybernetics: the poem as self-regulating machine. Concrete poems can be dull amusing grand satirical playful sad—anything except epic. 'Help serious thought & mind-play; concrete poet: play-expert making speech-rules' (Gomringer: Independently of Wittgenstein?). The constructed poem attracts: it is human, friendly, makes words move on the page—they move as quick as the eye the poem attracts. Eyeverse is not 'read'—it creates an impresson through the gestalt shape of the whole toy-tool, architected, poem—through each word as the eye wanders over them in any order.

coexistential overspill & boundary blurring: concrete poetry begins by being aware of graphic space as its structural agent, as the cosmos in which it moves, the universe into which it turns the page, the book. A printed concrete poem is ambiguously both typographic-poetry and poetic-typography—not just a poem in *this* layout, but a poem that is its own type arrangement. Hence many type layouts are poems. A concrete poem like ideograms, advertisements, posters, creates a specific linguistic area—*verbicovisual*—with the advantages of nonverbal communication. It advertises itself. Nonsemantically this overspills in direction of Diter Rot, of typograms & typikons.

Concrete poems: dynamic structures—exist in tension between poem-object & space-time: motorised semantic-poetry not around yet but concrete *is* mobile, kinetic-spatial, by its typographic life. Its effect on eye: perceptive ambivalence. The shrinking world: contracted/constricted negatively by bomb & spacefears, positively by jet-communications telstar space-probe. This makes coexistentialism inevitable, international: ie, all arts merge, barriers crumble, are scrambled (*sculpture sonore*, mechanised frescoes); new semantic eyeverse through new physiognomical typography & suprematist care for space, shares space-time spatial-kinetic concern of all forward-moving art. Battle of typograph & poet (form & content) is over—poet & typographer (soul & eye) must balance in same person: his the total responsibility before language, to create precise problems & solve them in terms of visible language. A general art of the word.

Nonsemantic concrete

This like Alan Davie's poesy (cf Michael Horovitz's new Methuen) can spill over into jazz & paint, & painting spill him over into life. Zen immediacy, the unwordable problem of the non & the non-non. Nonsemantic is even more concrete, more self-communicative. Overspill into EARVERSE (poésie à lire): sonorisms like f i sound poems invented by Hugo Ball 1915; n.1 gadgi beri bimba; Schwitters' beautiful priimiitittii (*transition* n.3): grim glim gnim bimbim (*mécano* 4-5 1923) & classical Primordial Sonata (Ursonate, based on Hausmann's *fmsbw*: 1924–33); or hans g helm's 'FA:M'AHNIESGWOW' structures developing this with stronger almost eyeverse typographic attention; all serial electronic music beginning early 50s at Radio Cologne (Stockhausen Boulez &c). Even Schwitters' *W* poem 1924 (began soft ended loud at 1st performance). EYEVERSE (poésie visuelle): like f i Francis Picabia's typographic poem-portrait of Tristan Tzara 1918, Diter Rot's *boks*, Japanese brush paintings, Alcopley's poetry without words, John Furnival's space elaborations, tornpaper dolly-poems. Reduced to suprematist ultimate, *white on white, & poème blanc for ian hamilton finlay.*

Nonsemantic overspills further to f i total nature/art ambituities of Kaprow's *Yard & Combines*, Rauschenberg's *Assemblages*; Dine's *Collages* & the Paris *New Realism*; New York *Happenings*; the Amsterdam *Dylaby* (dynamic labyrinths of Rauschenberg Raysse de Saint-Phalle Tinguel Ultveldt & Daniel Sporri himself a concretista); to current motorised painting & sculpture, mobile frescoes, sculptures sonores, pyromagnétiques, hydrauliques; lumino-dynamic creations lit from inside or outside; & true 3-d cinétisme plastique. All these: interart invasions, interpenetrations, coexistentialisms, mutual time-space interventions; kinetic, dynamic, spatial (cf useful survey of field work by Schöffer Malina Tinguely Calder Bury Le Parc Kosice Aubertin Takis Monari Vardenaga Boto & Hoenisch in UNESCO *Courier* September 1963) are concentric to nonsemantic concrete/spatial poetry: they are the background of pure concrete, the world of the 'création d'objets sonores poétiques ou visuels', a world where fauves & suprematists meet. [. . .]

First published in Typographica *new series no. 8 (London: December 1963).*

1964
SOMETIMES I PLAY THINGS
I NEVER HEARD MYSELF
William Bernbach

WILLIAM BERNBACH *(1911–1982), along with David Ogilvy, is considered the father of modern advertising. After working as a copywriter at the William H. Weintraub Agency, where his collaborators included the young Paul Rand, he founded his own agency with Ned Doyle and Maxwell Dane in 1949. Doyle Dane Bernbach went on to revolutionize the look and feel of American advertising with campaigns for Polaroid, Levy's Jewish Rye, Avis Rent-a-Car, and, most notably, Volkswagen. Speaking honestly and wittily in the tone of everyday conversation, the archetypal "Doyle Dane" ad contrasted sharply with the pompous hype and empty stentorian tone of 1950s advertising and was widely copied around the world. Bernbach's greatest influence, however, was not on the way ads looked but on the way they were made: breaking the pattern of traditional agencies, his copywriters and art directors worked side by side in collaborations designed to merge the communicative power of word and image. That the creative process championed by Bernbach was said to resemble nothing so much as jazz improvisation is underlined by the source of the title of this address to the 1964 Aspen Design Conference, bebop pianist Thelonius Monk.—MB*

When Eliot Noyes invited me to appear at this design conference, I asked him if he knew what he was doing. I am not a designer. I am an advertising man, and my knowledge of design is restricted to that field of communication. As a matter of fact, I have strong reservations about design, so strong that I informed Mr. Noyes that the theme of my talk would be: "Design can get in the way." He said, "Come anyway." So, here I am. At least, you know whom to blame. All I ask is that you remember my references to design are to design in advertising, and, if you see a relationship to design in other fields, that will be your doing and not mine.

Some time ago, in an interview, one of our great artists said: "Some people mistake neatness for art." With his usual genius this man brought to life for me, with one stroke of his brush, the danger in design. The danger is a worship of technique, a preciousness, a preoccupation with good looks. What I fear, and so often see, in an overconcern with design is a bloodlessness. The goal seems to be the presentation of a neat package, instead of a revelation of its contents. There seems to be a striving for a gentility, a good taste, a good manners. Well, there is nothing gentler or better mannered than a well-dressed corpse. The only trouble is that it's dead and inspires no one.

You just can't squeeze life into a package. It's going to ooze out here and there. I think it's terribly important to be aware of this. Not to be aware of it may lead to an overvaluation of rules and techniques, a tendency to distort and ignore life when it doesn't nicely fit into your system or theory. About a year ago a son of mine was graduated from prep school, and the main speaker was the Dean of MIT, and he told the story of this young man who just fascinated him up at MIT. This young man had a great design for living. He had divided his day not into hours, but into minutes. He knew precisely what he was going to do every minute of the day: so much time for study, so much time for socializing, so much time for sports, and he said he even knew precisely what kind of girl he was going to marry. He had this design down pat. She was going to be a girl about five-six, straight white teeth, black hair, her father had to have a certain income. His design was pat. And even a year later, the dean couldn't get this boy out of his mind. He came across the boy and said, "Well, John, how is everything going?" John said, "Just fine. Everything is working out just as I planned. I even met that girl I told you about, the one I designed. She has black hair, white teeth, she's five-six, her father works down on Wall Street, but I don't like her." Design can be dangerous.

In advertising, it takes more than a good design to provoke and persuade the consumer. I can remember—and it wasn't more than twenty years ago—when all an ad had to do was look good for it to be turned down by the client. He was suspicious of good-looking, well-designed ads. And he had every right to be. The early designers had begun to enter the field. They felt they had an easy job. It was no trick at all to make ads look better. Any change would be an improvement. The copy was to them merely a graphic element that must balance beautifully with the other elements in the ad. Making the copy inviting and easy to read was never an important consideration. Everything was lined up so evenly and neatly that the parts of the ad were completely overpowered by the total graphic configuration. Well, that may be good design, but it's bad advertising! And I question that it's good design. If you measure the effectiveness of any effort by how well its purpose has been achieved, then you cannot call some of these early efforts at advertising design successful. The purpose of an ad is to persuade people to buy your product, and everything, however expert, that slickly distracts from that idea and those words is, for my money, bad design.

About 85 percent of all ads today don't get looked at. This statistic was just revealed in a study made by the AAAA. This study was conducted by the advertising industry to find out what the public thought of advertising. We were worried about whether or not the public loved us. Our problem is they don't even hate us. The sad thing is that business is spending too much time and money on making advertising boring, and we're achieving this boredom with such great American efficiency. The scientific way we're going about it, we just can't miss.

Design is not the answer. This deplorable statistic—about 85 percent of ads not getting looked at—exists despite the fact that in the last ten years there has been a tremendous increase in the demand by business for more expertly designed advertising. As a principal in an agency that has won more than its share of art and design awards, I say I wouldn't hesitate for a minute to choose the plain-looking ad that is alive and vital and meaningful over the ad that is beautiful but dumb, whose vitality is buried in the neatness and self-consciousness of technically perfect design.

Of course, the ideal combination in an ad is beauty and vitality. But, the real danger is that we will be blinded by the beauty and forget that what really touches people and moves them is the idea and the warmth and sincerity and insight which we ourselves bring to the ad. Just because an ad looks good is no insurance that it will get looked at. How many people do you know who are impeccably groomed but dull?

I have seen firsthand the development of some of our industry's greatest art directors. And I am talking about industry and commerce. The pattern was always the same for these art directors. In the early stages they were preoccupied with design—and their work was self-conscious and pretentious. Then, they became concerned with the object of their design. They studied it; they analyzed it; they looked for ways to improve it. And then they searched for a way to put it down simply, believably, so that nothing would come between that product and the reader of the ad.

We have recently run a rather successful campaign for a firm called Avis Rent-A-Car, and people are coming to buy this product. And I'd like to make a very important point about the approach we took on this. We don't think just saying nice things or saying provocative things is going to make a product succeed. As a matter of fact, we believe firmly that a great advertising campaign will make a bad product fail faster—it will just enable more people to know how bad it is. We tell people in our ads that our windshield wipers work; our ashtrays are clean; we are only second, but we are trying harder; we want to be first. We took this campaign around to the people who deliver the cars to the consumer, the car washers and the mechanics. We told them we were completely dependent upon them; unless they delivered what we promised in the advertising, we would fail, and never did a company need its employees as much as we needed them. They then felt important for the first time in the company. They went to work; they produced a better product, and we have had rather a big success with this.

A few years ago I spoke before an art group in New York, art directors, and I said to them:

In the last decade we have seen a revolution of good graphic taste, so that today it occupies a position of unprecedented eminence. Today everybody is talking creativity, and frankly that's got me worried. I am jealous of the position you and I have reached in our profession, and I fear lest we lose it. I fear lest we keep the good taste and lose the sell. I fear all the sins we may commit in the name of creativity, and I fear that we may be entering an age of phonies. No one believes in you more than I do, no one has been helped by you and made you look good more than I. From my early work with Paul Rand about fifteen years ago right through the years, working with such commercial graphic giants as Bob Gage, Bill Taubin, Helmut Krone, and many others, I have watched you breathe vibrating life into my ideas with your talents. It is out of this great indebtedness to you that my concern springs. It can take very little time to lose all the ground we have gained. All we have to do is forget that good taste and advanced techniques are not ends in themselves, but wonderful tools with which to make vivid the advantage of a product. The purpose of an ad is to sell, and unless we sell, people will be suspicious of our ads once more. The primary responsibility of good creative people in advertising is not just to exercise creative freedom, but to know what is good creative work and what is merely pretentious acrobatics. With the tremendous increase in political and social pressures, with violence confronting us at every turn, with the fierce competition among advertisers, more and more it will take tremendous artistry with words and pictures to touch and move the reader. So exposed is he to banalities, to self-conscious, artificial attempts to arrest his attention, that he looks, but he does not see; he listens, but he does not hear; and what is worse, he does not feel. There has never been a greater challenge to your talent. To those of you who can meet that challenge, who through the magic of your artistry can make the reader see, hear, and feel, the rewards have never been greater, for you are the insurance an advertiser takes out on all the facts that he wants to tell the public, for only you, working honestly and imaginatively, can bring those dead facts to life and make them memorable to all who see them. And as a last word I'd like to quote my favorite philosopher, Thelonious Monk, when he said, "The only cats worth anything are the cats who take chances. Sometimes I play things I never heard myself."

Address to Fourteenth International Design Conference, Aspen (1964). From the archives of the IDCA (International Design Conference, Aspen).

1964
FIRST THINGS FIRST
Ken Garland

FIRST THINGS FIRST, *published by the British graphic designer Ken Garland in January 1964 in an edition of four hundred copies, was drafted during a meeting of the Society of Industrial Artists in London. Garland (b. 1929) asked to read out his manifesto, and the warm reception encouraged him to gather signatures in support from twenty-one designers, photographers, and students. The emergence of the British graphic design profession in the early to mid-1960s was accompanied by periodic soul-searching and discussion about the purpose of visual communication in magazines such as* Design, *where Garland was art editor from 1956 to 1962.* First Things First's *plea for a shift in designers' priorities away from the "high-pitched scream of consumer selling" into worthier forms of activity is the most concentrated statement of its kind. The manifesto was reprinted in* Design, *the* SIA Journal, Ark, *and* Modern Publicity, *and the Labour politician Anthony Wedgwood Benn wrote about it in his column in the* Guardian *newspaper. Garland was also invited to read the manifesto on the BBC's* Tonight *news program. Intermittently reprinted to this day, its still unanswered challenge to commercial graphic design has lasting resonance.—RP*

We, the undersigned, are graphic designers, photographers and students who have been brought up in a world in which the techniques and apparatus of advertising have persistently been presented to us as the most lucrative, effective and desirable means of using our talents. We have been bombarded with publications devoted to this belief, applauding the work of those who have flogged their skill and imagination to sell such things as:

cat food, stomach powders, detergent, hair restorer, striped toothpaste, aftershave lotion, beforeshave lotion, slimming diets, fattening diets, deodorants, fizzy water, cigarettes, roll-ons, pull-ons and slip-ons.

By far the greatest time and effort of those working in the advertising industry are wasted on these trivial purposes, which contribute little or nothing to our national prosperity.

In common with an increasing number of the general public, we have reached a saturation point at which the high-pitched scream of consumer selling is no more than sheer noise. We think that there are other things more worth using our skill and experience on. There are signs for streets and buildings, books and periodicals, catalogs, instructional manuals, industrial photography, educational aids, films, television features, scientific and industrial publications, and all the other media through which we promote our trade, our education, our culture, and our greater awareness of the world.

We do not advocate the abolition of high pressure consumer advertising: this is not feasible. Nor do we want to take any of the fun out of life. But we are proposing a reversal of priorities in favor of the more useful and more lasting forms of communication. We hope that our society will tire of gimmick merchants, status salesmen and hidden persuaders, and that the prior call on our skills will be for worthwhile purposes. With this in mind, we propose to share our experience and opinions, and to make them available to colleagues, students and others who may be interested.

Edward Wright
Geoffrey White
William Stack
Caroline Rawlence
Ian McLaren
Sam Lambert
Ivor Kamlish
Gerald Jones
Bernard Higton
Brian Grimbly
John Garner
Ken Garland
Anthony Froshaug
Robin Fior
Germano Facetti
Ivan Dodd
Harriet Crowder
Anthony Clift
Gerry Cinamon
Robert Chapman
Ray Carpenter
Ken Briggs

Self-published, 1964.

1964
THE RESPONSIBILITIES
OF THE DESIGN PROFESSION
Herbert Spencer

TOWARD THE END OF *his time as editor of* Typographica, *Herbert Spencer was asked by the magazine's publisher, Lund Humphries, to take on the editorship and design of the company's long-established* Penrose Annual *(founded in 1895). Spencer's first volume, published in 1964, included his article on the responsibilities of the design profession, in which the tensions of the fledgling discipline, so clearly exposed by the* First Things First manifesto, *are once again apparent. The British Designers and Art Directors Association, founded in 1962, had drawn regular criticism for the frivolous commercial concerns foregrounded by many of the designs featured in its annual awards, and Spencer's essay lends its weight to the attack on "designer's designers" whom he believes to be working not for the common good, but for the "approbation of their colleagues." He concludes by making a call for research into the practical and psychological aspects of communication design that would be often repeated, though less often heard, in the years that followed.—RP*

During the past ten or fifteen years, enormous changes have taken place in the practice of design. The great increase in the public awareness of the importance of good design, the effect of increasing international competition in trade. The influence of foreign magazines, post-war affluence and the ease and relative cheapness of travel, and opportunities for working abroad—all these things have helped to dissolve rigid attitudes and preconceived ideas towards the design of products and buildings and printing.

In a prosperous society, energetic and ambitious young executives and editors have emerged, determined to establish their reputations by the impact they can make rather than, as so often in the past, by the economies they can introduce. The efforts during the past twenty or thirty years of the designers' own professional organizations today ensure that designers who respond to this challenge with imagination and skill are generally adequately rewarded. In most sections of industry alert technicians are replacing frustrated handicraftsmen, and the role of the professional designer is accepted—in principle, at least.

Today's greater opportunities and rewards have attracted to the design profession large numbers of talented and imaginative young men and women, and since 1945 art schools have placed increasing stress upon graphic and industrial design in their courses. The majority of today's designers are formally trained and highly professional in their attitude to their work, and their training has given the best of them great fluency in the visual language of this age. This change in the status and training of designers is perhaps the most significant development in the profession during the past decade.

Many of the original aims and objectives of professional organizations such as the Society of Industrial Artists seem now to have been achieved. Design as a profession is established; the designer's status is respected; the payment of fees on a reasonable professional basis is generally accepted by industry; there is a large number of schools staffed and equipped to train students up to a reasonable professional standard; and most designers do adhere to a code of professional conduct. Seen in this rosy light—with so much already achieved and so little apparently still to be tackled—designers may feel encouraged to settle back and bask in the comfortable glow of their recently won respectability, with only occasional gentle bursts of activity in order to agitate for higher fees.

Fortunately, however, the design profession has acquired not only recognition but also responsibilities. And it is, I believe, through facing up to these responsibilities that the profession will escape from the cul-de-sac into which, in graphic design especially, it seems to have meandered.

Design, as a profession, is young. It has really only existed as an activity independent of painting or sculpture or architecture for about thirty years. Increasingly during the past twenty years, graphic and industrial design and typography have passed into hands that have been formally trained to serve the requirements of the profession and to produce work of a high standard of technical competence. But far too many art and design schools have been content simply to turn out skillful performers in an accepted idiom rather than men able to think out solutions in a logical and creative way. And the design profession as a whole has for too long been content to condone this situation instead of campaigning vigorously for design education of adequate breadth. By this neglect designers have created the situation which is at the root of their present dilemma.

If we examine the development of design over the past 150 years it is apparent that designers are faced today with a profound challenge not to their ability, but to their integrity. The design profession, emerging from a long period of adolescence, seems now to be wavering as though undecided whether to accept its adult obligations or to retreat to the nursery. And an alarmingly large number of designers everywhere seem to be content simply to turn their backs on the problem as though hoping that by diverting their eyes to their own—or their neighbor's—drawing board this threat to their profession's youth will somehow evaporate.

Let us look briefly at what we mean by the practice of design and see how this has gradually evolved.

There is of course no such thing as an 'undesigned' product or piece of printing. No matter how brief the message or how small the article (or how bad the end result) every product and every printed sheet is designed by somebody. Quite often many people contribute to the final result. Somebody has to decide the size, the shape, the color, the materials, and all the other visual details. Consciously or unconsciously considerations of taste, fashion, tradition, convention, convenience, efficiency, and expediency shape the final result. When industry was considerably less complex than it is today all these decisions were made by the master printer or master craftsman who personally discussed each job with his customer and personally instructed the members of his 'team' (and often carried out part of the work himself). The master craftsman's standards were higher and, generally, his personal skills were greater than those of his employees.

The engineers and inventors of the late eighteenth and early nineteenth centuries often gambled both their personal fortunes and their personal reputations on their enterprises: when they triumphed they decked out their products—whether locomotives or engines or machines—with ornament and decoration to make them worthy monuments to their success. These embellishments, it is true, were not always appropriate to the new materials they used, but generally they effectively expressed the vigorous enthusiasm of their promoters for their products and the honesty of purpose of the craftsmen who worked on them.

And with the mechanizing of production, new kinds of printing developed. First, in addition to the comparatively simple letterheadings, invoices, and trade cards already in use, the new mass production industries found necessary an increasingly wide variety of printed forms in order to control efficiently the processes of production and distribution. Then, as both production and competition increased, demand had to be stimulated by advertising.

After 1800, with advertisers using more and more superlatives, printing types grew bigger, fatter, and more exuberant, although layout continued to be based on that of the book—with display lines centered in width as on a title page and punctuated as in continuous text. The fat face type introduced in the first decade of the nineteenth century was the inevitable product of the printer's rigid adherence to symmetrical or centered layout and of the advertiser's growing demand for typography more compelling than that of his competitor.

Until the middle of the nineteenth century typographical experiments were largely confined to variations of the type design, but the invention of the platen machine led, about 1870, to a new kind of printing known as 'Artistic Printing.' This style made considerable use of colored inks and of elaborate ornament and decoration (often quite unrelated to the subject matter of the text), and incidentally brought about the first real departure from the centered layout of the book printer. Artistic Printing, at its best, encouraged high standards of craftsmanship and considerable technical ingenuity. But, especially in the diluted form of its commercial application, it was skill misapplied so far as the true purpose of printing is concerned.

It was not long before most printers had utterly lost all notion of true printing tradition. They had squandered their creative inheritance and were either imprisoned in a web of sterile convention or involved in an orgy of technical gimmickry without any discernible regard for the printed word as a means of communication.

Not surprisingly, quite soon they lost the respect of both the public in general and of their customers in particular. Aesthetically bankrupt and confused, the printing industry was quite incapable of picking up, or even of recognizing, the frayed ends of its severed traditions. It was ready to relinquish (though not without resentment) control of design to 'amateurs' such as William Morris and those who followed in his wake.

Unfortunately there are in several respects, as I shall later explain, close and uncomfortable parallels between late nineteenth-century typography and the situation in graphic design today.

But, broadly, what happened to printing design in the nineteenth century also happened to product and furniture design—not quite for the same reasons or following the same route, but none the less the result was a flood of designs wholly lacking in honesty of purpose or of function which deliberately disregarded the nature of materials and paid scant attention to the convenience or comfort of the user.

The flippant and irresponsible use of important technical innovations debased late nineteenth-century printing. The printing industry lost sight of its true function and allowed its compositors to manipulate words for their own and their colleagues' amusement without regard to the value of the results as communication. In the end, the word was rescued from all this gimcrackery by painters, writers, architects, and others who came to printing from outside the industry, and who, during the first half of this century, gradually eliminated vulgar affectation and restored to printing both logic and discipline.

Today we are in the throes of another technical revolution in printing. Metal is gradually being eliminated from composition. Released from its discipline the designer is free to place his lines of type at angles, and he can curve, cut, or split display lines and juxtapose one line of type closely against another or he can, if he wishes, superimpose one word upon another. This freedom from mechanical restriction provides the designer with wonderful opportunities for producing imaginative and sympathetic visual solutions and of conveying the author's message with great precision. But equally the designer can if he chooses use this new opportunity—as the late nineteenth-century compositors used theirs—not for better communication, but merely for superficial pattern making.

Unhappily, there are clear indications that both in the graphic and product design fields far too many designers are today working for the approbation of their colleagues rather than in an honest attempt to solve specific design problems to the best of their ability. They are motivated by fashion rather than conviction and they are rapidly undermining the basis and principles of twentieth-century design. Inspired by personal uncertainty, some of them are trying to turn the design process into a kind of professional mystique enclosed in a rigid yet ever-contracting circle which excludes all true creative activity. But the designer needs to have a heart as well as a head and his head should contain more than just a pair of eyes.

Just as I do not believe the honest designer can or should, or ever wants to, shed sound traditions nor do I think he ought ever willingly to embrace sterile or artificial conventions—not even newly created ones.

This, then, is the heart of the design profession's present dilemma. There are at present too many 'designer's designers' at work with the result that the public is in many cases being starved of the sound and aesthetically satisfying products to which it is entitled. This is a condition which can ultimately be cured only by design education of adequate breadth and vitality.

It is, of course, the principal aim of the new diploma courses which recently began in selected art schools in Britain to ensure that designers should in future be *educated* and not merely trained.

The men who emerge from these courses and others like them elsewhere during the late 'sixties will be well equipped to tackle many of the vital and fundamental tasks at which society and the design profession have so far barely begun to nibble.

Now is the time, therefore, for designers and their professional associations to examine the opportunities and obligations that lie ahead. As design has progressed from an amateur to a professional activity the jobs and the opportunities have grown larger, too. Most established designers now spend a substantial part of their time working not on single commissions, but on designs which relate to a corporate design policy or house style. The advantages of this situation are obvious. These larger exercises provide a sounder basis on which to conduct a design practice and, especially important, they allow time to be spent on research and experiment and investigation in a way that the single commission does not. Out of some of the largest schemes of this kind, promoted for quite legitimate commercial ends, much useful design knowledge and data have been established.

But the designers' contribution should be not only to the economy but also more directly to the health and happiness of our society.

There is, for example, remarkably little research being carried out into the practical and psychological aspects of lettering, or color, or pattern. The little that is being done is generally conducted by scientists without the participation of designers and the naiveté of their conclusions on matters of design often deprives the results of any practical value.

Tens of thousands of men, women, and children are killed or injured on the roads of Europe every year. Many of those who lose their lives or limbs are the victims of clumsy and inadequate signposting devised by engineers and civil servants. Of course these officials and engineers do their best but they fail because they try to solve unaided problems that are beyond their knowledge and experience.

Let us take just one example: in Britain and in many other countries pedestrians are encouraged to cross roads at places marked with white stripes. Indeed, in theory, the pedestrian has right-of-way on these 'zebra' crossings. But it is quite apparent that from a psychological point of view the stripes run the wrong way. Because they run in the direction of the traffic flow, they encourage the motorist to advance and act as a visual barrier to the pedestrian.

There are at least 10 million blind people in the world. Most of them live on charity of one kind or another—direct or disguised. Some of them are helped to lead useful, well-integrated lives through learning to read by touch and to operate machines, or carry out handicrafts. But there are thousands of ways in which trained designers by devising new and ingenious equipment and techniques could expedite the process by which these and other handicapped people are helped to fill a useful place in society. Many of the articles made by handicapped people could be better designed both in relation to the market and the abilities of those who produce them.

The elimination of illiteracy throughout the world is one of the greatest and most compelling needs of this century. How many designers are there, I wonder, actively engaged in this battle, in Africa, Asia, and South America. Teachers, missionaries, and Government officials spend years working out methods that would be obvious to a trained designer in thirty minutes, and other, original techniques lie wholly unexploited. Each year in Africa far more money is paid to artists and designers to boost the sales of Coca-Cola than is spent on designing and devising the weapons that will defeat illiteracy.

These are just a few of the tasks now facing society in which the design profession could make a vital contribution.

I am not suggesting that designers should embark on a mammoth campaign of charity. What I am saying is that in solving many of the real and exciting problems posed by twentieth-century society the designer—just as much as the scientist, the engineer, the doctor, or the teacher—has an important part to play. Designers should not quietly sit in the wings waiting to be asked to take the stage. *Somebody* should do something about it. And, as members of society, designers I suggest should now actively campaign for recognition of the role they ought to play. After all, nobody knows better than they do what as a profession they have to offer.

First published in The Penrose Annual *57 (London: 1964).*

1965
EDUCATION FOR VISUAL DESIGN
Gui Bonsiepe

THE HOCHSCHULE FÜR GESTALTUNG *in Ulm, Germany (1951–1968) was the first institution to make a significant attempt to develop a theory of design in the postwar years. Under its second director, Tomás Maldonado, and his colleague, design theorist Gui Bonsiepe (b. 1934), Ulm placed particular emphasis on the exploration of design's relationship with technology and science. In April and May 1964, Rudolf de Harak and the American Institute of Graphic Arts organized a series of five lectures with the title "Toward New Commitments and Disciplines in Design, Painting, and Art Education," and Bonsiepe's paper was later published, slightly abridged, in* Ulm, *the school's intellectually ambitious journal. Bonsiepe draws a fundamental distinction between the role of the designer, who attempts to improve the human environment, and the artist, who demonstrates the world's effect on the individual. He goes on to argue the limitations of the emergent view of advertising as "information" and suggests that commercial needs should be regarded as just one facet of design's responsibility to the society whose attitudes its messages both manipulate and shape.—RP*

RESERVATION AGAINST PROGRAMS

Education for visual design—these words could announce a manifesto. They could nourish the expectation that a program is presented here. But that is not my intention. We have become reserved in regard to programs, probably for the reason that our social environment is not conducive to the candor necessary to formulate and to present programs. My aim is more modest. I shall try to show some ways that might lead to a philosophy of visual design including education.

ALL-EMBRACING DESIGN

Using hitherto the term 'design' without specification, that is talking neither about architectural design, nor visual design nor product design, I am aware of the fact that this vague and undefined term could foster false ideas. 'Design' embraces a large variety of human activities. Its range reaches from the design of a wall carpet, to the design of an exhibition and ends in the most recent variant of design: the weapon and defense systems. In the course of my talk I will limit the often too loosely used term 'design.' Especially, I shall try to describe the content of the term 'visual design.'

ON THE HISTORY OF DESIGN

The history of design started officially in 1919 when Walter Gropius opened the Bauhaus. What was new and specific on this nowadays already legendary school was the fact that for the first time the total human environment was regarded as an object of design. For the first time the broad task was formulated that a human environment based on modern technology and industry has to be humanized. The impulses of the

Bauhaus people were directed towards improving the environment through the use of technology. The program of the Bauhaus contained political-social traits.

Of course the Bauhaus did not start from zero. The origins of the philosophy of the Bauhaus date back to the mid-nineteenth century.

AESTHETICS AND SOCIETY

It was Ruskin who terrified by the devastating aesthetic and social consequences of industrialization stated about 100 years ago: "Life without industry is guilt, and industry without art is brutality." But it was not only the aesthetic abhorrence of the rampant expansion of the world of machines which caused Ruskin to search for precautions against and remedies for the barbarian technique. Rather he felt that the aesthetic misery was an expression of the social misery. By improving the world aesthetically he hoped to improve the societal world. Ruskin might well have said that the human rights also include the right of a human environment, of an ordered and functioning environment.

A cynic today could easily renounce such ideas as naïve and false ideology. We should, however, not forget that the anchoring of aesthetics in society kept it from shriveling to an element of abstract anemic beautification or commercial exploitation as in styling.

THE CONSEQUENCES OF THE BAUHAUS

The basic course has proved to be the core of the Bauhaus concept. All the various art movements of the twenties have contributed to put a mark on this basic course, which are the German expressionism, the Russian constructivism and the Dutch Stijl. Only the French surrealism left at first sight no clearly visible traces if you disregard for a moment the photomontages of Moholy-Nagy. But to clarify this problem a more profound historical research is needed. It is difficult to evaluate exactly the extent of the Bauhaus influence on the whole art and design education. Although we still lack a historical study on these ramifications we might be justified in saying that there is hardly any art school which has not incorporated the basic course be it modified or not.

COMMUNICATION INDUSTRY

The Ulm School has conceived a program for visual design which not only differs from similar attempts of the Bauhaus but also is essentially new. The Bauhaus is not to be blamed for this, because the historical conditions simply did not allow it. The industry which we denote today by the term 'communication industry'—this is film, television, broadcasting, and mass printing—began to establish itself during the twenties respectively after the Bauhaus had been closed. And it is exactly in communication industry where dramas and farces of the communicative life take place today. Furthermore, the transition from an economy of scarcity to an economy of abundance placed advertising as a new institution of social control into the center of visual design. These changes in technology and economy prohibit the transplanting of the Bauhaus *en bloc*. But the new parts of the program of the Ulm School are not the cause for the reservations with which other schools of design regard Ulm. Causes for tensions and animosity are provided by the fact that the Ulm School gives greater attention to the question how design is related to science, than to the question how design is related to the arts.

DESIGN BETWEEN ART AND SCIENCE

Design is a newcomer, which does not fit into the scheme of traditional institutions. The right of autonomy, however, is not acknowledged and even refused by the representatives of the arts on the one hand, and by the representatives of the applied sciences on the other hand. The profession of the designer—hardly more than one generation old—has to defend itself continuously against usurpation tendencies from both. The beaux-arts-traditionalists take design as nothing more than a variant of art activity, overmore of a mediocre art activity because design is technologically infected. Product design appears to them as a continuation of sculpture with different means, and visual design as a subcategory of painting and graphics. The futuristic scientists now try to explain design as a phenomenon, the existence of which we have to attribute to the failure of an older profession, for instance engineering, and which therefore has to be brought back to its proper place. In both cases the autonomy of design is denied. But design cannot be reduced to either art or science. He who uses design primarily as a vehicle of self-expression the cool rationality—or what is believed to be the cool rationality of the Ulm School causes some uneasiness. For the high priest of relentless scientific method on the other side the Ulm School is not scientific enough, too much inclining to the intuitive side and too interwoven with some strange ideals. Thus the Ulm School moves in twilight. It stands between those who want to make out of design an art and those who want to make out of design a science.

ART AS UNPLANABLE INSTITUTION

The habit of the beaux-arts-traditionalists to classify design under the arts has now caused a paradoxical reaction in the field of design itself: the real art works of the 20th century—according to this opinion—are the design works; the previous art in form of painting and sculpture will be succeeded by the posters, packaging, trademarks, products, and machines; the scenery of the profane ordinary day will take the place of the elevated exception. Here, the essential difference between art and design is not recognized which does not exclude that between both areas of human activity fruitful relationships can exist. Art is one of the very few zones in which the individual is protected against the collision with the oppressive forces and in which the individual can hold open his horizon of experience. Since art emancipated itself—this process runs parallel to the process of industrialization—it is affected with doubts and exposed to insecurity. It resists the principle of administration which seems to be *the* principle of industrial society. One cannot plan art as one can plan the construction of Boulder dams. Art cannot be justified, cannot be derived from some functional scheme. Art and philosophy still permit the luxury of negation.

Baudelaire for instance insisted on the right of saying 'no' in an exemplary manner writing in his variations of the introduction to the 'Flowers of Evil': "it is not for my women, nor for my sisters, nor for my daughters that I have written these lines; nor for the women of my neighbor, nor for his sisters nor for his daughters. I leave this to those who have an interest in confusing the good intentions with the passion for the beautiful language." This negation contains more truth than any radiant positivity. The artist interprets. The designer does not interpret. The designer directs his efforts toward the immediate improvement of the human environment. The artist shows how this world afflicts the individual. Hitherto art was the archetypical area of aesthetic experience. This may have furnished the reason for the fact that design at first was regarded an art activity, because design too was involved in aesthetics. But it is misleading to force the aesthetics of art onto the aesthetics of design.

THE MEANING OF 'DESIGN'

At the beginning of my talk I emphasized the necessity of giving to the concept of design a precise meaning. This can be achieved by cutting off.

First I want to exclude from the activity of the designer the planning of weapon and defense systems. For from its beginnings the philosophy of design interpreted design as a design for living, less than for surviving and destruction. To the question: What has the designer to do with space rockets? there is today only one answer: nothing.

Secondly, I want to separate within the fields of design those sectors which remain under the influence of an arts and crafts tradition. Concerning visual design, these sectors are: calligraphy, the typography of the precious single book, woodcutting, etching, engraving, and illustration. In Ulm we have decidedly not introduced these design activities in our curriculum; first, there are already many schools offering an education in the mentioned fields; secondly, we want to concentrate our energies on the modern communication media and techniques, for which the term 'visual communication' has become customary.

PERSUASIVE AND NONPERSUASIVE COMMUNICATION

As Tomás Maldenado said in a seminar on the occasion of the World Design Conference in Tokyo 1960—we tend to equate visual communication with advertising. But there is a form of communication in which the problem is not to persuade consumers to buy this or that soap, or to elect this or that candidate. Without doubt, persuasive communication has the leading parts, and in such a manner that a few years ago there arose an increasing critique.

The reaction of the public mind against the oversupply of advertising messages could of course not wholeheartedly be welcomed by those which use advertising and which finance it. There was no lack of defenders of advertising. Apologies for and critiques of advertising disclose some antagonisms of our society. Most frequently advertising is criticized on the basis of economic considerations. Not only social critics are alarmed that the United States invest half as much money in advertising as in education of the whole nation (in 1963 about $12.5 billion). This doubt of the social function of design is disguised in economical terms. The apologists of advertising now argue that it does a considerable and important service to the whole society and economy. Broad layers of the population are informed by advertising about merchandises and services which otherwise they would never know of.

INFORMATION AND ADVERTISING

The conspicuously neutral concept of 'information' shall not seduce us to take the half truth for the whole truth. Nobody will deny that advertising gives information. This statement, however, does not tell us anything about the quality and societal necessity of these informations. Nobody will deny that advertising is an indispensable institution within a specific market system. But nobody can deny that advertising aims at influencing the preference behavior of consumers. In other words: advertising is willy-nilly chained to economical powers which can afford to enter at all the stages of the communication media, let alone the role they will play after that.

He who praises the educational and information giving role of advertising easily overlooks the fact that there are essential differences between education through an institution as school and education through an institution as advertising. Advertising as information does not make use of information in the way education does, or should do. For to persuade somebody, to manipulate somebody is anything else than making him an emancipated person. I do not intend to force reality into a rigid alternative.

The question is not about persuading, or not persuading, about influencing or not influencing, but about the intentions standing behind it.

THE TRIVIALITY OF COMMUNICATIVE LIFE

The visual designer is submitted to the drifts of antagonistic interests. Standing on an exposed spot he often serves as the scapegoat for all communicative evils. He is depicted thus as the man being the sole responsible for the triviality and vulgarity of the communicative life of the society. Although this global accusation simplifies the matters a great deal the reproaches of the visual designer to lend his aid to the spread of collective trance rather than for subjective humanization are not completely unfounded. Furthermore, it requires a sound quantity of naiveté or cynicism in order to identify oneself with a form of communication which consumes itself in the continuous praise of the qualities of laundry machines, cake-mixes, deodorants, detergents, painrelievers, charcoal filter cigarettes, hair dyes and rejuvenating face creams. No question, the spectrum of advertising is richer. But a philosophy of education cannot close its eyes in front of the extremes. On the contrary, it must face the uncomfortable and contradictory facts without, however, succumbing to these facts and without becoming an advocate of these facts.

CULTURAL TOTALITARISM

The statement: "Business is business, and nothing else" repels under the mask of alert aggressiveness the modest doubt whether this statement really covers the whole truth. An education for design should turn the student's mind to his social responsibility and make him immune against temptations to regard the production and distribution of goods and services exclusively as a matter of business. The visual designer is responsible for the visual culture of a society in which society business is but one facet and not—as it is often tempted to claim—the whole.

That the interests of business do not always coincide with the interests of society is a recognition nobody can avoid when working together with communication industry. Communication industry shapes the conscious—and the unconscious mind of the members of a society. It canalizes, it controls, and it manipulates. It enjoys much more power—and has therefore much more responsibility—than is generally known and that those people who use this industry for their purpose are ready to admit.

VISUAL DESIGN AND SALES PROMOTION

Some years ago the general public having hitherto rather nebulous ideas about the connections between power and communication was irritated by a series of publications. When there had existed a subliminal mistrust against the procedures and interests of communication industry the vague assumptions suddenly seemed to crystallize into an insight by using the really not flattering term 'the hidden persuaders.' Form and content of informations and in addition the intentional backing them turn to virulent problems in the work of the visual designer. Education has to prepare him not to accept carelessly the role offered to him in which he is abused for the relentless acceleration of the turnover of merchandise.

AREAS OF VISUAL COMMUNICATION

So far the notes on persuasive communication, its counterpart, non-persuasive communication is an almost untouched region. The world of sign-systems for traffic and displays on machines, the world of communication for educational purposes, the world of visual representation of scientific facts offer rich opportunities and challenges to the visual designer. Here, communication is not primarily economically motivated as in persuasive communication with its advertisements, billboards end TV spots.

In Ulm we could enter this new field of activity without difficulties because we follow the principle to educate a generalist rather than a specialist. We do not train a specialized typographer, packaging designer or photographer, but a visual designer having at his hand enough basic knowledge to adapt himself after graduation to certain areas and specialize himself when necessary.

First published in Ulm *no. 13/14 (March 1965).*

1965
VISUAL/VERBAL RHETORIC
Gui Bonsiepe

GUI BONSIEPE *(b. 1934) and Tomás Maldonado were among the first to attempt to apply ideas drawn from semantics to design. In a seminar on semiotics at the Hochschule für Gestaltung in Ulm, in 1956, Maldonado proposed modernizing rhetoric, the classical art of persuasion. Bonsiepe and Maldonado went on to write a number of articles on semiotics and rhetoric for the English publication* Uppercase *and the journal* Ulm *that were to prove an important resource for designers investigating this area. In his paper on visual and verbal rhetoric, first presented to the Arbeitsgruppe für Grafik Wirtschaft (Working Group for Graphic Design and Industry) in Stuttgart, in March 1965, Bonsiepe suggested the need for a modern system of rhetoric, updated by semiotic theory, as a tool for describing and analyzing the phenomena of advertising. Using this daunting but precise terminology the "persuasive structure" of an advertising message could be exposed. "Information without rhetoric," he concluded, "is a pipe-dream." The act of designing to communicate must inevitably bring rhetorical devices into play and the notion of impartial objectivity is consequently a myth. In a later version of his essay, published for American readers, in* Dot Zero *in 1966, Bonsiepe took the opportunity to revise and sharpen his text.—RP*

Rhetoric has fallen not so much into disrepute as into virtual oblivion. It has come down to us from ancient times with an aura of antiquity about it that makes it seem, at first sight, unsuited to handling the messages of the advertiser, which is the rhetoric of the modern age. Yet it can be shown that a modern system of rhetoric might be a useful descriptive and analytical tool for dealing with the phenomena of advertising. To explain how is the aim of this article.

The ancient Greeks divided rhetoric (the art of eloquence) into three parts: the political, the legal, and the religious. It was primarily the politicians, lawyers, and priests who were adepts in rhetoric, since it was their business to use speech to work on their public. Their object was to obtain a definite decision (on a campaign of war); to implant an opinion (concerning the prisoner at the bar); or to evoke a mood (in a religious ceremony). The domain of rhetoric is the domain of logomachy, the war of words.

Rhetoric divides into two kinds: one is concerned with the use of persuasive means (rhetorica utens) and the other with description and analysis (rhetorica docens). Practice and theory are closely linked in rhetoric. It is generally defined as the art of persuasion, or the study of the means of persuasion. The aim of rhetoric is primarily to shape opinions, to determine the attitude of other people, or to influence their actions. Where force rules, there is no need of rhetoric. As Burke says (in "A Rhetoric of Motives," New York, 1955), "It is directed to a man only in so far as he is *free*. . . . Insofar as he *must* do something, rhetoric is superfluous."

These conditions of choice are fulfilled by the situation on a competitive market where various wares come together. The consumer is given a wide range of choice among goods and services, and it becomes desirable to influence him in the selection he makes. This is the function of advertising. And so a new partner joins the classical triad of politics, justice, and religion in the domain of rhetoric; and that is marketing.

Of the listing of rhetorical processes there is no end. Shades of meaning have been set down with precision. Textbooks of rhetoric (and they are still textbooks of classical rhetoric) are as notable for their abundance of fine-spun distinctions as for their uncritical acceptance of traditional classifications. A terminology suited to Latin and Greek makes it difficult to use these concepts; rhetoric is weighed down by more than two thousand years of ballast. The time has come to bring it up to date with the aid of semiotics (a general theory of signs and symbols). For, apart from inconsistencies in the concepts it uses, classical rhetoric (which deals purely with language) is no longer adequate for describing and analyzing rhetorical phenomena in which verbal *and visual* signs, i.e., word and picture, are allied. Here the practice of rhetoric has far outrun its theory.

If one thinks of the unending spate of posters, advertisements, films, and television spots turned out by an industrial society with all the facilities of the communications industry at its command, and compares it with the very sporadic efforts made to throw light on the rhetorical aspects of this information, the discrepancy stares one in the face.

The five main sections of classical rhetoric can be reduced to only one useful for the analysis of advertising information: the third, covering the linguistic and stylistic formulation of the material. The rules for collecting, arranging, memorizing, and speaking, can be largely ignored. The stylistic aspects of rhetoric appear primarily as rhetorical figures, which can be defined (after Quintilian) as "the art of saying something in a new form" or (after Burke) as "changing the meaning or application of words in order to give the speech greater suavity, vitality and impact." According to classical theory, the essence of a rhetorical figure consists in a departure from normal speech usage, for the purpose of making the message more effective.

These figures fall into two classes: (1) word figures, which work with the meaning of words or the position of words in the sentence; and (2) idea figures, which work with the shaping and organization of information. The terminology of semiotics makes it easier to sort out these figures. Starting from the fact that there are two aspects to every sign, namely its shape and its meaning, we arrive at two basic types of rhetorical figure; for such a figure can operate through the shape of the sign or through its meaning. If we consider the shape, we are in the dimension of syntax. If we consider the meaning—or relata, to use the semiotic term—we are in the dimension of semantics. (Relatum is a term embracing everything a sign stands for; its subclasses are the things designated, the things denoted, and the things signified. The technical words for these are designata, denotata, and significata.) Using this classification, it follows that the two classes of rhetorical figure are the syntactic and the semantic. A figure is syntactic when it operates through the shape of the sign; it is semantic when it operates through the relatum (or referent). In traffic signs, we find that contours, colors and sign arrangements belong to the syntactic dimensions, and the meanings belong to the semantic.

Sifting and simplifying the ultrafine distinctions of classical rhetoric, we can catalogue the verbal rhetorical figures thus:

I. SYNTACTIC FIGURES

    A. Transpositive figures (departure from normal word order)
1. Apposition (explanatory insertions)
2. Atomization (treating dependent parts of a sentence as independent)
3. Parenthesis (enclosing one sentence in another)
4. Reversion or anastrophe (dislocation of a word for emphasis)

    B. Privative figures (omission of words)
1. Ellipsis (leaving out words which can be supplied from the context)

    C. Repetitive figures
1. Alliteration (repeating an initial letter or sound)
2. Isophony (repeating sounds of similar words, or parts of words, in a series)
3. Parallelism (repeating the same rhythm in successive clauses or sentences)
4. Repetition (repeating a word in various positions)

II. SEMANTIC FIGURES

    A. Contrary figures (based on the union of opposite relata)
1. Antithesis (confrontation in a sentence of parts having opposite meanings)
2. Exadversion (assertion by a double negative)
3. Conciliation (coupling of contradictory relata)

    B. Comparative figures (based on comparisons between the relata)
1. Gradation (words in ascending order of forcefulness)
2. Hyperbole (exaggeration)
3. Metaphor (transfer of a word to another field of application in such a way that a similarity of any kind between the two fields is assumed and given expression)
4. Understatement

    C. Substitutive figures (based on replacement of the relata)
1. Metonymy (replacement of one sign by another, the relata of both being in a real relationship)
2. Synecdoche (a special case of metonymy: replacement of one sign by another, the relata of both being in a quantitative relationship)

III. PRAGMATIC FIGURES

    A. Fictitious dialogue (speaker asks and answers himself)
    B. Direct speech
    C. Conversion of an objection into an argument in one's own favor
    D. Asteism (irrelevant replies to a question or argument)

With the aid of these definitions from the art of rhetoric, advertising copy can be analyzed and described in terms of rhetorical characteristics. In this way, its persuasive structure can be brought to light.

It is the usage among philosophers of language to contrast persuasion with information, opinion-shaping with documentation and instruction, and everyday speech with scientific language. In the eyes of orthodox representatives of a purified and unambiguous language, rhetoric is merely a handbook of verbal tricks, unworthy of the true scientist. In reply to this, the champions of rhetoric argue that the systematic ambiguity of linguistic signs is an inevitable consequence of the power of language, and is an indispensable part of the means of human communication. In thrashing out the theoretical question whether there can or cannot be any communication without rhetoric, the arguments seem to favor the latter alternative. The only examples of simple, dehydrated information, innocent of all taint of rhetoric, that come readily to hand are such things as logarithm tables, timetables, and telephone books. Fortunately communication is not limited to this; informative assertions are interlarded with rhetoric to a greater or lesser degree. If they were not, communication would die of sheer inanition.

"Pure" information exists for the designer only in arid abstraction. As soon as he begins to give it concrete shape, the process of rhetorical infiltration begins. It would seem that many designers—blinded by their effort to impart objective information (whatever that may mean)—simply will not face this fact. They cannot reconcile themselves to the idea that advertising is *addressed* information, and that its informative content is often secondary if it plays any role at all.

It is hard not to feel a little sympathy for this view, mistaken though it may be. It is the expression of a certain unease, a dissatisfaction with the role of the visual designer, felt in our competitive society, where his abilities are often wasted on the mere representation of the imaginary qualities of goods and services. And this representation often strikes a grandiloquent note in blatant contrast to the triviality and banality of the product offered. The prescribed, euphoric superlative is humbug. It is just as much humbug as "objective" information in advertising which is ashamed of its promotional purpose and tries to dissemble itself.

Once the point is yielded that there are various grades of rhetorical infiltration, then the question arises how these different grades can be assessed in terms of quantity. Mensuration and numerical data are the order of the day. They parade as the proud achievements of science. Despite a certain suspicion of figure-fetishism, which will accept new knowledge on the sole condition that it is in numerical terms, we can sketch out a simple possibility for measuring the rhetorical content of a text. In measurements one must keep to the ascertainable. And what is ascertainable in a text is the number of rhetorical figures of various kinds that it contains. The ratio of rhetorical figures to normal sentences in advertising copy is an index of its persuasiveness. If ten rhetorical figures and five normal sentences appear in a text, it may be said to have a persuasion grade of 2. What persuasion is, is not specified. It is not even defined. All that is given is the data needed to measure what is called persuasiveness.

Verbal rhetoric paves the way to visual rhetoric. As we said before, classical rhetoric was confined to language. But most posters, advertisements, films, and television spots contain linguistic and nonlinguistic signs side by side, and these signs are not independent, but interact closely. So it makes good sense to ask about typical picture/word combinations, typical sign relations, and visual/verbal rhetorical figures.

Visual rhetoric is still virgin territory. In what follows we shall make some tentative efforts to explore this new country. Our discussion is based mainly on interpretations of the analysis of a series of advertisements.

Taking the conclusions of verbal rhetoric as a guide, we dissected out figures having exclusive reference to the interplay of word and picture. The terms of verbal rhetoric were used to designate the concepts of this new rhetoric. New concepts were introduced where necessary. In this first approach, the visual/verbal figures were simply noted. The work of classifying and systematizing them still remains to be done.

To define a visual/verbal figure, it is no longer enough to apply the criterion of the "departure from normal usage" as in verbal figures; for it cannot be established what relations between verbal and visual signs form the standard from which one can depart. It would, therefore, seem more appropriate for purposes of definition to fall back upon the possible interactions already inherent in the signs. Thus a visual/verbal rhetorical figure is a combination of two types of sign whose effectiveness in communication depends on the tension between their semantic characteristics. The signs no longer simply add up, but rather operate in cumulative reciprocal relations.

[Captions to original illustrations follow. Due to the poor quality of the illustrations, they are not reproduced here.]

VISUAL/VERBAL COMPARISON

A comparison that starts with verbal signs and is continued with visual signs.

Advertisement: Young & Rubicam
The "sharp ideas" expressed verbally are represented by the sharpened pencil. The sameness of the advertisements from which an effective advertisement stands out is illustrated by the uniform row of unsharpened (= ineffective) pencils.

VISUAL/VERBAL ANALOGY

A relatum expressed verbally is paralleled by a similar relatum expressed visually.

Advertisement: Esso
"Refuel anywhere." The refueling of cars is illustrated by the analogy of the feeding hummingbird.

VISUAL/VERBAL METONYMY

A relatum indicated by verbal signs is visualized by signs in a real relationship to the verbal relatum; e.g., cause instead of effect, tool instead of activity, producer instead of product.

Advertisement: Esso
"Be precise!" The imperative expressed verbally is visualized by the tool (a micrometer) for carrying it out.

VISUAL/VERBAL CHAIN

A topic begun in words and continued and completed visually.

Advertisement: Time Magazine
"Where there's smoke"

VISUAL/VERBAL NEGATION

Verbal signs negate what is shown visually.

Advertisement: Kardex
"We don't do this." The picture is canceled out by the verbal statement.

VISUAL SYNECDOCHE

A relatum expressed verbally is visualized by a part representing the whole, or vice-versa.

Advertisement: Kardex
"You find Kardex in the most unlikely places." The baby is a visual sign standing for the whole nursery, and for the whole class of "unlikely places."

VERBAL SPECIfiCATION

A visual sign accompanied by only as much text as is necessary for its comprehension.

Advertisement: Elizabeth Stewart
"Elizabeth Stewart Swimwear"

VISUAL SUBSTITUTION

One visual sign replaced by another because of its formal characteristics.

Advertisement: Univac
"Geizkragen" ("Greedy-collar" = "skinflint"). The metaphorical word is illustrated by a punch card bent to look like a collar.

SYNTACTIC CLIMAX AND ANTICLIMAX

A purely visual figure.

Advertisement: General Electric
"How to have ice cubes without ever filling a tray." The series of pictures form virtually a mirror symmetry, with the middle picture the turning point. Up to this point the photography grows closer and more detailed; from this point, it recedes again into the distance.

VISUAL/VERBAL PARALLELISM

Visual and verbal signs representing the same relatum.

Advertisement: Dow
"We make plastic packages . . ." The verbal assertion is specified by the illustration of a plastic bottle. The assertion, "We make packages by the drumful . . ." is supplemented by the parallel illustration of a drum.

VISUAL/VERBAL PARALLELISM

Visual and verbal signs representing the same relatum.

Advertisement: VW

"You never run out of air." The abundance of air suggested verbally is visualized by an inserted area of light gray."

ASSOCIATIVE MEDIATION

One verbal sign out of a series is illustrated by a series of visual signs, which lead, in
turn, to another relatum of the verbal signs.

Advertisement: Smirnoff Vodka

"Take a holiday from everyday drinks!" The verbal element of "holidays" is
singled out of the series and illustrated by means of an open porthole, sunset, and a
calm sea. Thus vodka and holidays are linked together.

First published in Ulm *no. 14/15/16 (Ulm: December 1965). This revised version was published in* Dot Zero *no. 2 (New York: 1966).*

1966
DECLINE OF THE VISUAL
Marshall McLuhan

AFTER A BRILLIANT CAREER *in the 1960s as international media guru, Marshall McLuhan (1911–1980) lost favor. Then, in the digital 1990s, a new generation of readers began to notice the exceptional clairvoyance of the Canadian professor's views on technology, media, and society in the "global village." His status as mascot to the self-styled "digerati" was confirmed when* Wired *made him its patron saint.* Understanding Media *(1964) and* The Medium Is the Massage *(1967) were reissued (the latter by* Wired*) and academic studies appeared. McLuhan's collaborations with designer Quentin Fiore were also revisited as paradigmatic attempts to challenge publishing's established hierarchy of text and image. McLuhan's article for the New York design journal* Dot Zero *(1966–1968) reprises some familiar themes—electricity as global extension of man's nervous system—while spinning off insights that make more sense now than they probably did at the time. McLuhan's claim that the electrical revolution frees the typographer to exploit letters as "abstract sculptural designs" prefigures the experimental digital typography of the 1990s. His reflections on children's desire for involvement in the text foretell the graphic attractions of Nickelodeon and* MTV.*—RP*

A t a recent Delos conference the delegates met to consider the "crisis in human settlement." One basic consideration was that in the next forty or fifty years there will be more buildings erected in the world than in the previous six thousand years. At the present rate of building, each year sees more space enclosed than the previous forty or fifty years. What eludes the understanding of the architects and planners is that these rates of change and growth are even greater in other areas of human activity. While they worry about a population "explosion," electricity has imploded, or contracted, the world to the dimensions of a village.

One thing is clear to the builders and town planners. Enormous increase in the speed and volume of building requires a totally new approach to the problems of design. A jet crew has to use different resources of perception from a pedestrian. But the very speed that calls for advanced awareness and extended perceptions also makes possible the recognition of patterns that are not accessible to those moving at lower rates. At 12,000 feet the earth is still like representational painting. At 35,000 feet it begins to acquire abstract design. As the visual component is lowered, the tactile and kinesthetic components increase. Sheer design emerges as supreme. As change becomes our only constant, speed becomes a gyroscopic factor of stability in our world. And like the jet pilot, our entire society today lives by instrumentation, not by the unaided human senses.

With electricity, man extended his nervous system globally. Earlier extensions or technologies were fragmentary extensions of the body. Clothing extends the skin, the wheel the feet, script the eye. Thus the centuries of gradual mechanization by fragmentary extension have been reversed in a rush by the integral circuitry of the electric extensions of our system. With such electric circuitry we move swiftly out of the world of the wheel and of classified data into a world of pattern recognition. The learning process itself can move from the phase of the acquisition of data to the plane of discovery.

Instant communication insures that all factors of the environment and of experience shall coexist in a state of active interplay. It is interplay that yields an awareness of form and design, whereas at lower rates of movement one is left with facets and points of view. It is no paradox that pattern or design does not flourish in highly visual or highly literate cultures. Industrial societies push the visual sense into isolation because the fragmentation and analysis of the processes subjected to mechanization are managed by visual means. It is the visual power to isolate and arrest aspects of functions (a power not shared by the other senses) that is so indispensable to the mechanizing processes. And in this isolation design suffers. But with the electric extension of the nerves and of "feedback" the visual sense comes back into relation with the other senses, particularly with the sense of active touch. For the electrical is not mechanical or fragmentary but integrally "looped."

With television in particular there seems to occur an extension of the sense of active exploratory touch (which involves all the senses simultaneously) rather than of sight alone. But in all electric phenomena the visual is only one component in a complex interplay. And since in the Age of Information most transactions are managed electrically, the electric technology has meant for Western man a considerable drop in the visual component in his experience, and a corresponding increase in the activity of his other senses. Indeed, with the advent of electric technology we have entered a relatively dim, unconscious world in which the extension of everybody's nerves has involved him deeply in all other lives. And while this has threatened the sense of identity of many people, it has heightened our general awareness of the shape and meaning of lives and events to a level of extreme sensitivity.

In his new book, *The Beginnings of Architecture*, Siegfried Giedion cites several times the evidence that prior to script there is no architecture in any culture. With script comes the amplifying of the role of purely visual values and a diminishing of the audio-tactile complex. With script the vertical-horizontal planes can separate from the depth involvement of kinetic stress, and from touch and sound. The visual sense alone offers the uniformity, continuity, and connectedness needed in "rational" or visual organization of experience. Touch, sound, and the rest have neither the uniformity nor the connectedness needed for the architectural "enclosure" of space. But preliterate men have an unrivaled feeling for the unique life of forms, which visual man by his nature tends to reduce and enclose in uniform and continuous space. Writing itself is such a reduction of the complex sensory modes of words into a single visual mode. And now in the electric age when all sensory modes are simultaneously accessible, the tyranny of typography, which imposes its monotonous regime on all aspects of life and perception, can no longer be sustained. Yet the typographer can reap some advantage from the electrical revolution. For the first time, he is free to exploit letters as abstract sculptural designs.

I am suggesting that in the electric age men are able for the first time to perceive how their own sensory typologies, psychically and socially, have assumed their present patterns. And, furthermore, they are free for the first time to restructure the typical sensory ratios that their cultures happen to have imposed upon them. We have already become aware of the role of art as a kind of CARE package dispatched to undernourished areas of the sensorium. We now become aware of the possibility of arranging the entire human environment as a work of art designed to maximize perception and to make everyday learning a process of discovery. Town planners are applying the Montessori method to ordinary living. And, reciprocally, as we move into the new age of architectural planning for the inclusive needs of a community of continuous learning, design becomes as necessary to the educator as to the engineer. The age-old gaps between art and commerce are closing as fast as those between education and government.

With the electric extension of the nervous system men have not only become involved with one another in depth, they have had to shift their stress of attention from action to reaction. It is now necessary to know in advance the consequences of any policy or action, since the results of such policy and action are experienced without delay. This was not necessary in the former fragmented and mechanical age, when the consequences of actions were delayed. One could wait and see. At electric speed no wait is possible. The most luminous and harmonious designs, involving all factors and all senses at once, now become mandatory for the most ordinary situations. Thus the typographer, for example, is confronted with the need to devise types that can recapture the senses of children in the age of television. Types acceptable to the pre-TV child are of no relevance to the TV child with his myopic demand for involvement in the text.

Another way in which to describe the revolution of our senses in the electric Age of Information is to cite the fact that at the graduate levels of study our universities, which were in the Mechanical Age places for processing a few young people, have today become organs of perception for the entire society. The subject of their studies has widened to include all of society (for example, statistical means of audience research), and the results of their studies (from the predictions of the weatherman to the instruments for perceiving the structure of matter) more directly serve the whole society.

With this change of role of the university there has come a corresponding need to redesign every feature of the campus and the curriculum alike. It is a situation not unrelated to the one cited at the beginning of these observations. The new cities are no longer to be mere enclosures to house or contain populations of fragmented interests. They need to become immediate means of enhanced perception and enriched association.

First published in Dot Zero *no. 1 (New York: 1966).*

1967
TYPOGRAPHY IS A GRID
Anthony Froshaug

IN BRITAIN, ANTHONY FROSHAUG (1920–1984) was among the earliest to take up the New Typography of Jan Tschichold and others, making him a key figure in postwar British communication design. He set up his own printing press, which allowed him to pursue his mathematically precise typographic investigations with a control that could not be achieved within the framework of commercial printing. As a teacher at the Central School of Arts and Crafts, and later at the Royal College of Art, London, he exerted a lasting influence on a generation of British graphic designers. Resolutely uncommercial in his outlook, he was also, from 1957 to 1961, professor in graphic design and visual communication at the Hochschule für Gestaltung in Ulm. Froshaug wrote regularly, often to take issue, and this article was a response to a doctrinaire Tschicholdian exposition of the grid's usefulness by Design *magazine art editor Brian Grimbly in an earlier issue of the* Designer. *Froshaug's minute focus on the particularities of his typographic material (as well as something of his often difficult demeanor) can be seen in his decidedly non-doctrinaire meditations on the grid structures that he suggests are implicit in the word typography itself.—RP*

To mention both typographic, and, in the same breath/sentence, grids, is strictly tautologous. The word typography means to write/print using standard elements; to use standard elements implies some modular relationship between such elements; since such relationship is two-dimensional, it implies the determination of dimensions which are both horizontal and vertical.

Consider the problems which faced Gutenberg, some five hundred years ago, in helping 'the eternal God' to bring 'into existence the laudable art, by which men now print books, and multiply them so greatly. . . .'[1] Item, the said Johann Gutenberg knew of the invention of paper (which had reached Cologne by 1320); item, knew of the development of suitable inks . . . of the general features of the cloth- and wine-press, of the arts of the engravers, of the die- and punch-making of the goldsmiths (after all, he was a goldsmith himself).[2] What did Gutenberg invent?

In order that letters, characters, may be arranged in lines, line upon line, for printing, each letter must be of the same depth or body-size as its neighbors, irrespective of its individual width: the vertical dimension (y in Cartesian coordinates) is critical. If, as seems historically probable, Gutenberg's invention was that of the adjustable type-mould, tolerant of characters of differing widths, intolerant of divergence in body-size,[3] this invention acted as a vertical grid upon the setting, the forme, the page.

But the length of line, the width of setting, provided another

Die unregelmäfsigkeit diefes fatzes wird durch die typen der buchftaben a und e verurfacht; fie find zwar gröfser als die anderen lettern, bei genauer mefsung aber doch nur um dreizehn taufendteile eines zolls. Diefer verfchwindend kleine unterfchied wiederholt und vergröfsert fich mit jeder zeile, bis die zufammenhang der wörter und linien zum teil zerftört wird Wenn das gröfsere a und e noch zu einem dutzend linien verwendet werden follte, fo wäre der lefer gar nicht mer im ftande den fatz zu lefen.

dimension. It seems that this horizontal dimension (x) of the grid was determined by convention, and embodied in the Procrustean bed of the composing stick—probably at that time, as more lately in the case of 13-pica fixed newspaper sticks, an unadjustable hod into which the standard bricks of characters could be successively piled.

Of course, the fixing of a horizontal dimension or 'measure' demands conventions of variable spacing between words,[4] or of abbreviation of the words themselves,[5] if all the characters align at left, where the line begins, and are to end as lead-soldiers dressed by the right. The multifarious grids used by the scribes were directly translated into the techniques of metal setting. The scribes had long explored the two-dimensional axes, long before Gutenberg, long before Descartes described them as constraints.

This account restricts itself to those who used the Latin alphabet, who read from left to right; but only so far as concerns continuous narrative text. Quite early on, even in the days of incunabula, not only letters but other characters, for example numerals, needed setting—and in the attempt of mathematical conventions to show the sequence of a proof, equalities and tabulations were aligned, each below its antecedent step: centering a new implicit axis on the page.[6]

So during centuries: for the first ninety years of typographic printing saw the exploration and development of justified and unjustified setting, of italic, of new letters (*J* and *U* surviving; some, like the omega, left at last), of punctuation marks. After 1530, though, interest shifted toward experiment in letter-design and, later, mechanical improvement.

All later work, until the demands of writers such as Blake or Mallarmé[7] disrupted the conventions, considered the typographic grid unalterable. And even with the poets, their understanding of typography was such that they hardly considered the presentation of their personal desires a challenge to the grid.

And here's a sadness. Typography, as taught in schools of art, and captioned in the illustrated books, is mostly but a word delimiting a field of art-/craft-history; books of types, of typographic ornaments and rules, of title pages (fewer books of double-page spreads), sit on their shelves or presses. Typography (sic) has become the study of placing letters on a field: typography, a more precise form of lettering. And lettering, calligraphy, has died some sweet Roman death or letraset itself below the ground.

It is time, after half a millennium, for the reassessment of typography.

In architecture, stones, mud, plants humbled together, were governed; labor was delegated, craftsmen worked their feeling for materials on that material, builders organized, architects, later, chiefed constructions. After the decline of architecture, all major work nowadays is done by those who dreamed of white cathedrals or had an intimate experience or interest in their material, old or new.

So in typography: the early days were seasons of experiment; experiments became conventions, conventions rules—and after that, till now, almost always a play with shapes, with paper patterns, and the extraordinary facility of mechanical contrivance, to reach an end that is rarely worth attainment.

To print the slogan 're-assess' means nothing, of itself. Qualified, defined, means *know*, means *find the nuts of 'em*. What can be done, for instance, with these standardized components?—standardized before the military uniform, in fact. Accept is obviously the answer, accept the grid which is their essence.

'grid, n, Frame of spaced parallel bars . . . network . . . gridiron . . .'[8]

Or, 'net, plexus, web, mesh, twill, skein, sleeve, felt, lace; wicker; matting; plait, trellis, wattle, lattice, grating, grille, gridiron, tracery, fretwork, filigree, reticle; tissue, netting.'[9]

Having accepted, determine the conventions. For each text to be translated into typographic terms, determine not just how the text appears, but what it means to say. Discover if there be an existing typographic language which allows this fullest meaning to be set out. If not, how must the typographic syntax semantics be so changed that this most loved and fullest meaning is set clear. (And if the text is sacred, how does that text itself alter and enrich the typographic standards?) Follow the poets: they play the 'normal' language (as much as fools or advertising agents, they base their shocks and base their basic meanings on the norm, quite often by departing from it, but always allusive to it). Look at the length of line—consider the reader; look at the type, its size, the length of line it's set to (the horizontal) or the relation of the x-height of each line to neighbor lines (the vertical). Make all mistakes that can be made, while thinking that this trial, which afterwards may prove mistaken, is worth the most serious exploration (but never make mistakes deliberately with hooded, knowing eyes). Acknowledge all constraints.

Now all this may appear to be, but is not far from grids. (Only this latter word has lately become a conscious term.) I can't imagine any early printer using just such a word; I can only imagine such a concept informing his approach. To *find* the text, to stipulate the ways in which it gets manipulated, to cohere all the mutually-destructive (as they may, at first, seem) requirements into a still center of quiet meaning: this needs a knowledge and a recognition of typography. Admit constraints: then, having admitted, fill with discovery.

First published in the Designer *no. 167 (London: January 1967).*

Notes

1. *Chronicle of Cologne,* 1499.
2. Usher, A.P.: *A History of Mechanical Inventions,* Harvard 1954. Chapter X deals with 'The Invention of Printing;' however, Chapter IV on 'The Emergence of Novelty in Thought and Action' should not be missed.
3. Illegibility resulting from the mixture of types of differing body sizes (the 'a' and 'e' are 13 thou larger than the other letters).
4. Meisner, H. and Luther, J: *Die Erfidung der Buchdruckerkunst,* Bielefeld and Leipzig 1900.
5. Cover: thin, mid, thick, en and em spaces for 5, 6, 7, 8, 9, 10, 12, 14, 18, 24, 30, 36, 42, 48 and 60 point anglo-american. The spaces printed in gray are interchangeable with 2-, 3-, and 4-pica quadrats. Froshaug, A: *Typographic Norms,* Birmingham/London 1964.
6. Word and syllable abbreviations in Gutenberg's 36-line *Bible.* Note that the hyphens override the measure.
7. Ptolemy: *Cosmographia,* Ulm 1482. Note the comparatively small size of the numerator in fractions; compare Stock Exchange fractions in financial columns for one of the alternative solutions.
8. Mallarmé, Stefan: 'Un Coup de Dés,' *Cosmopolia,* Paris 1897. Consider also the problems necessarily raised by poets in a socio-religious sense, discussed by Themerson, Stefan: *Cardinal Pölätüo,* London 1961; note also the problems of relating the manuscript to typographical constraints, discussed by the same author in a most creative article 'Idéogrammes lyriques,' *Typographical 14,* London (December) 1966.
9. *The Concise Oxford Dictionary of Current English,* Oxford 1951.
10. *Tabular Synopsis of Categories:* Class 2, Space; 2. Dimensions; 2. Linear; 219. Crossing. Roget, P.M.: *Thesaurus,* London 1852.

1967
TRADEMARK DESIGN
Jay Doblin

JAY DOBLIN'S *(1920–1989) career spanned an extraordinary range of experiences: he held key positions at both the office of Raymond Loewy and at Lippincott and Margulies before cofounding Unimark International with Ralph Eckerstrom, Bob Noorda, and Massimo Vignelli in 1965. Throughout his life, Doblin was obsessed with reconciling the traditionally intuitive character of design practice with the analytic methods associated with science and business. A dedicated teacher, from his position as chairman of the Institute of Design at the Illinois Institute of Technology he conducted a rigorous and systematic exploration of design as a quantifiable discipline, a vision that proved appealing in turn to commercial clients like Amoco and Xerox. This essay is typical Doblin, with its skepticism of standard design practice and its attempts to order previously unclassifiable design methods. It appeared in* Dot Zero, *Unimark's de facto house organ and a pioneering vehicle for design criticism (this issue was dedicated to corporate identity and featured contributions from sources as various as Reyner Banham and John Kenneth Galbraith). Nearly forgotten today,* Dot Zero *(1966–1968) was itself an extraordinary expression of Doblin's commitment to design as an intellectual enterprise.—MB*

A trademark, well used, can be an enormously valuable business asset. It well may be the most valuable property of a corporation, more than its products, machines, factories, etc. A trademark can become the rallying point around which the meaning of the whole activity can be attached. As an example, the swastika, a mark that meant good luck, became the symbol for super-patriotism or terror depending upon which side the perceiver was on. William L. Shirer in the book *The Rise and Fall of the Third Reich* outlines Hitler's role as a graphic designer: "In the summer of 1920 Hitler, the frustrated artist but now becoming the master propagandist, came up with an inspiration which can only be described as a stroke of genius. What the party lacked, he saw, was an emblem, a flag, a symbol, which would express what the new organization stood for and appeal to the imagination of the masses, who as Hitler reasoned, must have some striking banner to follow and to fight under. After much thought and innumerable attempts at various designs he hit upon a flag with a red background and in the middle a white disk on which was imprinted a black swastika. The hooked cross—the hakenkreuz—of the swastika, borrowed though it was from more ancient times, was to become a mighty and frightening symbol of the Nazi Party and ultimately of Nazi Germany.

"Hitler reveled in his unique creation, 'A symbol it really is!' he exclaims in *Mein Kampf.* 'In red we see the social idea of the movement, in white the nationalist idea, in the swastika the mission of the struggle for the victory of the Aryan man.'" However ugly Hitler's intentions and results were, he must be credited with being the trademark designer of the century.

A trademark is a distinctive letter, word, device, or symbol used to identify the maker or owner, usually for commercial purposes. But this simple statement does not define how a trademark operates as a communications medium. From various sources in communications theory, interesting concepts can be cited that illuminate the role of the trademark. These concepts include the grid of communications, the eight forms of symbolism, the scale of ambiguity, and the semantic differential. The Grid of Communications shows how the trademark fits into the various communication forms.

THE GRID OF COMMUNICATIONS

The means by which we communicate are supported by two types of symbols—linear sequential and presentational. Linear sequential symbols are letterforms that include verbal and numerical. Presentational symbols are visual which include models, photographs, drawings, drafting, etc. Linear sequential symbols, letters and numbers, must be read symbol after symbol and their meaning accrued together into meaning. Presentational symbols work differently. They are perceived and understood as a whole, instantly (unless presented over a time sequence as often done in an illuminated sign, for example). These symbol types—verbal, numerical, and visual—can be set in a matrix against the four ways that communications function: *identification, instruction, meaning,* and *aesthetics.*

Identification is a utility of communications using symbols to describe a person, organization, object, or idea. Names, measurements, portraits are some forms of identification.

Instruction gives directions on how to proceed. Instruction can be in the form of verbal recipes, numerical formulas, or visual arrows.

Meanings, in communication, are messages and are factually uncheckable, requiring interpretations. The words "I love you," "unlucky 13" or the tail fins on a Cadillac are all messages conveying ambiguities obscured by emotions, biases, or attitudes, and generally subjective responses beyond the utility of communications.

Aesthetics is used in communication to make messages more beautiful and expressive, both in organization and in presentation. Poetry and painting are manifestations of aesthetic symbols.

Trademarks are clearly identification symbols—usually visual or verbal, and infrequently numerical. There is some confusion between trademarks that are visual identification symbols and those which are visual instruction symbols.

Presentational instructional symbols are now an important branch of visual design, especially for interlingual use. Traffic signs, machine controls, directional instructions, etc., are more and more being symbolized visually rather than verbally. These efforts at bridging verbal language problems through visual means are fascinating. However, it seems that many of these symbols fail because the complex messages they try to communicate are more obscure as signs than as words, and are not easily susceptible to a single presentational symbol. Many of these marks become pictographs rather than symbols. Instructional signing is a separate subject from trademarking—and, although subject to many of the same design concepts, is quite a different matter. The Grid of Communications helps explain this.

EIGHT FORMS OF SYMBOLISM

These two sets of trademark symbols, brandmarks and logotypes—parallel the divisions of all symbols into presentational and linear sequential symbol types.

Trademarks can be divided into two types—logotypes, distinctively designed letterforms; and brandmarks, distinctive graphic designs.

Letterforms, one of the eight forms, comprise a large segment of trademark symbols—whether they are a single letter or number, a letterlike mark, a monogram composed of a group of letters, or a logotype.

Presentational trademark symbols are divided into six possible visual groups that include object forms, man forms, vegetable forms, animal forms, inorganic nature forms and geometric forms. Any brandmark must be one of these, or a combination of these symbols.

Color, the eighth identificational element, is usually carefully specified to support both linear sequential and presentational symbols. Color identification is used on team uniforms, gas stations, racing cars, flags, etc. Color poses many interesting problems for identification that will not be explored here.

Presentational symbols are usually very specific and inflexible in their meaning as compared to the almost infinite communications capacity of sequential symbols. The two are usually used together to support each other. This is easy to see in advertising, textbooks, drama, etc.—the words and images are used together to make a comprehensive communication. This leads directly to the first problem of brandmarks.

Left to right: 1. Letterform for Westinghouse by Paul Rand. 2. Letterform of German steelwork Friedrich Heybring by A. Stankowski. 3–8. Object form for Creative Photographers, Inc. by E. Roch, human form for CBS by W. Golden, vegetable form for Nago, organic form for Swiss packaging competition by P. Wenger, geometric form for Milan Triennale by R. Sanbonet, animal form for Carr's Department Store by L. Sutnar.

DUAL TRADEMARKING

Most texts on trademarking start by telling the reader that the trademark is the keystone element in corporate identity. But then two trademarks—a brandmark and a logotype—are designed. Brandmark design is a challenging and rewarding game to play. Every graphic designer is asked to design brandmarks. Many graphic designers do virtually nothing else. Brandmark design is getting expensive these days. There are stories going around that some of the more luminous names charge upwards of $100,000 for a brandmark. Many designers concoct a brandmark and clear out, making no use applications or plan for control. This is the medicine man selling a portion that cures everything.

But management orders, even demands, the design of a brandmark because everyone has one. This also satisfies their need for eyework and is a rallying point for morale-boosting. There seems to be a deep psychological need for a brandmark, which requires satisfaction.

After an expensive and lengthy redesign program, most companies wind up with two trademarks, a brandmark and a logotype. Most corporate identity manuals show how to use both marks properly, separately and together. Dual trademarking is a fundamental mistake for communicating brand identity. The basic premise is to have one mark that is standardized and used consistently. Two trademarks are a nuisance to live with, and any plan that includes two is probably wrong. On such items as letterheads, sheets of raw material, packages, trucks, buildings, etc., the brandmark alone is probably insufficient to identify the company property. The logotype is always placed nearby to insure recognition. Few manufacturers dare use the brandmark alone. Dual trademarking leads to unclean and garbled design.

TACHISTOSCOPIC TEST OF BORDEN'S

Borden's is a company that typically uses two well-known trademarks—"Elsie" and a red logotype. A tachistoscopic test, a speed test used in visual laboratories, was conducted using three combinations of the brandmark "Elsie," the logotype "Borden's" and the two together. Ninety respondents were shown the three marks at one-half second durations.

The Borden's logotype alone was properly recognized by 97 percent of the respondents. The daisy with "Elsie" brandmark was recognized as Borden's trademark by 74 percent of the respondents. The Borden's logotype and "Elsie" brandmark when shown together drew 87 percent correct responses. The unsurprising conclusion that must be drawn is that the logotype has the highest identification rating: the brandmark has the lowest. When the two are shown together, the added eyework limits communications by lowering the correct responses to the logotype. This seems to jibe with other psychological studies—demonstrating that correct perceptions drop as the eye is required to do more work in a limited time period. Adding brandmarks on top of logotypes may lead directly to lower levels of communication. Considering the fact that the average shopper in a supermarket must screen two to three thousand items during a fifteen minute visit means that each item gets less than half a second exposure. Why load extra messages into the perceptual apparatus, considering that there is also other information beyond brand alone to be communicated?

THE SCALE OF AMBIGUITY

The scale of ambiguity is another analysis of symbols that helps to clarify the role of trademarks in relation to all forms of communication.

This scale relates closely to Martin Krampen's "Chart of Coding Techniques" [*Dot Zero* 1].

The scale is set up as a simple inversion from real to symbolic ($R=1/S$). As *real* decreases, *symbolic* increases—and vice versa. Notice that the ascending scale does not reach the bottom at the real end. This is because there is always a contribution of the perceiver to all incoming percepts. This biasing effect occurs when reality is converted to information by the perceptual apparatus. At the symbolic end, it is possible to have a 100 percent contribution of the perceiver as in a dream, a thought, an hallucination, etc.

This scale can be arbitrarily divided into four categories.

The first category called presentational models, includes symbols that are very close to real. At the most real level, the models are three-dimensional and duplicate the real object as closely as possible. This would include prototypes of mass-manufactured products, mannequins for displaying clothes, etc. Less real models would be mockups, scale models, etc., that communicate the general appearance of reality. Further away from real, up the scale, are presentational models such as dioramas, stage sets, etc., that begin to change depth, scale, color, etc.

The second category is presentational iconographs beginning with photography or cinematography. These images are usually two dimensional and yet convey a fairly large amount of information about reality. The next step up the scale would be icons ranging from handcrafted photograph-like renderings to sketchy impressions and cartoons.

The third category of symbols is presentational schematics including graphs, mechanical drawings, oscilloscope traces, etc. These demand a greater amount of contribution on the part of the perceiver in the form of training.

The fourth category includes presentational symbols. The Japanese flag, where a red circle on a white field stands for Japan, is such an example. Failure to know that a red circle on a white field means Japan is a 100 percent loss of information. This is the weakness of presentational symbols. The contribution of the perceiver must be very large or else all form of communication is lost.

It takes a far greater contribution on the part of the perceiver to participate at the symbolism end of the scale than at the real end. Models are relatively easy to understand, compared to symbols that may be meaningless unless the perceiver is prepared to contribute most of the information.

Linear sequential symbols occupy the same fourth category as presentational symbols. Both symbol sets must be known for any meaning to occur. The difference is that when the language is known the contribution of the perceiver can still be made, using the conventional meaning of the linear sequential symbols, as contrasted to the all-or-nothing mechanism of presentational symbols.

The requirement of preparing groups of perceivers to contribute to the symbols is called penetration.

PENETRATION

There are two things that impress me when looking through a book of trademarks. The first is the aesthetic cleverness of the designers at making clean and neat symbols. The second is the fact that I recognize so few of these symbols. Recently I purchased a copy of *Trademarks and Symbols of the World,* a nicely designed fat book containing 763 trademarks. I went through the book carefully counting those trademarks I knew. I could positively identify thirty-four of them. I skipped over a group of symbols for the Tokyo Olympics that are not trademarks but instructional signs. Many of the trademarks I recognized had a jet assist from the words built into the mark.

Learning to read trademarks is like learning to read Chinese characters. You must know 3,000 of them to be considered literate. The discovery of my trademark illiteracy leads me to take an unpopular position. I am suggesting that from a communications viewpoint a brandmark, for most companies, is not only a waste of time but can actually become a detriment. It can detract from better ways of communicating the company's brand messages. In addition, the enormous time and costs required to gain penetration throughout the target group may limit its communications effectiveness.

Most trademarks, with their indistinct and confusing forms combined with their low penetration, are of little more use than decorations. Decorations do play a useful role in graphics and on products. They give the designer a visual element to play with (like a piece of jewelry on a woman). This is related to man's need for eyework and for a visual climax—a center of interest. For no reason except the need for visual activity, the big blank door on a refrigerator calls for a crown, letter, shield etc., on its chest to counter aridity. The auto develops a horse, Indian rocket, coat of arms, etc., on the center of its front and back. In communications terms, most of these marks are incomprehensible. They are purely and only decorations, eyework for satisfactory visual closure.

Unless the meaning of a brandmark is communicated to everyone involved *before* perception, it becomes a meaningless decoration. This indoctrination can become a long and expensive process, and must be kept up because new viewers will be entering the market continuously.

There are brandmarks that have gained sufficient penetration for people to know their meaning instantly. If a brandmark can achieve great penetration (90 percent of its reference group) then it can do an important job. A classic example of a high-penetration brandmark is the Red Cross. Originally designed by reversing the Swiss flag, the Red Cross has developed powerful and instantaneous connotations. Whether the Red Cross appears on a letterhead an arm band, an ambulance, a hospital, etc., it gains instant recognition and communication of its comprehensive meaning. It would be hard to conceive a better means of communicating these messages than this brandmark provides.

But the Red Cross is unique. There are brandmarks in the United States that enjoy fairly substantial penetration. The American flag, Coca-Cola, the CBS eye, probably enjoy more than 80 percent penetration. But it is likely that most trademarks shown in books on trademarks enjoy less than 5 percent penetration. For most companies high penetration is impossible.

After a trademark has gained sufficient penetration, people stop seeing it as a design and see it as its meaning directly. This is particularly evident in good logotypes where people actually stop reading the words (sequentially) and simply recognize them (presentationally). This seems to be the goal of the designer to design a logotype that would be so distinctive, yet so readable, that it would do both jobs. From the article "Questions of Legibility," by Bror Zachrisson [*Dot Zero* 1], are some comments that support this idea. "That whole words are grasped as quickly as individual letters. That sense words are read at greater speed than nonsense material. That words could be perceived by indirect vision where single letters could not. That words with a char-

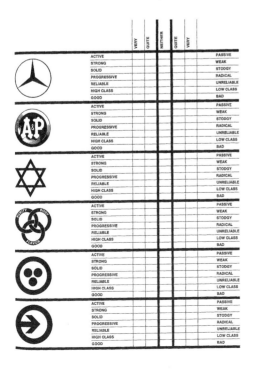

The semantic differential is an effective way to test the trademark. The semantic differential can be used to measure both the image and the penetration of trademarks. A series of test trademarks may be shown and scored on the semantic differential. Those marks with well known profiles will exhibit great stability among the respondents. Those marks with low penetration, that are not well known, will exhibit wildly varying profiles. The semantic differential can highlight the subjective responses to many of the attitudes that a corporation would be interested in knowing such as modern-old fashioned, strong-weak, big-small, active-passive, solid-stodgy, etc.

To test the penetration of a brandmark, apply this test to it. Brandmarks showing a consistent profile of answers over a large number of subjects have a high penetration. Those showing more inconsistent profile have lower penetration.

acteristic form are read at a distance more easily than words of a more even appearance. Evidently, the meaningfulness of a word or symbol, its configuration or gestalt
strength, plays an important part in perception."

A word (even multiple words) can transcend sequential reading and become
a presentational symbol since it can be perceived in one glance. For example Coca-
Cola is now seen by most people as a presentational symbol rather than linear
sequential symbol. It is not read, it is recognized. Even though Coca-Cola is an old-
fashioned, and rather corny and unclear logotype, it works because it has gained such
a high penetration. [. . .] Presentational brandmarks although intriguing looking and
decorative, often are very poor communicators. Without heavy penetration, a corporation is better off without a brandmark unless the letterform name is built into it.
Letterforms, on the other hand, leave little doubt in a literate society of their meaning; but in a conventional typographic form they can lose the personalized impact that
transcends to instant recognition.

The ideal trademark is a short word or combination of letters that can be read
and yet has distinctive presentational appearance. A new name might be coined for
these specialized letterform trademarks called "Logographs" or "Logograms." Neither
of these names are precisely correct according to the dictionary, but yet one of these
names could be made to stand for this special purpose symbol. The American trend is
toward better-designed logotypes. The old trick of fitting a line of lettering to some
shape (an oval or a circle, etc.) has died in favor of a crisp line with one of the letters
in a contrasting color or style.

The most modern European design is shunning brandmarks and communicating the corporate name via letterforms. A little Helvetica lower case lettering does
the whole job (the Müller-Brockmann syndrome). This is certainly pure and straightforward communications.

For me, either is better than the royal brandmarks of the past few decades. I
feel no loss of satisfaction by not having a crown, crest, horse, dog, tree, fish, arrow,
etc. stuck at some strategic place or on the machine.

First published in Dot Zero *no. 2 (New York: 1967).*

1967
HERE ARE SOME THINGS WE MUST DO
Ken Garland

THE VISION 67 *Design for Survival conference, held in New York in October 1967, took place against a background of "flower power" and protests against the war in Vietnam, in which conference speaker Ken Garland (b. 1929) also participated at Columbia University. Garland's paper, a development of some of the themes of* First Things First, *was made available in advance to delegates, in the conference literature, and rather than deliver it on stage, he chose to make an ironic presentation of the development of a package design for the entirely fictitious "Swiff" detergent, which grew ever larger and more elaborate even as its soap powder contents stayed exactly the same. In a hard-hitting critique of design and communication, which wryly evokes the observations of Karl Marx, Garland identifies four key tasks for the survival of a healthy contemporary culture: the need to resist the McLuhanesque celebration of the medium at the expense the message; the need to reduce the overproduction of meaningless broadcast and printed material; the need to redirect effort into the transmission of essential knowledge; and the need to circumvent media elites that act to exclude the mass of people.—RP*

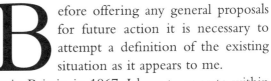

Before offering any general proposals for future action it is necessary to attempt a definition of the existing situation as it appears to me.

As a graphic designer working in Britain in 1967, I have to operate within the limits set by the capitalist system functioning not only in my country but also in the rest of western Europe, in North and South America, in Australasia and in some parts of Asia. The tasks which my clients pay me for are either (a) directly related to the purpose of making profitable business; (b) indirectly related to it as a form of commercial prestige-seeking or commercial goodwill; or (c) as part of a public service which is financed by an economy founded on the conduct of profitable business.

So when I think about my work in the short term I always have in mind this fact: that financial profit is the spur to industrial initiative, the reward for commercial achievement, the balm for battered professional consciences; and that lack of financial profit is a sign of failure, no matter what.

Of course it's possible to push the profit motive thing into the background as many of us do, and to concentrate on the job in hand as being a useful information task in its own right, or a means of experimenting with new graphic forms, or simply as a piece of fun that may give people pleasure. And of course a task may contain any or all of these qualities. But however enlightened the patronage and however open the brief may be, there is no getting away from the fact that in our society a business must show a healthy profit before it can indulge in such patronage; nor is it likely that any results of that patronage which prove hostile to business profitability will continue to be sponsored for very long.

For myself, I wish neither to remain outside the commercial world which forms the focus of capitalist society, nor to try and ignore the profit seeking which motivates it. It seems to me ridiculous to make apologies, as do so many business people in my country, for the profit motive. On the whole I'm much happier doing a specific selling task such as the design of a catalogue than when I'm working on a prestigious promotion piece loaded with cultural overtones. I've no quarrel with any client who points out that my work is valueless to him because, although it looks pretty, it doesn't help his sales figures. This is the vital factor to him, and so it is to me.

But I *do* quarrel with the artist, scientist, butcher, baker or candlestick-maker who claims that in his daily work he is unaffected by the dominant forces in capitalist society. Most especially will I take issue with those of my colleagues working in the communications field who minimize this influence. A prominent 19th century author wrote that:

> . . . the class which is the ruling material force of society, is at the same time its ruling intellectual force . . . Insofar, therefore, as they rule as a class and determine the extent and compass of an epoch, it is self-evident that they do this in their whole range, hence among other things rule also as thinkers, as producers of ideas, and regulate the production and distribution of the ideas of their age . . .[1]

It follows that there is no real difference between work done in the communication arts and science which is an integral part of the commercial system, and work which is done outside the immediate requirements of that system but nevertheless financed by it and so subject to its sanctions. Perhaps there is a marginal area of artistic and professional freedom in the latter situation; but both are utterly dependent on the health and resilience of a profit based economy, in which the real power, as Estes Kefauver demonstrated, is increasingly concentrated in the hands of a few people.[2]

Since I don't believe that there is any appreciable future in a so-called free enterprise system, there is no point in discussing its growth potential. But there are certain limited targets such as increased efficiency in social services, improved housing standards, better public transport system and so on, which can be described as survival operations.

I suppose you could say, 'If you're so damn unhappy about the present condition and future prospects of our capitalist society why do you come on with this "survival" bit? Why not just let it die of its own accord?' Well, I can't accept this notion of opting out of the system; nor can I agree with the revolutionary who claims that the whole setup is so rotten that we must kick it all to pieces before we can start on a new one. In a country plunged into a state of advanced social decay on the one hand, or of revolutionary chaos on the other, too many innocent people would suffer. A sudden dislocation of our delicately balanced society would result in the breakdown of our communication, transport, and distribution networks which alone could cause the death by disease and starvation of hundreds of thousands, maybe millions.

So until the majority of people in the western world become convinced (as they will) that they are victims of a self-perpetuating elite system, and find ways to get rid of it (as they will), what short- and medium-term survival tasks can we attempt?

First, let those of us who are employed in the information business get shot of any cockeyed nonsense that may have accumulated to the effect that the media we serve have any significant value in themselves apart from the messages transmitted through them. It seems to have become an occupational disease in our business, this urge to turn its operations into art forms and its devices into art objects in their own right. Eagerly we seize our camera, caressing its sensitive controls as we bring the searching lens to bear on—another equally skillful photographer aiming his equally superb camera at us! Yet another feature about trendy photographers, by trendy photographers, for whom? Or, darting into an art gallery, our straining eyeballs reach maximum blink-rate as their gaze fixes on our own exhibit: the advertisement for baked beans we designed last year, now transmogrified into this year's design award winner. No longer just a message about the unbeatable value of baked beans, it is now recognized for what it truly is: a prized gem in our environmental setting, a pacemaker in the race for new cultural symbols; which is more than can be said for baked beans, however tasty.

Flattering of course, for us in the business of processing information to be assured that the clever ways we have found to handle the media are very likely more important than the messages which we are commissioned to convey through them. Frequently, it is argued, the initial content of a film, or play, or TV program, or advertisement or what have you is of little or no value in itself, but that value accrues to it as a result of its processing for the medium, so that the content becomes something more, or something other than that at first intended.

But whether this observation has any grain of truth or not, it is surely no basis for a program of action. The implication of the misleading slogan 'The medium is the message' is that those of us working in the communication media may now treat with lofty condescension the initial content presented to us knowing that however trivial it may be we shall transform it into something significant; we can, in fact, welcome the triviality as being a fit challenge for our talents.

This is eyewash. Respect for the content is an absolute requirement in our business, whether it is about baked beans, or the future of mankind, or what you will.

Secondly—and this leads on from the first point—we must attempt a cure for the galloping elephantiasis from which the information media are now suffering. In 1955 Lewis Mumford wrote:

> Why should we gratuitously assume, as we so constantly do, that the mere existence of a mechanism for manifolding or mass production carries with it an obligation to use it to the fullest capacity? . . . to achieve control, we shall even, I suspect, have to reconsider and perhaps abandon the whole notion of periodical publication . . . as a needless incitement to premature or superfluous publication . . . we cannot continue inertly to accept a burdensome technique of overproduction without inventing a social discipline for handling it.[3]

I'm reminded of an occasion when I was the newly appointed art editor of a trade magazine. The editor thrust a few photographs into my hand and said, 'Lay out a six page feature using these.' Asked what was to be the text he told me to let him know how many column inches I would like, and they would write to fill. When I pointed out that even with the maximum conceivable amount of text there weren't anything like enough illustrations to fill six pages he said, 'Well, use your head—pick out some details and blow 'em up—give us a large fancy heading—that sort of thing.' 'That sort of thing' is now so familiar an operation to me that I have continually to remind myself that it isn't an integral part of the method by which information is handled, but rather the unhappy result of the way we abuse it.

Of course the main reason for the staggering over-production of broadcast and printed material is the stimulus of intensely competitive advertising. A well-known British press tycoon, when asked if he ever interfered in the editorial policies of the newspapers and periodicals he controlled, stated that as far as he was concerned the editorial content was just the thing that kept the advertisements apart, and that he left journalism to the journalist. We shouldn't be fooled by such disingenuous claims to impartiality: the very concept of news and comment as a purely quantifiable product like jam or toilet paper is itself a partial one. An increase in the volume of advertising booked requires an increase in the number of editorial pages—to help keep the ads apart—regardless of whether there is any news to fill them, and vice-versa.

The cure? Well, until we get rid of the conditions that favor the production of news and comment as though it were a species of plastic extrusion there can be no complete cure; but *something* can be done by the editorial staffs in publishing, radio, and TV. They surely can't be happy at being called on to engage in the tatty business of padding out their work in this way, whatever their political attitudes may be. If they can achieve enough solidarity in their unions and professional association, they will be strong enough to refuse to collaborate in the degradation of journalism into an aid to advertising.

Thirdly, we will not survive if we ignore the warning signs of dislocation in our *essential* information networks. Those signs are already becoming urgent. On 21 October 1966 a coal tip swept down a Welsh mountainside and killed 144 people, 116 of them children. The official report on the causes of the disaster said that the authority responsible 'should forthwith examine afresh its lines of communication to ensure that essential knowledge passes easily and automatically to those whose business is to become possessed of it and to eliminate those breakdowns and omissions which undoubtedly played a big part in bringing about the disaster.'[4]

Dare we hope that the kind of communication failure that contributed to the Aberfan disaster will not recur? I don't think we should. The responsible executives in this case were hard working, intelligent people; but they lacked an effective system of collecting, classifying, assessing, and acting upon information about the coal tips in the area, and about coal tips in general. Perhaps if some part of the vast amount of money spent on urging the British public to use gas as a domestic fuel rather than coal, or coal rather than gas, or electricity rather than either, had been diverted to the implementation of such a system, this disaster wouldn't have happened.

We must devote more energy and give higher priority to survival tasks of this kind. They may well demand the close cooperation of such unaccustomed colleagues as industrial psychologists, site workers, telecommunications engineers, specialist librarians, industrial and graphic designers, technical writers, politicians, and assorted civil servants. And those of us in the communications business who may be involved in such tasks need to know how to tackle them.

It isn't only a matter of bringing together hitherto unfamiliar skills; a change of attitude is needed as well. To take a small example: like many graphic designers I'm familiar with the problem of arranging lettering and symbols on commercial vehicles as part of a corporate identity program, in order to achieve the greatest possible impact on the travelling public. But if I were asked to assess road safety factors relating to the design of vehicle livery of this kind and to ensure that they were fully taken into account, I would hardly know how to begin because the concept behind such a consideration is at such variance with any previous considerations involved.

But it is no excuse to say that no one has ever before asked me to think about this problem. We should be able to *anticipate* incipient social needs in our sphere of activity, in the same way as some far-sighted architects have done in theirs; then we won't be so badly thrown by them when they arise. So often, I believe, it is the minor factors that matter because they build up to a serious total problem. To continue the example of road safety: what about such problems as the effective (as against merely flashy) design of vehicle dashboards; the consideration of the conflicting effect of store and street lighting on traffic sign systems; the presentation of vehicle operation and maintenance manuals; and the measurement of visibility requirements in design of vehicle windows and rear view mirrors?

Are not these some of the components in what is literally a major survival task? Yet how much effect have we in the visual communications field spent on this task in contrast to the time we have spent on designing detergent packs or advertisements for deodorants?

Fourthly, we of all people must see the danger in the urge to form in-groups and join exclusive elites. It can be one of our especial functions in society not only to help in devising new communication techniques, but also to keep open lines of communication which are threatened with extinction or which are becoming dangerously one-way-only. Speaking of the trend in western society (and there is every reason to believe that the same thing has happened in the U.S.S.R.), C Wright Mills pointed to the following development:

> (1) Far fewer people express opinions than receive them . . . (2) The communications that prevail are so organized that it is difficult or impossible for the individual to answer back immediately or with any effort. (3) The realization of opinion in action is controlled by authorities who organize and control the channels of such action. (4) The mass has no autonomy from institutions; on the contrary, agents of authorized institutions penetrate this mass, reducing any autonomy it may have in the formation of opinion by discussion.[5]

There is no reason why we have to connive at these authoritarian trends; our skills can be equally useful to those voluntary bodies and local associations that stand outside the operations of mass communication media and their controlling elites. In particular, we can find ways in which hitherto unvoiced yet deeply felt opinion may be made clear. The great success in Britain of the Consumers Association, based on pioneer American organizations of the same kind, shows the urgent need of effective feedback in the producer-consumer link.

In so far as we cut ourselves off from the feelings and hopes of those not in authority or positions of privilege, we reduce our usefulness to society. It is a bitter irony that many creative people who feel strongly about the threat to our social life caused by authoritarian pressures are unable to give expression to their feelings in any but esoteric forms. In stylish films like *The red desert* Antonioni attempts to describe the plight of human beings isolated and estranged in a world where machines are more at home than they are; but the films are littered with in-group symbols, fashionable illusions and smart visual tricks, to such an extent that they are only understandable (if at all) to a resolutely sophisticated middle class audience. Yet more than thirty years before, in *Modern times*, Charlie Chaplin dealt with the same vital theme in a clear, unpretentious and universally understood form. And even the best of film-makers may find that in their work they have lost touch with common experience; for example, the vivid simplicity of Fellini's *La strada* has turned into the weird, self-indulgent nonsense of his 8½. In my own sphere of graphic design we often find ourselves trapped in a similar kind of closed circuit, so that we are designing for, and seeking the approval of, our fellow designers to the exclusion of any consideration for those to whom the work is ostensibly directed. But the trap is mostly of our own making, and the relief when we escape it is enormous. It is not that our work is thus free from hard criticism; quite the reverse. The in-group of professionals and professional critics can often be too indulgent over those aspects of work about which lay-men would be ruthless in their judgment. The toughest design critics I've ever come across were the children who live in my street, whom I consulted about a toy I was designing. But they were also by far the most helpful critics I know, unimpeded by consideration of taste and current trend, scornful of irrelevant detail and delighted by any evidence of careful thought for the wishes of *them*, the destined users of the toy.

What I am suggesting as the fourth survival task in my list is that we make some attempt to identify, and to identify *with*, our real clients: the public. They may not be the ones who pay us, nor the ones who give us diplomas and degrees. But if they are to be the final recipients of the results of our work, they're the ones who matter.

If you detect a common attitude running through these proposals, and feel sympathetic towards it, you will no doubt add your own items to the list. What I must say in conclusion, though, is this. These tasks operate in the short and middle-term. They might play some part in preventing the disintegration of our society which will surely take place if it hardens into its present unhappy mold. In the long term there must be vast, probably painful changes. And I cannot agree with Buckminster Fuller when he says:

> All politics are obsolete as fundamental problem solvers. Politics are only adequate for secondary housekeeping tasks.[6]

We cannot hope, nor should we try, to effect fundamental changes in our society by side stepping the issues of government. Political change is the inevitable outcome of economic pressures; and the economic effects of the technological revolution will themselves result in political decisions. Those of us who believe in an egalitarian society will not bring it nearer by scorning the political instruments by which it will be attained.

On one historic dictum I think we at this Vision 67 Congress will all agree:

> The philosophers have only interpreted the world in various ways: the point, however, is to change it.[7]

Reprinted in Ken Garland, A Word in Your Eye *(Reading: University of Reading, 1996).*

Notes
1. Marx, Karl, *The German Ideology* (1846).
2. Kefauver, Estes, *In a Few Hands* (1965).
3. Mumford, Lewis. 'Technics and the future of Western civilization,' *Perspectives* II, New York 1955.
4. *Report of the Tribunal Appointed to Inquire into the Disaster of Aberfan on October 21, 1966* (1967).
5. Mills, C. Wright, *The Power Elite* (1956).
6. Fuller, R. Buckminster, Final summary at Vision 65 Congress on 'New challenges to human communications' (1966).
7. Marx, Karl, *The German Ideology* (1846).

1967
VISUAL POP
George Melly

REVOLT INTO STYLE *by the British writer George Melly (b. 1926) is one of the definitive accounts of the evolution of Pop style in postwar Britain. Melly—jazz singer, authority on Surrealism, and critic—brought a sharp journalistic eye to the visual manifestations of this seismic upheaval in popular culture, social attitudes, and taste. His 1967 report on Pop's graphic dimension, first published in a British newspaper, is an early example of commentary that addresses graphic communication not from the designer's perspective as a professional activity, but as a form of coded subcultural expression in the lives of its intended audience. Melly might, by his own admission, have been an observer of this culture, rather than an active participant in the "Underground" music scene, but his sympathetic assessment and insights come from a critical consumer's point of view.—RP*

Sometime in the early summer of 1966, I went along to the Victoria and Albert Museum to look at the Beardsley exhibition and was rather surprised to find it packed with people. I was puzzled, not only by the size of the public, but because I found them impossible to place. Many were clearly art students, some were beats, others could have been pop musicians; most of them were very young, but almost all of them gave the impression of belonging to a secret society which had not yet declared its aims or intentions. I believe now, although I was not to realize it for several months, that I had stumbled for the first time into the presence of the emerging Underground.

That this confrontation should have taken place at an art exhibition is, again in retrospect, significant. The Underground is the first of the pop explosions to have evolved a specifically *graphic* means of expression, and Beardsley, while not as it turned out the most important element, was one of the earliest formative influences in this openly eclectic process.

I use the word 'graphic' advisedly. Every British pop moment, from Rock 'n' Roll on, produced its own visual style. Until the Underground, this had affected only the clothes, hairstyles, facial expressions, or the choice of this scooter or that transistor. Naturally this visual selection reflected an attitude while, at the same time declaring allegiance to the movement it externalized, but the Underground consciously set out to evolve a graphic imagery which would provide a parallel to its musical, literary and philosophical aspects.

Inside the pop world, even as early as 1965, there were several pointers to the way things were moving which I—by both age and inclination a friendly outsider— had taken in only to misinterpret. Yet, however unperceptive, my misunderstanding was at least explicable. Ever since the early days of Presley, the intellectual 'pop' movement, which was largely graphic in its means of expression, had paid frequent pictorial homage to the heroes of pop music, and it was for this reason that, when pop-record sleeves in particular had begun to show signs of visual sophistication, I imagined that this was merely because the record companies had decided to put the enthusiasm of pop painters and designers to commercial use.

Nor was I entirely mistaken. The coming together of the two edges of the pop spectrum was initially a slow process, but what I hadn't realized was that it was a case of mutual attraction and not simply an unacknowledged intellectual offering laid at the shrine of pop music.

The sleeve of *Sergeant Pepper,* the Beatles' recent LP, could stand as the fruit of this cross-pollination. It has become not so much a sleeve as an art object with its card of cutouts and double-spread photograph of the Beatles in nineteenth-century military uniforms (John Lennon wears a daisy in his epaulette). What is more, the front of the sleeve is almost a microcosm of the Underground world.

This collage-photograph was 'staged' by the pop artists Peter Blake and his wife Jan Howarth, and acts as a sign that the liaison between the two wings of pop is complete. Yet Blake remains an established painter who has become accepted by the objects of his admiration. He is not a product of the Underground but an ally. The real graphic artists are completely of it, and dedicated entirely to the concept of total involvement. Their medium is the poster.

'Hapshash and the Coloured Coat' is the curious trade name of two young men called Nigel Waymouth and Michael English. They are musicians in the avant-garde pop idiom, but also, and it is this aspect which is relevant here, poster design-ers. They are cool, polite, and very beautiful to look at with Harpo hairstyles, unironed marbled shirts, tight trousers, loose belts, and two-tone Cuban boots. I talked to them in their house in Notting Hill and within a few sentences felt, as is usual when in con-versation with the Underground, that I had tumbled into a world where time oper-ates at a different speed.

English, who has been at Baling Art School, met Waymouth when the latter was painting the shopfront of the Chelsea boutique, Grannie Takes a Trip, in December 1966, and by March 1967 they had decided to join forces and design posters. But what were these posters for? Superficially the answer was to advertise the activities of UFO, which stands, among other things, for 'Unlimited Freak Out,' and which was the first spontaneous and successful attempt to produce a total environ-ment involving music, light and people.

What interested 'Hapshash' was *using* this environment as a launching pad. Unlike conventional poster designers they weren't concerned with imposing their image on a product out of the environment. It must be emphasized here that the aim of UFO was mind expansion and hallucination at the service of the destruction of the non-hip and the substitution of 'love,' in the special, rather nebulous meaning that the word holds for the Underground.

Waymouth and English set out to discover a visual equivalent, but their meth-od of doing so showed them to be very much the children of the technological soci-ety. Their street posters revived the use of Day-glo, an invention which had had a short burst of commercial life in the mid-1950s, and which they hoped would 'blow the public's mind.' But, inside the club, a chance revelation of the effect of the all-pervasive ultraviolet light on certain colors interested them in how they might exploit this accident. Yet why display posters *inside* the place they are intended to advertise?

The answer is that the Underground poster is not so much a means of broad-casting information as a way of advertising a trip to an artificial paradise. The very let-tering used (a rubbery synthesis of early Disney and Mabel Lucie Attwell carried to the edge of illegibility) reinforces this argument, and suggests that, even in the streets, the aim of the Underground artists is to turn on the world.

However, this a-commercial approach to the poster should not be taken to indicate a belief in improvisation and shoddiness in the technical sense. On the contrary, the Hapshash posters are of a standard that makes most contemporary commercial advertising look both uninventive and sloppy. Yet when it comes to imagery there is no attempt to conceal a magpie approach to any artist past or present who seems to strike the right psychedelic note. As a result the Hapshash posters are almost a collage of other men's hard-won visions: Mucha, Ernst, Magritte, Bosch, William Blake, comic books, engravings of Red Indians, Disney, Dulac, ancient illustrations of treatises on alchemy; everything is boiled down to make a visionary and hallucinatory bouillabaisse.

Nor are more contemporary sources despised. Pop and comic books have played their part, and the modern commercial designer Alan Aldridge,[1] himself a brilliant pasticheur of the thirties, is heavily drawn on. (It may be of interest here to point out that it was Aldridge who first conceived the idea of painting designs on a girl to advertise Penguin Books. It's an omnivorous eater, the Underground.)

Yet this open eclecticism has surely a built-in flaw, and that is the drying up of a supply of new spices to add to the pot. What amazed us in the spring of 1967 is already beginning to do no more than charm, and what charms must eventually pall. Furthermore, as the influence of Hapshash spreads into commercial advertising, the inevitable law of pop culture has begun to operate; that which spreads becomes thinner.

Another point in his favor is that, whereas Waymouth and English are associated with *International Times,* Sharp is connected with the magazine *Oz,* and while *Oz* is extremely sympathetic to the Underground it has a less childlike confidence in mind expansion as the whole answer to the crisis in our society. As if to confirm this analysis, Sharp's posters seem divided between a bitter political disillusion and the more agreeable if hackneyed universe of the flower children. Yet in the latter field, his 'Dylan' poster is outstanding for its richness of imagination, and if such a deliberately transitory art form as the Underground poster can produce a work of permanent interest, this could well turn out to be it.

Firmly dedicated to a way of life which itself shows signs of dissolution, it will be interesting to see if the mind-expanding poster goes down with the scene or succeeds in clambering aboard whatever may be sailing towards us over the horizon.

The 'Nouveau Art-Nouveau' may have already begun to decline in popularity, but the idea of the 'mass-produced unsigned object' is probably here, if not to stay, then at least to be thrown away and replaced by its successor. The Underground poster has succeeded in destroying the myth that the visual imagination has to be kept locked up in museums or imprisoned in heavy frames. It has helped open the eyes of a whole generation in the most literal sense. It has succeeded, however briefly, in fulfilling the pop canon; it has operated in 'the gap between life and art.'

First published in the Observer Colour Supplement *(London: December 1967); Reprinted in George Melly,* Revolt into Style *(London: Allen Lane, 1970).*

Notes
1. Aldridge too is perfectly conscious of his course, see *The Penguin Book of Comics.*

1970
POSTERS: ADVERTISEMENT, ART,
POLITICAL ARTIFACT, COMMODITY
Susan Sontag

IT HAS BECOME ROUTINE *for observers of graphic design to call for criticism able to situate graphic production in the wider matrix of culture, but this has rarely been achieved as convincingly as in Susan Sontag's essay on Cuban revolutionary posters. Sontag (b. 1933), one of the United States' best-known cultural critics, visited Cuba and, in 1969, wrote about the country—controversially—in the left journal* Ramparts. *Asked by* Ramparts's *art director Dugald Stermer to contribute an introduction to his large-format collection of Cuban posters, Sontag delivered a forensic, partly historical analysis of the medium, showing how a capitalist invention, which began as means of encouraging "a social climate in which it is normative to buy," ended up becoming a commodity itself. She relates this popular new Cuban art form designed to raise and complicate consciousness to developments in film, literature, and fine art, before turning to the problematic position of the non-Cuban viewer. Posters, Sontag concludes, are substitutes for experience; collecting them is a form of emotional and moral tourism, and Stermer's book is implicated in a tacit betrayal of the revolutionary use and meaning of images now consumed as just another dish on the left-liberal bourgeois menu.—RP*

Posters are not simply public notices. A public notice, however widely circulated, may be a means of signaling only one person, someone whose identity is unknown to the author of the notice. (One of the earliest known public notices, found in the ruins of ancient Thebes, is a papyrus advertising a reward for the return of an escaped slave.) More typically, most pre-modern societies mounted public notices to circulate news about topics of general interest, such as spectacles, taxation, and the death and accession of rulers. Still, even when the information it carries concerns many people, rather than a few or just one, a public notice is not the same as a poster. Both posters and public notices address the person not as an individual, but as an unidentified member of the body politic. But the poster, as distinct from the public notice, presupposes the modern concept of the public—in which the members of a society are defined primarily as spectators and consumers. A public notices aims to inform or command. A poster aims to seduce, to exhort, to sell, to educate, to convince, to appeal. Whereas a public notice distributes information to interested or alert citizens, a poster reaches out to grab those who might otherwise pass it by. A public notice posted on a wall is passive, requiring that the spectator present himself before it to read what is written. A poster claims attention—at a distance. It is visually aggressive.

Posters are aggressive because they appear in the context of *other* posters. The public notice is a freestanding statement, but the form of the poster depends on the fact that many posters exist—competing with (and sometimes reinforcing) each other. Thus posters also presuppose the modern concept of public space—as a theater of persuasion. Throughout the Rome of Julius Caesar, there were signboards reserved for posting announcements of general importance; but these were inserted into a space that was otherwise relatively clean verbally. The poster, however, is an integral element of modern public space. The poster, as distinct from the public notice, implies the creation of urban, public space as an arena of signs: the image- and word-choked façades and surfaces of the great modern cities.

The main technical and aesthetic qualities of the poster all follow from these modern redefinitions of the citizen and of public space. Thus posters, unlike public notices, are inconceivable before the invention of the printing press. The advent of printing quickly brought about the duplication of public notices as well as books; William Caxton made the earliest known *printed* public notice in 1480. But printing alone did not give rise to posters, which had to await the invention of a far cheaper and more sophisticated color printing process—lithography—by Senefelder in the early nineteenth century; and the development of the high-speed presses which, by 1848, could print ten thousand sheets an hour. Unlike the public notice, the poster depends essentially on efficient, inexpensive reproducibility for the purpose of mass distribution. The other obvious traits of a poster, apart from its being intended for reproduction in large quantities—its scale, its decorativeness, and its mixture of linguistic and pictorial means—also follow from the role posters play in modern public space. Here is Harold F. Hutchinson's definition, at the beginning of his book *The Poster, An Illustrated History from 1860* (London, 1968):

> A poster is essentially a large announcement, usually with a pictorial element, usually printed on paper and usually displayed on a wall or billboard to the general public. Its purpose is to draw attention to whatever an advertiser is trying to promote and to impress some message on the passer-by. The visual or pictorial element provides the initial attraction—and it must be striking enough to catch the eye of the passer-by and to overcome the counter-attractions of the other posters, and it usually needs a supplementary verbal message which follows up and amplifies the pictorial theme. The large size of most posters enables this verbal message to be read clearly at a distance.

A public notice usually consists entirely of words. Its values are those of "information:" intelligibility, explicitness, completeness. In a poster the visual or plastic elements dominate, not the text. The words (whether few or many) form part of the overall visual composition. The values of a poster are first those of "appeal," and only second of information. The rules for giving information are subordinated to the rules which endow a message, any message, with impact: brevity, asymmetrical emphasis, condensation.

Unlike the public notice, which can exist in any society possessing a written language, the poster could not exist before the specific historic conditions of modern capitalism. Sociologically, the advent of the poster reflects the development of an industrialized economy whose goal is ever-increasing mass consumption, and (somewhat later, when posters turned political) of the modern secular centralized nation-state, with its peculiarly diffuse conception of ideological consensus and its rhetoric of mass political participation. It is capitalism that has brought about that peculiarly modern redefinition of the public in terms of the activities of consumption and spectatorship. The earliest famous posters all had a specific function: to encourage a growing proportion of the population to spend money on soft consumer goods, entertainments, and the arts. Posters advertising the great industrial firms, banks, and hard commodities came later. Typical of the original function are the subjects of Jules Chéret, the first of the great poster makers, which range from cabarets, music halls, dance halls, and operas to oil lamps, apéritifs, and cigarette papers. Chéret, who was born in 1836, designed more than a thousand posters. The first important English poster makers, the Beggarstaffs—who began in the early 1890s, and were boldly derivative of the French poster makers—also mostly advertised soft goods and the theater. In America, the first distinguished poster work was done for magazines. Will Bradley, Louis Rhead, Edward Penfield, and Maxfield Parrish were employed by such magazines as *Harper's, Century, Lippincott's,* and *Scribner's* to design a different cover for each issue; these cover designs were then reproduced as posters to sell the magazines to the expanding middle-class reading public.

Most books on the subject flatly assume the mercantile context as essential to the poster. (Hutchinson, for instance, is typical in the way he defines the poster by its selling function.) But even though commercial advertising provided the ostensible content of all the early posters, Chéret, followed by Eugene Grasset, were quickly recognized as "artists." Already in 1880, an influential French art critic declared that he found a thousand times more talent in a poster by Chéret than in most paintings on the walls of the Paris Salon. Still, it took a second generation of poster makers—some of whom had already established reputations in the serious, "free" art of painting—to establish for a wide public that the poster was an art form, not simply an offshoot of commerce. This happened between 1890, when Toulouse-Lautrec was commissioned to produce a series of posters advertising the Moulin Rouge, and 1894, when Alphonse Mucha designed the poster for *Gismonda,* the first of his dazzling series of posters of Sarah Bernhardt in her productions at the Théâtre de la Renaissance. During this period the streets of Paris and London became an outdoor gallery, with new posters appearing almost every day. But posters did not have to advertise culture, or present glamorous or exotic imagery, to be recognized as works of art themselves. Their subjects could be quite "common." In 1894, work with such lowly commercial subjects as Steinlen's poster advertising sterilized milk and the Beggarstaffs' poster for Rowntree's Cocoa were being hailed for their qualities as graphic art. Thus, only two decades after they began appearing, posters were widely acknowledged as an art form. During the mid-1890s there were two public art exhibits in London entirely devoted to posters. In 1895 an *Illustrated History of the Placard* came out in London; between 1896 and 1900 a publisher in Paris issued a five-volume *Les Maîtres de l'Affiche.* An English journal called the *Poster* appeared between 1898 and 1900. Amassing private collections of posters became fashionable in the early 1890s, and W. S. Roger's *A Book of the Poster* (1901) was specifically addressed to this already sizeable audience of enthusiastic poster collectors.

Compared with the other new art forms that arose toward the end of the last century, posters achieved the status of "art" rather more rapidly than most. The reason, perhaps, is the number of distinguished artists—such as Toulouse-Lautrec, Mucha, and Beardsley—who quickly turned to the poster form. Without the infusion of their talents and prestige, posters might have had to wait as long as movies did to be recognized as works of art in their own right. A longer resistance to the poster as art would probably have been inspired less by its "impure" origin in commerce than by its essential dependence on the process of technological duplication. Yet it is precisely this dependence which makes the poster a distinctively *modern* art form. Painting and sculpture, the traditional shapes of visual art, inevitably had their meaning and aura profoundly altered when they entered, in Walter Benjamin's classic phrase, "the age of mechanical reproduction." But the poster (like still photography and the cinema) carries no history from the pre-modern world; it could exist only in the era of mechanical duplication. Unlike a painting, a poster was never meant to exist as a unique object. Therefore, reproducing a poster does not make a second-generation object, one aesthetically inferior to the original or diminished in its social, monetary, or symbolic value. From its conception, the poster is destined to be reproduced, to exist in multiples.

Of course, posters have never won the status of a major art form. Poster-making is usually labeled an "applied" art, because, it is assumed, the poster aims to put across the value of a product or an idea—in contrast to, say, a painting or sculpture, whose aim is the free expression of the artist's individuality. In this view, the poster maker, someone with artistic skills which he lends, for a fee, to a seller, belongs to a different breed from the real artist, who makes things which are intrinsically valuable and self-justifying. Thus, Hutchinson writes:

> A poster artist (who is not merely an artist whose work happens to be used on a poster) is not drawing and painting solely for self-expression, to release his own emotions, or to salve his own esthetic conscience. His art is an applied art, and it is art applied to the cause of communication, which may be dictated by the demands of a service, message, or product with which he may be out of sympathy but whose advocate he has temporarily consented to be, usually in return for suitable financial remuneration.

But to define the poster as being, unlike "fine" art forms, primarily concerned with advocacy—and the poster artist as someone who, like a whore, works for money and tries to please a client—is dubious, simplistic. (It is also unhistorical. Only since the early nineteenth century has the artist been generally understood as working to express himself, or for the sake of "art.") What makes posters, like book jackets and magazine covers, an applied art is *not* that they are single-mindedly devoted to "communication," or that the people who do them are more regularly or better paid than most painters and sculptors. Posters are an applied art because, typically, they apply what has already been done in the other arts. Aesthetically, the poster has always been parasitic on the respectable arts of painting, sculpture, even architecture. In the numerous posters they did, Toulouse-Lautrec, Mucha, and Beardsley only transposed a style already articulated in their paintings and drawings. The work of those painters—from Puvis de Chavannes to Ernst-Ludwig Kirchner to Picasso to Larry Rivers, Jasper Johns, Robert Rauschenberg, and Roy Lichtenstein—who have occasionally tried their hand at posters is not only not innovative but mainly casts into a more accessible form their most distinctive and familiar stylistic mannerisms. As an art form, posters are rarely in the lead. Rather, they serve to disseminate already mature elitist art conventions. Indeed, posters have been one of the main instruments during the last century for popularizing what is agreed on, by the arbiters of the worlds of painting and sculpture, as visual good taste. A representative sample of posters done in any given period would consist mostly of work that is banal and visually reactionary. But most of what are considered *good* posters bear some clear relation to what is fashionable visually, not merely popular—fashionable, though, only up to a point. The poster never embodies a really new style—high fashion is, by definition, "ugly" and off-putting at first view—but fashion at a slightly later stage of assimilation or acceptability. For example, Cassandre's famous posters for Dubonnet (1924) and the transatlantic liner *Normandie* (1932), clearly influenced by Cubism and the Bauhaus movement, employed these styles after they were commonplaces in the fine art scene, already digested.

The relation posters have to visual fashion is that of "quotation." Thus, the poster artist is usually a plagiarist (whether of himself or others), and plagiarism is one main feature of the history of poster aesthetics. The earliest good poster makers outside Paris, who were English, freely adapted the look of the first wave of French posters. The Beggarstaffs (a pseudonym for two Englishmen who had studied art in Paris) were heavily influenced by Toulouse-Lautrec; Dudley Hardy, best remembered for his posters for the Gilbert and Sullivan productions at the Savoy Theater, owed to both Chéret and Lautrec. This built-in "decadence" continues unabated to the present, as each important poster artist partly feeds on earlier schools of poster art. One of the most remarkable recent examples of this functional parasitism on earlier poster work is the brilliant series of posters done in San Francisco in the mid-1960s for the great rock ballrooms, the Fillmore and the Avalon, which freely plagiarized Mucha and the other Art Nouveau masters.

The stylistically parasitic trend in the history of the poster is additional confirmation of the poster as an art form. Posters, good posters at any rate, cannot be considered mainly as instruments for communicating something whose normative form is "information." Indeed, it is precisely on this point that a poster differs generically from a public notice—and enters the territory of art. Unlike the public notice, whose function is unambiguously to say something, the poster is not concerned ultimately with anything so clear or unequivocal. The point of the poster may be its "message:" the advertisement, the announcement, the slogan. But what is recognized as an effective poster is one that transcends its utility in delivering that message. Unlike the public notice, the poster (despite its frankly commercial origins) is not just utilitarian. The effective poster—even one selling the lowliest household product— always exhibits that duality which is the very mark of art: the tension between the wish to say (explicitness, literalness) and the wish to be silent (truncation, economy, condensation, evocativeness, mystery, exaggeration). The very fact that posters were designed to have instant impact, to be "read" in a flash, because they had to compete with other posters, strengthened the aesthetic thrust of the poster form.

It is hardly accidental that the first generation of great posters was made in Paris, the art capital but hardly the economic capital of the nineteenth century. The poster was born out of the aestheticizing impulse. It aimed to make of selling something "beautiful." Beyond that aim lies a tendency which has continued throughout the hundred-year history of poster art. Whatever its origins in selling specific products and performances, the poster has tended to develop an independent existence as a major element in the public decor of modern cities (and of highways, as the nature-effacing links between cities). Even when a product, service, spectacle, or institution is named, the ultimate function of the poster may be purely decorative. Only a short step separates the posters done in the 1950s for London Transport, which were more ornaments than advertisements for their subject, from the Peter Max posters of the late 1960s mounted on the sides of buses in New York City, which advertised nothing at all. The possible subversion of the poster form by its drift toward aesthetic autonomy is confirmed by the fact that people began so early, already in the 1890s, to collect posters; thereby removing this object preeminently designed for public, outdoor space, and ostensibly for the cursory passing glance of crowds, to a private, interior space—the home of the collector—where it could become the subject of close (i.e., aesthetic) scrutiny.

Even the specific commercial function of posters, in their early history, strengthens the aesthetic basis of the poster form. Alongside the fact that posters, at their origin a device of commercial advertising, reflect the intensity of a single-minded didactic aim (to sell something) is the fact that the first task of posters was the promoting of goods and services that were economically *marginal*. The poster originates in the effort of expanding capitalist productivity to sell surplus or luxury goods, household articles, nonstaple foods, liqueurs and soft drinks, public entertainments (cabaret, music hall, bullfights), "culture" (magazines, plays, operas), and traveling for pleasure. Hence, the poster frequently had, from the beginning, a light or witty tone; one main tradition in poster aesthetics favors the cool, the amusing. Evident in many of the early posters is an element of exaggeration, of irony, of doing "too much" for their subject. Specialized as it may seem, the theatrical poster is perhaps the archetypal poster genre of the nineteenth century, beginning with Toulouse-Lautrec's harsh Jane Avril and Yvette Guilbert, Chéret's suave Loïe Fuller, and Mucha's hieratic Sarah Bernhardt. Throughout the history of the poster, theatricality has been one of its recurrent values—as the poster-object itself may be viewed as a kind of instant visual theater in the street.

Exaggeration is one of the charms of poster art, when its tasks are commercial. But the theatricality of poster aesthetics found its heavy as well as playful expression, when posters became political. It seems surprising how late the political role of the poster followed the advertising role it fulfilled from its origins around 1870. Public notices continued to serve political functions, like calls to arms, throughout this period. An even closer precedent for the political poster had been flourishing since the early nineteenth century; the political cartoon, which, in the burgeoning weekly and monthly magazines, had reached a masterly form in the hands of Cruikshank and Gillray, and later Nast. But despite these precedents, the poster remained largely innocent of any political function until 1914. Then, almost overnight, the newly belligerent governments of Europe recognized the efficacy of the medium of commercial advertising for political purposes. The leading theme of the first political posters was patriotism. In France, posters appealed to citizens to subscribe to the various war loans; in England, posters exhorted men to join the army (from 1914 until 1916, when conscription was introduced); in Germany, posters were more broadly ideological, arousing love of country by demonizing the enemy. Most posters done during World War I were crude graphically. Their emotional range moved between the pompous, like Leete's poster of Lord Kitchener and his accusatory finger with the quotation "Your country needs YOU" (1914), and the hysterical, like Bernhard's nightmare anti-Bolshevik poster (same year). With rare exceptions, such as the poster by Faivre (1916) urging contributions to the French war loan of that year under the slogan "*On les aura*," the World War I posters have little interest now other than historical.

The birth of serious political graphics came right after 1918, when the new revolutionary movements convulsing Europe at the close of the war stimulated a vast outpouring of radical poster exhortation, particularly in Germany, Russia, and Hungary. It was in the aftermath of World War I that the political poster began to constitute a valuable branch of poster art. Not surprisingly, much of the best work in the revolutionary poster was done by collectives of poster makers. Two of the earliest were the "November group," formed in Berlin in 1918, among whose members were Max

Pechstein and Hans Richter, and ROSTA, formed in Moscow in 1919, which included as active artists the poet Mayakovsky, the Constructivist artist El Lissitzky, and
Alexander Rodchenko. More recent examples of revolutionary poster work produced
by collectives are the Republic and Communist posters made in Madrid and
Barcelona in 1936–37 and the posters turned out by revolutionary students at the
Ecole des Beaux Arts in Paris during the revolution of May 1968. (Chinese "wall
posters" fall into the category of public notices rather than posters, as the terms are
used here.) Of course, many individual artists have made radical poster art outside the
discipline of a collective. Recently, in 1968, the revolutionary poster was the subject
of a large and impressive retrospective exhibition at the Museum of Modern Art in
Stockholm.

　　The advent of political posters may seem like a sharp break with the original
function of posters (promoting consumership). But the historical conditions which
produced posters first as commercial advertising and later as political propaganda are
intertwined. If the commercial poster is an outgrowth of the capitalist economy, with
its need to attract people to spend more money on nonessential goods and on spectacles, the political poster reflects another specifically nineteenth- and twentieth-century
phenomenon, first articulated in the matrix of capitalism: the modern nation-state,
whose claim to ideological monopoly has as its *minimal*, unquestioned expression the
goal of universal education and the power of mass mobilization for warfare. Despite
this historical link, however, there is a major difference of context for commercial and
political posters. While the presence of posters used as commercial advertising generally indicates the degree to which a society defines itself as stable, pursuing an economic and political status quo, the presence of political posters generally indicates that
the society considers itself in a state of emergency. Posters are now a familiar instrument, during periods of crisis for the nation-state, for promulgating political attitudes
in summary form. In the older capitalist countries, with bourgeois-democratic political institutions, their use is mainly confined to wartime. In the newer countries, most
of which are experimenting (not too successfully) with a mixture of state capitalism
and state socialism and are undergoing chronic economic and political crises, posters
are a common tool of nation-building. Particularly striking is the extent to which
posters have been used to "ideologize" relatively unideological societies in the Third
World. Two examples from this political year are the posters being put up all over
Egypt (most of them blown up newspaper cartoons), as air war in the Middle East
escalates, identifying America as the enemy who stands behind Israel, and the posters
that swiftly appeared throughout relatively poster-free Phnom Penh in April 1970,
after the fall of Prince Sihanouk, inculcating hatred of the resident Vietnamese and
rousing the Cambodians to war against the "Viet Cong."

　　Obviously, posters have a different destiny where they disseminate the official
view in a country, as do the British recruiting posters of World War I or the Cuban
posters for OSPAAAL and COR in this book, than they have where they speak for
an adversary minority within the country. Posters expressing the majority view of a
politicized society (or situation) are guaranteed mass distribution. Their presence is
typically repetitive. Posters expressing insurgent, rather than establishment, values get
less widely distributed. They usually end being defaced by irate members of the silent
majority or ripped off by the police. The chances for the insurgent poster's longevity
and its prospects of distribution are, of course, improved when it is sponsored by an
organized political party. Renato Guttuso's anti-Vietnam War poster (1966), done for
the Italian Communist Party, is a less fragile political instrument than the anti-Vietnam

posters of freelance dissenters, like Takashi Kono in Japan and Sigvaard Olsson in Sweden. But however dissimilar in context and destiny, all political posters share a common purpose; ideological mobilization. Only the scale of this purpose varies. Maxi-mobilization is a realistically feasible goal when posters are the vehicle of a ruling political doctrine. Insurgent or revolutionary posters aim, more modestly, at a mini-mobilization of opinion against the prevailing official line.

One might suppose that political posters produced by a dissenting minority would need to be, and often are, more appealing visually, less strident or simplistic ideologically, than those produced by governments in power. They have to compete for the attention of a distracted, hostile, or indifferent public. In fact, differences of aesthetic and intellectual quality do not run along these lines. State-sponsored work may be as lively and loose as the Cuban political posters or as banal and conformist as the posters in the Soviet Union and East Germany. A similar range of quality occurs among insurgent political posters. Very distinguished poster work was done for the German Communist Party in the 1920s, by John Heartfield and Georg Grosz among others. During the same period, only naïve agit-prop posters, like William Gropper's poster urging support for the striking textile workers in Passaic or Fred Ellis' poster demanding justice for Sacco and Vanzetti, both from 1927, were being made for the American Communist Party. The art of propaganda is not necessarily ennobled or refined by powerlessness, any more than it is inevitably coarsened when backed by power or when serving official goals. What determines whether good political posters are made in a country, more than the talent of the artists and the health of the other visual arts, is the cultural policy of the government or party or movement—whether it recognizes quality, whether it encourages, even demands it. Contrary to the invidious idea many people have about propaganda as such, there is no inherent limit to the aesthetic quality or moral integrity of political posters—no limit, that is, separate from the conventions that affect (and perhaps limit) all poster-making, that done for commercial advertising purposes as much as that done for the purposes of political indoctrination.

Most political posters, like commercial posters, rely on the image rather than the word. As the aim of an effective advertising poster is the stimulation (and simplification) of tastes and appetites, the aim of an effective political poster is rarely more than the stimulation (and simplification) of moral sentiments. And the classic means of stimulating and simplifying is through a visual metaphor. Most commonly, a thing or an idea is attached to the emblematic image of a person. In commercial advertising, the paradigm occurs as early as Chéret. He designed most of his posters, no matter what they were selling, around the image of a pretty girl—the "mechanical bride," as Marshall McLuhan named her twenty years ago in his witty book about contemporary versions of that image. The equivalent in political advertising is the heroic figure. Such a figure may be a celebrated leader of the struggle, living or martyred, or an anonymous representative citizen, such as a soldier, a worker, a mother, a war victim. The point of the image in a commercial poster is to be attractive, often sexually attractive, thereby covertly identifying material acquisitiveness with sexual appetite and subliminally reinforcing the first by appealing to the second. A political poster proceeds more directly and appeals to emotions with more ethical prestige. It is not enough for the image to be attractive, even seductive, since what is being urged is always put forth as more than merely "desirable;" it is imperative. Commercial advertising imagery cultivates the capacity to be tempted, the willingness to indulge private desires and liberties. The imagery of political posters cultivates the sense of obligation, the willingness to renounce private desires and liberties.

To create a feeling of psychic or moral obligation, political posters use a variety of emotional appeals. In posters featuring a single model figure, the image can be heart-rending, like the napalmed child in posters protesting the Vietnam War; it can be admonitory, like Lord Kitchener in Leete's poster; it can be inspirational, like the face of Che in many posters made since his death. A variant of the poster focusing on one exemplary persona is the type that depicts the agon or struggle itself, juxtaposing the heroic figure with the figure of a dehumanized or caricatured enemy. The tableau usually shows the enemy—the Hun, the capitalist in frock coat, the Bolshevik, LBJ—either being pinned down or in flight. Compared with posters featuring only exemplary figures, posters with agon imagery usually appeal to cruder feelings, like vindictiveness and resentment and moral complacency. But depending on the actual odds of the struggle and the moral tone of the culture, such imagery can also bypass these emotions and simply make people feel braver.

As in commercial advertising, the image in political posters is usually backed up by some words, the fewer (it's thought) the better. The words second the image. One handsome exception to this rule is Sigvaard Olsson's black-and-white poster of Hugo Blanco (1968), which superimposes a lengthy quotation in heavy type over the face of the jailed Peruvian revolutionary. Another exception, even more striking, is the COR poster reproduced here on p. 18, which dispenses altogether with an image and makes a bluntly colorful, nearly abstract arrangement of the words of a sophisticated ideological slogan in maxim form: "*Comunimo no es crear conciencia con el dinero sino crear riqueza con la conciencia.*"

II.

In capitalist society, posters are a ubiquitous part of the decor of the urban landscape. Connoisseurs of new forms of beauty may find visual gratification in the unplanned collage of posters (and neon signs) that decorate the cities. It is an additive effect, of course, since few posters to be seen outdoors nowadays, regarded one by one, give any aesthetic pleasure. More specialized connoisseurs—of the aesthetics of infestation, of the libertine aura of litter, and of the libertarian implications of randomness—can find pleasure in this decor. But what keeps posters multiplying in the urban areas of the capitalist world is their commercial utility in selling particular products and, beyond that, in perpetuating a social climate in which it is normative to buy. Since the economy's health depends on steadily encroaching upon whatever limits people's habits of consumption, there can be no limit to the effort to saturate public space with advertising.

A revolutionary communist society, which rejects the consumer society, must inevitably redefine, and thereby limit, poster art. In this context, only a selective and controlled use of posters makes sense. Nowhere is this selective use of posters more authentic than in Cuba, which has, by revolutionary aspiration (abetted by, but not reducible to, the cruel economic scarcities imposed by the American blockade), repudiated mercantile values more radically than any communist country outside of Asia. Cuba obviously has no use for the poster to inspire its citizens to buy consumer goods. That still leaves a large place for the poster, though. Any modern society, communist no less than capitalist, is a network of signs. Under revolutionary communism, the poster remains one principal type of public sign: decorating shared ideas and firing moral sympathies, rather than promoting private appetites.

As one would expect a large proportion of the posters in Cuba have political subjects. But unlike most work in this genre, the purpose of the political poster in Cuba is not simply to build morale. It is to raise and complicate consciousness—the highest aim of the revolution itself. (Leaving out China, Cuba is perhaps the only current example of a communist revolution pursuing that ethical aim as an explicit political goal.) The Cuban use of political posters recalls Mayakovsky's vision in the early 1920s, before Stalinist oppression crushed the independent revolutionary artists and scrapped the communist-humanist goal of creating better types of human beings. For the Cubans, the success of their revolution is not measured by its ability to preserve itself, withstanding the remorseless hostility of the United States and its Latin American satraps. It is measured by its progress in educating the "new man." To be armed for self-defense, to be on the slow arduous road to some degree of agricultural self-sufficiency, to have virtually abolished illiteracy, to have provided the majority of people with an adequate diet and medical services for the first time in their lives—all these remarkable accomplishments are just preparations for the "avant-garde" revolution Cuba wishes to make. In this revolution, a revolution in consciousness that requires turning the whole country into a school, posters are an important method (among others) of public teaching.

Posters have rarely voiced the avant-garde of political consciousness, any more than they have been genuinely avant-garde aesthetically. Left-revolutionary posters usually occupy the middle and rear portions of political consciousness. Their job is to confirm, reinforce, and further disseminate values held by the ideologically more advanced strata of the population. But Cuban political posters are not typical. In most political posters, the level of exhortation has not greater amplitude than a few simple emotive words—a command, a victory slogan, an invective. The Cubans use posters to convey complex moral ideas (notably some posters made for COR, like "Crear consciencia . . ." and "Espiritu de trabajo . . ."). Unlike most political posters, the Cuban posters sometimes say a great deal. And, sometimes, they say hardly anything at all. Perhaps the most advanced aspect of Cuban political posters is their taste for visual and verbal understatement. There seems no demand on the poster artists to be explicitly and continuously didactic. And when didactic, the posters—in happy contrast to the Cuban press, which seems seriously to underestimate the intelligence of people—are almost never strident or shrill or heavy-handed. (This is hardly to argue that there is no proper place for bluntness in political art, or that stridency always betrays intelligence. One of the most important means of changing consciousness is to give things their proper *names*. And naming may, in certain historical situations, mean name-calling. Broadcasting relevant invective and insult, like the French posters from May 1968 which pointed out "*C'est lui, le chienlit*" and "CRS=SS," had a perfectly serious political use in de-mystifying and delegitimizing repressive authority.)

In the Cuban context, however, such stridency or heavy-handedness would be an error, as the poster makers often avow. The posters mostly keep to a tone which is sober and emotionally dignified while never detached, while being put to most of the high-keyed uses political posters conventionally have in revolutionary societies actively engaged in ideological self-transformation. Posters mark off important public spaces. Thus, the vast Plaza de la Revolución, which can hold a million people for a rally, is largely defined by the huge colorful posters on the sides of the tall buildings bordering the Plaza. And posters signal important public times. Since the revolution each year is given a name in January (1969 was "The Year of the Decisive Effort," referring to the sugar harvest), and a poster announcing this is put up all over the island. Posters also supply a set of visual commentaries on the main political events in the course of the year: they announce days of solidarity with foreign struggles, publicize rallies and international congresses, commemorate historical anniversaries, and so forth. But despite the plethora of official functions they fill, the posters have a remarkable grace. At least some political posters establish an astonishing degree of independent existence as decorative objects. As often as they convey a particular message, they simply express (through being beautiful) *pleasure* at certain ideas, moral attitudes, and ennobling historical references. For just one example, look on p. 22 at the poster "Cien Años de Lucha 1868–1968." The sobriety and refusal to make a statement in this poster is quite typical of what the Cubans have done. Of course, even the brief text of a poster can convey an analysis not just a slogan but a genuine piece of political analysis, like the Paris posters from May warning people against the ideological poisons of the press, radio, and television—one showed a crude drawing of a television set, above which was written "*Intox!*" The Cuban posters are much less analytic than the posters from the recent French revolution; they educate in a more indirect, emotional, graphically sensuous way. (Of course, Cuba lacks a tradition of intellectual analysis comparable to the French.) Rare are the political posters which do not involve some degree of moral flattery of their audience. The Cuban political posters flatter the senses. They are more stately, more dignified than the French posters from May 1968—which cultivated, for reasons of practical exigency as well as ideological motives, a raw, naïve, improvised, youthful look.

That posters of this deliberate aesthetic ambition appear frequently in Cuba, even that any are made at all, should hardly be taken for granted. The look that the Cuban posters aim at, and usually achieve, requires—besides talented artists—careful technical work, good paper, and other costly facilities. It is perhaps comprehensible that even a country coping with such severe economic shortages might allocate so much time and money and scarce paper to do political posters (and other forms of political graphics—like the exuberant layout of *Tricontinental* magazine, done by Alfredo Rostgaard, who makes most of the OSPAAAL posters). But the important educational role of political graphics in Cuba hardly explains altogether the high level, and expensive means, of Cuban poster art. For the Cuban poster is certainly not exclusively political, nor even (like the poster output of North Vietnam) mainly so. Many posters have no political content at all, and these include some of the most expensively and carefully produced posters—those done to advertise films. Advertising cultural events is the task of most of the altogether nonpolitical posters. In appealing, sometimes whimsical and sometimes dramatic, images and playful typography, these posters announce movies, plays, the visit of the Bolshoi Ballet, a national song contest, a gallery exhibit, and the like. Thus Cuban poster artists apparently perpetuate one of the earliest and most durable poster genres: the theatrical poster. But there is an important difference. The Cubans make posters to advertise culture in a society that seeks *not* to treat culture as an ensemble of commodities—events and objects designed, whether consciously or not, for commercial exploitation. Then the very project of cultural advertising becomes somewhat paradoxical, if not gratuitous. And indeed, many of these posters do not really fill any practical need. A beautiful poster made for the showing in Havana of, say, a minor movie by Alain Jessura, every performance of which will be sold out anyway (because movies are one of the few entertainments available), is a luxury item, something done in the end for its own sake. More often than not, a poster for ICAIC by Tony Reboiro or Eduardo Bachs amounts to the creation of a new work of art, supplementary to the film, rather than to a cultural advertisement in the familiar sense.

The élan and aesthetic self-sufficiency of the Cuban posters seem even more remarkable when one considers that the poster is itself a new art form in Cuba. Before the revolution, the only posters to be seen in Cuba were the most vulgar types of American billboard advertising. Indeed, many of the pre-1959 posters in Havana had English texts, addressing themselves not even to the Cubans but directly to the American tourists whose dollars were a principal source of Cuba's earnings, and to the American residents, most of them businessmen who controlled and exploited Cuba's economy. Cuba, like most other Latin American countries—the weak exceptions are Mexico, Brazil, and Argentina—had no indigenous poster tradition. Now, the best posters made anywhere in Latin America come from Cuba. (The efflorescence of Cuban poster art in recent years is hardly known, however, due to the isolation of Cuba from the non-communist world imposed by American policy. Writing as recently as 1968, Hutchinson does not exempt Cuba from his general dismissal of Latin America as a place where posters of high quality originate.) What accounts for the extraordinary burst of talent and energy in this art form in particular? Needless to say, other arts beside the poster are practiced with great distinction in Cuba today—notably, prose literature and poetry, with flourishing traditions that long predate the revolution, and the cinema, which, like poster making, had no roots at all. But perhaps the poster provides, better than any other form at this time, an ideal medium for reconciling (or at least containing) two potentially antagonistic views of art. In one, art expresses and explores an individual sensibility. In the other, art serves a social-political or ethical aim. To the credit of the Cuban Revolution, the contradiction between these two views of art has *not* been resolved. And in the interim, the poster form is one where the clash is not so sharp.

Posters in Cuba are done by individual artists, most of whom are relatively young (born in the late 1930s and early 1940s) and some of whom, notably Raúl Martínez and Umberto Peña, were originally painters. There seems to be no impulse to make posters collectively, as they are made in China (along with most other art forms, including poetry) or as they were by the revolutionary students of the Ecole des Beaux Arts in Paris in May 1968. But while Cuban posters, whether signed or unsigned, remain the work of individuals, most of these artists use a variety of individual styles. Stylistic eclecticism is perhaps one way of blurring the latent dilemma for the artist in a revolutionary society of having an individual signature. It is not easy to identify the work of Cuba's leading poster makers: Beltrán, Peña, Rostgaard, Reboiro, Azcuy Martínez, and Bachs. As an artist moves back and forth between designing a political poster for OSPAAAL one week and a film poster for ICAIC the next week, his style may change sharply. And this eclecticism within the work of individual poster artists characterizes, even more strikingly, the whole body of posters made in Cuba. They show a wide range of influences from abroad which include the doggedly personal styles of American poster makers like Saul Bass and Milton Glazer; the style of the Czech film posters from the 1960s by Josef Flejar and Zdenek Chotenovsky; the naïve style of the *Images d'Epinal;* the neo-Art Nouveau style popularized by the Fillmore and Avalon posters of the mid-1960s; and the Pop Art style, itself parasitic on commercial poster esthetics, of Andy Warhol, Roy Lichtenstein, and Tom Wesselman.

Of course, the poster makers have an easier situation than some other artists in Cuba. They do not share in the burden inherited by literature, in which the pursuit of artistic excellence is partly defined in terms of a restriction of the audience. Literature, in the centuries since it ceased to be a primarily oral and therefore public art, has become increasingly identified with a solitary act (reading), with a withdrawal into a private self. Good literature can, and often does, appeal only to an educated minority. Good posters cannot be an object of consumption by an elite. (What is properly called a poster implies a certain context of production and distribution, which excludes work, like the pseudo-posters of Warhol, produced directly for the fine arts market.) The space within which the genuine poster is shown is not elitist, but a public—communal—space. As they testify in numerous interviews, the Cuban poster artists remain very conscious that the poster is a public art, which addresses an undifferentiated mass of people *on behalf of* something public (whether a political idea or a cultural spectacle). The graphics artist in a revolutionary society doesn't have the problem the poet has, when the poet uses the singular voice, the lyrical *I* the problem of *who* is speaking and being spoken for.

Beyond a certain point, however, the place of the artist in a revolutionary society—no matter what his medium—is always a problematic. The modern view of the artist is rooted in the ideology of bourgeois capitalist society, with its highly elaborated notion of personal individuality and its presumption of a fundamental, ultimate antagonism between the individual and society. The further the notion of the individual is driven, the more acute becomes the polarization of individual versus society. And for well over a century, the artist has been precisely the extreme (or exemplary) case of the "isolated individual." The artist, according to the modern myth, is spontaneous, free, self-motivated—and frequently drawn to the role of the critic, or outsider, or disaffected nonparticipant. Thus, it has seemed self-evident to the leadership of every modern revolutionary government, or movement, that in a radically reconstructed social order the definition of the artist would have to change. Indeed, many artists in bourgeois society have denounced the confinement of art to small elite audiences (William Morris said: "I don't want art for a few, any more than education for a few, or freedom for a few.") and the selfish privatism of many artists' lives. The criticism is easy to agree to in principle, hard to translate into practice. For one thing, most serious artists are quite attached to the "culturally revolutionary" role they play in societies which (they hope) are moving toward, but have not yet entered, a revolutionary situation. In a prerevolutionary situation, cultural revolution mainly consists of creating modes of *negative* experience and sensibility. It means making disruptions, refusals. This role is hard to give up, once one has become adept at it. Another particularly intransigent aspect of the artist's identity is the extent to which serious art has appropriated for itself the rhetoric of revolution. Work that pushes back the frontier of negativity is not only defined, throughout the modern history of the arts, as valuable and necessary. It is also defined as revolutionary, even though, contrary to the standards by which the merits of politically revolutionary acts is measured—popular appeal—the avant-garde artist's acts have tended to confine the audience for art to the socially privileged, to trained culture consumers. This cooption of the idea of revolution by the arts has introduced some dangerous confusions and encouraged misleading hopes.

It is natural for the artist—who is, so often, a critic of his society—to think when caught up in a revolutionary movement in his own country, that what he considers revolutionary in art is akin to the political revolution going on, and to believe that he can put his art at the service of the revolution. But so far there exists, at best, an uneasy union between revolutionary ideas in art and revolutionary ideas in politics. Virtually all the leaders in the great political revolutions have failed to see the connection at all, and indeed quickly sensed in revolutionary (modernist) art a disagreeable form of oppositional activity. Lenin's revolutionary politics coexisted with a distinctly retrograde literary taste. He loved Pushkin and Turgenev. He detested

Russian Futurists, and found Mayakovsky's bohemian life and experimental poetry an affront to the revolution's high moral ideals and spirit of collective sacrifice. Even Trotsky, far more sophisticated about the arts than Lenin, wrote (in 1923) that the Futurists stood apart from the revolution, though he believed they could be integrated. As everyone knows, the career of revolutionary art in the Soviet Union was extremely short-lived. The final fling of "formalist" painting in post-revolutionary Russia was the Moscow group exhibition "5 × 5 = 25" in 1921. The decisive step away from nonrepresentational art was taken that year. As the decade wore on, the situation worsened steadily, and the government banned the Futurist artists. A few of the great avant-garde geniuses of the 1920s were allowed to continue working, but under conditions which promoted the coarsening of their talents (like Eisenstein and Djiga Vertov). Many were intimidated into silence; others chose suicide or exile; some (like Mandelstam, Babel, and Meyerhold) were eventually sent to death in labor camps.

In the context of all these problems and disastrous historical precedents, the Cubans have taken a modest tack. The debate on Cuban graphic art in the July 1969 issue of *Cuba Internaccional,* cited later in this book by Dugald Stermer, goes over the traditional problems raised by the task of reconceiving art in a revolutionary society, of determining what are the legitimate freedoms and responsibilities of the artist. One-sided options are condemned; pure utilitarianism as well as pure aestheticism, the frivolity of self-indulgent abstractness as well as the aesthetic poverty of banal realism. The usual civilized pieties are advanced: the wish to avoid sledge-hammer propagandism but to remain relevant and understandable. It is the same old discussion. (For a more ample discussion, with reference to all the arts, see issue #4, from December 1967, of *Unión,* the magazine published by the Union of Writers and Artists.) The analysis is not particularly original. What is impressive, and heartening, is the Cuban solution; not to come to any particular solution, *not* to put great pressure on the artist. The debate continues, and so does the high quality of the Cuban posters. Comparisons with the poster art of the Soviet Union for more than forty years— indeed with the public propagandistic art of all the countries of Eastern Europe—puts in an almost monotonously favorable light the Cuban government's achievement in resisting an ethically and esthetically philistine treatment of its artists. The Cuban way with artists is pragmatic, and largely respectful.

Admittedly, one cannot take the relatively happy relation of the poster artists to the revolution as uniformly typical of the situation of artists in Cuba. Among all the Cuban artists, the poster makers have a particularly easy time integrating their identity as artists with the demands and appeals of the revolution. Every society in the throes of revolution puts a heavy demand on art to have some connection with public values. The poster maker has no fundamental difficulty in acceding to this demand, posters being both an art form and also an extremely literal means of creating values. After the poster, the art form that seems almost as comfortable with this demand is the cinema—as evidenced by the remarkable work of Santiago Alvarez and the young directors of feature films. With other art forms, the situation is less unequivocal. As relatively permissive toward artists as the Cuban Revolution is, more individual voices (even among artists whose commitment to the revolution is unquestionable) have run into opposition. Last year, ugly pressures were brought to bear on Hubert Padilla, probably the best of the younger poets. It should be mentioned that during Padilla's ordeal, which included being attacked in the press, temporarily losing his government job, and having his book, after it received a prize from the Casa de las Americas, printed with a preface criticizing the award of the prize to him, there was never any question of refusing the print his book, of censoring his poetry—much less of jailing him. One hopes, and has good reason to believe, that the Padilla case is an exception; though it is perhaps significant that Padilla was not totally vindicated, and did not get his job back, until Castro personally intervened in the matter. Lyric poetry, the most private of arts, is perhaps the most vulnerable in a revolutionary society as poster making is the most adaptable. But this is hardly to say that only poets can be frustrated in Cuba. The conflict between aesthetic and sheerly practical, even more than ideological, considerations has created problems even for the other public arts—for example, architecture. Probably, Cuba simply cannot afford buildings like the School of Fine Arts in the suburbs of Havana done by Ricardo Porro in 1965, which is one of the most beautiful modern structures in the world. The priority now given to the design of, say, aesthetically banal low-cost prefabricated houses over the construction of another original, glamorous, and expensive building like that one is hardly unreasonable. But the conflict of utility (and economic rationality) versus beauty seems hardly to have affected the policy toward posters—perhaps because poster production represents much less of an expenditure, and seems more obviously useful; and because "individuality" is traditionally a less important norm of poster esthetics than it is in modern literature, cinema, or architecture.

In their beauty, their stylishness, and their transcendence of either mere utility or mere propaganda, these posters give evidence of a revolutionary society that is not repressive and philistine. The posters demonstrate that Cuba has a culture that is alive, international in orientation, and relatively free of the kind of bureaucratic interference that has blighted the arts in practically every other country where a communist revolution has come to power. Still, one cannot automatically take these attractive aspects of the Cuban Revolution as an organic part of revolutionary ideology and practice. It could be argued that the relatively high degree of freedom enjoyed by Cuban artists, however admirable, is not part of a revolutionary redefinition of the artist, but does no more than perpetuate one of the highest values claimed for the artist in bourgeois society. More generally, the liveliness and openness of Cuban culture does not mean that Cuba necessarily possesses a revolutionary culture.

Cuban posters reflect the revolutionary communist ethic of Cuba in one obvious respect, of course. Every revolutionary society seeks to limit the type, if not the content, of public signs (if not actually to assure centralized control over them)— a limitation that follows logically on the rejection of the consumer society, with its phony free-choice among goods clamoring to be bought and entertainments demanding to be sampled. But are the Cuban posters "revolutionary" in any further sense than this? As has already been noted, they are not revolutionary as that idea is used by the modernist movement in the arts. Good as they are, the Cuban posters are not artistically radical or revolutionary. They are too eclectic for that. (But perhaps no posters are, given the tradition of stylistic parasitism in poster-making of all genres.) Neither can they be considered manifestations of a politically revolutionary conception of art, beyond the fact that many though hardly all of the posters illustrate the political ideas, memories, and hopes of the revolution.

Cuba has not solved the problem of creating a new, revolutionary art for a new, revolutionary society—assuming that indeed a revolutionary society *needs* its own kind of art. Some radicals, of course, believe that it does not, that it is a mistake to think that a revolutionary society needs a revolutionary art (as bourgeois society had bourgeois art). In this view, the revolution need not and should not reject bourgeois culture since this culture, in the arts as well as the sciences, is in fact the highest form of culture. All that the revolution should do with bourgeois culture is democratize it, making it available to everyone and not just a socially privileged minority. It is an attractive argument, but unfortunately too unhistorical to be convincing. Undoubtedly, there are many elements of the culture of bourgeois society that should be retained and incorporated into a revolutionary society. But one cannot ignore the sociological roots and ideological function of that culture. From a historical perspective, it seems much more likely that, precisely as bourgeois society achieved its remarkable "hegemony" through the splendid achievements of bourgeois culture, a revolutionary society must establish new, equally persuasive and complex forms of culture. Indeed, according to the great Italian Marxist Antonio Gramsci—the foremost exponent of this view—the very overthrow of the bourgeois state must wait until there is first a nonviolent revolution in civil society. Culture, more than the strictly political and economic institutions of the state, is the medium of this necessary civil revolution. It is, above all, a change in people's perceptions of themselves, which is created by culture. It is self-evident to Gramsci that the revolution demands a new culture.

In Gramsci's sense of a change of culture, Cuban poster art does not embody radically new values. The values represented in the posters are internationalism, diversity, eclecticism, moral seriousness, commitment to artistic excellence, sensuality—the positive sum of Cuba's refusal of philistinism or crude utilitarianism. These are mainly *critical* values, arrived at by rejecting two opposing models: the vulgar commerciality of American poster art (and its imitations in the billboards multiplying throughout Western Europe and Latin America), on the one side, and the drab ugliness of Soviet socialist realism and the folkloric and hagiographic naïveté of Chinese political graphics, on the other. Nevertheless, the fact that these are critical values, those of a society in transition, does not mean they cannot be, in a stronger or special context, also revolutionary values.

Talking about revolutionary values in the abstract, without being historically specific, is superficial. In Cuba, one of the most powerful revolutionary values is internationalism. The promotion of internationalist consciousness plays almost as large a role in Cuba as the promotion of nationalist consciousness plays in most other left-revolutionary societies (like North Vietnam, North Korea, and China) and insurgent movements. The revolutionary élan of Cuba is profoundly rooted in its *not* settling for the achievements of a national revolution, but being passionately committed to the cause of revolution on a global scale. Thus Cuba is probably the only communist country in the world where people really care about Vietnam. Ordinary citizens, as well as public officials, frequently make a point of belittling the severity of their own struggle and hardships, comparing them with those endured for decades by the Vietnamese. Among the mammoth posters that dominate the great Plaza de la Revolucíon in Havana, equal prominence is given to a poster of Che, a poster honoring the struggle of the Vietnamese people, and a poster hailing the goal of ten million tons for the 1970 sugar harvest. Those posters which illustrate Cuba's own revolutionary history are not intended simply to inspire patriotic feeling, but to demonstrate the Cuban link with international struggle. Equal in importance on the political calendar to the days commemorating the martyrdoms in Cuba's own history are the days of solidarity with other peoples, for each of which a poster is designed. (Examples, in this book, are posters for the days of solidarity with the people of Zimbabwe, of the United States' black colony, of Latin America, and of Vietnam.) An inverse measure of this theme of solidarity is the fact that the Cuban political posters rarely divide the world into black and white, friends and enemies—like the "Love the Fatherland" posters in East Germany, or the Vietnamese poster images of the American "pirate aggressor." The imagery on the Cuban political posters is almost always affirmative, without being sentimental. Practically none are devoted to invective or caricature. As few of them resort to crude exhortation, practically none depend on Manichean moral polarizing.

Thus, even the very eclecticism of the Cuban poster artists has a political dimension, in that it too reaffirms Cuba's distinctive refusal of national chauvinism. The claims of the nationalist versus the internationalist perspective is perhaps the most acute issue in Cuban art today. In almost all the arts, there is a sharp division of attitude on this issue, which tends to run—like so many conflicts these days—along generational lines. The rule seems to be that whatever the art form, the older generation tends to be nationalist, that is, folkloric, more "realistic," while the younger generation tends to be internationally minded, avant-garde, "abstract." In music, for instance, the split is particularly severe. The younger composers are drawn to Boulez and Henze, while the older composers press for a distinctively Cuban music based on Afro-Cuban rhythms and instrumentation and the *danson* tradition. But in the poster, as in the cinema, such a split hardly exists—a fact which may have helped to make these art forms particularly distinguished in Cuba now. Nobody from an older generation is making movies, because the only movies made before 1959 were stag films (Cuba was North America's principal supplier). In less than a decade, the new Cuban film industry has already turned out several very good feature-length fiction films and some impressive short films and documentaries. All Cuban films reflect a diverse range of foreign influences, both from the European art cinema and the American underground. And all Cuban poster art, also lacking any roots prior to the revolution and similarly free of a conflict between older and younger artists, is international in influence.

Contrary to what older artists in Cuba often allege, it is internationalism—not nationalism—in art which best serves the revolution's cause, even its secondary task of building a proper sense of national pride. Cuba suffers profoundly from a complex of underdevelopment, as the novelist Edmundo Desnoes has called it. This is not just a national neurosis, but a real historical fact. One cannot overestimate the damage influenced on Cuba by American cultural, as well as economic, imperialism. Now, though isolated and besieged by the United States, Cuba is open to the whole world. Internationalism is the most effective and most liberating response to the problem of Cuba's cultural lag. The fact that the theaters in Havana play Albee as well as Brecht is neither a sign that the Cubans are still hung-up on bourgeois art nor a symptom of revisionist soft-mindedness (as a similar-looking cultural policy is in nonmilitant Yugoslavia). It is a revolutionary act for Cuba, at this historical moment, to continue to accommodate works of bourgeois culture from all over the world, and to draw on the aesthetic styles perfected in bourgeois culture. This accommodation does not mean that the Cubans don't want a cultural revolution, but only that they are pursuing this goal in their own terms, according to their own experience and needs. There can be no universal recipe for cultural revolution. And in determining what a cultural revolution would mean for a given country, one must take into particular account the available resources of the national past. Cultural revolution in China, with its magnificent culture stretching back through the millennia of history, must necessarily have different norms than a cultural revolution in Cuba. Apart from the strong survivals of Yoruba and other African tribal cultures, Cuba possesses only the bastardized remnants of the culture of oppressors—first the Spanish, then the Americans. Cuba has no long, prideful national history to look back on, as do the Vietnamese. The history of the country is little else than the history of one hundred years of struggle, from Martí and Maceo to Fidel and Che. Becoming international is then Cuba's indigenous path to cultural revolution.

This concept of cultural revolution is, of course, not the usual one. Far more common is the view which assigns to art in a revolutionary society the task of purifying, renewing, and glorifying the culture. Such a demand on art is a familiar part of the program of most fascist regimes, from Germany and Italy in the 1930s to the Greek colonels today, as well as of Soviet Russia for over forty years. In its overtly fascist form, this project is usually conceived along strictly nationalist lines. Cultural revolution means national purification: eliminating unassimilable, dissonant art from the nation's cultural past and foreign corruptions of the country's language. It means national self-renewal, that is, reconceiving the nation's past so that it seems to lend support to the new goals proposed by the revolution. Such a program for cultural revolution always criticizes the old bourgeois culture of the prerevolutionary society as being both elitist and essentially empty, ephemeral, or formalist. This culture must be purged. A new culture is summoned to take its place, one that all citizens will be capable of appreciating, whose function will be to increase the individual's identification with the nation, to simplify consciousness in the hope of reducing private disaffection (by reducing the dissonance of ideas and moods and styles in the country), and to promote civic virtue.[1] This, perhaps the most common notion of cultural revolution, is the policy not only of fascist revolutions, but, all too often, of societies that have mounted revolutions from the left. But genuine left-revolutionary societies and movements have, or ought to have, a quite different notion of cultural revolution. The proper goal of a left-wing cultural revolution is not to increase national pride, but to transcend it. Such a revolution would not seek to systematically revive old cultural forms (nor practice selective censorship of the past), but to invent new forms. Its purpose would not be to renew or purify consciousness, but to change it—to raise or educate people to a new consciousness.

According to the view of some radicals, the only authentic forms of revolutionary art are those produced (and experienced) collectively; or at least, it is felt, revolutionary art forms cannot wholly originate from the work of a single individual. In this view, the organizing of collective spectacles would be the quintessential form of revolutionary art—from the spectacles celebrating the Goddess of Reason devised by Jacques-Louis David during the French Revolution to the long Chinese film epic of the early 1960s, *The East is Red*. But the example of Cuba, which has pretty much rejected the organization of spectacles as a valuable form of revolutionary activity, leads one to question this view. Spectacle, the favorite public art form of most revolutionary societies, whether of the right or the left, is implicitly understood by the Cubans as repressive. What replaces a taste for revolutionary spectacle is the fascination with the scenario of revolutionary action. It may be the scenario of a great public project, like the anti-illiteracy campaign in 1960, the settling by militant youth of the Isle of Pines, and the 1970 sugar harvest. (In such projects, the whole population, as far as it is feasible, participates—but not as something seen, something organized for the eye of a viewer.) Or it may be the scenario of an exemplary struggle by an individual, in the history of Cuban liberation, or by a movement abroad with whose agon the Cubans identify and by whose victories they feel morally nourished. What interests the Cubans, as a resource for political art, is the dramatically exemplary aspect of radical activity. The dramatically valid spectacle may be the life and death of Che, or the Vietnamese struggle, or the ordeal of Bobby Seale. For radical activity can take place anywhere, everywhere—not just in Cuba. This is the fundamental dramaturgic identification that fuels their internationalism.

In this political conception, poster art plays a particularly useful, compact role. Political posters in Cuba give a lexicon of the important scenarios—the struggle of blacks in the United States, the guerrilla movement in Mozambique, Vietnam, and so forth, down a long list—which are going on right now. The retrospective themes of many of the Cuban posters are no less international in orientation. A poster asking people to remember the victims of Hiroshima has the same purpose as a poster recalling the martyrs of the Moncada assault in 1956 which launched the Cuban revolution. Political posters in Cuba function to enlarge moral consciousness, to attach the sense of moral responsibility to an *increasing* number of issues. This enterprise may be regarded as impractical, gratuitous, even quixotic for a small, beleaguered island of seven million people barely managing to subsist under the American siege. The same spirit of gratuitousness is revealed, in a specific instance, in the decision to make beautiful posters advertising cultural events which everyone wants to see and will attend anyway. One only hopes the Cuban genius for the impractical moral ambition, for limited, seemingly arbitrary, yet extravagant gratifications of the senses—from the posters to the Coppelia ice-cream palaces—can be sustained, that it will not diminish. For just this taste for the gratuitous gives life in Cuba a feeling of spaciousness, despite all the severe internal and external restraints; and gives the Cuban Revolution, more than any other communist revolution in progress, its inventiveness, youth, humor, and extravagance.

III.

If the task of a cultural revolution and of conceiving a politically revolutionary role for artists is full of difficulties and contradictions *within* the context of an ongoing political revolution, the prospects for a genuine cultural revolution outside (or before) a political one are even more problematic. The history of virtually all the ostensibly revolutionary movements in art and culture to have arisen in non- or prerevolutionary societies is hardly encouraging. It is, more or less, simply the history of cooption. The fate of the Bauhaus movement is only one example, among many, of how revolutionary forms of culture arising within bourgeois society are first attacked, then neutralized, and finally absorbed by that society. Capitalism transforms all objects, including art, into commodities. And the poster—including the revolutionary poster—is hardly exempt from this iron rule of cooption.

At the present time, poster art is in a period of renaissance. Posters have come to be regarded as mysterious cultural objects, whose flatness and literalness only deepen their resonance, as well as inexhaustibly rich emblems of the society. In recent years, the eye of film-makers has turned more and more to posters. They appear as magical, partly opaque references; think of the use of posters as key objects in almost all Godard's films. They are cited as eloquent and exact sociological and moral evidence; a recent example is Antonioni's tour of Los Angeles billboard fantasies in the early part of *Zabriskie Point*. (This new, enriched role of the poster in movie iconology since 1960 has little to do with the traditional use of the poster in cinema narrative—to convey briefly some necessary information—that begins with the shot of the poster of Irma Vep, played by Musidora, in Feuilade's *Les Vampires* [1915].) But the extent to which poster images come to be more and more frequently incorporated within other arts is only one, fairly specialized, index of interest. Posters have appeared increasingly interesting not only as points of reference, but as objects in themselves.

Posters have become one of the most ubiquitous kinds of cultural objects—prized partly because they are cheap, unpretentious, "popular" art. The current renaissance of poster art derives its strength less from any more original type of production or more intensive public use of posters than from the astonishing surge of interest in collecting posters, in domesticating them.

The current interest differs in several ways from the first wave of poster collecting, which started two decades after posters began to appear. First, it is simply much bigger in scale, as befits a later, more advanced stage in the era of mechanical reproduction. Poster-collecting in the 1890s may have been fashionable, but it was hardly, as it is now, a mass addiction. Second, a much broader range of posters is being collected. The collections of the 1890s tended to be from the collector's own country. Recent poster collections tend to be ostentatiously international. And it is hardly accidental that the beginning of the craze for collecting posters, in the mid-1950s, coincides with the rising tide of postwar American tourism in Europe, which has now made regular trips across the Atlantic as banal a prerogative of middle-class life here as vacations at American seaside resorts had been in an earlier age. This archetypal public object, once collected by only a small band of connoisseurs, has now become a standard private object in the living rooms, bedrooms, bathrooms, and kitchens of the young American and European bourgeoisie. In such collections, the poster is not simply—as it once was—a new, exotic kind of art object. It has a more special function. As poster art is itself usually parasitic on other forms of art, the new fashion of collecting posters constitutes a meta-parasitism—on the world itself, or a highly stylized image of it. Posters furnish a portable image of the world. A poster is like a miniature of an event: a quotation—from life, or from high art. Modern poster-collecting is related to the modern phenomenon of mass tourism. As collected now, the poster becomes a souvenir of an event. But between the poster of El Codobes or the great Rembrandt retrospective hanging on the wall and the photographs the middle-class tourist took of his summer vacation in Italy mounted in an album, there is one important difference. Somebody had to be there to take the photographs; nobody had to go to Seville or Amsterdam to buy the poster. More often than not, the collector never actually visited the art exhibit or attended the bullfight advertised in the posters he has hanging on his wall. The posters are, rather, substitutes for experience. Like the photographs taken by a tourist, the poster functions as a souvenir of an event. But the event is often which has taken place in the past and which the collector first learns about when he acquires the poster. Since what the poster illustrates is often not part of his personal history, the collection becomes instead a set of souvenirs of imaginary experiences.

What spectacles and events and people one has chosen to hang in miniaturized form on one's wall does not merely constitute a facile kind of vicarious experience. It is also, plainly, a form of homage. By means of posters, everyone can easily and quickly select a personal pantheon—even if he cannot be said to have created it, since most poster buyers are confined to choosing among the numerically limited, already selected assortment of mass-produced posters offered for sale. What posters one choose to nail up in his living room indicates, as clearly as his choice of a painting might have in the past, the *taste* of the owner of the private space. It is, sometimes, a form of cultural boasting—a particularly cheap example of a use to which culture has traditionally been put in all class societies: to indicate or affirm or lay claim to a given social status. Often the purpose is more cool, less pushy than this. As a cultural trophy, the display of a poster in one's private space is, at the very least, a clear means of self-identification to visitors, a code (for those who know it) by which the various members of a cultural subgroup announced themselves to each other and recognize each other. The display of good taste in the old bourgeois sense has given way to the display of a kind of calculated bad taste—which, when it accords with or is just in advance of fashion, becomes a sign of good taste. One does not necessarily lend one's approval to the subjects represented in the posters hanging on his walls. It suffices that one indicates an awareness of the worldly value, with some nuances, of these subjects. In this complex sense posters become, when collected, a cultural trophy. Far from indicating any simple approval or identification with the subject, the range of posters displayed in someone's private space may mean no more than a kind of lexicon of nostalgia and irony.

As might be expected, even in the relatively brief history of the modern revival of poster collecting, the choice of the kind of posters to hang is subject to marked changes in fashion. The bullfight posters and posters of Paris art exhibitions, almost ubiquitous a decade ago, evidence rear-guard taste now. Some time ago these were over-taken by Mucha posters and by old movie posters (the older the better; Saul Bass posters from the 1950s are too recent). Then came the vogue of posters advertising exhibits by American not European artists (for example, the famous posters of Warhol, Johns, Rauschenberg, and Lichtenstein shows). After that came the rock ballroom posters, which were succeeded by the head posters, for looking at when stoned. Starting in the late 1960s, a major part of collecting interest has shifted to radical political posters. It seems odd, at first, that the radical political poster has such apparently diverse uses. It appeals to the populations of economically under-developed, ex-colonial societies, many of whom can barely read. It also appeals to the most literate young people in the most advanced industrial nation, the United States, who have challenged the preemi-nence of discursive language in favor of more emotive, nonverbal forms of saying.

In the succession of poster fashions it is rare for one type of poster to displace another. Rather, the interest in a new poster subject is added on to the already exist-ing interest in others. So the audience grows. Every big city in America and most major cities in Europe now have numerous places where posters can be bought. The head shop is one type of outlet common in the United States; its distinctive, if narrow, mixture of wares includes—besides posters—cigarette papers, pipes, roach holders, strobe and op lights, peace symbol jewelry, and buttons printed with satiric, inso-lent, or obscene slogans. Posters are now sold in the rear of discount bookstores and some metropolitan drug stores. For more serious or at least more affluent collectors, stores like Posters Original Unlimited in New York City stock only posters; these come from all over the world. Recently, though, the mass printing of large blow-ups of photographs has somewhat cut into the poster market, while serving much the same function. These poster-size photographs are even cheaper, and therefore more widely sold, than the mass-reproduced reprint runs of posters. Perhaps, too, the poster-size photograph is inherently more attractive than a poster to many younger people—members of a generation marked by its profound experiences of nonverbal psychic states, notably through rock music and drugs—because it is a pure image: direct, frontal. The photograph posters are more neutral, more low-keyed, simply by virtue of always being black-and-white, than posters, which have colors. Posters still carry some residual traces of their origin in, and influences by, high arts such as painting. But the big blow-up photographs of famous people that are now being hung up on the wall, poster fashion, are about as neutral and impersonal as any image can be (though the image is of a person), and carry not the slightest stigma of art.

In collecting posters, there seems to be no risk of cultural indigestion. As in the crowded, haphazard arrangements of public space for which posters are originally designed, each poster in the collector's casual private space is innocent of its neighbor. A reprint of a poster from the Russian Revolution, bought at a Marboro bookstore, may hang alongside a poster sold at the Museum of Modern Art of its Magritte show several years ago. The same eclecticism, the same disregard of any notion of compatibility, marks the use of poster-size photographs. These are almost all photographs of celebrities, a category into which Huey Newton is fitted as easily as Garbo. Radical political leaders have the same status as movie stars. Though one comes from the world of politics and the other from the world of entertainment, both are celebrities, both are beautiful. This standard, of popularity or glamour, by which photographs are selected for reproduction in poster-size and marketed is reflected in their use. The poster is an icon—as it is in Cuba, where practically every home and office building has at least one poster of Che. But in the contemporary style of collecting posters (and poster-size photographs) almost uniform throughout the capitalist world, from Boston to Berlin, from Madison to Milan, the icons represent many kinds of admiration. These juxtapositions, whereby Ho Chi Minh is in the bathroom and Bogart is in the bedroom, while W. C. Fields hangs next to Marx over the dining room table, produces a kind of moral vertigo. Such morally startling collages indicate a very particular way of viewing the world, now endemic among the educated young bourgeois of America and Western Europe, that is one part sentimentality, one part irony, one part detachment.

Thus, collecting posters is related to tourism in yet another way than the one already mentioned. Modern tourism may be described as a means for a kind of symbolic appropriation of other cultures which takes place in a brief time, conducted in a state of functional alienation from (or nonparticipation in) the life of the country visited. Countries are reduced to places of "interest," and these are listed in guidebooks and graded. This procedure allows the tourist, once he has touched on these principal places, to feel he has actually had contact with the country visited. That specifically modern (indeed post–World War II) way of traveling which is modern mass tourism is something quite different from foreign travel as understood in earlier periods of bourgeois culture. Unlike travel in its traditional forms, modern tourism turns traveling into something more like buying. The traveler accumulates countries visited as he accumulates consumer goods. The process involves no commitment, and one experience never contradicts or excludes or genuinely modifies the one that came before or will come after. This is exactly the form of the modern avidity for the poster. Collecting posters is a species of emotional and moral tourism, a taste for which precludes, or at least contradicts, serious political commitment. The collecting of posters is a way of anthologizing the world, in such a fashion that one emotion or loyalty tends to cancel out another. Events and human beings represented in a poster are miniaturized or scaled down in a stronger sense than the literal, graphic one. The desire to miniaturize events and people incarnated in the current vogue of poster-collecting in bourgeois society is a desire to scale down the world itself, particularly what is alluring and disturbing in it.

In the case of radical political posters, this miniaturization of the events or persons incarnated in poster-collecting represents a subtle or not so subtle form of cooption. The poster, at its origins a means of selling a commodity, is itself turned into a commodity. The same process is taking place in the publication of this book—which involves a double reproduction (and miniaturization) of the Cuban posters. First, an

anthology is made of the available Cuban posters. Then, those which have been chosen are reproduced in a scaled-down size. This group of posters is then converted into
a new medium, a book, which is prefaced, typographically packaged, printed, distributed, and sold. The present use made of the Cuban posters is thus at least several steps
away from it original use, and involves a tacit betrayal of that use. For, whatever their
ultimate artistic and political value, the Cuban posters arise from the genuine situation of a people undergoing profound revolutionary change. Those who produce this
book, those like most people who will buy it and read it, live in counter-revolutionary
societies, societies with a flair for ripping any object out of context and turning it into
an object of consumption. Thus, it would not be altogether just to praise those who
have made this book. Especially Cuba's foreign friends, as well as those who merely
lean toward a favorable view of the Cuban Revolution, should not feel altogether
comfortable as they look through it. The book is itself a good example of how all
things in this society get turned into commodities, into forms of (usually) miniaturized spectacle and into objects of consumption. It is not possible, say, simply to regard
the "contents" of this book with sympathy, because the notion that the Cuban posters
make up the books content is really a spurious one. However much those who have
made this book may like to think of it simply as presenting the poster art of Cuba, to
a wider audience than ever before, the fact remains that the Cuban posters reproduced
in this book have thereby been converted into something other than what they are—
or were ever meant to be. They are now cultural objects, offered up for our delectation. They have become one more item in the cultural smorgasbord provided in affluent
bourgeois society. Such feasting eventually dulls all capacity for real commitment,
while the left-liberal bourgeoisie of such countries is lulled into thinking that it is
learning something, having its commitments and sympathies extended.

There is no way out of the trap, of course, as long as we—with our unlimited resources for waste, for destruction, and for mechanical reproductions—are here,
and the Cubans are there. No way out is possible as long as we are curious, as long as
we remain intoxicated with cultural good, as long as we live inside our restless, negative sensibilities. The corruption embodied in this book is subtle, scarcely unique, and
in the sum of things hardly even important. But is a real corruption nevertheless.
Caveat emptor, Viva Fidel.

First published in Dugald Stermer, The Art of Revolution: 96 Posters from Cuba *(New
York: McGraw-Hill, 1970).*

Notes

1. A concise, and little known, example of this idea of cultural revolution is the speech Pirandello gave in Rome in October 1935,
in the presence of Mussolini, at the inauguration of the new theatrical season at the Teatro Argentina. It can be found in the *Tulane
Drama Review* #44. . . . A less emphatically nationalist form of this right-wing conception of cultural revolution is used by conser-
vatives, like André Mairaux during his tenure as Minister of Culture under De Gaulle. For a devastating analysis of Mairaux' conception of bringing elite culture to the masses, and of the ideological purposes of the Gaullist conservative politics of culture, see
the essay by Violette Morin, "*Le culture majunscule: André Mairaux*," in *Communications* #14, 1969.

1972
HOW CAN ONE MAKE SWISS TYPOGRAPHY?
Wolfgang Weingart

A RADICAL THINKER, DESIGNER, *and pioneer of postmodernism, Wolfgang Weingart (b. 1941) attended the Künstgewerbeschule in Basel where he studied and later taught with Emil Ruder and Armin Hofmann. In the late 1960s, Weingart began a series of typographic experiments that challenged the rational principles and strict geometries that had previously characterized Swiss typography, introducing alternative models based on a reconstructed verbal/visual syntax. The ideas espoused in this particular lecture, originally given during a 1972–1973 tour of American design schools, are notable for questioning the fundamental theoretical suppositions upon which the Swiss school had long based its teaching. Using less predictable mannerisms—diagonal placements, randomized letterspacing—Weingart developed, both in his own work and in his teaching curricula, a series of syntactic, semantic, and pragmatic exercises that paved the way for what would later be considered, in the late 1970s and early 1980s, the New Wave in America.—JH*

WHAT IS 'SWISS TYPOGRAPHY'?

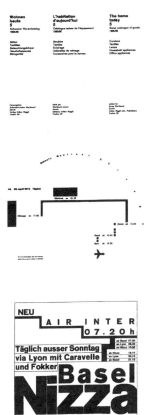

I am happy that I can be with you today, especially because your invitation has given me my first opportunity to visit America.

I have not come here to bring you something like the typographic message of salvation from the Old World, but instead to inform you about my school activities in Basle.

I deliberately do not say 'teaching activities' because the thinking, ideas, and typographic models that I want to show you are not only the results of my teaching in Basle, they are also the results of my intensive, private occupation with typography and graphic design. Both sides are not as separated from one another as I seem to imply—on the contrary, as you will see for yourself later.

Because I come from Switzerland and because the concept 'Swiss Typography' is probably connected with a fixed idea for you, I would like to supplement my introduction. I want especially to show you that not only one conception of typography exists in Switzerland. Simply stated, at least two directions exist. One direction is the well-known, moderate-objective or rational direction, with its design principles and methods. Another direction is a newer tendency towards a lively, relatively free kind of typography that renounces extensive design dogma, and tends to look unorthodox. But this second direction is unthinkable without the classical 'Swiss Typography,' in that it is a logical further development of it. That is the kind of typography which, together with my students, I have tried to develop for the past five years. With that, I end my introduction.

I would like to summarize what you can expect in the next sixty minutes: a confrontation with the legendary concept of 'Swiss Typography,' and a very personal statement of a very personal concept of typography and typography education. (For some people, maybe too personal).

But first, the answer to a question which I am repeatedly asked, and perhaps one that may be in the minds of some of you here: 'How did you come to teach typography in Basle, Weingart?

The short answer is that in 1963, by chance, I met Armin Hofmann. Actually, I only wanted to inquire about his and Emil Ruder's classes. I showed a few typographic designs that I had brought from Germany, and as far as I can remember there were three designs in particular (right) which enabled me to begin study with both teachers one year later. The attempt to learn typography with Emil Ruder failed. I felt myself less of a student, and more of an observer. In this role I remained free from typographic dogma, and critical in the face of design criteria. Also, the contact with Armin Hofmann was, at that time, very short—he left our school for some time and went to the national Design Institute in Ahmedabad, India. In that respect, I feel that I am neither a Hofmann student, nor a Ruder student, but instead, self-taught.

Through my way of making typography, and through publications in technical journals, my relationship to the Basle School was distant but friendly, especially with Armin Hofmann, who has actively supported my ideas all along. I can still remember the question in 1963 as to whether I would like to teach typography for him in the near future.

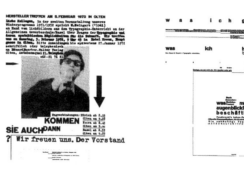

In spring 1968 the Advanced Course for Graphic Design was started, and today, as far as I know, it remains a solitary model in Switzerland, as well as the rest of Europe. It is attended predominantly by foreign students, the majority from America. Within this course, a position in the typography faculty was open, and so I began.

Up until that time it was accepted that the typography teachers and students would teach and learn typography according to the patented concept of 'Swiss Typography.'

What then, is to be understood by the term 'Swiss Typography?' We can attempt to explain this complex concept perhaps with the aid of these five especially typical examples:

With them, you can see that certain design principles are very predominant. That is, certain characteristics like the type style, design structure and gray value became immediately obvious in the trained observer. Everything is based on the right angle, and everything is ordered with regard to materials and the hand-setting process. The essential goal is to implicate the unprinted white space as a design factor. The criteria for this are the two rather puritanical concepts of 'information' and its 'readability,' which, in their complex meaning, are simplified. We are in agreement that today, in spite of all the progress and knowledge in communications research, there is no reliable definition of what is a reasonable, fair, unmanipulated message, completely aside from the question of whether there could, or even should be such a definition. Furthermore, it is also difficult to explain how a message could be translated, typographically, yet remain effective.

Here is where I began, because when all of the previous questions are unanswered, then 'Swiss Typography' can be only one of many possible directions, and in no way, as some of its advocates assume, the absolute typography. The deciding factor for me is to take the design criteria of 'Swiss Typography' as a sensible point of departure, and through teaching and experimentation, to develop new design models. Since the beginning, I have been conscious of what my responsibilities are as a typography teacher in Basle. It was never the idea to throw either 'Basle' or 'Swiss Typography' overboard, but rather to attempt to expand them—to enliven and change them with the help of intensively considered design criteria and new visual ideas. Finally, the reason for this lecture is to present the results of a relatively short period of development in both our class work and my own experimentation.

I think I should explain what I understand by the terms 'teaching method' and 'school.' It seems important to me, because such a definition will make the following pictures and theories more understandable.

Eidg. Schützenfest
Zürich
24. Juli bis
12. August 1963

'School,' for me, is an institution which, through a certain teaching program, attempts to clarify certain information. This information is essentially independent from the concrete demands made by existing professional standards. The teaching programs are open, not bound by fixed opinions. The content of the program is determined and constantly developed in the school. It is important that 'school' maintains an experimental character. The students should not be given irrevocable knowledge or values, but instead, the opportunity to independently search for such values and knowledge, to develop them, and learn to apply them.

The result of such schooling is not a programmed typography, but instead, a typography or graphic designer who, as a starting-point in his practical work, has the possibilities and potentialities of typography design in his grasp. This view is actually the trademark of the Basle school: providing thorough basic knowledge about design possibilities and constantly developing and building upon this knowledge. Not just the finding of pre-set design patterns, but instead, the attempt to train the senses to recognize alternative design directions, and to use each of these directions with equal importance, instead of searching for typographic expression, our educational goal is to find differentiated typographic solutions.

1972
Hausmitteilungen
Allgemeine
Gewerbeschule
Basel

In my typography class one can find both middle-axis and strong grid styles beside the freer, more flexible exercises. The prerequisite, exclusively, is that for every solution a design criterion must be developed. With that, the individual freedom is so large that, for example, an 'ugly' design can become a 'beautiful' design.

I hope that my short definition has made clear to you what kind of 'school' we are striving for in Basle, and how these ideas operate relative to the goals, methods and criteria of my typography course. Then, when you know these didactic ideas, you will find that the abundant possibilities of 'Swiss Typography,' which I will show you, are a natural consequence of them.

Grafik	Arts	Graphic art
einer	graphiques	of a
Schweizer	d'une	Swiss
Stadt	ville	town
	suisse	

With that, I believe I have clarified why I must speak about typography instruction, if I want to speak about typography. For me, one is not possible without the other.

Back to our theme: 'How Can One Make Swiss Typography?' Obviously the question has a double meaning. Its first objective is 'Swiss Typography,' although, as we have seen, no one actually knows exactly what 'Swiss Typography' is today. The second aim of the question is that of the 'making' of typography, which is in itself questionable, in that it is quite difficult to make something that one cannot exactly define. The answer to my two-sided question is: Firstly, all of the examples from my typography courses and my personal work are 'Swiss Typography'—they have been made in Switzerland, and stem from classical Swiss typography. Secondly, you will learn about the 'making' of this typography, in that I shall discuss its entire design process—that is, the preliminary, conceptual, and design considerations, as well as our final criteria.

I do not want to overlook a discussion about typography's right to exist. I think that its existence has a sense, as long as we have something to communicate—and that is as human beings, with very differentiated sensual needs, not as automatons with factual information needs, capable of being mechanically satisfied.

Despite this, I am not sure about the value and position of typography in today's communications scene. Certainly, typography today does not have, and cannot lead, its own life; much less so than in earlier times. But what does this 'own life' mean? Actually nothing more than life from itself, for itself, sufficient.

In contrast, this inside cover of the Rolling Stones' record *Exile on Main Street*

is exactly the opposite. The attempt is much more to express visually those specific Rolling Stones' qualities of hard-rock subculture aesthetics and nonconformist attitudes: 'shabby-beautiful.' A German music critic and non-designer said of this 'anti-design idea,' 'This cover, with all its vulgarity and tastelessness, works like an ironic comment on the polished image which the Rolling Stones acquired, in the eyes of many critics, after their last English tour.'

This cover questions the conventional concept of typography, which commonly means that which can be set and printed. As we knew, this idea is very limited. It originated from a handcraft ideology, in which there was no place for important modern reproduction methods.

In contrast, we define typography today as one of many design fields in which the object is to produce communication. We, the typographers, determine what the specific typographic means are, and which of these are to be used.

This is an example from the 1971 Peter Stuyvesant campaign in West Germany, which is probably unfamiliar to most of you. This campaign, which was one of the most successful ever in German advertising, ran for almost ten years with the slogan 'The Aroma of the Great Wide World.' After the firm had decided to develop a newer, more modern campaign, the problem was how to retain, at least partially, the old and successful conception. One does not just throw away that which has functioned so well. As you can see in the solution, only 'The Aroma' is placed above the Peter Stuyvesant pack with the words 'of the Great Wide World' being supplied by the mind of the German consumer.

The result in advertising, as strong conceptual ideas move to the foreground, design is pushed into the background. What is the function of typography here? For example, is readability a problem in this case, which must be solved with sensitivity?

It is because I think this way that my relationship with typography remains unbroken. I see the uncertainty, but I have it less than many other typographers. For me there have never been any typography problems, but instead, only typo*graphic* problems. There is no competition between text and picture, but instead, an alliance.

Although there is no picture involved, this example demonstrates clearly what I mean. At first, one recognizes only a kind of technical organization of the typographic elements, but with more critical observation, one realizes that the life of the design lies in its syntactical values. That is, from the connection between such elements as type, format and placement. I believe it is exactly here, in the expression of the syntactic moment, that the decisive criteria lie, in that here the graphic or total configuration comes to fruition.

A parallel example: a printed word can only function when the letters are placed in the correct syntactic order. But upon viewing the word, one is not conscious that the syntactic plays such a role. In other words, it becomes evident only when one of the letters is in the wrong position. Basel is readable for a German speaking person, and embodies a geographical location, whereas the world Basle is not. On the

BASEL

BASLE

other hand, the word Basle is understandable to an English speaking person. Basel: German, Basle: English.

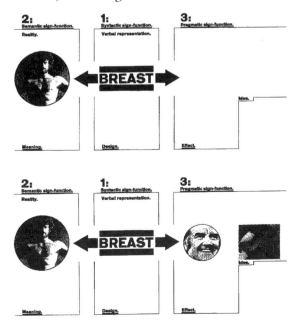

I would like to introduce the theoretical concept of syntax here, because it is something of a key concept in understanding my view of typography. It is a kind of fixpoint in my design goals, and the drive behind my didactic work. From now on, I will be repeatedly speaking about syntactic, semantic, and pragmatic relationships in typography. Some of you are probably not familiar with these elementary concepts in relation to a so-called communications theory, so I have made a diagram which should help illustrate the functions of signs. The point of departure is what one means by a 'sign.' In this case the word 'breast' has two meanings: the man's breast and the woman's breast. It is a word with two completely different meanings. This printed word does not just stand there; it means something, a certain 'breast,' which in our case will be a man's breast. The fact that a sign only functions as a sign when it refers to something, or should mean something, is called its 'semantic sign-function.'

This sign, or typographic word-picture, 'breast,' is composed of different basic signs, or letters. The relationship of the letters to one another and to the paper, is called the 'syntactic sign-function' of a sign. And of course it's clear that a sign can only function as a sign when there is someone there to read it, which means a sign must be made in such a way that it can be seen, read and understood. This 'effect' of a sign belongs in the area of 'pragmatic sign-function.' This simple model demonstrates a communication process that does not function very well. The receiver (3) of the message 'breast,' understands a woman's breast, which is something different than the sender (1) actually intended. This is a problem which we all share. Our designs produce different effects. Our signs can acquire a meaning other than that intended.

In answer to the question posed as the theme for this lecture, I would like to say that one can only make typography today if one understands its syntactic dimension. More simply stated, the syntactic dimension in typography is, for me, a new territory. Here I see an undiscovered, surprising visual vocabulary, with more effective design methods for supplying information. Naturally, these new possibilities are not within easy reach; these first bits of knowledge and first new patterns cannot immediately be transposed to a practical level, especially not in today's world of consumer advertising, which is based upon immediate visual exhaustion. The syntactic differentiation of typographic material is more difficult to achieve in such fields as consumer advertising, and is only plausible where there is a receptive, thinking audience. Here I close the range of ideas.

What is the essence of my method of teaching typography? My most important goal in the typography class is to show the interested students—and it is only possible for me to work with such students—all the possibilities that lie in a typography workshop. And then, to place these possibilities in connection with the individual design problems of each student. By possibilities, I mean both the materials and technical processes available in a workshop.

For me, typography is a triangular relationship between design idea, typographic elements, and printing technique. Every problem in my class is handled from these three aspects, none of which should ever fail. The thing that is so special for me, with regard to the value I place on typographic syntax, is the variability of the materials under the influence of idea and technique. This means finally, the flexibility with which typography can function and still retain its meaning, in relation to different kinds of problems. All of the following examples were made with these considerations in mind. They are free from every fashionable tendency found in advertising and design. They are neutral, and comparable in a visual sense with basic mathematical exercises.

I hope that this introduction has sufficiently prepared you for the following examples. It was bit longer than I had planned, but I will confine my discussion of the pictures to only that which is necessary. I have divided the picture material into chapters. These chapters relate to the different problem areas found in my classes. The themes that are dealt with in these chapters increase in complexity, in the same way that the problems and methods in my classes over the years have become more complex. In this way you can become a student of mine for a while. Forget that you already know something about typography—possibly too much. Put aside your typographic experiences, prejudices and aesthetic preconceptions, at least for the next forty minutes.

TECHNICAL WORK AND ELEMENTARY TYPOGRAPHY

Imagine that you need my course and have no ideas about typography. As your most important goal you want to experience as many typographic possibilities as you can in perhaps two years, and become independent.

Our first exercise is as follows:

In the first few hours I instruct you in typesetting techniques and related problems. You set a ragged-right composition, print it and attempt to improve it optically. From this ragged-right composition you now make compositions of block, middle-axis, and free line placements.

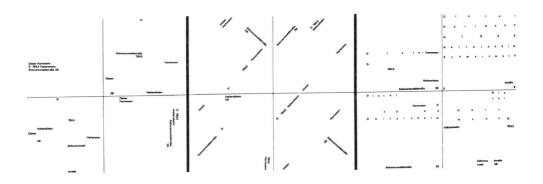

When you have these abilities at your command, we can proceed to the second exercise. I give you a typewritten manuscript which you set in one type size. That is why you have learned to set type during the first exercise. Only the printed word is reality, not that which has been sketched or made from blind text. Only with a set and printed word can you realize its actual length, its relationship to other words and to the entire text, as well as to your predesignated space.

The text and format of the next exercise (above) is also devised to deepen your first experiences of the division of space; through the study of the placement of letters and lines and their interrelationships, and with the aid of a certain self-determined program, you attempt to organize visually your name and address within a given area.

With the same limitations, you attempt to solve a more complex, practice-orientated problem. You attempt to visualize the logic and content of the text. You try to find functional typographic design possibilities, based on criteria like readability, text organization, and visual quality.

At this point, a slight digression is necessary: it is a mistake to assume that typography instruction for graphic designers is not very meaningful, or to say that the teaching of elementary typography problems is superficial, in that any intelligent student can master them by himself. To this I would like to reply that the

more basic a problem is stated, the more difficult it becomes to solve. Complex problems allow mistakes and superficialities to be more easily hidden.

Because we have already pushed these elementary exercises somewhat too far, let us solve another functional problem as an end to this first chapter. You have to design a business letterhead conforming to the DIN system, the German industrial Norm system, which is also valid in Switzerland.

As already stated, I am convinced that such elementary typographic exercises are a prerequisite for the solution of complex typographic design problems. Only here can the eyes, mind and feelings be equally and gradually trained, and only here can one learn to deal confidently with format, space, proportion and composition. Beyond that, these basic exercises provide insight and knowledge into general typographic problems, and are indispensable in the execution of concrete practical problems. Only when the student has understood that making typography means the visual organization of a given space with regard to a specific functional intention, will he be in a position in the future to make independent typographical decisions, regardless of whether the emphasis lies on dealing with complex practical problems or on experimental work. Obviously, I see that a bit idealistically.

The most important result of these basic exercises is that the student develops a relatively open relationship to everything that has to do with typography. He is in a position to explode the old venerable concept of typography—at least in the syntactical sense. In opposition to fixed traditions, he is less rigid in dealing with the materials and technical opportunities of the workshop. He has learned that a composed word need not look like a composed word. For example (far left), the conventional word-picture for Swissair, and with it the word Swissair set with an increasing progression from bottom towards top, which becomes a semantically changed word-picture. In this case Swissair is an airline company which, through the progression of the letters, has a part of its most typical activity visualized—that of flying; the form rises into the air. The student has now realized that the material is not, as in classical typography, stiff and only applicable in a very limited way.

This picture shows the technically limited possibilities of hand-setting—the horizontal and vertical. The student should have the courage to violate the respected laws of lead typography when it is necessary

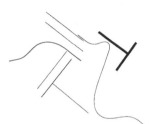

for the effectiveness of the typographic composition. He then knows that in letterpress almost everything can be printed, and in offset, *everything*.

THE SYNTACTIC DIMENSION IN TYPOGRAPHY

As you can see, the arrangement of examples into chapters is not meant so precisely. Naturally in the basic exercises we began working with the connection of typographic elements to one another. Next, I began to distribute different problems to the students—more complex problems that demand greater effort—naturally, with consideration to levels of talent and interest. Our fifth problem is really an expansion of the previous ones. The text is more complex and you have first one, then two, and finally many type sizes at your disposal, to develop a series of very different results.

In these Swissair advertisements for a daily newspaper (right), you have the possibility to completely exhaust the interpretative possibilities contained in the text and flight-plan. There are fewer restrictions in relation to type material and design freedom.

These further examples (left) demonstrate a strong contrast and clear tension in the typographic design material used. They show advertisements for the Swiss Post, Telegram and Telegraph Service (PTT), which are published on the back covers of telephone books. They contain information about the different services offered by PTT.

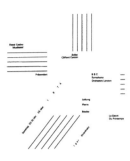

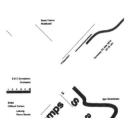

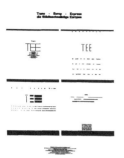

Here is a poster for the Trans-European Express (TEE). We have set ourselves the goal of connecting different semantic interpretations with one another. The method for this should be the application of different syntactic design material: middle-axis composition (upper left and at the bottom); block composition, with extreme word and line spacing (upper right); block composition, spaced in decreasing progressions (lower left); block composition without additional manipulation (lower right).

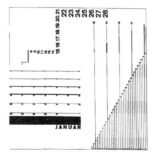

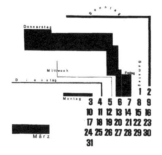

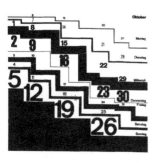

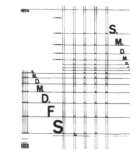

The work that I have shown you is very diverse because the students themselves are very different from one another. They differ in their basic educations, interests and abilities, as well as their nationalities. Often there are as many as six different nationalities on one course. On average, I figure on one-fourth convinced opposition, one-fourth convinced support, one-fourth not convinced support, and one-fourth misdirected professionals. As you can imagine, this is a fundamental handicap for any lesson or teaching method. There are some students—often the majority—who are very dependent on their respective teachers and constantly want to be led. Only a few are in a position to search, find, and decide independently.

This frequently intense student-teacher relationship is naturally the cause of a certain uniformity in the results from the class. To this often-made reproach against both the school and myself, I would say two things: Firstly, what teaching method does not lead to a certain uniformity? Regardless of where I look I see only gradual differences. Secondly, these more or less evident traces of uniformity in the work are not of primary importance, but instead, what is important is the foundation upon which they are built. I admit that our school does in a certain sense produce uniform results—in a visual sense. But at the same time I think that the exercises enable the students to transfer their underlying knowledge and ability to a position whereby, during practical work, each can reach completely different kinds of results. Obviously, this is not so easily generalized—it is important to take into consideration the extent to which the personality, intelligence, and ability of the student has been developed.

As I've already mentioned, I place great importance on these examples and the working process that leads to them. They are loosening-up exercises for the design student, similar to elementary exercises in which the emphasis is placed not so much on familiarity with the materials and technical aspects, as on expanding the typographical design vocabulary. The student discovers a visual language—the visual language. I mean that when the lesson functions correctly, every student should learn how to assert himself. When the teacher is colorful and stimulating enough in what he does, the student will receive enough stimulus for the development of his individual abilities and ideas.

Finally, I do not give the student any recipes to take with him, but instead only models for the solution of specific problems. Within the different kinds of problems set, the student has enough opportunity to practice coming to terms with both the problems and himself. But as I said, I see the problem very clearly and I am conscious that it cannot be fully explained with a few quick sentences. The so-called school crisis talked about today is not as noticeable in Basle as in other similar institutions. From what I have seen, the crisis is visible in other countries, especially in Europe. Today, few schools can or want to function as in earlier times. Obviously, the reason is that both classical understanding of one's self and the social role of the school as an adaptable institution have broken down. But I believe—and risk saying it—that there is another reason: not only has this 'self-understanding' broken down, but also, so has 'discipline.' There is no reliable teaching concept any more, no program on which an education can be based—not even a reliable direction which one could follow.

Everyone does what he wants. What is missing are good teachers and lecturers. I do not know of one school today in Germany, for example, which continues the methodical pioneer work begun by the Bauhaus. It was attempted by *Ulm,* but with different prerequisites and in another environment—and you know how that ended. With the example of *Ulm* you can see what I mean, in that *Ulm* was ruined by, among other things, the loss of its three dominant personalities: Max Bill, Tomás Maldonado, and

Bonsiepe. Certainly, today's students want nothing to do with such strong domineering personalities. But I am opposed to this. If we want to reconstruct, to not only look for but also realize new directions, we need strong, flexible, and active personalities.

THE SEMANTIC DIMENSION IN TYPOGRAPHY

The basic exercises in my classes are syntactic exercises. But in working with the synthetic dimension the semantic cannot be excluded. By that I mean activating that part of typography dealing with the meaning of the design elements.

As I mentioned at the beginning, what is decisive for me in my instruction is the *typographic* aspect of typography. This is not just a question of syntax, but instead, a question of semantic evaluation of the syntactical elements.

Naturally, our exercises on this theme are very limited in that we are not a scientific institution, which could, with large technical expenditure, conduct tests related to the semantic quality and effectiveness of typographic signs. In that respect our exercises remain relatively subjective. But with experience and a healthy human understanding at our disposal, we experiment with the character of letterforms, their sizes and associations, as semantic factors. One could say that we are expanding the visual vocabulary of design alternatives. But, in certain respects, we go much further than any scientific testing can, in that empirical science with its social-scientific testing methods can in general deal only with the expectations and known experiences of those tested. Only in rare cases can something new be deduced from such information.

As an example, some years ago I received a hint from the disciplined and intelligently solved logotype for Arabian Airlines. I tried to determine if the Arabic association function only because the *i* dot was turned on its corner.

Or is it perhaps just as good with simple round dots, which are not normally used with this typeface, Helvetica?

I am sure you find, as I do, that the effect of the turned square cannot be surpassed. As proof of the quality of this visual idea—which is definitely an idea, and not a product of so-called syntactic research—I placed it in confrontation with a line of Arabic script.

One realizes where the connection of this most ingenious microaesthetic invasion into our western lettering structure lies—in the dots—which in Arabic script, are determined by the writing implement.

Here are some other examples that I found in Israel. They support my theory that certain graphic modifications in typography, or lettering, can intensify the semantic quality of typography as a means of communication. Conversely, the lack of such modifications in normal typography reduces the associative semantic dimension of typography as a means of communication. The famous Coca-Cola trademark looks different in Hebrew—but still awakens an immediate association—because we identify

Arabian Airlines

Arabian Airlines

Arabian Airlines

Arabian Airlines

Arabian Airlines

يون فى لبنـــان

Arabian Airlines

certain essential characteristics of this well-known supersign. We are all able to recognize such associations, either consciously, or, as in the case of the less visually aware, subconsciously.

It is completely different with the internationally known concept 'Police'. Although this lettering appears on a jeep, we would not be able to decode the Hebrew word for police if the English word was deleted. To us, it could just as well be a military jeep. The typographic signs in the English version are then without semantic value.

A similar situation occurs with the geographical concept 'Tel Aviv', which when spoken evokes a large number of associations, none of which can be found when looking at this street sign. In order to orientate ourselves in Israel, we need letterforms that are familiar to us.

Although they are still in the early stages, here are some examples of what has resulted from our exercises with the semantic dimension and its syntactic associations. I will explain the concepts and adjectives that served as semantic goals for each of the respective problems. Shown here are two semantic interpretations of the three letters, TEE, for Trans-European Express. Comfortable sleeping: the round forms represent 'clouds,' which are soft and should lead to the association with 'soft bed.' The quarter moon supports this idea of 'bed' and a 'night's sleep,' through associations with 'dreaming' and 'romantic nights.' Fast to the destination: the extreme perspective of the capital letters and the movement 'towards a point' or 'towards a goal,' should help visualize the racing tempo of this long-distance, high-speed train.

Obviously, these examples do not have much to do with 'typographic design,' but they do offer a very good view of the overlap between graphic design and typography, especially with reference to problems that emphasize the semantic. To that extent they function as preliminary design exercises, or as 'building blocks' in the design process of a poster or logotype.

This example illustrates the type of development in our design process. You can see the steps with which we came to the desired result of a semantic interpretation of the concept 'Bible.'

Firstly, we set the word 'Bible' as it is commonly known. That is, readable, and with the normal letters of our alphabet.

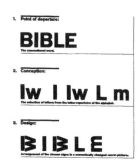

Secondly, we considered how we could best interpret this concept visually. We selected one possible interpretation; the 'classical' origins of the Bible. Then we considered with which letters of the alphabet it is possible to visually define this specific semantic interpretation.

Finally, we placed the selected basic letters together to form the new supersign 'Bible.' This new word-picture awakens semantic associations with 'old greek lettering' or 'classical' Bible.

We attempt to stimulate and secure our ideas through material studies during the design process—that is, to convey the individual idea in a generally understandable form. In the case of the word 'Athens,' we investigated the structure and then the written origins of the Greek letterforms. In the typography workshop, we attempt to properly represent the characteristics which we discover, with the letters and line material at our disposal.

THE FORMATION OF SIGNS AS A SYNTACTIC PROCESS

The steps we have taken in syntactic change, which until now have been concerned mostly with complex typographic problems, are also possible with single letters. The limits of the possibilities, except for a few examples, are determined by the extent of the material in the typography workshop, and the creative ability of the individual students.

To what degree can we change the nature of the letter *ö*? At which point can we still identify it as an *ö*? In other words, what is the most typical visual characteristic necessary for it to be recognized?

Can the semantic value of the capital letter *H* be changed? In what way does its meaning develop through differentiation in weight and proportioning of the typographic line material?

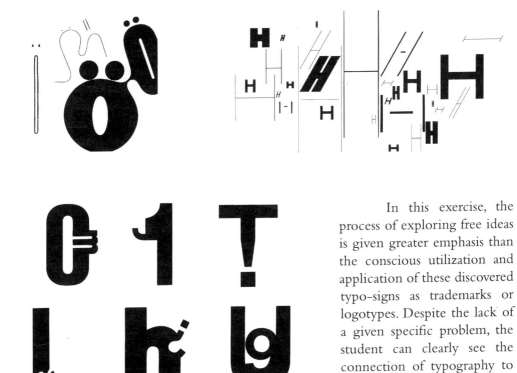

In this exercise, the process of exploring free ideas is given greater emphasis than the conscious utilization and application of these discovered typo-signs as trademarks or logotypes. Despite the lack of a given specific problem, the student can clearly see the connection of typography to graphic design.

PURE DESIGN—TYPOGRAPHY AS 'PAINTING'

In case you sometimes have the impression that we work in a bit of a vacuum, I would like to show you what working in a vacuum really means. In all of our work we are conscious that we have an empty space, a vacuum, which we must fill with typographic elements.

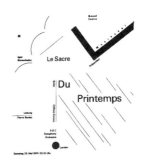

For both myself and my students, I would say that the fascination of typography lies in its ability to transform a silent, unprinted piece of paper, with the aid of rigid signs, into a dynamic form of communication.

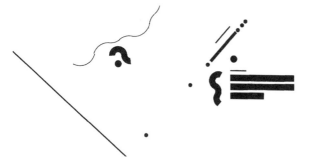

HOW DOES BASLE DIFFER FROM
OTHER SCHOOLS?

I have already spoken to you many times about 'Swiss Typography' in relation to our work in Basle. But there are many different schools in Switzerland, each with very different concepts of typography.

How do my ideas differ from the others? In reply, I would like to show you some more typical examples of 'Swiss Typography:' five designs from Emil Ruder and his students (opposite page). The main criterion for the form of typographic design is 'readability.' It is the dominant factor in the selection and optical organization of the typographic signs. The 'message' to be communicated is not intensified through the use of additional syntactic or semantic material.

To question the motive behind such an attitude towards typography, is to question the attitude towards communication in general. For a long time there has been a tendency in 'Swiss Typography' to deliver a message in a 'value-free' manner. 'Value-free' means to present a message simply, and not to equip it with additional visual characteristics to heighten its semantic and persuasive effectiveness. Here the ethics of the designer are very much involved.

Without bringing ethics into question, we can say that this 'value-free' attitude towards a 'message' is only one of many. However, even the most objective information, with the most sober visual presentation, still connects the receiver with personal values.

This idea, contained in 'Swiss Typography' and striven for in Switzerland and other countries—of pure functional organization, with its grid, unified typeface, type size, and semantic restraint—is a vain wish. It can only be one part of the complex function that distinguishes typography as a means of communication.

The human being has more than just technical and economic needs. He has very differentiated psychological needs, especially in those areas that have to do with culture and aesthetics. That is, those areas which we call 'design.' This is a social-psychological platitude from which advertising, with intelligent ideas, lively texts and visualizations, has already

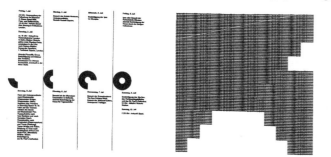

profited greatly. (This was very amusingly formulated as well as ideally practiced by the grand advertising philosopher, Howard Luck Gossage.)

Of course these are only some examples from an abundance of other designs with which I could have illustrated the concept of 'Swiss Typography.' In contrast, these designs from the Basle advertising agency GGK (bottom), show how something can look when one tries to make interesting typography from cold and objective subject matter.

These last two examples show clearly that 'Swiss Typography,' at least in Switzerland, is in a state of radical change. Or differently stated today, in Switzerland at least, no one knows anymore what the specialists actually mean when they bestow the honorable predicate 'Swiss Typography.'

Returning to the actual question: How does my concept of typography and typography instruction differ from other such concepts in Swiss schools?

Basically, these concepts do not differ. Good or bad, we are all building on the classical 'Swiss Typography.' We completely accept the fundamental principles of the purity and precision of typographical material, its logical and disciplined structure, and the meaning of the white space in a design. We are all sure that these 'values' will never be false.

Perhaps the reason for this is that Switzerland offers every person working creatively very special conditions, which for these people means something like a unified 'fertile base.' In both its domestic and foreign policy, Switzerland is an extremely stable country. In a positive sense, peace and order prevail and a respect for people

who think differently is still guaranteed. For the individual, that means the freedom to work uninterruptedly on his or her own projects.

After having recognized the similarities to other schools, I would now like to discuss the differences. You can see from the examples of work which I've shown you from my students and myself that we consciously emphasize the syntactic possibilities in typography. Occasionally, you have probably thought that this is harmful to the readability of a text. But I think that the relatively high stimulus of such a text is adequate compensation for low readability. What good is readability when nothing in the text attracts one to even read it? Naturally this attitude leads to continued attempts to break away from trusted design patterns. We attempt to test experimentally the semantic and syntactic possibilities of typography, and to break through its ideological borders by consciously ignoring the traditional limits and recipes for typographic design. Also, we try to remain blind to the gags and trends of the international advertising and design scene. With my definition of 'school,' I have attempted to explain why we are so logical and sometimes a bit too self-conscious in our work.

It would be unfair to present our school and its typography teaching methods only in a positive light. We also have ideas about how we can better reach our teaching goals through improved didactic means.

One of the problems is our almost exclusive occupation with syntactic and semantic design problems in typography. But this is only an outward expression of something completely different. That is, the real problem of the meaning of a text. In my opinion one cannot make really good typography without exact knowledge and precise understanding of a text. The study of the meaning of texts, through special and theoretical lectures, seminars, and exercises, is completely missing in our programs. Our action-radius of 'typographic design' is quite small within a theoretical model for a communications process.

As you can see from my self-critical remarks, we are aware of the deficiencies at our school. The attempt to remedy this situation has been frustrated by many problems. Firstly, by the organization and institutional structure of our school. Secondly, by the very limited time at our disposal to cover the various areas of our typography program. And finally, the entire problem is embedded in the general social process of changing consciousness and the new order of social and cultural values. Thus, we are again confronted with the questions of the definition and goals of 'school,' and with the value and nature of typography.

IN CONCLUSION: WHAT SHOULD THE
CORRECT TYPOGRAPHY EDUCATION CONTAIN?

What should an ideal design school be like? And with reference to my own field of activity, what should a 'correct' typography education consist of? Perhaps I can outline a definition of the goals that the typography course must fulfill. Basically, I see three categories:

1. The value of typography within the most diversified communication processes, and its efficiency as a means of communication, must be redefined. Such a redefinition would be an attempt to expand the meaning and range of the concept 'typography.'

2. In the future, new information technology and changing forms of communication will obviously require additional new typographic standards in relation to the syntactic and semantic. The substance of typography must change, along with the information it has to convey, and the general cultural scene in which it must function.

3. Finally, although it may be a subjective and perhaps provocative statement to make, I feel strongly that this new typography must also—and I emphasize also—be the result of a very personal thought process in design. By that I mean those efforts based upon individuality, imagination and artistic qualities.

In the second half of this century, as in the first, we need personalities who can influence the development of typography through their personal contributions. From the simplified goals I have outlined above, one can begin to see possibilities for change in the educational system. Certainly in the future, a study of typography must include a study of the meaning of 'text.'

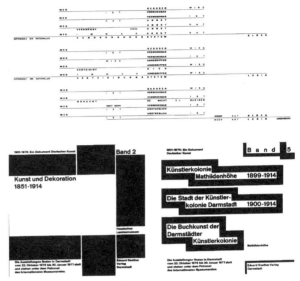

If we want to build upon the theme of 'text,' and expand in the direction of conceptual work and communications planned, we will need input from new fields such as: sociology, communications theory, semantics, semiotics, computers, and planning methods. Furthermore—as experience has shown in the more advanced schools—we need flexible technicians who are capable of combining specialized knowledge with an understanding of design problems.

But first and foremost, we need schools in which such challenges can be instigated and realized. I know that these challenges are not new, but I place them here at the end of my statement because they are derived from personal experiences within my typography course. My

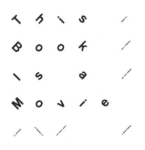

own work and that of my students, as a typographic development process, can only logically progress, when, with the aid of our acquired experiences and knowledge, we can reform both the educational system and its teaching methods. Concepts of typography, such as those we are trying to develop in Basle, contain more than simply the expansion of the syntactic and semantic vocabularies. We do not want to produce a kind of 'design cream' to be skimmed off by the agencies and studios.

We attempt to educate human beings who can, with imagination and intelligence, make responsible typographic contributions to the formation of the environment, especially the future environment, whose problems are already becoming evident.

First published in 1972 in a photocopied edition of two hundred copies and distributed during a lecture tour of design schools and universities throughout the United States. Reprinted in Octavo no. 4 (London: 1987).

1973
SOME ASPECTS OF DESIGN FROM THE PERSPECTIVE OF A WOMAN DESIGNER
Sheila Levrant de Bretteville

SHEILA LEVRANT DE BRETTEVILLE *(b. 1940) is a graphic designer and educator whose work is principally concerned with social issues, most notably concerning women. She studied art history at Barnard College and received her MFA in graphic design from Yale, where, since 1991, she has been director of the Graduate Program in Graphic Design. In 1971, she founded the first design program for women at the California Institute of the Arts, and two years later cofounded "The Woman's Building," a center for female culture in Los Angeles. In this essay, published in the British periodical* Icographic, *de Bretteville examines the limitations of modernism which, in its effort to clarify and simplify (she calls it "visual fascism"), represses and restricts the communication needs of a fragmented and culturally eclectic audience. The scarcity of women writing on design before the early 1980s makes this essay—as much a diatribe against the sterility of modern design as an attack on white/male supremacy—all the more valuable. The ideas espoused here would continue to surface in her own projects and in the writings, teachings, and design work of designers and critics for the next twenty-five years.—JH*

INTRODUCTION

The design arts are public arts, and as such are major vehicles for forming our consciousness. Consciousness, in turn, is illuminated by communications, object, buildings and environments. The design activity stands between us and our material existence, affecting not only our visual and physical environment but a sense of ourselves as well.

The process by which forms are made, and the forms themselves, embody values and standards of behavior which affect large numbers of people and every aspect of our lives. For me, it has been this integral relationship between individual creativity and social responsibility that has drawn me to the design arts. It is possible and profitable to reinforce existing values through design. In my work, however, I try to project alternative values into society in the hope of creating a new, even utopian culture, by acting in accordance with values of my own choosing.

We can look at design and actually read its messages—thus we can locate, create and use positive modes which reject the repressive elements of dominant culture. I have been trying to use forms and processes which project and reassert aspects of society which—though of essential value—have been repressed, devalued and *restricted to women* in the private realm of the home.

As I become increasingly sensitive to those aspects of design which reinforce repressive attitudes and behavior, I increasingly question the desirability of simplicity and clarity. The thrust to control almost inevitably operates through *simplification*.

Control is undermined by ambiguity, choice, and complexity, because subjective factors in the user become more effective and the user is invited to participate. *Participation undermines control.*

The oversimplified, the unremittingly serious, the emphatically rational are the consistent attitudes associated with work adopted by major institutions and the men and few women who inhabit them. In the circle of cause and effect, these attitudes are reinforced and reproduced as they are visually and physically extended in our environment.

One means of simplification is to assign attributes to various groups and thereby reinforce divisions. The restriction of certain behavior to the home and the making of women into the sole custodians of a range of human characteristics create a destructive imbalance. The design arts reinforce this imbalance by projecting the 'male' tone only in the public realm of our large institutions: business, science, the military and even education, valuing their anonymous, authoritarian aspects and separating themselves further and further from the private realm, thus continuing to isolate women, female experience and 'female' values.

MASS MEDIA AND COMMUNICATIONS:
A DIAGRAM OF SIMPLIFIED SEPARATION

The mass media have a tradition of visual simplification in order to isolate their messages to attract attention. This simplification denies the complexity of life's experience. Simple statements, familiar and repeated imagery, sell the product and the idea most efficiently. They also reinforce restricting separations.

In advertising, women are described as, or permitted to be, laughing, crying, doubting, making mistakes, hesitating: women alone are seen as nurturing or as providing emotional support for children and men. When, for example, a company represents itself in a service capacity or as particularly accommodating, it uses a female figure and reinforces traditional attitudes by this symbolic imagery.

The iconography for men is equally rigid. Men in work situations are shown as serious, decisive, professional, assured. No emotions, no fantasy; the few moments of relaxation or emotion permitted to men are relegated to leisure and the home.

Likewise, the home becomes devalued as a place where no serious work can be done. As the woman is virtually seen only in the home, she too is devalued. By depicting women as exclusively emotional, doubting, cooperating, and helping others, by only showing these activities in private, in the home, the polarities of what men and women are thought to be are reinforced and legitimized. In fact, the very characteristics that are allowed in women in the home, prevent success in the competitive public sector.

If the idea and the design are simple, complete and set, there is no opportunity to bring one's own values to the forms. If there is no ambiguity the eye is attracted once, the message understood and accepted quickly. When visual material is ambiguous the different nuances often encourage multiple and alternative reactions to the same communication. Were the mass media to include contradictions; were its images to contain suggestions rather than statements, the viewer could make an effort to bridge the gap, to interpolate, extrapolate, participate. But this is not the goal of mass media communication. Design as a problem-solving activity is assumed to involve only the acceptance by the designer of the aims of the client. If the client's goal is to sell a product or idea quickly, the problem does not include the encouragement of a thinking audience.

The modern movement in design encouraged a simplicity and clarity of form. This mode was embraced by some of the most creative and intelligent designers. It became fashionable to simplify for the clarity and power of the image, but as design becomes fashion, simplification becomes pernicious. This simplification in form and process leads to restricting and limiting separations and boundaries. By relaxing boundaries, by allowing more complexity in the image, designers could prevent this kind of visual fascism.

The reawakening of feminism has renewed the demand that the social expectations for both men and women be broadened, enabling all to participate freely in the social system according to the full range of their personalities, and allowing all individuals to create their behavior from the whole spectrum of possibilities. Not only will we not know what immutable differences exist until expectations change, but the very values which are devalued and suppressed are consequently unavailable in viable form to both men and women.

Designers could help to revalidate what have been designated as 'female' values and devalued as such.

PUBLICATIONS: SOME ALTERNATIVE MODES

People aware of design and its responsibilities are developing a design activity based on an ideology which encourages the emergence of the direct voice of the individuals who compose society.

The movements of the sixties questioned the structures and institutions that engender conformity. Alternative modes began to be developed that pointed out the limitations of hierarchical, one-directional channels of communication. For example, modern offset printing technology has begun to be used to create a model for participatory politics. By compiling a catalogue of goods and services recommended by a large number of contributors across the country, *The Whole Earth Catalog* reestablished the value of individual subjectivity and designed a structure that encouraged user participation. This effort, as well as others of the youth, hippie, human-potential, counter-culture movements, helped validate some repressed 'female' values, and encouraged the growth of the women's movement.

A similar attitude pervaded my design for a special publication for the International Design Conference in Aspen. Usually, six months after the conference, the participants receive a booklet containing excerpts of the speeches and comments by established and rising stars. Rather than impose my own understanding through this kind of control and simplification, I composed a newspaper of the direct voices of those participants who chose to record their experiences.

Cards were distributed on which any comments a participant might want to make could be written, drawn or typed. On the last night, these panels were glued together directly, forming pages. Then, through the use of an inexpensive, quick, rotary form of offset lithography, the newspaper was available in the morning. The distribution and assemblage of standardized panels created a nonhierarchical organization. All spreads were virtually alike, not one dominated, and all invited the readers to participate through choosing which entries to read and in what order.

It is the readers who must create and combine these fragmented responses into their own personal picture of the conference. It was the participants who chose the fragments, the reader who organized them individually.

As a designer, I created the structure that facilitated this process. The visual form of this newspaper was not the result of an effort to use a new form; new material, or new technological process, nor to develop a new or personal style. The forms were developed first to accord with a social context, to help achieve by their existence, the standard of behavior they reflected. The forms are the visual expression of an effort to project information in such a way as to emphasize alternative standards of behavior, alternative modes of design.

An increasing number of periodicals have begun to have guest editors, guest designers—*Radical Software, Design Quarterly, Arts in Society,* and others. As in the structure of *The Whole Earth Catalog,* special issues of publications provide alternatives to the small authoritarian establishment and expand the number of sources of information.

For example, I edited and designed a special issue of *Arts in Society* about California Institute of the Arts, a new community of the arts. The schools of this new institute were to open in one year, and I tried to create a graphic model that would reflect the formation of an alternative learning situation. These schools were being created by men who had been successful in the cultural establishment and were now creating an institution by working out some other ideas and goals, among them those of the movements of the sixties. I wanted to devise a design which would project the concepts of a horizontal person-centred community. Every design decision was made to reinforce these concepts through the form of the publication.

I chose several types of visual and textual material and organized them in waves of information. Letters between the Provost and future faculty members were scattered throughout the magazine, as well as taped fragments of dean's meetings, memoranda, student applications. These were interspersed with photographs from television and newspapers that described the social context of the United States during the decade in which the institute was being planned.

The organization of the magazine purposefully avoided the presentation of information in a simple, clearly logical linear manner. Instead, it was diffuse and depended on repetition of similar content, similar forms, cycles, leitmotifs, in both the writing and the imagery. Many aspects of the book had to be reconceptualized and reorganized. The traditional table of contents, and its position in the book was not an appropriate form for introducing material. I substituted an alphabetical index placed after the first signature that included each type of information to be encountered in the book. Throughout the magazine, the author is listed by name only, and in the index, in alphabetical order. This was done in an effort to avoid hierarchy and authority and to guide the reader to a different way of reading.

The tentativeness of fragmented organization encouraged the reader to participate in the ultimate conceptualization of the community. Since California Institute of the Arts was yet to open, and consequently, was not clearly defined, its character could, in some sense, be shaped by the individual reader's subjective response. I felt that it was possible to establish a real and dynamic relationship between the institute and a readership. The nonhierarchical, fragmented organization, the diffusion of formal elements had become attractive to me as a visual projection of alternative modes of relationship. Certainly it is an alternative to the method of projecting set, simplistic messages that distort communications in the mass media.

Projecting data in a clear, systematized manner is most sensible in the communication of certain types of information, such as maps and catalogs, but when it is used to communicate ideas or information about people and their relationships, it distorts.

Designers are taught to reduce ideas to their essence, but in fact that process too often results in the reduction of the ideas to only one of their parts. A more diffused manner of organizing material maintains enough complexity, subtlety, and ambiguity to entice the readers who normally dart away with someone else's encapsulated vision, rather than remaining long enough and openly enough with the idea to make it their own.

I invited students in my class at CalArts to investigate this form and process, using content that was personally meaningful to them. I asked them to create a whole of their own. The whole was to be greater than the sum of the parts. A woman student explained her solution;

> Its cryptic presence overshadows that of its ingredients. We recognize these symbols in an understanding of their total symbology (or at the very least, in a resolution that they may be unified meaningfully). . . . Masculine hands describe, define, offer, repulse, threaten . . . the only feminine elements are solely and grotesquely sensual—bodies fulfilling a seemingly obligatory sexual role, and hair-do's delineating a faceless area, a nonexistent identity. . . . It seems that many of the superficial accoutrements of a culture are present, and yet little of the whole human being is seen. Despite the constant sexual innuendo, despite the care given to the tools of a communicative sort . . . despite the hands that gesticulate and promise or threaten . . . there is no real touching . . . the accoutrements, the parts have less graphic, linguistic, and psychological importance than the whole.

As the community becomes used to ambiguity, complexity, subtlety in design and content, it will be more able to support the formation of individual conclusions, the expression of individual subjective opinions and will advocate the sharing of authority. For me this is a good: that Design can encourage.

The organization of material in fragments, multiple peaks rather than a single, climactic moment, has a quality and rhythm that may parallel women's ontological experience, particularly her experience of time. Although I came to use this fragmented organization in an effort to reflect a community of the arts in formation and to encourage the reader to participate, this form of visual organization corresponds more to a woman's world.

There are several genres of women's work, quilts and blankets, for example, which are an assemblage of fragments generated whenever there is time, which are in both their method of creation as well as in their aesthetic form, visually organized into many centers. The quilting bee, as well as the quilt itself, is an example of the essentially nonhierarchical organization. Certainly the quality of time in a woman's life, particularly if she is not involved in the career thrust toward fame and fortune, is distinct from the quality of time experienced by men and women who are caught up in the progress of a career.

The linearity of time is foreign to the actual structure of a day as well as to the rhythm of women's monthly biological time. Thought processes released from the distortions of mechanical progress are complex, are laminated with myriad strings, are repetitive and permeated with the multiple needs of others as well as oneself. Unbounded relationships cause most women to think not only about work, but about the groceries needed, dinner, a child's dental problems, etc., in between thoughts about work. Women's tasks in the home are equally varied and open-ended—child-rearing is the classic example—while a man's work in the home has a beginning and an end, it has specific projects, like the fixing of windows, appliances, or plumbing. The assemblage of fragments, the organization of forms in a matrix, projects this experience of time, suggests depth and intensive as an alternative to progress.

When the design arts are called upon to project aspects of the women's movements, it is particularly appropriate to challenge existent assumptions about form and process. When I was asked by a group of women artists to design a special issue of *Everywoman,* a feminist newspaper, I tried to incorporate the visual projection of the egalitarian, collective form of the small group process. In weekly meetings, small groups of women throughout the country talk in turn so that those easily dissuaded from speaking by more vibrant, dominant personalities, are assured of being heard. In this *Everywoman* design I avoided the associations of space and length of article with quality, and gave each woman a large photo of herself and a two-page spread, regardless of the length of her copy, I tried to link the spreads visually and to make no spread dominant. Looking alike, the articles did not visually compete with each other for the reader's attention; it was left to the reader to discern differences which might be subjectively more meaningful. In addition, I encouraged the women artists to stay within the limits of the budget and printing process used by the ongoing publication, even though they had access to special funds. It seemed that we could provide a more viable model if we did not inflate the object and participate in the existent attitude that whatever is technologically or financially possible must be made available—at least to a few.

Designing a structure that will encourage participating, nonhierarchical, nonauthoritarian relationships between the designer and the user, also results in visual and physical forms that are outside the mainstream of design as much as these ideas and attitudes are outside mainstream culture. The way these publications look is different from the way our national publications look: this difference is much less the result of creating another style of designing structures which encourage different values. Desirable as it is that these values become diffused into society, such design structures are often modest in appearance, rather than powerful, elegant, simplified, clear and dynamic forms. perhaps the importance of dynamic visual relations should be questioned and quiet, literary forms reevaluated.

Design appears to be a particularly ambiguous enterprise—and design for social change, even more so—in comparison with the other arts. The designer is often paid by those very institutions that would be affected by her attitudes in forming and shaping design: the contradictions for a freelance designer who wishes to effect social change is thus apparent. Because design is attached to the world of business and industry in this way, it is difficult to know in advance if one's design will be used to reinforce values that the designer opposes.

Designers must work in two ways. We must create visual and physical designs that project social forms but simultaneously we must create the social forms that will demand new visual and physical manifestations. Those designs of mine which I have discussed are the products of situations in which I was called upon to give physical form to efforts to create new social contexts. In this case, the major thrust was to rethink assumptions—profit was not a consideration and the budget was modest, and the audience (unfortunately) was limited. In this way I was exempt from the pressures that make it difficult for a larger, moneymaking project. But as such situations are rare and because I could no longer separate physical and social design, I found myself needing to create an interface. I wanted to investigate the possibility of working with other women. I allowed myself to indulge the notion that this method would locate problems and design solutions free of the design system in which both commercial stars and commercial hacks were always subject to the pecuniary ethos. Further, without losing the social context implied in the activity of design, I had actively to erode the idea of design as a private activity. It has always been the public nature and responsibility of design that I have believed definitive. Accordingly, I initiated a *Women's Design Program* at California Institute of the Arts.

In this program I was able to explore the relationship between design and feminism. The personal and ideological involvement offered the opportunity of finding a sphere of action that allowed these values to survive, I wanted to give attention not so much to what could be produced as to an operative ethic. That does not mean that we were not to design using concrete forms, but points to the need to protect these ideas from being buried under the subservient design process. Working with communications, rather than object-making, made it easier to infuse a design with these attitudes.

It was clear to me that women designers could only locate and solve design problems in a responsive way if they simultaneously studied their own history, tried to isolate female values and worked cooperatively. I designed procedures and projects which could reinforce the idea that design is a social activity and that women working in the design arts must have an understanding of the technical, as well as the social aspects of media technologies.

The design and printing of *Broadsheet 1* documented this investigation of design and feminism. Several of the early projects recorded in *Broadsheet* seem, on the surface, to have primarily technical goals, but they incorporated other values. Through the simple manipulating of bright red dots on a white ground, the women eased into an understanding of the simultaneous organization that allows people to see an image out of the dots and intervals in the half-tone process used in most publications. They learned this in an atmosphere that was intentionally playful and unthreatening. In an effort to recover a personal connection with work, the women investigated typographic conventions using language that had strong meaning for them individually. Playing with these meanings, they manipulated the forms to construct their own interpretations of it.

Just as these two ostensibly technical exercises were necessarily based on social values and contents, so the project of creating a photo-essay of another woman in the program was designed to help each woman gain control of the photographic medium as well as to express a relationship between the photographer and the subject which reflected their growing understanding of each other.

I planned a group project for the *Women's Design Program:* the problem was to be defined and explored in terms of our experiences as women, and the solution attempted as an ensemble. As a result, I suggested that we should design a presentation of menstruation to girls. While we looked at material currently in use, the examination of our own experience was the real starting point for this group. We found it necessary to create material which would provide an alternative to the films and brochures linking menstruation with uncleanliness and an incapacity for physical and emotional self-control, while the 'positive' aspects were linked to marriage and childbearing.

We videotaped our own discussions of this material and later, looking at videotapes of our talks, we were struck by the cogency of hearing about the variety of experience of menstruation in the context of real people's lives. We decided on this format as our design solution.

We invited groups to the studio and videotaped their discussions of menstruation, calling the project *Learning from Women's Experience.* Technical proficiency was

acquired in the process of making videotapes, as each woman had a turn at being director, assistant director, camerawoman, or in charge of sound, light, etc. We taped young
girls talking about the deficiency of information on menstruation, about their conflicts
and questions. The talk ranged—some wanted to remain tomboys, others felt uncomfortable with the boys who had been their friends until this time, and many were confused about their capability to have children when they felt they were too young then
or might never desire them. We tried videotaping discussions with males in the hope
that including them in the talk would encourage integrated audiences where young
boys and girls could engage in open discussion of their feelings after seeing the tape.
But the tapes with both younger and older males were very strained by the difficulty
they encountered in understanding this experience for which they had no analogy in
their own lives, and from which they felt excluded, shameful, fearful, and yet curious.

We taped a group of older women who reminisced about the conspiracy of
silence on the subject and their experiences, including the menopause. Their tape was
the most exciting, not only because they generously shared their richness of longer
lives, but because their open and honest exchange of experience illuminated the
problem of menstruation as a continuum in women's lives.

Even in this project we had to wrestle with the linking of emotionality and
women. When we learned from a woman doctor that there were psychological causes for the emotional intensity some of us experience before menstruation, our first
judgement was that this emotional reaction was unfortunate. But soon we saw this as
good—perhaps this menstrual state would not seem deviant in a society that was not
so committed to controlled rationality. In this project of designing educational material, we realized how important it is to provide an alternative to the presently available materials that oppose the devaluation of 'female' characteristics as an instrument
in the unthinking discrimination against women. We were also, perhaps obliquely, providing more emotional latitude for men.

The work of the *Women's Design Program* was, to some extent, a retreat from
the public world of business and industry where most of the design activity takes
place. Our progress led me to realize how vulnerable women were to those values,
which coalesce to deny us, in even our most private sectors, an appreciation and an
understanding of our femaleness. Originally, I had been sensitive to the relegation of
'female' values to the home, but now I saw that even in her most private house (her
body), woman is not able to live openly and knowledgeably. I knew that to liberate
the private self, we must understand and alter the public realm.

One way for design to alter the public realm is to develop images of the
future which embody female values and can permeate our contemporary society. To
do this successfully, we must know what forms most communicate the discrepancy
between male and female values, devaluate femaleness, and cannot incorporate such
modes as emotionality, complexity, and supportive cooperation.

The rigid separation of work and leisure, attitudes and values, male and
female—which we noted above, is reinforced by the tradition of simplification in the
mass media and it also operates in product and environmental design. A few new voices
were raised in the sixties who appreciated, not only complexity and contradiction, but
the value of participation in the popular vernacular. However, the connection and
response to the multiplicity of human potential was lost as their attitude became style
and fashion. [. . .]

First published in Icographic 6 *(Croydon, England: 1973).*

1975
GOOD DESIGN IS GOOD BUSINESS
Thomas J. Watson, Jr.

OF ALL THE CORPORATE *design patrons in postwar America, few were admired by the profession more than Thomas J. Watson (1914–1993). The combination of IBM, a company virtually synonymous with American economic hegemony in the second half of the twentieth century, with Watson's personal commitment to quality architecture, industrial, and graphic design was widely seen—especially by designers—as a potent object lesson in the inseparability of good design and good business. Watson himself asserts this now legendary formulation in this essay, first presented as a lecture sponsored by Tiffany & Co. at the University of Pennsylvania's Wharton School of Business, and cites IBM-funded work by a pantheon of designers including Eliot Noyes, Charles Eames, and Paul Rand as evidence. Interestingly, however, the case made is at best one of the compatibility of design and business, as Watson neither claims nor proves the cause-and-effect relationship implied by the essay's title. Nonetheless, designers to this day invoke Watson, often unknowingly, in their efforts to persuade hesitant clients to make design a commercial as well as an aesthetic imperative.—MB*

After entering a business which, fortunately for me, was headed by my father, I eventually came to see design become one of the major reasons for the success of the IBM Company over the past eighteen or nineteen years. We had relatively good design in the days before I ever got there, but one night in the early 1950s, as I was wandering along Fifth Avenue, I found myself attracted to typewriters sitting in front of a shop window. They were on stands with rolls of paper in them for anybody's use. They were in different colors and very attractively designed. (In those days you could have an IBM typewriter in any color as long as it was black, as Henry Ford said about his "Tin Lizzie.") I went into the shop and also found attractive, modern furniture in striking colors with a kind of collectiveness. The nameplate over the door was Olivetti.

Subsequently, I went to Italy and met Mr. Adriano Olivetti, one of the great industrial leaders of Italy. He had a completely organized design program that included company buildings for employee housing—which was popular in Italy at that time—as well as Olivetti offices, products, colors, brochures, and advertisements.

Shortly after this, in 1955, a close IBM friend of mine, manager of our IBM business in Holland, sent me a very thick letter in which he said: "Tom, we're going into the electronic era and I think IBM designs and architecture are really lousy. I've collected a lot of Olivetti brochures and pictures of their buildings, as well as brochures and pictures of IBM. Put them all out on the floor and have a look down each column and see if you don't think we ought to do something." The Olivetti material fitted together like a beautiful picture puzzle. At that time we didn't have a design theme or any consistent color program. All we had were some very efficient

machines, not too well packaged, and some competence in the new field of computers. In fact, we were building our first family of computers—the 700 series. They
worked on vacuum tubes, which seemed from the inside design to be the very epit-
ome of modern technology. We thought it was time for the outside to match the
inside. That was a design problem. We took all of the top-level people in the IBM
Company to a hotel in the Pocono Mountains where we considered IBM design in
contrast with that of Olivetti and a number of other companies. We wanted to
improve IBM design, not only in architecture and typography, but color, interiors—
the whole spectrum.

The only person in my experience who knew anything about design was
Eliot Noyes. During the war, I had become interested in gliders. Eliot Noyes was head
of the glider program in the Air Force and we had flown gliders a few times together. After the war he became a prominent industrial designer, so I had asked him to
join us in the Pocono Mountains. At the end of three days, he convinced us to do an
about-face in our design trends. From that day to this, Eliot Noyes has given fifty percent of his time to the IBM Company, never as an employee, always as an independent consultant. It has been a wonderful relationship.

With Eliot's arrival, we organized our design plans. We had just three factories in those days. In every IBM factory and laboratory today, there is a design section
free to change the exteriors of our machines, if it does not hinder their function, in
order to make them fit a cohesive and attractive design. It is done autonomously at
each lab and plant, but always under the general supervision of Eliot Noyes. Eliot also
travels, lectures, and advises people to come to the various centers of design here and
abroad and to keep their ideas modern and fresh. Furthermore, as we design these
machines, we are aware of our position at the cutting edge of technology in elec-
tronics, a technology which can often be physically beautiful. The actual mechanisms
themselves make lovely pictures, so we finally put in safety glass and let the customer
or observer look into the machine mechanism itself, rather than try to hide it under
a cover. At the same time we began to work on good office and showroom interiors.
We have used probably hundreds of interior decorators over the past twenty years.

After Eliot Noyes, we took on Paul Rand to work on design and Charles
Eames to do films, exhibitions, and museum activity. Charlie has designed the exhibit called "Computer Perspective," which was on display in our Manhattan office
building. He knows how to explain computers to the public. Charlie can put what a
computer does into a little cartoon-like film and in the course of twelve minutes have
everybody in the room understanding the main computer functions, what the world
is looking for from computers, and how they work.

In the course of fifteen years, from 1956 to 1971, we built about 150 plants,
laboratories, and office buildings. Whenever we had one to build, we would get the
names of three good architects from whom our own design people would pick as
appropriate for our needs. The names that we picked from were familiar names: Mies
Van Der Rohe; Breuer; Eero Saarinen; the late Egon Eiermann of Germany; Jacques
Schader of Switzerland; Marco Zanuso of Italy (who is an excellent interior decorator as well as a designer); Jorgen Bo of Denmark; Sten Samuelson of Sweden; Shoji
Hayashi of Japan, and the late Henrique Mindlin of Brazil.

[. . .]

What is the definition of a good design in the IBM Company? We feel that
good design must primarily serve people, and not the other way around. It must take
into account human beings, whether they be our employees or our customers who

use our products. Our machines should be nothing more than tools for extending the powers of the human beings who use them. As a consequence, our design, our colors, our building interiors are intended to complement human activity, rather than dominate it. Naturally, we are interested in the cost per square foot of a plant we intend to build, but we are equally interested in good design. We try to balance the two considerations. We also know that you have to pay a premium for good design, but that premium is paid back as many different benefits to the corporation in its activities.

A good architect wants to experiment, to pioneer. There is always a dialogue—even a conflict—between a good, strong-minded architect and a good, purposeful company. We have had some lively conflicts with some of those better known architects. For example, we have a plant in Boca Raton, Florida, done by Marcel Breuer. It was the third building he did for us. He has a perfectly delightful personality. He appears to be disarmingly soft, but he is like a piece of steel inside. Part of his intended design included a large lake in front of this building with an island on it and some mobiles on the island. I thought it was a great idea but it was going to add as much as $600,000 to the cost of the plant, which was already about $40 million. About that time the country also went into that economic recession of 1969 and 1970. So I had to eliminate the island, a decision which almost lost me my friendship with Marcel Breuer, which I prized highly. I made a promise to him that at some point in the future the island would be installed along with the mobiles. If any of you visit that plant in Boca Raton, feel free to visualize an island in the middle of that lake. It will be there one day.

There has to be a certain amount of conflict in such matters, and one has to cajole, persuade, and even insist that the architect move only a reasonable distance beyond the last best thing he has seen or done. I have just been in Rome and have seen plenty of historical reasons for not letting architects get too far ahead of you. You may remember that the Renaissance Pope, Julius II, had his problems with Michelangelo. (It can be argued that Michelangelo had his problems with the Pope, too.) For Julius II, he designed a sarcophagus, larger than Saint Peter's basilica in which it was supposed to rest, and so a new basilica had to be planned. The time schedule got completely out of hand, and Michelangelo lost some of the support of the Pope. In the IBM Company, we would call that a loss of both cost and account control.

If a corporation decides to be a design leader, it must have a good advisor, which is why you are hearing the name "Noyes" frequently throughout this lecture. Without a good advisor, the design program may be garish, or what designers call "kitsch," as a result of trying to go a bit too far. Experimental design, carried beyond disciplined control, often becomes nonfunctional, wasteful, and expensive. Good design has to meet functional requirements. It has to serve as good background and be subordinated to the human and machine activities it supports. It ought to create a pleasant atmosphere, whether it is a building, a computer, a piece of furniture or an interior. In all cases, the design plan is there only because people are there.

We built, for example, a very modern monolithic circuitry plant in Endicott, New York. In this plant, production was on a highly automated basis with very few people and highly mechanized production lines. The factory interior looked almost like a modern drawing room. While building it, we decided the cafeteria of our oldest plant, also in Endicott, was outdated and that we would put a cafeteria in the lower floor of the new plant. The beautiful theme of monolithic circuitry production was projected into the new cafeteria. There were three tiers for the tables and unusual colors on the walls. The place looked unbelievably clean, but in our other Endicott installations there are many oily, greasy screw-machine type operations. When that cafeteria was opened, many of our employees from the older plant operations refused to come in and eat because they were afraid, and embarrassed, that they would soil it. It was overdesigned and we had to "unplush" it. It caused an uproar. Many of our oldest IBM employees are in Endicott and most of them own IBM stock. When they see money being wasted, many write immediately to me saying, "Somebody has lost his mind here in Endicott. They're taking the shrubbery and plants out of this lovely cafeteria and tearing down the walls." But we finally converted it to a place that was designed appropriately and was comfortable for people. Only then did it become popular. This is a good example of how overdesign wastes money.

Design in industry usually encompasses a mixture of the practical and the aesthetic. Even the way an organization is designed can determine whether it is ugly or beautiful. If it is well designed, it can respond to the future. It can change its form and it remains competitive. But if it is rigidly designed and inflexible, an industry can go out of business within a few decades. Certainly good design flavors the relationship of a corporation with its many publics—its employees, its stockholders, its customers, its social critics, and the multitudes of business watchers.

My father headed IBM from 1914 until his death in 1956. Because I worked a number of years for him, I can tell you some of his goals for the IBM Company which relate to our design program. Business growth alone was far from his top objective. What he wanted was to win a place for IBM in the estimation of people, and he realized that we had to earn it not only by what we did, but also how we looked. So we wore white shirts and dark suits and even stiff collars. Father felt that nonconservative dress might confuse a sales prospect, whose mind might stray, even enviously, away from the product that the salesman was trying to sell, to the cut of the salesman's coat or the design of the shoes. I did manage to break away from the stiff collar. We now wear more comfortable collars. People still smile at our dark suits and white shirts. But we in IBM smile along with them. The stockholding public also smiles happily at our growth and success.

Long before we had enough money to launch a design program, we tried to look more successful than we really were. We had an unusually fine showroom on Fifth Avenue by 1926. I remember standing on the balcony to watch the parade for Lindbergh after his flight to Paris in 1927. I am sure if we used the same percentage of our earnings today that we used on that Fifth Avenue showroom, we would own about two blocks on Fifth Avenue. And yet it caused people to look up and say, "What do those letters 'IBM' mean?" The windows helped get our products known and this in turn helped to sell them.

[. . .]

I think it is relatively easy to measure the impact of design on a product. As I said, we could not get our typewriter division out of the red until we had it packaged in a way that made typists want to use it. Their hands have to provide only an ounce of pressure instead of the seven ounces that a manual typewriter requires. But it should also look attractive on her desk.

Design is good business in countless other ways. How much business did a good-looking exhibit attract to the IBM Company? To what extent do good-looking facilities invite people to apply for work at IBM? These are intangible things that we believe are genuine dividends of a good design program.

Everybody wants to be a part of, or do business with, a winning organization. If the organization looks the part with good design, people begin to think the company is going somewhere in the world. History alone is the ultimate judge of what good design is. We can only act on our tastes and instincts, temper them with business consideration and hope for good results. The Egyptian pyramids survived because of sound engineering. But I think one reason we go to see them is their design—very simple, very attractive, very pleasing to the eye.

We remember the merchant cities of Venice and Florence, not because of their sophistication and wealth, but because of what resulted from that sophistication and wealth in the arts and in design—in painting, architecture, pottery, sculpture. Nobody can consciously design for posterity. But it behooves anyone in business today to pay full attention to the value of design, as long as he means for that business to go on serving the nation and the world in all of the relevant ways that spell business survival.

On several occasions I have summarized my belief in design as a strong business success force: "In the IBM Company, we do not think that good design can make a poor product good, whether the product be a machine or a building or a promotional brochure or a business man. But we are convinced that good design can materially help make a good product reach its full potential. In short, we think that good design is good business."

First published in The Uneasy Coalition: Design in Corporate America, *edited by Thomas Schutte (Philadelphia: University of Pennsylvania Press, 1975).*

1975
EDUGRAPHOLOGY—THE MYTHS OF DESIGN AND THE DESIGN OF MYTHS
Victor Papanek

IN HIS BOOK Design for the Real World, *Victor Papanek (1925–1998) suggests that only one profession is "phonier" than industrial design: advertising design. Subtitled "human ecology and social change," Papanek's seminal 1971 critique was published in twenty-one languages and he gained an international reputation—and earned scorn from many designers—as an impassioned advocate of "design for need." "Edugraphology," published four years later, summarizes some of Papanek's central complaints about the wastefulness of industrial design while returning to the problems of two-dimensional design, which his book had touched on only in passing. With a palpable sense of exasperation and urgency, he details and debunks the self-serving "myths" that design education helps to instill. Designing is a "basic human ability," he suggests, and by perpetuating these myths—chief among them that design as now practiced is really intended for ordinary people—designers and design educators conspire to fence off design and keep nonprofessionals out.—RP*

> They want production to be limited to "useful things," but forget that the production
> of too many "useful" things results in too many "useless" people.
>
> —Karl Marx

Design philosophy and the designer's self-image have been victim to a series of shocks. Some twenty years ago designers saw themselves primarily as artists, able to close the gap between technology and marketing through their concern with form, function, color, texture, harmony, and proportion. For an industrial designer or architect, a further concern was with cost, convenience, and "taste." Within ten years the designer's role had broadened into a systems approach, showing greater interest in production, distribution, market-testing, and sales. This opened the door to team–design, although with the team largely made up of the technocrats, sales specialists, and modish "persuaders."

More recently a very few designers have attempted to create a new design coalition in which users of tools and makers of tools (read: consumers and workers) participate in the shaping of the design process together with social anthropologists, ecologists, and others.

Elitist circles in design have even more recently given rise to such gimmicks as the "Nostalgia wave," "Kitsch Nouveau," "New Brutalism," and other fashions carefully manipulated to increase hedonistic ethnocentricity.

In the Western world the concept that "designing things" and "making things" are different is only about 250 years old. From then on the idea of design was increasingly connected to the appreciation of things deemed "beautiful" by an upper-class culture that created a moral and ethical basis for the concept of beauty.

Louis Sullivan's "Form-follows-Function," Frank Lloyd Wright's "Form-and-Function-are-one" and "Truth-to-Material," like the Bauhaus' "Fitness-for-Purpose" and "Unity-in-Diversity" were all basically ethical and moral imperatives. Often the moral imperatives ousted the practical reality, as anyone who ever sat on a Frank Lloyd Wright chair or read by a Bauhaus *Kugellicht* can testify.

Our future job in design education is made easier, not harder, by these changes design has experienced. For now the nexus between autonomous man and the benign environment has emerged as our new moral imperative.

Now the whole formal concept of design is under attack. Increasing numbers of people feel that design no longer serves them: that modern planning and architecture are alienating (they are); industrial design class-oriented (it is); and graphic design trivial and boring (it is). Design is further and further removed from people and the real world and it seems that "they up there" are out of touch with "us down here" (and all that is all too true).

Design education and the design establishment have responded to this in two ways:

1. Relabeling: a frenzied search for new words or labels to cloak an essentially unchanged activity. "Commercial Art" has become "Advertising Design," then "Graphic Design," more recently "Visual Design," "Communications Design," more absurdly "Environmental Graphic Communications," etc., *ad absurdum*.

"Industrial Design" has been relabeled "Product Design," "Product Development," or "Form-giving" and, in an increasingly frantic attempt to make it acceptable to new constituencies: "Alternative Design," "Alternate Design," "Appropriate Technology," "Social Design," "Intermediate Technology," or "Advocacy Design," *ad nauseam*.

It can be said that relabeling doesn't work: you can call a Crematorium the "Final Departure Lounge," or an idiot: "educationally under-advantaged" but nothing changes except for exposing the manipulative character of language.

2. "Business-as-usual" on one level, with increasing preoccupation by small design sectors with artificially invented "Third World" design, playground planning, aids for the handicapped, or other minority groups.

About concentrating on an invented Third World and other "needs," one can say that this has to do with what Freud called *Verdinglichung* and when I translate as "Objectification." It involves the change from knowing one's real needs into a demand for consumer goods. It makes survival of marginal or oppressed groups or countries dependent on the knowledge-monopoly of a professional elite and on the production-monopoly of specialists.

"Basic needs" thus are redefined as those that can be solved only by internationalized professions. (Since *local* production of internationalized products is highly profitable to native, highly trained elites, such groups will defend this as a "legitimate struggle against foreign domination.")

Finally, by flipping out into *only* designing for real or invented minorities, the mainstream of design is left to the mercy of establishments and their valuation.

Graphic design and graphic design education seem generally dedicated to six discernible directions:

1. To persuade people to buy things they don't need with money they don't have to impress others who don't care.

2. To persuasively inform about the class-merits of an artifact, service, or experience.

3. To package in a wasteful and ecologically indefensible way, artifacts, services, or experiences. (Look at any undertaker's coffin!)

4. To provide visual delight or visual catharsis to those classes taught to respond "properly."

5. To undo with one hand what the other has done. (Anti-pollution posters, anti-cigarette commercials).

6. To systematically research the history, present, and future practices in the five fields listed above.

In design education we have accepted myths that exist in the public about design, as well as invented new ones about ourselves.

I now plan to list ten of these myths and propose also ten remedies:

1. THE MYTH THAT DESIGN IS A PROFESSION. Design fails to satisfy people to the degree to which it is professionalized and it can satisfy people only to the extent to which it can again be made participatory. This particular myth is most propagated by Professional Design Societies that often turn out to be geriatric clubs, dedicated to legal tax-evasion and similar self-help schemes.

2. THE MYTH THAT DESIGNERS HAVE TASTE. On record, designers do seem to have taste (whatever that means) but only for the work of a few other designers. Students are exposed to "function formalism," "radical software," "romantic primitivism," or "socialist (–imperialist) realism."

In all these cases people and designers drift apart, since "taste" is always manipulative in the end.

3. THE MYTH THAT DESIGN IS A COMMODITY. A commodity exists to be consumed. The more we make design into a commodity, the more it will be consumed, measured, divided, eaten, eaten-up.

Styles, fashions, fads, and eccentricities will follow one another at an ever-increasing pace, subject to the same market-manipulations that govern other commodities.

4. THE MYTH THAT DESIGN IS FOR PRODUCTION. With some of the balance having gone awry we may now well ask: Mass Production or Production by the Masses?

The industrialized countries, containing one third of the population of Earth, threaten the economy of the entire planet. Mainly the threat is to people: through noncreative work; through making people subservient to technology; and by making believe that "Growth" can solve problems. In terms of the environment; production (as we have come to know it) harms the environment by concentrating people in cities; and treating nonrenewable (capital) resources as if they were renewable (income resources).

5. THE MYTH THAT DESIGN IS FOR PEOPLE. Design is mainly for designers.

All designers know how hard it is to persuade marketing people to accept their designs. Marketing people in turn know how hard it is to get people to buy the goods. Right now millions carry expensive fountain pens that must be softly sand-papered from time to time to be kept "good-looking," just so that its designer might win a prize in Milano or a magazine page in Britain or a Museum of Modern Art award in New York.

If Design were really for people it would enable people to participate in design and production; help conserve scarce resources; and minimize environmental damage.

6. THE MYTH THAT DESIGN SOLVES PROBLEMS. It does, but only problems that are self-generated. A graphic designer "solves the problem" of advertising rail-travel as ecologically saner than automobile-travel, but at the cost of neglecting walking or bicycling, *and in so doing diminishes the choices people can make.*

7. THE MYTH THAT DESIGNERS HAVE SPECIAL SKILLS AND THAT THESE SKILLS ARE DEVELOPED THROUGH SIX YEARS OF HIGHLY SPECIALIZED EDUCATION. What we *do* have is the ability to tell things (via poster, film, technical drawing, rendering, printed page, spoken word, or prototype model); and to organize parts into a meaningful whole.

But these are innate human potentials. On the other hand: "trick-of-the-trade" skills are taught by many vocational schools in one year.

8. THE MYTH THAT DESIGN IS CREATIVE. In reality design schools (teaching such subjects as "Creativity 101") direct students into analytical and judicial modes of thought and permit creativity only with narrow institutional limits. ("How do you spell: Cat?" or "What is the square root of minus one?" are analytical questions; "Who is right?" a judicial one; whereas creativity involves synthesis rather than cloning). Education tends to turn out competent and competitive consumers rather than creative and autonomous individuals.

9. THE MYTH THAT DESIGN SATISFIES NEEDS. It does, but at great social cost; furthermore the needs satisfied are invented ones. An airbrush, for instance, is an expensive, specialized, and hierarchical tool. It takes months to really master it (or to be mastered by it). it makes its user into a professional specialist whereas a plain sable brush is cheap, easy to use, open to all, and has infinitely more creative scope for the user.

10. THE MYTH THAT DESIGN IS TIME-RELATED. Much design is concerned with creating artificial obsolescence. But obsolescence always creates devaluation, leading to alienation, and finally existential *Angst.*

When design is for permanence, permanence is interpreted as five to ten years, whereas in reality a good tool (say: a bicycle, a motorized pushcart, a community freezer, or an axe) should minimally last a lifetime.

Design is a basic human ability to help autonomous self-realization. Designers and design educators are engaged in withdrawing this ability from all but a carefully screened group of people, through mythologizing who we are and what we do. We must de-mythologize and de-professionalize our work and our training.

I would like to list ten ways of bringing design back into the mainstream of life:

1. Some designers will be able to connect themselves differently in the future: why do thousands of us work for industry, but almost none of us for trade unions? Why do we work *directly* for cigarette companies or carmakers, but almost never for cancer clinics or autonomous groups or pedestrians or bicyclists?

2. Designers will have to concern themselves consistently with the important differences between non-renewable and renewable resources, as mentioned earlier.

3. Design must enable people to participate directly both in the design development and the production stages of objects. Cross-disciplinary teams must contain makers and users.

4. Designers will form new coalitions with makers and users; new coalitions between users and reusers.

5. A well-designed technology must be one of self-reliance. That is a technology that is capital saving (the word "capital" is used here to denote nonrenewable resources). It will further be a technology that is simple, small in scale, and aware of ecological, social, and political consequences of the design act.

6. Design must cure people of product addiction. This can only be done by demythologizing not only design but also the object itself.

7. Some of us can through schools bring our students into direct and continuous contact with real people's real needs in a real world, instead of manufacturing needs for them.

8. Design will still be concerned with tools. But they will be as unlike most of today's products as feasible: products and tools that only create the very demands they are specialized to satisfy and thus eliminate or diminish human labor, participation, and ability.

9. As I have said somewhere else: all men are designers. All that healthy men do is design. We must take note of that and through our own work enable more and more people to design their own experiences, services, tools, and artifacts. *The poor countries need to do this to find work for their people, the rich countries in order to survive.*

10. Technology as such need not be feared; the alphabet, Arabic numbers, moveable type, typewriter, photocopier, tape-recorder, and camera have given us the "open-ended" tools to move design from myth to participation, from participation to a joyous, autonomous way of personal fulfillment.

Let me close by quoting a proverb from China that sums up why design and design education must be directly tied to meaningful work and participatory life:

I hear and I forget,
I see and I remember,
I do and I understand.

First published in Icographic *no. 9 (Croydon, England: 1975).*

1976
THIS TYPEFACE IS CHANGING YOUR LIFE
Leslie Savan

IF CRITICISM HAS BEEN *historically in short supply in graphic design trade maga-*
zines, it has been virtually nonexistent in the popular press, where the ephemeral nature of
logos, page layout, and typefaces seems to have discouraged serious scrutiny. One writer
unafraid to focus on what others might consider the detritus of mass media has been Leslie
Savan (b. 1951), advertising columnist for the Village Voice. *While Savan's brief primar-*
ily has been the cultural and political implications of print advertising and television com-
mercials, she has written about graphic design as well, most notably in this piece, her first
published in the Voice. *This meditation on Helvetica, so ubiquitous by 1976 as to be near-*
ly invisible to the lay public, is an unlikely but persuasive demonstration of the goal Savan
set for herself when she began writing about media: to expose "how commercial values
infiltrate our own beliefs and desires." It remains, twenty years later, a model of how the
sometimes impossibly esoteric world of graphic design can be made accessible and relevant to
a wider audience.—MB

The quest for a clean public restroom is usually in vain. We assume a restroom to be dirty and disease-rid-den, and settle for what we have to. Occasionally, though, I've found a restroom that, before I'd even entered, I've assumed with relief was not dirty but clean. I realize that it was a restroom sign, with its mod-ern, Teflon-smooth letters spelling "women," that led me to expect a clean toilet. Although it was surely no different from any other toilet, I thought it had to be more sanitary. It was similar to the way an attractively packaged cleansing cream, like Helena Rubinstein's "Deep Cleanser," could convince me that what was inside was the best of all possible creams. It was those same clean, modern letters on the package.

These letters seem to be everywhere. They tell us "This is a dial tone first phone," this box is for "U.S. Mail," and to "Enjoy" Coke, "It's the real thing."

Along with NBC's well-publicized logo change, the lettering used on all NBC-produced programs and printed material is being converted to the exact same style. This lettering style, or typeface, is graphically renovating or coordinating every-thing from newspapers (including the *Village Voice* logo) to "new towns" to multina-tional corporations.

The typeface is called Helvetica. From more than nine thousandwidely vary-ing typefaces, a few "modern" ones have become designers' favorites. But Helvetica is by far the most popular and biggest selling typeface in the last ten years. It comes in a variety of widths, weights, and spacing arrangements. The basic form is Helvetica Medium, and it seems "most itself" in lowercase letters.

The "signs of the times" can be found on the literal signs of the times. The use of Helvetica on so many of them expresses our need for security, for visual proof—if nothing else—that the world's machinery still runs. Subliminally, the perfect balance of push and pull in Helvetica characters reassures us that the problems threatening to spill over are being contained.

Helvetica was designed by a Swiss, Max Meidenger, and first produced by the Haas Typefoundry in 1957. Haas says it was designed specifically for the Swiss market ("Helvetica" means Swiss), and was intended to be a "perfectly neutral typeface without any overly individual forms and without personal idiosyncrasies."

Helvetica is a "sans serif," as it lacks the little extra strokes, called serifs, at the end of its letters' main strokes. Since serifs lead the eye from one letter to the next, they are supposedly more legible, particularly for small print. But the difference is minimal for most sign size letters, and many designers say they use Helvetica precisely because it's so easy to read. As Ed Benguiat, a leading typeface designer and the art director of Photo Lettering, Inc., says, "You don't read the word, you read power. . . . For that one or two-word display message, for buckeye and force, you use sans serif."

But why is Helvetica the most popular of the sans serifs? "It's beautiful," said Benguiat. "It's a pure letter."

Other designers describe Helvetica as "contemporary," "easy to read," "no-nonsense," "neutral," and even "cold." The first word that comes to their lips, though, is "clean." It is not surprising, then, that when Walter Kacik redesigned New York City's garbage trucks in 1968 he used Helvetica. The trucks are all white except for one word, which is in black, lowercase Helvetica: "sanitation." Photographs of them were exhibited at the Louvre and at the Museum of Modern Art. Kacik chose Helvetica, he said, "because it was the best of the sans serifs and it didn't detract from the kind of purity we wanted." The result was that "people trusted these trucks."

Indeed, cleanliness implies trust. We've been brought up to associate the two ("I'm clean, officer.") and their opposites ("You dirty, rotten, two-timing dame!"). Cleaning up images is the main business of some marketing and design firms. Probably the most influential of them is Lippincott and Margulies (L&M). It is not an advertising agency; it bills itself as a "pioneer in the science of corporate identity."

Finding a corporation's identity almost always means redesigning its graphics. (Occasionally a name change itself is in order—L&M gave us such newspeak sounds as Amtrak, Pathmark, Cominco, and Uniroyal.) In its own brochures (in Helvetica), L&M denies that it offers "face-lifts" or "standardized solutions." It claims to work from the inside out. Considering the expense to its clients ("Coca-Cola spent over a million dollars for a little squiggle," a former L&M executive said), its soundproof-room confidentiality, and its scientific bent, L&M might be regarded as a corporate shrink.

L&M's list of more than five hundred identity-seeking clients includes: American Motors, General Motors, Chrysler, Exxon, Amtrak, Chase Manhattan, First National City Corporation, Bowery Savings Bank, Chemical Bank, American Express, U.S. Steel, ITT, the Internal Revenue Service, the New York Stock Exchange, RCA, NBC, MGM, J. C. Penney, Coca-Cola, and Con Ed.

Only a few of these companies, such as Amtrak or Con Ed, use Helvetica for the logo itself—a logo is almost obliged to be unique and most are specially designed. But as a supporting typeface (and, in most cases, *the* supporting typeface) on everything from annual reports to cardboard boxes, nearly every one of the companies listed above uses some form of Helvetica.

For instance, "Coca-Cola" is distinctive, but Helvetica says "It's the real thing." The new American Express logo is specially drawn, but everything else is in Helvetica. (And when non-Roman alphabets like Chinese cannot take direct Helvetica letters, they will be drawn as closely as possible to it.)

L&M vice-president in charge of design, Ray Poelvoorde, said Helvetica "already has sort of become an unofficial standard." Asked if using such a pervasive typeface wouldn't undermine the costly corporate identity, he said, "You're offering a very nice courtesy to the general public who is bombarded with many messages and symbols every day. And for a company not well-known, to ask the public to memorize more symbols . . . is fantasy."

But if he is right, then the companies that are remembered, that are finding their identities, are doing so by looking more and more alike—almost like one big corporation. A unilook for Unicorp.

Some designers do think Helvetica is overused. Some are even bored with it. But few believe that it is a mere fad. Most companies choose Helvetica in the first place because they expect it to remain contemporary for quite a while. And most companies cannot afford more than one identity change. This is especially true for New York's Metropolitan Transportation Authority.

Since 1967, the MTA has been gradually standardizing its graphics from about a dozen typefaces to a combination of Helvetica and Standard Medium. (The two are almost identical, but the latter was more available to the MTA.)

In contrast to the subway's filth and potential for violence, the cleanly and crisply lettered signs lend a sense of authority. They assure us that the train will come and diminish the chaos created by the graffiti-scrawled walls. (It's no accident that the designer of Norman Mailer's "The Faith of Graffiti" branded the book's covers with Helvetica.) The subway-sign renovation alone, less than a quarter complete, is conservatively estimated to cost from $500,000 to a million dollars.

This MTA graphic system was originated by Massimo Vignelli, who founded, and has since left, an appropriately named design firm, Unimark International, with Walter Kacik, the man who revamped the garbage trucks. Vignelli created Bloomingdale's logo and, more recently, the graphics, in Helvetica, for the Washington, D.C., Metro, still under construction. He thinks Helvetica is not merely a fad but that it can be used faddishly. "As good as it is when used properly, it becomes very bad looking when used badly," as, he suggested, in a wedding invitation.

What is its proper usage? "All kinds of signage are fine." In fact, a system of "symbol signs," with supporting Helvetica letters, intended to replace the numerous sign systems around the world, has been devised by Vignelli and other leading designers. (The design committee is headed by Thomas Geismar, whose firm, Chermayeff & Geismar, is L&M's chief competitor for the corporate identity market.)

Symbol signs are simple silhouetted pictures that act as signs: a knife and fork will mean restaurant; a question mark, an information booth. The symbols are scheduled to be tested at various terminals in New York, Boston, Philadelphia, Williamsburg, Virginia, and the state of Florida this summer. Helvetica is already used at airports such as Seattle, Dallas-Fort Worth, and Kennedy, but the symbol system might usher it into other transportation facilities.

The symbols will often need lettered support, but, in deference to varying cultural styles, the system's guideline manual does not recommend any one typeface. When other cultures shop around for a typeface, however, they will probably be influenced by the example used throughout the manual itself, one deemed "legible, aesthetic, and compatible" with the symbols: Helvetica.

The U.S. Department of Transportation, which commissioned the system, will ask other federal agencies and state governments to adopt it. Then, in order to become an official standard, the symbols will be submitted to two standardization organizations (the American National Standards Institute and the International Organization for Standardization), which certify and promote standards in everything from abbreviations to industrial parts. Helvetica, riding the back of a symbol, might pass through a well-guarded standards stronghold.

Meanwhile, it already headlines all publications of the Departments of Labor and Agriculture. It's also the only standard style for the U.S. Post Office. With an eagle it appears on the new mailbox stickers saying "U.S. Mail" and "Air Mail."

Governments and corporations rely on Helvetica partly because it makes them appear neutral and efficient, partly because its smoothness makes them seem human.

This chic, friendly aspect of the typeface bothers one designer, James Wines, codirector of SITE (Sculpture in the Environment) and a Pulitzer Prize winner for graphics (the category has since been discontinued), said about Helvetica, "It represents an update authority. Not old government, but new government." He goes further: "Helvetica is part of a psychological enslavement. It's a subconscious plot: getting people to do, think, say what you want them to. . . . It *assumes* you accept some system. It means it's predetermined that you're on their route, that it's not casually happening to you."

Helvetica signs ease us not only through building corridors, but through mental corridors. Ready for any mistaken move in a modern maze, a sign greets us at the point of decision, a mental bell rings in recognition, and down we go through the right chute! A slick-looking sign lubricates our grooves of thought and taste, making the product whose name it bears easier to accept. After transforming ugly garbage trucks into slick sanitation vehicles, Walter Kacik should know when he says, "Helvetica enhances things that normally wouldn't work."

It serves to tone down potentially offensive messages: "Littering is filthy and selfish so don't do it!" And Lenny Bruce's autobiography is packaged in Helvetica.

Helvetica skims across all categories of products and places to stamp them "sanitized," "neutralized," and "authorized." Cleanly trimmed of all excess until only an instant modern classic remains, its labels seem to say, "To look further is in vain." As Vignelli said, "What you see is different from what you perceive. You see Helvetica and you perceive order." With more unusual lettering, "you perceive fantasy."

Fantasy and a well-ordered society have always been at odds. And, as James Wines says, by designing fantasy out of our society, we are headed in a dangerous direction. "Our world is a designed extension of service," he said. "Other worlds are an aesthetic extension of spirit."

The writing's on the wall.

First published in the Village Voice *(New York: 7 June 1976). Reprinted in* The Sponsored Life *(Philadelphia: Temple Press, 1995).*

1977
LAY IN—LAY OUT
Piet Schreuders

ORIGINALLY PUBLISHED IN AN *edition of just 1,250 copies, Dutchman Piet Schreuders' booklet enjoyed a cult reputation among design students for many years. Long out of print, it was reissued in 1997 in an expanded version with other material by the author. Schreuders (b. 1951) came to graphic design as a writer, researcher, and self-publisher of magazines such as* De Wolkenkrabber *and* Furore, *keen to master all aspects of their production. Some regarded his early design work, with its extensive use of vernacular styles, as risible; others saw him as an influential alternative—an antidote even—to the aesthetic dogma of Dutch graphic design epitomized, in the 1970s, by Wim Crouwel and Total Design. Certainly, Schreuders always stressed that, for him, graphic design flowed from the content itself. Crouwel is one of those satirized, along with other well-known Dutch designers, in a loose collection of observations and asides that wittily elaborate Victor Papanek's contemporaneous conviction that the graphic design profession is indefensible ("criminal" says Schreuders) and ought not to exist. This is the first full-length English translation of Schreuders' notorious text, slightly abridged with the author's encouragement.—RP*

> *Day in—day out—*
> *Same ol' hoodoo follows me about;*
> *Same ol' pounding in my heart*
> *Whenever I think of you,*
> *And darling, I think of you,*
> *Day in and day out . . .*
>   —Johnny Mercer, *Day In—Day Out* (1939)

The profession of graphic design is criminal and really ought not to exist. We will devote a booklet to it.

A hundred years ago it did not exist; in another hundred years it will probably be long gone. But just now it is flourishing.

Anyone who writes a letter with a left margin of four centimeters is creating a design. Anyone who lays the dining table in a certain way is doing a layout. Anyone who spray-paints provocative text on brick walls is applying typography. In this sense, ever since man was conscious of form, graphic design has always existed. But because "design" has developed into a commercial enterprise in which time is money and business is business, design for print has become more a matter of efficiency than clarity and beauty. This has led to new typefaces being designed not for typographic but for commercial reasons. Developments such as these can only be called criminal.

Graphic designers are criminal insofar as they practice a highly specialized profession that the world could well do without. They manage to sell their work with words such as "planning" and "objectivity," while drowning the content of their given material in a tasteless sauce. Nowhere are chaos and subjectivity more powerful than in contemporary designers' circles. In the name of Design, countless magnificent existing designs were either tampered with or replaced by a "house style," "visual identity," or "pictogram." There is even an organization of designers: organized crime!

I believe it is exactly this criminal aspect which makes graphic designers so appealing to the layman, like the cowboys or gangsters of yesteryear. It is more than likely that in thirty years' time, we will mention names like Jan van Toorn, Wim Crouwel, and Pieter Brattinga just as wistfully as those of John Dillinger, Al Capone, and "the Godfather" today.

Graphic designers: it is advisable not to deal with them directly, but they can be quite entertaining when observed from a certain distance.

★

Graphic design has a similar effect on printed materials as speech lessons on someone's speech. Believing there is something wrong with one's articulation, one makes a conscious effort to pronounce the words clearly, only to make matters worse in the process. Defeating your own object—clarity and intelligibility—is practiced in the designers' world more than anywhere.

To the famous maxim "Good typography is invisible," one might add: "Good typography is secret." Because most typography and graphic design are applied consciously, because every day more companies feel obliged to hire a "designer," and because the notion that whatever is not "designed" does not count at all, the profession really ought not to exist. It should be practiced only in secret, and only by unassuming men who have never been told what exactly it is that they are doing.

★

If a design is ugly, not functional, confusing, unclear, tasteless—in a word, inadequate—one can always call it "art." There will always be those who believe it. But the question of art and design is fraught with difficulty. Design can indeed sometimes be art. Viewed in isolation, graphic design products can in fact be truly beautiful. Not only that, but without any artistic inspiration graphic design would amount to nothing more than a collection of odd planes, frames, borders, rules, and lines on paper.

There are "good" designs that are, strictly speaking, inadequate and even disturbing. Yet such a design can have a certain worth if it can shed new light on one thing or another, for instance on design itself. The terms "innovation," "revolutionary," and "pioneering" apply here. And then you might as well call it "art."

Yet the best art has usually been made by people who would rather die than be called "artist;" they prefer words like "professional." That's a question of terminology. A professional, by tradition, is someone who always does just a bit more than merely practicing his trade at one hundred percent. A graphic designer, however, goes into a trance at the word "artist." I happen two know two graphic designers who have been bickering for years about their own identity, focusing on just this item: is it preferable for a graphic designer to be an "artist" member or an "art-loving" member of the Amsterdam arts club, Arti et Amicitæ?

All things considered, it isn't surprising that you often see graphic designers sporting a beard.

★

Magazine covers are living proof that, if things go well, the commercial requirement of standing out in a magazine rack can actually be combined with typographic excellence. As with any graphic design, first your eye is caught (and it attracts you), then you might read it (and it doesn't disappoint). The first stage is the province of design, and the second stage depends on the first. If a reader does not "read" the design, then the whole thing fails.

Fruit crate label art, as preserved in Gielijn Escher's famed private collection, is a prime example of this. Have graphic designers ever been employed to "develop" a suitable typeface for these labels? Were these designs preceded by design meetings? No, these labels were made with one object only: to stand out in a store. The fact that the labels are also very beautiful, that they must have been made by artists of genius, was only discovered after the fact. Too late: whoever attempts to create such labels now (and it does happen), irrevocably fails.

Fruit crate labels, c. 1925: no meetings . . .

★

With the tools of his trade, a graphic designer has all the necessary ingredients to turn something into printed matter. To design is to execute power. Ideally there should be a balance of power between designer and reader. In principle, a designer can push his activities as far as he likes, but there will always come a point at which the reader no longer accepts his efforts. The designer can go on designing to his heart's content, but his product will have lost its function.

What the designer and the reader have in common are conventions. The more the designer practices a certain modesty and keeps within certain conventions, the bigger the chance that a reader will be responsive to his work.

Designing is playing with conventions. This can be clearly seen in American newspapers, where language and layout of headlines flow easily and with great effect. In the United States, a variety of English called "American" is spoken, about which British-born writer Raymond Chandler once remarked:

"It is a fluid language, like Shakespearean English, and easily takes in new words. [. . .] It is more alive to clichés. Its impact is emotional and sensational rather than intellectual. It expresses things experienced rather than ideas.

"It is a mass language [. . .] It is a language which is being molded by writers to do delicate things and yet be within the grasp of superficially educated people. [. . .] [C]ompared with it at its best, English has reached the Alexandrian stage of formalism and decay."[1]

Not surprisingly, American newspaper typography can be like a refreshing shower. It can be described in one American word: "impact." Newspaper typography—in a sense superior to other forms of typography because its goal is to sell things as they are as opposed to making them beautiful, tasteful or attractive—has reached its zenith in America. American language that defies the rules of grammar and typography is being used in newspaper headlines.

Headlines in 144pt font size, screaming layout, slang headlines: American newspaper typography can be carried pretty far without being insulting to the reader, which cannot be said about English tabloids. Papers like the *Daily Mirror*, boasting oversized headlines like their American counterparts, reek of vulgarity. The 133rd birthday of a Japanese woman was once introduced with the headline: "Bravo, Old Jap!" And even that is a gem of wit and good taste when compared to the Dutch tabloid press.

On Thursday, September 3, 1959 this was the front page of the 'home edition' of the Chicago Sun-Times. Five different headlines compete for your attention. The front page was changed for the 'street edition'. The layout of the revised front page is so symmetrical as to be almost boring, but it can be very effective if used sparingly. (From: Quentin P. Gore, Chicago Sun-Times Type and Makeup Manual, 4th printing, March, 1964)

In 1954, the *Chicago Sun–Times* (born in 1947 of a fusion between the Chicago *Sun* and *Times* newspapers) introduced a form of newspaper typography that was slightly more well-considered than the previous method of "big and black." Front pages started heaving more than one headline; sometimes a front page would contain nothing but headlines. This practice has since been abandoned, but it looked great.

[. . .]

One can make something good out of any system of design: even the so-called "Swiss" typography, the most tasteless invention since the cuckoo clock. Embroidering on the sympathetic notion that it is typography and design's goal to organize thoughts, "Swiss" designers believed that the world would benefit from a kind of global design style, created out of a very limited set of elements (one typeface, one manner of setting, one kind of picture: a hard-printed photo). There have been one or two designers capable enough to artistically translate this nonsense in a way which, at the time, had its merits. But the "Swiss" dogma turned out to attract additional hordes of idlers, car drivers, managers, dimwits, accountants, and copycats, so that "Swiss" typography, if it ever amounted to anything, soon developed into a pseudo-religion. Suddenly the graphic profession was overcrowded with fast-talking men in loud neckties who proceeded, as if remotely activated by a mother lode in Zurich, to restyle airports, show programs, newspapers, and labels. No single fashion has been as overpowering as the fashion of restyling, and once a restyling process was underway, it became easier and easier to re-restyle the same things, and again, and again. Finally, the point was reached where all existing graphic design had been reduced to either a period point, a line, or a paper clip.

★

Long ago, in the period when the year 2000 was popular, Wim Crouwel invented the "typeface of the future." This font was nameless, but it did have a code number: 7/3/11/3/7. Although it was impossible to read, it was executed in the so-called Martian style, familiar from animated cartoons: a style that seems to suggest that

Wim Crouwel's typeface 7/3/11/ 3/7, designed to be understood by machines—and machines only?

man has finally been defeated by machines. In hindsight it is difficult to guess whether or not Crouwel had intended the 7/3/11/3/7 as a practical joke, but if he had, it would have been an especially sick joke. It is one of the few typefaces in the world requiring subtitles.

★

Like those in many new professions, graphic designers often try to wrap their activities in a haze of self-importance. They have the need for self-assurance like everybody else, yet they have a profession which, according to the man in the street, does not even exist. This explains their pompous tendencies, the establishment of special design "offices," their special clothes and showy spectacle-frames. Often this urge overshadows the content of their work. Such a designer treats a text with soap and water, puts it in the freezer, then cuts it in slices and then deep-fries it in a home-made batter consisting of rules, headlines, and hard-contrast photos.

This is why graphic design often resembles instant mash and powdered meat.

★

As soon as the notion took hold that a designer can work with a so-called "grid," the lid was off.

A grid!

Having to think only once, after which you can cut and paste text, photographs, ads, headlines, and illustrations according to a pre-set scheme!

A grid, to be sure, is the answer to everything: it removes the necessity to think; the design looks "well-planned;" and you have yet another jargon word with which to impress your client.

★

A paradox: the Dutch Post Office has an "aesthetic department," and yet this body has never designed any of the postal forms that are among the high points of the graphic design of their period (mid-1960s).

What is a form? A piece of paper, the front of which is never used, and the back rarely, by post office workers wishing to jot down sports results. A request for a receipt for the amount spent on stamps will result, not in the form specially designed for this purpose, but a blank piece of paper with a stamp mark. This piece of paper often turns out to be the backside of form #P2201, "Proof of posting by registered mail," a masterpiece of composition and typography. It was designed in 1962.

Dutch Post Office form #2201, edition 1962: Proof of shipment by Registered mail.

The "aesthetic" department has certainly been responsible for the design of Dutch stamps; and the Netherlands has excelled in ugly stamps. Among the beautiful Dutch stamps is the series of standard numeral stamps, designed by Jan van Krimpen between 1946 and 1957. A few years ago, afraid of seeming old-fashioned, the Post Office commissioned a replacement, and chose an ugly design, if not the very ugliest.

In 1960, Christiaan de Moor put down his "Twelve Commandments for the postage stamp designer."[2] It may be useful to reprint commandments one and two here:

1. As a symbol of the state, the stamp should be dignified in character.

2. A postage stamp is a piece of graphic art requiring the utmost attention to detail, technically as well as aesthetically.

They can't say they hadn't been warned.

Postage stamps as they ought to look: the numerical stamps from a series designed by J. Van Krimpen, 1946–1957

In olden days, typography was a craft beginning and ending with metal typesetting. Nowadays, in the era of phototypesetting, rub-down, and paste-up, typography has a hard time even attaining the level of metal typesetting. One is glad if the text is straight, well-spaced, with a sharp image.

Of course, you can't stop technical progress, and I am still pleased with the fact that someone once invented the wheel. But the way in which printers have converted to phototypesetting and have thrown their old metal installations out the window is reminiscent of the era of American gangster terrorism, when gambling machines were installed in many cafés under threat of violence. Likewise, the development and distribution of phototypesetting machines was not promoted by typographers, but by electronic engineers, with financial backing from large electronic companies. This does not bode well for typography and, indeed, letterpress type is still much more beautiful than phototypesetting. Reproducing existing metal typefaces will always lead to quality loss. One type designer who drew a logical conclusion from this dilemma is Dutchman Gerard Unger. He prefers to introduce new letterforms, especially designed to take account of the new techniques and to withstand photographic distortion. Unger has designed a number of new typefaces. His pioneering work must be praised here, although only time can tell if his fonts are really useful.

★

A good method of producing text in the new conditions is to get a specimen of letters printed in many copies, then cut and paste them up: just as kidnappers make their demands out of cut-up newspaper headlines. The rest is a matter of perfectionism in good spacing: something that is almost impossible with rub-down letters. Further, they often use bastardized forms of familiar metal typefaces.

[. . .]

There are those who say that graphic design must never stand out, that the text should be the focus of attention in a piece of print, and that any influence a designer might have on it is bound to be a bad one.

Should design limit itself to just presenting the text? Can it not be positively attractive? In a good piece of design, you see the quality at first glance. It is like music: you recognize it at once, just by hearing the so-called "sound." Just as writers reach readers because they write well, so good design brings printed matter closer to readers and bad design scares them off.

Attempts to find objective grounds of judgement lead to confusion. Graphic design is a highly individual activity, just like writing. A writer reaches readers because he can write; if he can't write, there is no contact.

In his pamphlet "Design and Print" Wim Crouwel proposes: "Especially in this day and age, words like 'beautiful' and 'ugly' can only be used from a purely personal viewpoint. For a mass medium like print, 'objective norms' are necessary."[3] In the present booklet, however, objective norms are totally absent, and I will most happily use words like "beautiful" and "ugly." Mr. Crouwel's own designs, incidentally, are quite personal, quite individual, very much of their time—and yes, really ugly.

For design to be timeless, all mannerisms of the day must be thrown overboard. At each step of the way, we must ponder: "How will this look in ten years' time?" For design to be good, it must be well thought out and tastefully assembled. I cannot reveal anything useful about "taste" here, and even the meaning of the term "thought out" is more complicated than it seems. For often a piece of wonderful design which looks well-balanced and thoroughly planned actually came about almost by accident. And the reverse can be true as well.

★

No one knows what makes a good popular song, but it's more than likely a happy combination of text, music, arrangement and interpretation. Only very rarely do all these ingredients work so well together that the song becomes more than a sum of its parts (as we say: it "swings"). All the notes are in place, the harmonies are perfect, vocal and accompaniment form an entity. It could be a sentimental, romantic ballad, lovingly played late at night after having cleaned the record carefully. It could be a pop song making the top of the charts. "Please, Mr. Typographer, play that song for me!" And so we can discern Latin-American (samba) design, big band design, or the monumental Bach design.

What is good design? There is no formula for it. Design is the sum of all kinds of small but important decisions. Often the best pieces come when one is not concentrating too hard on the task, perhaps listening to the radio. Design is like film-direction or mixing tracks of sound-recording, to make a whole out of diverse elements.

Graphic design! It is not the oldest, but certainly the nicest profession in the world.

So what are the essential rules for making a good design?

1. Take a piece of paper.
2. Start laying out.

First published as Lay In—Lay Out *(Amsterdam: Gerrit Jan Thiemefonds, 1977). Reprinted in* Lay In—Lay Out (En Ander Oud Zeer) *(Amsterdam: De Buitenkant, 1997).*

Notes

1. "From Chandler's working notebook: notes on English and American style." In: Dorothy Gardiner and Kathrine Sorley Walker (Ed.), *Raymond Chandler Speaking* (London: Hamish Hamilton, 1962, p. 80).

2. Christiaan de Moor, *Postzegelkunst* ('The Art of the Postage Stamp'). The Hague: Staatsbedrijf der Posterijen, Telegrafie en Telefonie, 1960.

3. "Ontwerpen en Drukken," part one in a series of pamphlets on design, published by Gerrit Jan Thiemefonds in 1975.

1983
THE AGE OF PLUNDER
Jon Savage

WHILE IT CONTAINS MANY *details that are socially specific to Britain—particularly in its opening paragraphs—Jon Savage's article, written for the* Face *at the height of its cultural impact, is one of the most incisive commentaries on the graphic design of the early 1980s. The few years since punk had seen a groundswell of design activity in the music business, and graphic imagery created in the subcultural context of the musical "new wave" soon began to exert a powerful influence on the international mainstream of design, which by the end of the 1970s lacked energy and innovative thinking. Savage (b. 1953) wrote as a music critic with a broad awareness of style's coded role in popular culture and a tenacious grasp of the political meanings of visual form. Even by the standards of more recent design writing, his article is unflinchingly direct in its criticisms of designers who engage in the postmodern plunder of historical styles, casually stripping them of their original meanings, and reducing the past to a playground of consumable commodities.—RP*

A Beatles 12-inch flops on to my desk, sporting a rather fetching color pic of those well-known faces in their velvet collar Burtons and their famous pink tab collars. The record contains their first—not very good—single "Love Me Do" with an *alternative take.* Train-spotting sleeve notes and a facsimile of the original label add up to a product that is perfectly anachronistic (they didn't have Beatles" collectors *or* 12-inchers in 1962, but that's another story). It's perfectly aimed: backed up by a clever campaign on the London buses—youthful pics of the Four with the captions "It was 20 Years Ago" and "Did You Know that John Lennon was in the Beatles?"—the record charted and peaked at number five. I thought it was shit in 1964, but now?!

This alerts me, and I start noticing things. A few days later, I'm on a quick shoot: Manchester's Christmas lights are being switched on in the city center. There's a bit of razzmatazz: a brass band, an electric organ, appearances by the stars of *Coronation Street.* What gets me is the large crowd, and how it's behaving: this is after all, only a low-key event but there are thousands more out than have been expected and they're ravening.

The crowd is pinched, cold and in sections obviously very poor. As they surge and yell, I catch a note of real desperation and chilling frenzy beneath the surface jollity that could turn any which way. Things are nearly out of control. And, supreme irony, this crowd, which has been ground down by Tory policies reinforcing the divide between the two nations, started singing and bawling between the carols; *Beatles songs,* those songs of hope from another age: "She Loves You" and "A Hard Day's Night." "Help" might have been more appropriate.

You wouldn't catch them singing ABC songs. Back to the wonderful world of pop. I turn to the *Daily Mail* of 16 November. A full-page feature trumpets Mari

Wilson as "The Girl Behind the Return of the Beehive." The piece adds, revealingly, that "Mari, 25 . . . is dogged by the fact that her hairstyle has always been bigger than her recording success." *Quite.* A few days before, she has appeared on *The Old Grey Whistle Test*: a quick interview reveals that she's done all the homework necessary on the beehive and the late 1950s/early 1960s, that she really wants to emulate Peggy and Judy and that she is going to perform one of her fave songs, "Cry Me a River."

She perches on a stool, surrounded by her violinists, the "Prawn Cocktails"— so *Ealing*—who actually looked like punks. It's not bad, but nothing like Julie London. But then Mari is one camp joke that has transcended as things tend to at present. She records for a very studied little label called Compact, which has also done all the necessary homework: silly cod sleeve notes by "Rex Luxore," silly inner sleeves with 1950s curtain patterns and a name taken from a cruddy early 1960s television serial that is hop enough to drop.

The thing that really floors me is that in the same *Daily Mail* of 16 November there is a tiny news item: *Compact,* the twice-weekly TV serial set in a women's magazines office, is to be brought back by the BBC in the spring of 1984. The original series was killed off seventeen years ago. Clearly, we are dealing with something quite complex, that is beyond the bounds of parody.

We are inundated by images from the past, swamped by the nostalgia that is splattered all over Thatcherite Britain. Everywhere you turn, you trip over it: films, television series of varying quality, clothes, wars, ideologies, design, desires, pop records. A few more examples, to make your hair really curl: the Falklands War—*so* Empire, so 1940s war movie; *Brideshead Revisited* and *A Kind of Loving,* two Granada serials that looked at the 1920s and the 1950s respectively through rose-colored glasses with the design departments having a field day with all this "period" nonsense. The British film of 1982 that has the Yanks drooling is *Chariots of Fire,* a 1920s morality play. There's a rush of public-school and working-class boys into the army, an event unthinkable ten years ago and a new confidence in the middle classes, just like the 1950s, with the rise of formerly moribund magazines like the *Tatler,* and the runaway success of the *Sloane Ranger Handbook.* It's all underpinned by a reinforcement of the old class and geographical divisions by the most right-wing government since the war. And I haven't even *mentioned* the 1960s.

Craving for novelty may well end in barbarism but this nostalgia transcends any healthy respect for the past; it is a disease all the more sinister because unrecognized and, finally, an explicit device for the reinforcement and success of the New Right.

Part of this is a response to increased leisure. Because we don't produce solid stuff any more—with the decline of the engineering industries—we are now all enrolled in the Culture Club. In the gap left by the failure of the old industries comes Culture as a Commodity, the biggest growth business of the lot: the proliferation of television, video (especially in the lower income groups), computers, and information. But this flow of information is not unrestricted: it is characteristic of our time that much essential information is not getting out, but is instead glossed by a national obsession with the past that has reached epidemic proportions.

Pop music, of course, reflects power politics, and it is fascinating to see how it has toed the line. As elsewhere, 1982 has been the year of the unbridled nostalgia fetish: consumers are now trained—by endless interviews, fashion spreads, "taste" guides like the *NME*'s "Artist as Consumer" or our own arch "Disinformation'—to spot the references and make this spotting *part of their enjoyment.* It is not enough to flop around to "Just What I've always Wanted," no, you have to know that Mari has done her homework and you should be able to put a date to the beehive. Thus pop's increasing self-consciousness becomes part of the product and fills out nicely all the space made available by sleeves, magazines, and videos.

These days, it is not enough to sling out a record: it has to be part of a discrete world, the noise backed up by an infrastructure of promotion, videos, and record sleeves that has become all-important and now is in danger of making the product top-heavy with reference. Basically, it's mutton dressed as lamb: do ABC *really* have to dress up (badly) as country squires to promote "All of My Heart?" Of course not: but it sells the product like the wrapping on a chocolate box. But this is ABC's third or fourth image: when do they stop, and when does the audience have enough?

Record sleeves have been an integral part of this tendency towards mystification and an overloading of meaning: in this Tower of Babel the designer, too, has become all important. Designers even have two books to celebrate their role—the *Album Cover Albums*—and they win design awards and stuff like that. If—like me— you remember when records came in plain white sleeves, it's nice to see people trying, but it is getting a bit silly when the sleeve is more important than the record. Or maybe not: here is perhaps the ultimate recognition of the disposability of today's pop *music,* an acknowledgement of the victory of style over substance.

Here we refer, as always, to punk rock: because in those turbulent nine months the ground rules were laid. Punk always had a retro consciousness—deliberately ignored in the cultural Stalinism that was going on at the time—which was pervasive yet controlled. You got the Sex Pistols covering Who and Small Faces numbers and wearing the clothes from any youth style since the war cut-up with safety-pins; the clash wearing winklepickers and sounding like the Kinks and Mott the Hoople on *better* speed; Vivienne and Malcolm buying up old 1960s Wemblex pin-collars to mutate into Anarchy shirts. Partly this was a use of deliberate reference points—an age before country-rock, session musicians, and dry ice. It was also a reflection of the revivalist groundwork already put in by labels like Stiff and Chiswick, who were the first to reintroduce picture sleeves and customized labels, just like those French or Portuguese Rolling Stones EPs you'd find in *Rock On.*

Thus you will find items like the *All Aboard with the Roogalator* sleeve, at the time much more interesting than the record itself: a direct crib of Robert Freeman's famous picture for *With the Beatles.* Or, rather more wittily, the sleeve notes written by Paul Morley for *The Good Time Music of the Sex Pistols,* a 1977 bootleg, which are a word-for-word steal from *The Pretty Things* album of 1965: "Exactly one year ago, as we write, the Sex Pistols were raw, unexposed, and latent. They were like the atom, ready to ecstatically disclose to the world punk rock, a religion of fast moving people . . ."

By this time, picture sleeves were, like "Limited Edition" 12-inch singles or coloured vinyl, an established part of the record company come-on to the consumer and, thanks to designers like Jamie Reid for the Sex Pistols and Malcolm Garrett for Buzzcocks, an integral part of the way the product was put over. Sleeves like Jamie's "Holidays in the Sun" and "Satellite," and the Buzzcocks' "Orgasm Addict" (designed by Garrett around a montage by Linder) complemented perfectly what was inside, as nostalgic and found elements were ripped up and played around with to produce something genuinely new.

The energy that had created punk and, as an unintentional byproduct, revitalized the music business couldn't sustain: by the time the channels were fully opened, there wasn't really very much left to say. Punk's quite careful, instinctive constructions were unraveled stitch by stitch in a series of revivals, renewals, and plain fads as every youth style since the war was paraded for emulation and consumption. The references that had been a means to an end became an end in themselves. Instead of trashing the past, pop music started to celebrate it—an act formerly unthinkable in such a tawdry, transient medium. The Age of Pillage had begun: so many sleeves to fill, so many images to construct—where better to go than pop's *own* rich past.

This was and is simple enough. Images from pop's unselfconscious past are invoked as some kind of ritual, or key to a time when pop was still fresh and all a gogo: money, sex, and fame beyond measure. Key figures recur: thus you will get the Ray Lowry sleeve for the Clash's *London Calling* directly imitating that of Elvis Presley's first HMV LP, or the sleeve for "Armaggideon Time" reproducing the blithe young dancers that are to be found on any pre-1958 HMV single sleeve. These references are further compounded by genuine reissues, like HMV's own *It's Only Rock 'n' Roll: 1957–62,* which reproduces the dancers again, but in a different context: Collectors' Corner.

The Beatles are also ripe for plunder. The *With the Beatles* sleeve, perhaps the most famous and monolithic piece of cover art—a symbol from the exact moment when pop went *mass* for the first time—reappears everywhere. Little stylistic devices like the white band on top of the front sleeve, with the name of the group and a mono/stereo designation or silly sleeve notes surrounded by ads for "Emitex" and notices that this is "Microgroove" or "33⅓ Extended Play" have become so familiar as to be hardly worth remarking upon. What the Beatles signify also becomes a matter for comment: thus the Residents felt it necessary to graffiti-ize the *With the Beatles* sleeve for their own insect ends to make the *Third Reich'n'Roll* point: that pop music as epitomized by the Beatles has become a dread, totalitarian hand upon the minds of the youth. Perhaps they protest too much, but then a group like Haircut 100 will invoke the rear sleeve of *Rubber Soul* to reinforce their "pure-pop" Monkee pretensions.

It is worth pointing out the difference in meaning between the original and the copy or homage. When *Rubber Soul* or *With the Beatles* came out, the design was innovative: not shocking perhaps, but thought-provoking. Its invocation by Haircut 100 or even the Residents shows how the Beatles have taken on, with time, a meaning very different from their original one and how falsely current pop views the past, redefining that past in its own contemporary image. Similarly, when the Elvis HMV sleeve appeared, it was simultaneously surprising and instinctive—not a matter for comment. Lowry's sleeve captures the *feeling* well—mainly because he is a genuine obsessive—but there's no getting away from the fact that the Clash are putting themselves in the "Great Rock 'n' Roll Tradition" with all that *that* implies. It's ironic for a group that had said "No Elvis, Beatles, or Rolling Stones in 1977," but even that was giving the past a little too much credence.

Another example of the way this plunder works can be seen in the sleeve for the recent Bauhaus hit, "Ziggy Stardust." The group's pretensions in naming themselves after the architectural school—particularly when their work has no conceivable reference to it—can be dismissed as another example of pop's demented pillage of all twentieth-century art, but the mechanics of this particular "revival" are quite interesting. The record was an unabashed tribute by the group, as they admitted, to glam rock in general and Bowie in particular and an astute choice as the Great Single that Bowie himself never released. The packing reflected this: the Bauhaus "corporate" logo—another recent trend, this—was overlaid by the *Aladdin Sane* flash, typically inaccurate and out-of-sync, as "Ziggy Stardust" came from the previous album. The package was then topped by lettering taken directly from Edward Bell's *Scary Monsters* sleeve, thus matching three different periods of Bowie into one "authentic" package. The group made a very good job of it on *Top of the Pops*—all of David's mimetic gestures, and "Ronno" lurches—but by then it was all beside the point. This *was* glam rock for 1982.

Pop's own past has not been sufficient: perhaps the most irritating manifestation of the Culture Club is the way that the whole of twentieth-century art and—more recently—any amount of ethnic material have been used with increasing desperation to tart up product that has increasingly less meaning. In this, Bauhaus are only small offenders.

Take the spearheads of last year's obsession with style, for instance: Spandau Ballet, before they got wise and changed direction, connived in sleeves by Graham Smith that peddled the worst kind of neo-neo-Classical pomposity in their frank debt to John Flaxman's lithographs. or consider Chris Sullivan's poor Picasso—cubist period, please—pastiches on any blue Rondo à la Turk sleeve. These were obvious enough and made the mistake of being much too "fine art:" anybody with an Athena poster on the wall could see where they came from; just like all the progressive groups used to do bad Dali in the early 1970s. Much more clever and systematic is the work of Peter Saville, perhaps the best-known sleeve designer in England today, and one whose work on the new Ultravox album gained, hardly surprisingly, more comment than the record itself.

Saville began work on designing Factory posters and sleeves, where his frank debt to Futurist posters and typographer Jan Tschichold fitted in perfectly with Factory's "industrial," "machine" image. Tschichold published the book that is regarded as the foundation of modern typography in 1928: *Die neue Typographie* proposed a new, almost classical simplicity and a rejection of Victorian ornament—like the Futurist movement in Italy, it was a celebration of the age of the machine. Thus it comes as no surprise that Saville's brilliant sleeves for Factory Records—*The Factory Sample,* New Order's *Movement* and "Everything's Gone Green'—reproduce Futurist and Tschichold designs fairly closely. They gave Factory one of the highest, if not *the* highest, graphic profile and made Saville's name.

Peter Saville sleeve for New Order's "Movement" LP, 1981

If on occasions the sleeve became not an ornament but a prison, then it was because the product didn't come up to the Factory "specification:" a very good example of this occurs on Section 25's tentative, delicate *Always Now* album, which is all but swamped by a Saville sleeve that is an object exercise in overdesign, and a clear indication that the designer has become more important than the group.

With time, this process has become clear as Saville becomes more important and more influential: his recent designs for Ultravox's "Quartet" and "Hymn" are perfect examples of cover art that matches

Fortunato Depero's original Futurist poster, 1932

the interior product in a way that is far from flattering. Like Ultravox, these sleeves are grandiose, cod neoclassical exercises perfectly executed for the erection of false pillars of worship. Like the ABC sleeve for "All of My Heart," which has them parodying the classical grandeur of a Deutsche Grammophon sleeve, they represent some kind of nadir of style over content. Boys, my congratulations!

The past, then, is being plundered in pop as elsewhere in order to construct a totality that is seamless, that cannot be broken. It is a characteristic of our age that there is little sense of community, of any *real* sense of history, as the present is all that matters. Who needs yesterday's papers? In refashioning the past in our image, in tailoring the past to our own preconceptions, the past is recuperated: instead of being a door out of our time, it merely leads to another airless room.

The past then turned into the most disposable of consumer commodities, and is thus dismissable: the lessons that it can teach us are thought trivial, are ignored among a pile of garbage. A proper study of the past can reveal, however, desires and spirits not all in accordance with Mrs. Thatcher's mealy-mouthed ideology as it spreads like scum to fill every available surface, and it is up to us to address ourselves to them.

First published in the Face *no. 33 (London: January 1983).*

1983
CALL FOR CRITICISM
Massimo Vignelli

MASSIMO VIGNELLI *(b. 1931) is inevitably associated with the popularization of Swiss modernism in the United States throughout the 1960s. Indeed, his landmark programs for American Airlines, Knoll International, and the New York Metropolitan Transportation Authority, among others, are credited with establishing Helvetica as the default typeface for corporate America by 1970. Yet Vignelli, trained as an architect, was always impressed by what he perceived as architecture's superior level of discourse, as well as the professional respect that critical thought seemed to engender. By the 1980s, it was impossible for Vignelli, a frequent collaborator with Michael Graves and Robert A. M. Stern, to ignore the rise of postmodernism and the obvious parallels between the banality of corporate glass box architecture and the limitations of sans-serif typefaces set on a three-column grid. An invitation from Walter Herdeg to write a preface to the 1983–1984 edition of* Graphis Annual *provided Vignelli with a forum to call for a more rigorous approach to graphic design criticism. Vignelli was prescient: the years that followed saw a gradually accelerating growth in thoughtful writing about graphic design.—MB*

The extremely exciting, seductive, and dangerously probing attitude of the eighties has brought us a devouring desire to reassess the philosophy of our profession, its origins, and its meaning as it stands today.

We feel a tremendous need for historical investigation into the roots of our profession, not only of the modern movement, but even before the industrial revolution. We need to rediscover the friendliness of design prior to the industrial revolution. We need to understand the motivations of the creative minds that preceded the modern movement. We are all offspring of the modern movement and we want to know more about our intellectual forebears. We need our roots. We need to know who the protagonists were, what prompted them to operate as they did, who their clients were, and how their rapport generated a climate of creativity which affected others.

Historical information, introspection, and interpretation are almost totally missing in our profession, and I think we feel a tremendous need to fill that gap.

The development of graphic design theory in this century is a corollary of the development of the major arts. This condition has culturally humiliated our profession. The consequences are a total vacuum of theory and a surplus of transitory superficial fads. It is time that theoretical issues be expressed and debated to provide a forum of intellectual tension out of which meanings spring to life. Pretty pictures can no longer lead the way in which our visual environment should be shaped. It is time to debate, to probe the values, to examine the theories that are part of our heritage and to verify their validity to express our times. It is time for the word to be heard. It is time for Words and Vision.

The emergence of semiotics could and will have a deep impact on our profession. It will establish a discipline of awareness and expression unreached before. The theoretical implications of new technologies for the way we conceive and express the printed word and the graphic image are a tremendous field of exploration which is still to be tapped. Again the lack of appropriate professional publications deprives all of us of the stimulation that could emerge from dialogue.

It should be no surprise that, along with the lack of history and theory, criticism is totally missing. The main function of criticism is not that of providing flattering or denigrating reviews but that of providing creative interpretations of the work, period or theory being analyzed. Out of those creative interpretations a new light is cast on the objects, and new nuances and reflections are brought to our notice.

With criticism, designers will be offered the possibility of multilayered reading of the work of other designers, or the opportunity of focusing on the meaning of particular expressive movements. Criticism will prevent, to a great extent, the superficial spreading of fads, or in any case will provide ground for their evaluation in the proper context. Graphic design will not be a profession until we have criticism.

The need for reassessment calls for documentation. We are thirsty for documentation that could provide us with sources of information for the re-evaluation of periods, people, or events. Graphic design publications around the world provide a good source of documentation, although most of the time in a very disengaged way.

We need to arouse the awareness that every gesture of the present is a document for the future, and that our present will be measured only by these gestures.

First published in Graphis Annual 83/84 *(Zurich: 1983).*

ABOUT THE EDITORS

MICHAEL BIERUT is a partner of Pentagram, the international design consultancy, and a coeditor of *Looking Closer 2* and *Looking Closer*. He lives in New York.

JESSICA HELFAND is a partner of William Drenttel/Jessica Helfand, a multimedia and print media company. She is the author of *Six Essays (to 12) on Design and New Media*. She lives in Falls Village, Connecticut.

STEVEN HELLER is a senior art director at the *New York Times* and the editor of the *AIGA Journal of Graphic Design*. He is the author or editor of more than seventy books on graphic design, including *Design Dialogues, Design Literacy,* and *Paul Rand*. He lives in New York.

RICK POYNOR is the founding editor of *Eye* magazine and a writer on design and the visual arts. His books include *Typography Now: The Next Wave, The Graphic Edge,* and *Design Without Boundaries: Visual Communication in Transition*. He lives in England.

INDEX

Page numbers in italics refer to illustrations

Books from Allworth Press

Looking Closer 2: Critical Writings on Graphic Design
edited by Michael Bierut, William Drenttel, Steven Heller, and DK Holland
(softcover, 6¾ × 10, 288 pages, $18.95)

Looking Closer: Critical Writings on Graphic Design
edited by Michael Bierut, William Drenttel, Steven Heller, and DK Holland
(softcover, 6¾ × 10, 256 pages, $18.95)

Design Literacy (continued)
by Steven Heller (softcover, 6¾ × 10, 288 pages, $19.95)

Design Literacy: Understanding Graphic Design
by Steven Heller and Karen Pomeroy (softcover, 6¾ × 10, 288 pages, $19.95)

The Swastika: Symbol Beyond Redemption?
by Steven Heller (hardcover, 6¼ × 9¼, 256 pages, $21.95)

Sex Appeal: The Art of Allure in Graphic and Advertising Design
by Steven Heller (softcover, 6¾ × 10, 288 pages, $18.95)

**Design Culture:
An Anthology of Writing from the AIGA Journal of Graphic Design**
edited by Steven Heller and Marie Finamore (softcover, 6¾ × 10, 320 pages, $19.95)

Design Dialogues
by Steven Heller and Elinor Pettit (softcover, 6¾ × 10, 272 pages, $18.95)

The Education of a Graphic Designer
edited by Steven Heller (softcover, 6¾ × 10, 256 pages, $18.95)

Selling Graphic Design, Second Edition
by Don Sparkman (softcover, 6 × 9, 256 pages, $19.95)

AIGA Professional Practices in Graphic Design
The American Institute of Graphic Arts, edited by Tad Crawford
(softcover, 6¾ × 10, 320 pages, $24.95)

Licensing Art and Design, Revised Edition
by Caryn R. Leland (softcover, 6 × 9, 128 pages, $16.95)

Business and Legal Forms for Graphic Designers, Revised Edition
by Tad Crawford (softcover, includes CD-ROM, 8½ × 11, 224 pages, $24.95)

**The Trademark Guide: A Friendly Guide for Protecting
and Profiting from Trademarks**
by Lee Wilson (softcover, 6 × 9, 192 pages, $18.95)
